ELIJAH
the Tishbite

Books by F. W. Krummacher

Elijah the Tishbite
The Suffering Saviour

ELIJAH
the Tishbite

F. W. Krummacher

kregel PUBLICATIONS
Grand Rapids, MI 49501

Elijah the Tishbite reprinted 1992 by Kregel Publications, a division of Kregel, Inc., P.O. Box 2607, Grand Rapids, MI 49501. This edition, with minor improvements, is reprinted from The Religious Tract Society's 1838 edition published in London.

Cover and book design: Alan G. Hartman

Library of Congress Cataloging-in-Publication Data

Krummacher, F. W. (Friedrich Wilhelm), 1796-1868.
   Elijah the Tishbite / F. W. Krummacher.
      p.   cm.
Originally published: 1836.
   1. Elijah (Biblical prophet) 2. Bible. O.T.—Biography.
I. Title.
BS580.E4K7   1992   222'.5092—dc20   92-16137
                                                 CIP
   ISBN 0-8254-3059-3 (pbk.)

1 2 3 4 5 printing / year 96 95 94 93 92

Printed in the United States of America

To the Reader

In preparing this translation, some of the least important passages have been omitted which has made it necessary, in some instances, for the sake of preserving the consecutiveness, to make some alterations in the context. The peculiar style of Dr. Krummacher has also made it requisite to use considerable freedom in the translation of some parts in order to do justice to the spirit and liveliness of the original. The editors have also added sub-heads and made minor corrections in the text.

Contents

7

1

Elijah's First Appearance

It is a brilliant description which the Lord gives us of his true church here on earth, when, in the Song of Solomon 4:4, he says, "Thy neck is like the tower of David, builded for an armory, whereon there hang a thousand bucklers, all shields of mighty men." He compares it to that stronghold of the Jebusites, on mount Zion, which David took. Thus the church of God also stands founded on a rock, and that rock is Christ and his blood. It rests upon the power and word of God; the eternal triune Jehovah bears it in his hands, and the gates of hell shall not prevail against it.

The tower of David was builded for an armory, whereon hung the shields of his heroes by thousands. And when was ever the fortress of the church of Jesus Christ unprotected? For nearly six thousand years has the infernal adversary bent his bow against it and shot at it with his fiery darts; but it stands unimpaired to this day. For there is one shield over it, which is better than a thousand; where is the lance that will penetrate it? That shield is He who is the Alpha and the Omega, and his protection who can disannul?

But David's tower was hung with all kinds of weapons of mighty men of valor. The weapons of vanquished foes were there displayed, as trophies, to be made a show of openly; and there were also the arms of crowned conquerors, who had fought for Zion, and which were hung up as encouraging mementos for children's children. The living tower of the church of God is hung with similar decorations for the spiritual eye; behold them hanging upon the turrets, the scathed and broken weapons of many thousand vanquished mighty ones; here, the two-handed sword of the murderer from the beginning, the old dragon; there, the envenomed sting of death, the king

9

of terrors; here, the ponderous ordinance that thundered from the seven hills; there, the shivered spears of many false prophets and seducing spirits, together with their tattered banners; and from year to year the number of these broken weapons swells and multiplies. But contemplate also upon this tower the trusty swords of those who once fought the battles of Zion, and to whom, as instruments of the living God, we owe the preservation of our light and the maintenance of the true sanctuary; behold how they bristle on the battlements for the joy and consolation of us their remote descendants and for our encouraging examples! Here, the sword of Noah, the preacher of righteousness; there, of Moses, the meek and much tried man; here, the armor of Daniel; there, of Judas the Maccabee; here, of Paul, who fought the good fight; there, of Peter, divinely surnamed a rock; here, the helmets, breastplates, and other equipment of the reformers, a Huss and a Wickliff, a Luther, a Calvin, and a Zwinglius, all zealous for the truth and for the honor of God, all valiant defenders of the citadel of Zion.

And behold! amongst the swords of these spiritual heroes, one which presents itself with peculiar effulgence to the eye; one which has wrought mightily for the glory of the kingdom of God, and was as sharp and piercing as any could be in arduous and evil times. Who once handled that noble weapon? It was Elijah the Tishbite; a man mighty in word and deed, and in miracles besides; who broke forth like a fire, and whose word burnt like a torch, and who was so eminently distinguished by Divine grace, that, when the Lord of glory himself appeared upon earth, the Jews said, "It is Elias!"

The life of Elijah may be made an abundant source of animation and encouragement, of strength and refreshment to our faith; we intend therefore to notice the history of this man of God in a series of discourses. We shall accompany him at one time into the streets of the royal city and to the prince's throne; at another, into the solitary wilderness; to the public and tempestuous scene of his labors, and into the quiet chamber and to the humble couch watered with his tears; and learn of him how the Lord guides his people, and how his imparted strength is perfected in weakness.

May the Spirit of the Lord God bless and seal these our meditations, imparting to them such a life and power that many a weary heart may be refreshed, and that the feeble knees of many may be strengthened!

1 Kings 17:1

> And Elijah the Tishbite, who was of the inhabitants of Gilead, said unto Ahab, As the Lord God of Israel liveth, before whom I stand, there shall not be dew nor rain these years, but according to my word.

Thus commences the brief record of the prophet Elijah, abruptly setting us at once in the midst of his life. At this very first mention of him we see the whole man living and moving, in spirit and in conduct. This manner of his introduction to our notice is itself remarkable. In the preceding chapters, the inspired historian had, as it were, dug through the wall, and discovered to us the horrible abominations in which Israel, during those melancholy times, was so deeply immersed. Clouds and thick darkness cover the whole land; the images of Baalim and Ashtaroth fearfully gleam on every side; idolatrous temples and heathen altars occupy the sacred soil; every hill smokes with their sacrifices, every vale resounds with the blasphemous yells of a cruel priesthood. The people drink in iniquity like water, and sport in shameless rites around their idols. Alas! alas! how is the glory of Israel departed! how is Abraham's seed no longer discernible! their light is become darkness, the salt has lost its savor, the fine gold has become dim! And now, while darkness reigns throughout the land; while no cheering star gleams through the universal blackness, on a sudden the history changes, with the words, "And Elijah Said"—The man seems as if dropped from heaven into the midst of this awful scene, without father, without mother, without descent, as is written of Melchisedec. Lo, he stands forth in the midst of the desolation, but not without his God. Almost the only grain of salt in the general corruption, the only leaven that is to leaven the whole mass; and that we may learn at once who he is, he commences his career with an unheard-of act of faith, by closing, in the name of his Lord, the heavens over Israel, and changing the firmament into iron and brass. Thanks be to God! the night is no longer so horrible, for a man of God now appears, like the rising moon, in the midst of it.

Let us meditate for a few moments on what is here related of Elijah: I. His name and circumstances; II. His spiritual character; III. The prophetic denunciation with which he comes to our notice.

I. *His name is Elijah.* It is no useless action to attach importance
to the names of sacred personages, and to inquire into their meaning.
The names of Scripture characters were often given by God himself.
Such names served to convey a divine promise or assurance, or
taught some rule of life, or carried some divine memorial, or indicated
the character and predominant disposition of the persons who
received them, or expressed some divine calling. Thus the name of
Noah signified a comforter; the name of Abraham, a father of many
nations. Names were to the people like memoranda, and like the
bells on the garments of the priests, reminding them of the Lord and
his government, and furnishing matter for a variety of salutary reflections. To the receivers of them they ministered consolation and
strength, warning and encouragement; and to others they served to
attract the attention and heart to God.

I am aware that to make things of this kind the subject of any religious consideration, at present, is to expose ourselves to the
imputation of weakness and superstition. How few there are, even of
professed Christians, who practically believe that the very hairs of our
head are all numbered, that God's providence extends to matters the
most minute, and that he is often specially glorified in the "day of
small things!" But he who possesses this childlike faith, accounting
nothing as really little in God's sight, realizing his heavenly Father's
gracious presence in his house and garden, under his vine and his fig-
tree—blessed indeed is that person! He possesses much joy and peace
and divine delight at all times; wherever he is, he beholds the signs
and hears the voice of God.

The name of this wondrous man was Elijah—that is, being inter-
preted, "My God of power," or, "Jehovah is my strength." A great and
excellent name, and he bore it in deed and in truth. He was a man
like you or me; nothing in himself, but the strength of God was his;
he could do nothing, and yet deeds of omnipotence proceeded from
his hands; he lay in the dust, a worm, but was commissioned with
Divine authority and power; he was a royal personage, who had
power to open and shut heaven, to bid the dead to live, the living to
die, and to hold judgment upon the enemies of God. Thus he might
justly be called "Elijah." And is the force of this name merely, "God
strengthens me"? Certainly not; but rather, "God himself is my
strength." Here is a distinction with a difference. It is not the same
thing to say, "God holds his shield before me"; and to say, "God him-

self is my shield." If he holds his shield before me, not a hair of my head can be touched; and the evil I dread shall not come nigh me. But if God himself be my shield, I then lift up my head in the raging storm, as under a serene sky, and am a partaker of the happiness of God as much in the midst of tribulation as out of it. Peter, when released from prison, when his chains fell from his hands, and the prison doors opened to him of their own accord, might shout for joy as he went on, and say, "The shield of the Lord is around me." But Stephen, when stoned to death by his enemies, might cry out, with the countenance of an angel, "God is my shield!"

It is not one and the same thing, "God gives me peace," and to say, "God is my peace." If God gives me peace, the proud waves of my soul subside, the storm is allayed, the conflagration is extinguished, a still small voice, as from the top of Horeb, breathes through my spirit, and the spices diffuse their precious odors in my garden. But if the tempest should still rage in the firmament of my animal soul; if it should thunder and lightning in all directions; if conscience accuse, the flesh be rebellious, my thoughts reproach me, and the fiery darts of the wicked one be hurled through my recoiling spirit— if I am troubled on every side, yet not distressed; perplexed, but not in despair; if, lifted in the chariot of faith above the tumult, I hold fast by the glorious sufferings of my Lord; if I save myself in the rec- ollection, that He is the God, "yea, and amen," keeping covenant with a thousand generations, and lay up the weather-worn and shat- tered bark of my mind in that haven of faith, the free grace of God, casting anchor under the rocky shelter of the unchangeable promis- es—then, yes then, Jehovah is my peace.

The same difference of meaning applies to the expressions, "God strengthens me," and "God is my strength." If God strengthen me, then, through his grace, I experience within me a Divine power, by which I can accomplish something, and feel myself arrayed and armed with a courageous and joyful spirit; I smile at partition-walls that would confine me, and at barricades that would exclude me, and fear nothing. But if, finding nothing but weakness in my soul, and trembling at the sight of the danger that surrounds me, and at the immense mountains of difficulties which lie before me yet, with all the shrinking of nature, I advance with holy boldness to meet them, hoping on against reason and feeling, in simple faith on Him who is eternally near, who will go with me, and to whom it is an easy thing to rebuke, with a word, the ocean's waves, and to thrash the moun-tains so that they shall become a plain; and if I walk by faith on the waves of nature's terrors, destitute of courage and yet a hero, out of weakness made strong, and out of despondency valiant—then I can exult and say, "God is my strength"; and my feet are placed upon a rock. What a wonderful thing is faith, which lays hold of a power to do all things, through Christ strengthening us; which brings man, who is a worm, into fellowship with the Father and with his Son Jesus Christ, and is the means whereby strength is ordained, and praise perfected out of the mouth of babes and sucklings!

Elijah owed not his greatness to high birth or station, or a native place of renown. He was born, as we see from the text, among the mountains of Gilead, on the other side Jordan; a region which, though famous for its plants, and its balms and spices, was mostly inhabited by blind idolators, and overspread with the abominations of the Amorites. It lay not far from the country of the Gergesenes, where, in the time of our Lord, the devils entered into the swine; and it may be supposed that, unless from extreme necessity, no Israelite would take up his dwelling among these mountains. It was probably in some poor abode, possibly in a wretched banished Jewish family, that Elijah was born and brought up. His birthplace, Tishe, may be considered as only a mean and obscure village in the mountains; and the prophet in his childhood could not have known much of schools, or seats of learning, or of worldly grandeur. But it has constantly been the way of our God in all ages, to take those by whom he purposes to do great things rather out of the dust than from off the throne, that all may see how everything depends upon his choice, and know that flesh and blood have not wrought his mighty works, but that to him alone belongs the glory. Hence it was that he thus prepared, in Gilead, the balm which should recover the health of the daughter of Zion; and in that den of murderers, the country of the Amorites, he raised up the man by whose instrumentality he proposed to beat down altars, execute judgment upon kings, and destroy the priests of Baal. If we translate the word "Tishbite," it means a converter; and how well does this name befit the whole life and vocation of our prophet!

Elijah enters on the stage of history with a word of faith and power: "And Elijah the Tishbite said"—and where was it he spake; and to whom, and when? Here surely is "the voice of one crying in the wilderness." Ever since the death of Solomon the evil of idolatry had been coming in like a flood, and no barrier could any longer avail to keep out the torrent of general corruption. The despotic declaration of Rehoboam, the son of Solomon, upon coming to the throne—that if his father scourged the people with whips, he would chastise them with scorpions—had occasioned such a disaffection that the ten tribes had revolted, and formed a separate kingdom under Jeroboam. Only the two tribes of Judah and Benjamin remained subject to the house of David, and formed the kingdom of Judah; while the ten rebellious tribes styled themselves the kingdom of Israel. The kings of Judah, who possessed the south of the promised land, resided at Jerusalem, on mount Zion. The kingdom of Israel comprised all the northern districts, and its royal residence was first the fortified hill of Thirza, and afterwards the city of Samaria. The two kingdoms were at almost perpetual war with each other; but this was not the greatest evil. A thousand times worse was their internal disorder.

Jeroboam began his reign by introducing, from political motives, a new idolatry. He was apprehensive that, if the people continued in connection with the temple, and the worship of God at Jerusalem, they would gradually fall away from him again, and return under the dominion of the house of David. He therefore made an imitation of the golden cherubim of the temple, transferred some of the festivals to other seasons, and chose priests out of all the tribes of the people, at his own pleasure, without restriction to the tribe of Levi. This unlawful worship became open idolatry, when in the year 900 before the birth of Christ, king Ahab, that tame obsequious slave of his bloodthirsty wife Jezebel, ascended the throne of Israel. Then it was, at the instigation of this ungodly woman of Sidon, that the worship of Baal became the established religion of the country, and the worshipers of the true God were persecuted with fire and sword. Oh the sad and evil times which now came on! the gross darkness which now covered the land; the horrible abominations which now went on accumulating! Gloomy idol temples rose in every direction; profane altars, stained with the blood of prophets and holy men, bade defiance to the Most High, and called for Divine jealousy and vengeance. It seemed as if Satan transferred his residence from hell to earth, and was striving to obscure the light of heaven with the smoke and vapor of the most horrible idolatry.

Such were the times, and such the awful state of things, when Elijah, the man of God, stood up. The kingdom of Ahab and Jezebel is the dark field of labor on which he enters, in the name of God, and where we are to behold him employed. How will he conduct himself in the midst of such a crooked and perverse generation? How will he navigate this stormy sea? How will he surmount walls and barriers like these? Such questions will be fully answered as we proceed, and by every answer I trust we shall be strengthened in the faith, and be constrained joyfully to exclaim, "Jehovah, he is God! Jehovah, he is God!"

II. Let us now take a view of *Elijah's spiritual character*, the relation in which he stood towards God. This he indicates himself in the text, where he exclaims, "As the Lord God of Israel liveth, before whom I stand." Elijah stood before the God of Israel; such was his spiritual position and situation; such the characteristic state of his inward life. Do you ask who the God of Israel is? Do you know the Angel who conversed with Abraham in the plain of Mamre, and the mysterious Person in the form of man, who wrestled with Jacob till daybreak, and said to him, "Thy name shall be called no more Jacob, but Israel: for as a prince hast thou power with God and with men, and hast prevailed"? Gen. 32:28. Do you know the appearance in the burning bush at the foot of Horeb, and that bright and wondrous Presence, of which God the Father said unto Moses in the desert, "My Presence shall go with thee, and I will give thee rest," Exod. 33:14? Do you know that living Rock, which followed the people of Israel through the wilderness in their journey to Canaan; or that Captain of the Lord's host who appeared with a drawn sword in his hand unto Joshua, and who was himself the sword of Joshua's victories and the shield of his help? Josh. 5:13-15. Do you know him? Christ is his name! He is the Lord, the God of Israel! Before him stand the thousands of thousands; before him, the angels whom he makes as the winds, and his ministers whom he makes as the flames of fire; before him stood Elijah.

"Happy are thy men, and happy are these thy servants, who stand continually before thee!" So spake the queen of Sheba to Solomon, 1 Kings 10:8. But a greater than Solomon is here! and how much happier are those servants who stand always in the presence of the God of Israel! But no one can ever stand before him in his own strength. Those whom he suffers to appear before him, stand on the foundation of the Lord; stand in his righteousness and beauty. For with an iron scepter he casts down all who dare present themselves before him on their own footing, or behold him in their own strength, or lift up the head before him in their own righteousness.

But to the worm in the dust, to the poor self-renouncing penitent, lying in his blood, he says, "Lift yourself up, stand before me, behold my face with comfort, and be not afraid!" He who desires to stand before him, and to lift up his head in his presence, must first have lain prostrate before him in the dust, must have abased and humbled himself before him. How often may Elijah have fallen on his face before him among the mountains of Gilead, how many tears may he have shed in solitary caves and caverns, before he could say, "As the Lord liveth, the God of Israel, before whom I stand!" Elijah was a man reconciled to God in Christ Jesus the promised Messiah, and clothed with his righteousness. This is implied in his words, "I stand before the Lord God of Israel"; and is further evident from his having received the honor a thousand years afterwards, to be a witness with Moses, on mount Tabor, of the transfiguration of his Lord.

But the standing before the Lord expresses something more than a state of reconciliation in general. I stand before the Lord when I desire, above all things, that the will of the Lord may be at all times plainly manifested to me, and that I may do nothing, from one moment to another, but what shall please him, and promote his glory; when I keep my eyes waking, and place myself as it were at my post, to watch for the tokens of my King, and listen attentively with my spirit to his voice, and his commands within me and without; when I desire, according to the least of his intimations, to run the way of his commandments; I then stand before the Lord. Thus Elijah stood before the Lord. To be an instrument for the accomplishment of the Divine will, and for the glorifying of his name, was his ardent desire; he could say with Isaiah's watchman, "Lord, I stand continually upon the watch-tower in the day-time, and I am set in my ward whole nights," Isa. 21:8. His life was a hearkening to God's voice; he passed his days in the presence of his eternal King, and "Lord, speak! for thy servant heareth," was his watchword. Such was Elijah, by the grace of God, and thus did he stand before the Lord God of Israel.

III. We shall consider *the denunciation Elijah proclaimed.* Let us direct our eyes to Samaria, that idolatrous city. There stands the man of God in the midst of foes, before the tyrant Ahab, and opens his mouth, boldly and valiantly, and exclaims in such a manner as to make the people's ears tingle, "As the Lord God of Israel liveth, before whom I stand, there shall not be dew nor rain these years, but according to my word." Elijah—What are you doing? What a risk you are incurring! Is not this putting the honor of Jehovah at stake? Will they not ridicule not only you, but him also, if there be any delay in what you have announced? Yes; but Elijah is not afraid of this. He knows that the word of the Lord in his mouth is truth.

But how was it that Elijah was empowered to make such an announcement? The prophet, full of holy jealousy for the honor of his God, felt an inward assurance that such a chastisement upon the land would tend to melt the hardened hearts of the people, and to restore the glory of Jehovah's name. He brought this matter before the Lord, as St. James tells us at the end of his epistle, 5:17. "Elias was a man subject to like passions as we are, and he prayed earnestly that it might not rain" and Amen! was the answer from above in his soul. Amen, be it so! It is given into thy hands to shut and to open heaven. Elijah took this Amen of the living God as a sword in his hand; depending upon this Amen, he prophesied drought with Divine infallibility. The whole country of Samaria seemed to shake her head at it, and to laugh at his prediction. The luxuriant pastures and the well-watered fields seemed to exclaim together, "This judgment shall not be executed!"—and a thousand springs and brooks, flowing through the land, and the vapory hills, which form and attract the clouds, all seemed to join together to falsify his word. But Elijah was not confounded; with the Amen of his God in the hand of his faith, what were natural appearances or reasonings to him! His voice was more mighty than that of many waters, for it was the voice of God within him; neither springs, nor brooks, nor clouds, nor the richest luxuriance of vegetation, could avail against that word, "As the Lord God of Israel liveth, over this land shall come a drought."

So, sincere Christian, do you also believe the Amen, which you have received from God in your heart respecting his adoption of you, and his grace toward you. Do not be confounded either by your objecting nature, or by the weakness of the flesh; either by the scruples of reason, or by the devil, the spirit that is always arguing. Keep a firm hold, by faith, of the Divine Amen once given you, and abide by it, and say, "As the Lord God of Israel liveth, and endureth for ever, nothing shall condemn me, or separate me from the love of God in Christ Jesus."

"As the Lord liveth before whom I stand, there shall not be dew nor rain these years, but according to my word!" Elijah said it, and immediately heaven and earth changed their appearance. The one became as iron, and the other as brass, and the dew of heaven was restrained. The word of the prophet struck, like a fever, into the heart of the earth, withering and scorching, and all that was fresh and green faded and hung its head; every stream and rivulet dried up, and all that had breath lay gasping and languishing on the ground. Neither dew nor rain fell during three years and six months. Such were the effects produced by the voice of man; but a man who was in communion and accord with the Almighty.

In conclusion, I say unto you, my people; whom the Lord hath so highly favored; verily, if the high places in your hearts are not removed, the idolatry rooted out, the Baalim demolished, before which, alas, so many of you, secretly or more openly, bow the knee, it will be more tolerable for the land of Samaria and Israel, than for you. Oh it is already as if heaven had begun to close upon us. How sparingly does the dew of the Spirit fall! how few arise from the dead! and how long is it since a plenteous shower of heavenly rain has refreshed our vale![1] My friends, what is the cause of this? Has an Elijah stood forth in the midst of us with his word, "As the Lord liveth, there shall not be dew nor rain these years"? Or does Elijah sleep, forgetting to re-open what was shut up? Church of God, you little flock of Israel, you people of his possession, you are as Elijah. Yes, your voice can call forth clouds and rain. Arise, and call upon your God! for "the effectual fervent prayer of a righteous man availeth much!" James 5:16. Pray for dew and rain upon the dry land, and then announce it from the "Amen" of your heart, and say, The drought will soon be at an end; get up, eat and drink, and be joyful, for there is a sound of abundance of rain. May God graciously grant it! Amen.

---

1. The Vale of Barmen, where the author resided.

2

Elijah at the Brook Cherith

At that awful moment, when Israel stood at the brink of the Red Sea, perplexed with which way to turn; while before them the deep waters roared, behind them the enraged Egyptians were rushing upon them with chariots and horsemen, and on either side of them perpendicular rocks rising up like walls on high, making retreat impossible, the Lord came to Moses and said, "Wherefore criest thou unto me? Speak unto the children of Israel, that they go forward," Exod. 14:15.

There seems something very surprising in this command. No vocal cry had proceeded from the prophet's lips; on the contrary, he seemed firm and resolute, endeavoring to comfort and animate Israel with all his might, and to set before them the promises with which God, who is "Yea and Amen," had so solemnly bound himself to them, to be their defense and their help. "Fear ye not," he cried through all their ranks; "stand still and see the salvation of the Lord, which he will show to you today; for the Egyptians whom ye have seen today, ye shall see them again no more for ever. The Lord shall fight for you, and ye shall hold your peace," Exod. 14:13, 14. And while he was thus crying through all their companies, apparently so firm, so courageous, and so joyful in his God, the word of the Lord came, saying, "Moses, wherefore criest thou unto me?"

Moses alone was capable of understanding this Divine address, and Moses understood it well. From his voice, indeed, there had been no cry to God; but so much the louder was the cry of his heart; and, though in appearance he was courageous, valiant, and intrepid, like a young hero, for the people's sake, that they might not despair—in the spirit of this man of God there was the very opposite; there was distress and disturbance, perplexity and fear. His faith struggled in arduous conflict with the billows which impetuously broke in upon him, threatening to overwhelm him; while the promises of his God—though it seemed as if he had them like a rock under his feet, and as a staff in his right hand—alas, they were to his spirit only as the broken moonbeams on the surface of a stormy ocean. The Lord saw clearly what was passing in the soul of his prophet, and before Moses had time or opportunity to lament over it before him, or to hasten to him with the cry, "Lord, I believe! help thou my unbelief!" the Lord was already preparing to rebuke the storm in his heart; and he did rebuke it, by saying to him, "Wherefore criest thou unto me? Speak unto the children of Israel, that they go forward!"

We have a God, who is perfectly acquainted with the most secret thoughts of our hearts, and whose eyes, like a flaming fire, dart through the chambers of our soul, and descend into the most secret recesses of our nature. Even before we have opened to him our distress, he is already making arrangements for our help, regarding our very uneasiness as a cry to him, and giving ear to our inward groanings. He always knows exactly, and much better than we do, what is good and necessary for his children; and, in truth, he never leads them otherwise than they would wish him to lead them, if they were able to see as clearly into their hearts and their necessities, as he does. But we very seldom know what is good for us; and therefore the ways by which God leads us are generally mysterious and obscure, just because the why and the wherefore are concealed from us. But however severe, painful, and dark the Lord's guidance of us may occasionally appear, it is in reality nothing less than an answer, if not to our express petitions, yet to our wants, and to those necessities of ours with which we may be unacquainted. They are all ways of mercy, and their simple end is salvation and blessing.

"Wherefore criest thou unto me? Speak unto the children of Israel, that they go forward!" Thus spake Jehovah unto Moses: and what a commission was this! Lord, behold the sea with its billows at our feet! "Let them go forward!" Lord, are we able to walk upon the waves, and to find a highway upon the mighty waters? "Let them go forward!" Lord, Lord! but where is the passage over the flood, or where are the vessels for our conveyance? Is it your will that your people perish in the sea, and that the Egyptians triumph? "Speak unto them, that they go forward!" says the Almighty; but still he does not touch

a single wave to quell it, nor does he dry up the sea, but lets its waves
roar at their pleasure, and pointing to its troubled surface he commands that "all the hosts of Israel go forward!" They must venture
upon his word, they must believe before they see, and go forward in
faith. They venture, and lo! the very moment they prepare to
advance in the name of their God, and to step upon the boisterous
element—the waves, struck by the rod of Moses, part asunder, and
become a wall on their right hand and on their left, a highway in the
sea is opened before them, and the people pass over joyfully.
This is the way of our gracious God. We must venture upon his
word; and verily, however much we seem to hazard in his name,
nothing is really hazarded. And when he commands us to go forward,
be it into fire, tempest, or the sea, let us advance boldly and be of
good cheer: the result will be glorious. Truths like these, of the most
consolatory kind, we shall see confirmed, as we now proceed with the
history of our prophet.

1 Kings 17:2-6

> And the word of the Lord came unto him, saying, Get thee hence, and
> turn thee eastward, and hide thyself by the brook Cherith, that is before
> Jordan. And it shall be, that thou shalt drink of the brook; and I have
> commanded the ravens to feed thee there. So he went and did accord-
> ing unto the word of the Lord: for he went and dwelt by the brook
> Cherith, that is before Jordan. And the ravens brought him bread and
> flesh in the morning, and bread and flesh in the evening; and he drank
> of the brook.

How refreshing a stream of instruction may this narrative prove to
those who have to tread in any similar path, or to bear any similar trials to those of Elijah! Draw near then, you who dwell in a desert, and
are solitary in the midst of this wilderness world. Bring vessels with
you, and draw abundantly, and drink, and let your sorrows cease.
The subjects to which we would now direct your attention, are, I.
Elijah's perplexity; II. God's command; III. The prophet's faith; IV
The triumph of his faith.

Elijah's Perplexity

I. Elijah had prayed; in zeal for the honor of God he had prayed
that it might not rain; and, being assured of an answer to his prayer,

he had gone to Samaria to meet Ahab. There, in his presence, he declared with holy boldness—and no doubt the whole country was soon filled with the report of it—"There shall not be dew nor rain these years, but according to my word," v. 1.

The word was spoken in God's name, and the judgment denounced immediately followed: first, in appalling harbingers; then, in complete desolation. The sun glared upon the earth with its scorching beams, a memento of the eyes of the Lord the righteous judge which are described as "a flame of fire"; those rays which heretofore had diffused a smile over the whole face of nature were now changed into arrows of destruction and death while the sultry winds dried up with their burning gusts every rivulet from its bed and every fountain from its source; the plants and trees dropped their leaves and withered away; the lowing herds and bleating flocks explored every spot upon the parched fields; the wild beasts moaned in the forests; the dearth rose to its height, and it was not long before the famine became universal and turned every place into mourning and woe.

And where is Elijah? Where should he be? He is sharing in the common calamity. No angel has come to convey him away—no chariot of fire has taken him up. There he stands with the criminals on the place of execution, apparently himself a sacrifice to the wrath he had drawn down, and exposed, with the ungodly, to famine and death. There he stands, panting and groaning like the rest, exposed to the same dangers, and, over and above, hated by a whole nation, and devoted to ruin by the infuriated populace. He seemed likely to suffer the fate of Samson, who pulled down upon himself the pillars of Dagon's temple-roof, and was buried in the common ruin of his enemies. Surely it was no small matter, in such circumstances, to keep faith alive. What a commotion must have arisen in his soul, at beholding the universal misery around him, and his own personal danger! How easily may we suppose natural pity at one time, and natural fear and despondency at another, suggesting to him, "Why did you pray for this?" It is not difficult to realize the perplexity in which the prophet must have felt himself. His joyful elevation of spirit must well nigh have subsided, and no support was left him, but simple faith in the "Amen" of his God; the consciousness that all had been done in God's name, and that now, the Lord would provide.

Similar experiences to that of which Elijah was probably the subject are not uncommon to the children of God. Something like this every Christian occasionally undergoes, in one way or another. An individual is inwardly constrained to say or do some particular thing. The impulse is strong—the inward call seems not to be resisted. Stimulated by holy zeal, he cheerfully enters, in the name of God, upon a duty or a course of action without any cold calculation of consequences—the measure is adopted, the word is uttered. Then all at once he is made aware of what he has risked; he finds himself cast into difficulties and dangers, which seem far to exceed the measure of his faith and ability; he has stepped with Peter upon the open sea: the wind becomes boisterous, and he is threatened with destruction. He wants to retrace his steps, but retreat is out of question. Then that cheerful zeal which actuated us seems to have burned down into the socket, and the soul desponds and cries, "Lord! save us, we perish!"

This was the case with some excellent men, who very lately, on account of their faith, were obliged to leave their native land. In opposition to the spirit of the great and mighty of this world, and of the ignorant multitude, they preached to their congregations the pure gospel—repentance towards God, and faith towards our Lord Jesus Christ. In so doing they had exposed themselves to danger which, however, was somewhat held back by their prudently refraining from publicly attacking the national church and the unchristian inroads which their superiors were making upon its ancient doctrine and discipline. But, all unexpectedly, their lips were opened by Another, so that they could not refrain from preaching what they had been reluctant to bring out, and would otherwise have shrunk from doing; and, carried away by a holy zeal, they declared the danger by which the national church was menaced. All mischiefs and abuses were then exposed without fear of consequences, so that the people's ears tingled.

Uzziah was denounced for his unpardonable presumption in seeking to associate the censer with the sword. They could no longer keep silence respecting the insidious design of reducing the religion of Christ ultimately to mere heathenism; they roundly declared nothing else was intended, than craftily to bear away the ark of the covenant, and to smuggle images of jealousy—false doctrines and precepts—into the sanctuary. They complained openly, that the churches had been robbed of that valuable treasure, the Heidelberg catechism; that books were imposed upon teachers and scholars, which were infected with the spirit of antichrist; that the last pillars of their ancient ecclesiastical constitution were being shaken, in order that the church of Christ might become a mere political institution; and many of the worthy preachers so lost sight of themselves, and gave themselves up so entirely to the impulse of the Spirit of God, that they openly avowed they could not conscientiously belong to such a church any longer.

The words were uttered, the match thrown into the mine; and who would fetch it back? The people were amazed and confounded; many hastened to their teachers as soon as the sermon was ended, and expressed their determination to separate from such a church; others wavered, and were much perplexed. The mass of the people vented abuse and curses, threatening to stone those intrepid witnesses; and the strong arm of civil power came upon them with ejections, imprisonments, and exile. The worthy men had not thought of consequences like these. Consternation came upon them like an armed man. The heroic zeal, which had carried them away in their pulpits, and in which they regarded God only and his cause, but not themselves or their own lives, had now so subsided under the pressure of these floods of affliction, that they were forced to say, "Had we foreseen the consequences, we would have held our peace." Nothing now remained to them but the conviction that God had directed them; for their own prudence would have had it otherwise; and this assurance, that God would have it so, is the pilgrim-staff which has supported and comforted them in their banishment and wanderings to the present hour.

Now, that which happened to these worthy men upon a public scale, happens to thousands of Christians in a more private way continually. One, under the influence of the Spirit of love, confidently entrusts his property to a brother in embarrassment, for Christ's sake; but subsequently he experiences the temporal inconveniences of such an act in his own privations or those of his children, and in other perplexing circumstances; then his joy departs, and his heart is terrified. Another, animated by holy zeal, stands up at length among his friends or relatives, with a confession of Christ crucified, or even with a serious call to repentance; but afterwards, when he finds what misunderstandings and wrong feelings he has thus raised against himself, his zeal subsides, and he is wretchedly cast down. What now must he do? Must he recall what he has uttered? This he cannot, this he dare not do, for his Lord's sake; no, he must let the fire burn. A third is constrained, from the fullness of his heart, to entreat the Lord to unite him more closely to himself; and if it cannot be done by gentle means, to effectuate it through affliction. The affliction comes—the waves of trouble roll over him; but alas! affliction, while he is under its chastening, no longer seems joyous, but grievous. The cheerful emotion, with which he once prayed respecting it, is gone; he is ready to repent of such a prayer; his heart can do nothing but mourn and complain.

Are we then to begin nothing without first calculating the consequences? I reply: Where it is possible previously to sit down and count the cost, do so. But as this is not always possible, it cannot be made a universal rule. The lion roars—who can keeps from trembling? The Lord gives the word—who can refuse to publish it? The stream rushes along—who shall impede it? The love of Christ constrains—who shall restrain it? The Spirit is as a fire in the bosom—who shall quench it? What a man is bound to do—he must do; and if any evil result from it, he may then say, "I was bound to do it; it was God's command; it was not the dictate of flesh and blood." With faith like this, much difficulty and perplexity may be overcome. And you may rely upon this, that if the arm of God is ready to assist any, it is those who, upon his call to "Come hither!" confer not with flesh and blood, but with joyful alacrity venture upon the waves; and at his bidding, risk all consequences. This we may learn from the example of Elijah.

God's Command

II. He did not remain long in this solitary condition, left to the musings of his heavy heart. When he knew not what to do, counsel was given him; and when he saw no way of escape, the gates were opened to him. Such is usually the case. We read, that now "The word of the Lord came to him." What a cheering visitation in a land overspread with desolation and misery! For when the word of the Lord comes to us, we are visited by nothing less than God's eternal love and compassion; for the word of the Lord is Christ. Nothing is so beautifying to the spirit of a man at any time as the visitation and manifestation of Christ. But this is especially blissful and desirable, when we have undertaken something in his name, and have thereby kindled a fire, which threatens to consume ourselves and others—when, at his bidding, we have ventured upon a duty, the consequences of which are such as to perplex us, and make us doubt whether it was really the will of God, and at his bidding. Such a perplexity is indescribably painful, and raises our distress to the highest pitch. How gladly is He welcomed under such circumstances, when he unexpectedly knocks at our door, and permits us again to hear the sweetness of his voice; when he again, in some way of his own, gives us to understand that we have acted rightly; causing something to transpire which leaves us no longer in doubt as to his approval of our conduct, and either by some external help, or by some spiritual testimony and assurance of his grace, giving us an evidence that he regards us not with displeasure, but with complacency; and that what we have done has been well done, for he has pronounced it good. Oh! this surpasses all other joy in this world, and though our temporal burdens may remain as they were, we are wonderfully strengthened to bear them!

"The word of the Lord came to Elijah." He had not to seek for it, but it came to him; and the Lord is kind indeed, thus to comfort his children uninvited, and to anticipate their suit with his own counsel; for he does not always wait until they ask, any more than that saying is always true, that "Distress will compel men to pray." Oh how are men even at their wit's end, when the waves of trouble come suddenly upon them, and imminent dangers encompass them! They are confounded at the winds; they shrink at the waves; they seize the rudder of human strength; they cling to the brittle anchor of human hope; but, "Master, awake, we perish!" is forgotten, or, if the Lord is thought of, there is a lack of faith, or filial courage and confidence, or something else; and scarcely one step is taken toward seeking the Lord. How justly might he be offended at this, and requite us accordingly! But, no! He rather protects his children with the blessings of goodness, and heaps coals of fire on their heads. He often visits them uninvited, and breaks in with his light and salvation, where he was not only not sought after, but even affronted with misgivings. Such visits of the Lord are surely well suited to humble and abase us, to melt the heart and stop the mouth, so that we have not a word to say for shame and confusion of face. Free and unmerited grace then appears in all its brightness; the Christian can find nothing in himself worthy to be thought of as a meritorious cause of the afforded aid—no prayer, no sigh, no looking up to the Lord; and this humbling acknowledgment of mere unmerited grace, which our proud nature is so unwilling to make, how salutary is it, how good, how conducive to our spiritual welfare!

But to return to the narrative. The Lord interposed, not only to comfort the prophet, but to rescue him from extreme danger. This, however, was to be done in a way which should glorify the name of the Lord, as well as serve for a beneficial exercise of faith to Elijah. No fiery chariot was yet to bear him above his troubles; he was not yet to rise aloft amidst a convoy of angels. Here would have been little room for the exercise of faith. God, therefore, showed him another path. "Get thee hence, and turn thee eastward, and hide thyself by the brook Cherith, that is before Jordan. And it shall be, that thou shalt drink of the brook; and I have commanded the ravens to feed thee there." A singular direction, as it would seem, from a bad condition to a worse. But you remember it was said to Manoah, "Why askest thou after my name, seeing it is wonderful?" Judg. 13:18. And as is his name, so is his way: "Thy way is in the sea, and thy paths in the deep waters, and thy footsteps are not known!" Psa. 77:19.

Do we inquire whether the Lord directs his children still, as thus in old time? Undoubtedly he does though not by any audible voice, yet with equal certainty and evidence; and this commonly by closing up, inwardly or outwardly, all other ways, and leaving only one open to us. And is not this equivalent to our hearing a voice behind us, saying, "This is the way, walk ye in it, when ye turn to the right hand, and when ye turn to the left," Isa. 30:21? When he inwardly leads us—he impresses a Scriptural conviction on the judgment as to what we ought to do, and it is scarcely possible for us any longer to hesitate. Would our feelings lead us in a different course? Then peace immediately departs; and such disquietude arises within us that we are compelled to retrace our steps. When he outwardly leads us—he brings us into such circumstances, connections, and situations, that only one way remains open, for we see every other obstructed by visible providences. The ways which the Lord thus points out to us seem, therefore, like that to the brook Cherith, selected and appointed purely for the exercise of our faith, and the crucifixion of our old man. Only follow on courageously! Whenever the Lord says to any of his children, "Get thee hence, and hide thyself," he also adds, either expressly or by implication, "and the ravens shall feed thee there." Every duty which He commands has its promise appended to it; and we need be under no concern except to know that the Lord has directed our way.

The Prophet's Faith

III. And how did Elijah obey this command of his God? There was doubtless in him, as well as in every other man, something that would oppose this Divine direction, and be dissatisfied with it. Elijah was a man subject to like passions as we are, and therefore his nature would have much to say against it. How could it please him, that instead of an instantaneous and supernatural deliverance, he is obliged to make a long journey on foot, like any ordinary person? And why he should be directed to turn eastward into the land of Judea, which participated in the judgments of Samaria, he could not discover. To be directed into the lonely wilderness, and to the brook Cherith, amidst gloomy, uninhabited woodlands, was far from inviting. And even his security there, from the pursuit of Ahab, and from the general drought, was not warranted by any natural appearances; while the prospect of being fed by ravens, those unclean and voracious creatures, must have appeared as disagreeable as it was contrary to reason and experience. But, however much nature might oppose, or the old man murmur and recoil, these were silenced and crucified within him. For there was a Spirit imparted to Elijah, which taught him that his own nature was wrong, and that God's will was right.

Not, perhaps, that Elijah was able, with fervency of joy, to thank God for the command given him, and triumphantly to rejoice in it. Possibly, his mind was much tried and depressed by it; but it proved courageous in the faith by which he endured, as seeing Him that is invisible. "As it is the Divine command," he might think, "therefore it is holy, just, and good. God's commissions to his children, what are they but hidden promises? Since he saith to me, 'Get thee hence' I am well assured that he will make a way for me, succor me, and preserve me on the way. Since he commands me to turn eastward, I am certain, though I seem to be going towards the setting rather than the rising sun, still it will be morning over my head. Forasmuch as he bids me hide myself by the brook Cherith, which is before Jordan—that brook must be a safe place of refuge, though it were in the midst of Samaria itself. I am directed to drink of the brook; here then I have a pledge that the sun will not be permitted to affect this brook with his scorching rays." Thus might the prophet think, and then he would conclude further that "God's promises are, virtually, obligations which he imposes upon himself. If he say, 'I will do this or that for thee,' he must necessarily bring it to pass for his own name's sake. Therefore the ravens will certainly come, and sooner will they themselves die of hunger, than I shall be suffered to starve." In this manner might Elijah have conversed with his own heart; and so, taking the word of the Lord into the hand of his faith, he made it the staff of his pilgrimage. Whenever he grew weary, he leaned upon this staff, and his courage revived. When danger appeared in his way, he feared not, while he had this staff to support him. And have you such a staff in your hands? Are you assured, with this prophet, that the path you tread has been pointed out to you of God, and has any Divine promise been applied to you, and become your own, either a particular promise, or a general one, like this, "Fear not: for I have redeemed thee. When thou passest through the waters, they shall not overflow thee" Isa. 43:1, 2? Oh then of a truth, all is well, sure, and certain! But now look at Elijah as he takes his journey, a solitary traveler. It seems almost as if we hear the sound of his footsteps, while we read, that "He went and did according to the word of the Lord: for he went and dwelt by the brook Cherith, that is before Jordan."

The Triumph of His Faith

IV. Come, let us pay a visit to this man of God in his new dwelling-place. A dreary wild, near the banks of the Jordan is the scene now opened before us. Dead silence reigns around, interrupted perhaps by the cry of the solitary bittern, while among the heath and the juniper bushes broods the ostrich, no hunter disturbing its repose. No pathway opens to the view—not a human footstep is seen—all is wilderness and solitude. Let us follow him, in imagination, toward the Jordan. Yonder lies our track, where the naked rocks rear their lofty heads, and the forests frown. Then, through one thicket and another, through one narrow pass and another, we come at length down into a deep and narrow glen, overhung with tangled wood, where a brook runs murmuring along, and finds its way between the rocky masses. Oh look! there sits the man of God! Here is his appointed dwelling. The blue sky his roof, the bare rocks his walls, the stone his seat, the shady wood his bedchamber, the grass

his couch; his company, the purling brook and the hoarse ravens aloft
among the trees. There he sits in his hairy mantle, silent and reflecting; and whenever solitude becomes wearisome, or the hissing of
serpents, or the distant roar of the lion, would inject terror into his
soul, he remembers, "I am imprisoned here for the Lord's sake, and
his footsteps are among these rocks" and thus by faith and hope he
regains courage.

For twelve months did Elijah dwell there. This may seem to you
incredible, and almost dreadful! But how would you be astonished,
were Elijah to assure you, that the whole time never appeared
tedious; that solitude daily became to him less solitary—nay, lively
and cheerful! And doubtless this was the case. He needed neither
books nor society; neither labor nor diversion to entertain him. Silent
nature around him, and the treasure of his own experience, supplied
him with an ample volume. Self-examination, prayer, and converse
with Him who seeth in secret, were employment enough for him. His
Lord and God, whose gentlest whispers and footsteps he could far
more readily perceive in his solitude than amidst the noise of the
busy world, was sufficient company for him. The works of creation
which encompassed him soon served as a living epistle, which he
found it employment enough to study. The rock, by which he dwelt,
preached to him of a Rock that ever lives, and whereon he himself
had built. The brook had something to say to him, and spoke many
sweet and comfortable things to him of the truth and faithfulness of
God, and told of other waters that were still to come—of waters that
God would pour upon the dry ground, and of floods upon the thirsty
land, and of springs which he would cause to break forth in the
desert. At one time, the shady trees would preach to him, and suggest to him the comforts of the tree of life, and of those heavenly
palls from whose tops eternal peace would at length breathe upon
him. At another, the cheerful songsters of the air, and the wild roses
in the brakes, would sing to him, "Be calm, Elijah, and free from care.
How can He who is so faithfully mindful of us in this wilderness,
feeding the one and giving fragrance and beauty to the other, be forgetful of you?" In short, everything began to live, and breathe, and
talk around him: the stars in the firmament, the flowers on the banks,
the drops on the leaves, and the zephyrs among the shrubs; so that
Elijah experienced what the apostle says, "There are so many kinds
of voices in the world, and none of them is without signification," 1

Cor. 14:10; and was able to sing with David, " The voice of the Lord is powerful. The voice of the Lord shaketh the wilderness," Psa. 29:4.8.

After having thus pleased and delighted himself awhile in the exterior world and its speaking emblems, he would then return to another world within him, and be absorbed in listening to what was stirring and passing there. At one time a new insight was afforded him into his deep poverty of spirit and natural corruption; and then he would be led to weep, and mourn, and wrestle in prayerful conflict. At another time, he would contemplate the work of Divine grace within him, and the clear evidences of the indwelling and operation of the Holy Spirit in his soul; and now the cliffs of the wilderness would resound with psalms, like a temple of God, and with pious hymns of thanksgiving, which vibrated strangely with the mountain echo, far into the depths of his solitude.

Let no one be too much cast down, should the Lord ever direct him to the wilderness, by the river Jordan, and to the brook Cherith! For he still is accustomed to do so with his children in a variety of ways. If he visit us with sickness, so that we must be alone upon our bed and in our chamber; or if our friends forsake us, and forget us; if we become regarded as outcasts, having neither house nor heart opened to us any longer; or if we are called to sojourn in Mesech, and to dwell amongst those who are of a different mind from ourselves, who do not understand us, and who ridicule our way of life—in such situations we are shut in with Elijah, by the brook Cherith. But be not alarmed; rather be of good courage! Such seclusion, or exclusion, how blissful and salutary may it become! Numberless Christians have been constrained to declare that it was in their imprisonment, or place of exile—in their lonely sick chamber, or in the days when they were forsaken by men, and cast out by the world—that they entered really into their own hearts, and ascertained their true spiritual state.

The leaven of the Pharisees was then put away from them, and worship was no longer paid to an imaginary Savior. They began to long in earnest for close communion with him; and the wrestling prayer of Jacob, lasting until daybreak, which they had only talked of before, now became a matter of reality and experience, an event in their own personal history. And a hundred other things pertaining to inward religion, which they had only in imagination appropriated hitherto, were then individually realized. They were then also first truly brought into the number of those sheep who hear His voice, and were never so conscious that he really lives and speaks to his children, and walks and dwells with them; nor did they ever experience his tender consolation and support, or ever feel his love so strongly, as at that very time, when their path was so solitary and through the wilderness, when they were obliged to be with their Lord alone. Therefore be of good cheer, you who dwell by the brook Cherith in solitude, for God's dew can drop upon the dwellings of the wilderness, as David sings, and the pastures in the wilderness do spring with blessings.

"Thou shalt drink of the brook, and the ravens shall feed thee there." Thus said the Lord; and, however marvelous and unheard of it might sound, Elijah bowed himself and believed, and his faith did not deceive him. All that the Lord had promised was "yea, and amen," and nothing remained unfulfilled. It was not long before the whole country was like a heath, and fields and woods became scorched as by fire. One spot alone continued green and cool; that spot was the prophet's rocky vale. Every fountain was exhausted, and every forest stream dried up by the sultry heat; one brook alone continued to flow—the brook Cherith that remained as fresh and as full as if nothing had happened. And the ravens also fulfilled their office. How wonderful! those ravenous carrion birds, impure according to the law, and so voracious and unfeeling, that they would leave their own young to starve, did not God interpose, as we read in the book of Job, "Who provideth for the raven his food? when his young ones cry unto God, they wander for lack of meat," Job 38:41—these creatures we find employed here in an occupation of disinterested kindness, dead as it were to the natural voracity of their species, coming and going at God's bidding, denying their own appetites, and performing a most beneficent office. No sooner does the morning dawn in Cherith's rocky vale, than their cry is heard aloft in the trees, and when Elijah wakes, he beholds the provision for the day lying before him. And when the evening shades advance, these black liveried servants again appear, laden with meat and bread. And this takes place not merely once, but a whole year round, without intermission. O wisdom of God, which carnal reason would account foolishness, how precious you are! Let the world imagine to itself a magnificent Deity "whose government is only general" we adhere to

the Lord God of Elijah, and rejoice in his providential superintendence of the smallest matters.

And this God still lives, a living Savior, who is always to he found
of them who seek him, and is nigh unto them that call upon him;
and whose delights are with the sons of men. About his servants and
handmaids is encamped a mighty host and when he says, "Come,"
they come; or, "Go!" they go and there has been no end to his wonders, even to this day. Who else was it but the God of Elijah, who,
only a short time ago, in our neighborhood, so kindly delivered a
poor man out of his distress; not indeed by a raven, but by a poor
singing bird?

The man was sitting, early in the morning, at his house-door; his
eyes were red with weeping, and his heart cried to Heaven for he was
expecting an officer to come and imprison him for a small debt. And
while sitting thus with his heavy heart, a little bird flew through the
street, fluttering up and down, as if in distress, until at length, quick
as an arrow, it flew over the good man's head into his cottage, and
perched itself on an empty cupboard. The good man, who little imagined who had sent him the bird, closed the door, caught the bird, and
placed it in a cage, where it immediately began to sing very sweetly.
It seemed to the man as if it were the tune of a favorite hymn, "Fear
thou not when darkness reigns"; and as he listened to it, he found it
to soothe and comfort his mind. Suddenly someone knocked at his
door. "Ah, it is the officer," thought the man, and was sore afraid. But
no, it was the servant of a respectable lady, who said that the neigh-
bors had seen a bird fly unto his house, and she wished to know if he
had caught it. "O yes," answered the man, "and here it is"; and the
bird was carried away. A few minutes after, the servant came again.
"You have done my mistress a great service," said he; "she sets a high
value upon the bird, which had escaped from her. She is much obliged to you, and requests you to accept this trifle, with her thanks."
The poor man received it thankfully, and it proved to be neither
more nor less than the sum he owed! And when the officer came, he
said, "Here is the amount of the debt; now leave me in peace, for
God has sent it me."

The God of Elijah still lives! and under this truth I may rank other
experiences also. Help has often come to others in a wonderful manner, from persons who were not only strangers, but even disaffected
and bore some ill-will; from unbelievers, who, in general, cannot

endure them that are "quiet in the land," Psa 35:20. But, all at once, it suddenly occurred to one, he himself knew not how, that he must bring someone some particular thing; or another could not sleep for the thought of not having done something for another, and however much he strove to drive the idea from his mind, he could not succeed in kicking against the pricks. Yes, He who turns men's hearts as the rivers of water, sent them aid; and His purpose who shall defeat? What they did for others was not done because they intended it, but because they were constrained by conscience, that is, by the God of conscience; and thus we experience that the God of Elijah, who can provide for his servants even by the ravens, still lives.

Therefore let every child of God be strong and of good courage! Only believe, you who are at the brook Cherith and in the wilderness! for faith can supply the want of everything temporal, and faith is the grave of care. And remember, dear friends, that it is in vain for you to rise early and sit up late, and eat the bread of Sorrows; for as David says, "He giveth it to his beloved sleeping,"[1] Psa. 77:2. May He who gives songs in the right, teach us all the song of the royal psalmist, "I will both lay me down in peace, and sleep; for thou, Lord, only makest me dwell in safety !" Psa. 4:8.

---

1. German Version.

3

The Departure for Zarephath

Once, when the children of Israel did evil in the sight of the Lord, he delivered them into the hands of the Midianites, a fierce and warlike people; these God employed to drive back his erring and straying sheep under the crook of the Chief Shepherd. There was great distress in Israel at that time. A considerable number of the people forsook house and home, fled to the woods and mountains, or skulked into caverns and rocks; and a few intrenched themselves in deserted fortifications! Whenever they attempted to cultivate the land, the Midianites soon fell upon them, like locusts, destroying all growth in the field, and leaving no sustenance for man or beast. This severe scourge produced its effect. The Israelites acknowledged their sin and smote upon the thigh, every hand was stretched to heaven, and every tongue prayed, "Return, O Lord! to thine oppressed inheritance!" And God, who is faithful, heard them, and sent them relief.

In the field of Ophrah stands a solitary oak, and near it is a threshing-floor, where a young farmer is threshing his father's corn; and while thus engaged, he has to look about him every moment, with no little anxiety, for he fears to be surprised by the marauding Midianites. His name is Gideon. In the midst of his busy and anxious occupation he is surprised by the sudden appearance of a stranger of benevolent and noble aspect. The stranger sits down beneath the oak, and says, "The Lord be with thee, thou mighty man of valor!"

Gideon, with the regard of a true Israelite for his country, replied,

"O my Lord, if the Lord be with us, why then is all this befallen us? and where are all the miracles which our fathers told us of, saying, Did not the Lord bring us up from Egypt? But now the Lord hath forsaken us, and delivered us into the hands of the Midianites," Judg. 6:12,13. Then, we are told, the Lord looked upon him, and said: "Go in this thy might, and thou shalt save Israel from the hand of the Midianites: have not I sent thee?" ver. 14.

To be looked upon by the Lord is not always a source of comfort and pleasure. When he once looked upon the Egyptians, it was as if the arrows of the Almighty had struck through the whole host. Then were the hearts of the mighty troubled, and the wisdom of the prudent "as brought to naught. He looketh upon the mountains and they tremble," Jer. 4:24. When a look of the same kind alighted upon Daniel's attendants, such a terror came over them that they fled and hid themselves. And how affectingly does Job complain, "Thine eyes are upon me and I am not! Am I a sea, or a whale, that thou settest a watch over me? How long wilt thou not depart from me, nor let me alone till I swallow down my spittle? I have sinned; what shall I do unto thee, O thou Preserver of men! Why dost thou not pardon my transgression, and take away my iniquity?" Job 7:8. 12:21. And still does the Majesty of heaven look upon man who is a worm; yes, he who is holy, holy, holy, looks into our darkness; the eye of his everlasting righteousness still beholds the sinner; and an awakened consciousness of this is the most awful of all terrors that a miserable soul on earth can experience; and yet it must in some measure be experienced, before we can ever truly rejoice in the light of his countenance.

But the look which was here given to Gideon, under the oak, was one of kindness and grace: and he who gave it directs him, saying, "Go in this thy might!" In what might?

"In the might which my beholding thee communicates; which has assured thee of my gracious favor." Verily, a power thus communicated, which gives to its recipient a consciousness of Divine grace and love, is great indeed. The heart, which hitherto had been like the troubled sea, is now changed into an abode of heavenly peace; and the soul, which a little before had sat down in sackcloth and in ashes, suddenly rises in joy and transport as on eagles' wings, now that the eye of Divine commission has beamed upon it. A person, very simple, it may be, in other respects, will then unfold himself like a blossom of paradise, diffusing around the most delightful and salutary fragrance, and will discover, all at once, such gifts and powers as seem to have come immediately from above. Reserved and retiring persons seem at such times to have had their lips touched and their tongues unloosed, and will express themselves in such a lovely manner, that one is never tired of hearing them; yes, the most modest and timid will then come forward and confess Christ and his love, with such a holy boldness and sober joy, that one cannot but admire their courage and liberty of spirit. And what real sacrifices do we then see, such persons make, what self-denial! what patience! what resignation! what fervent brotherly love will they evince! But whence does all this proceed? We answer, from the power of one gracious look of God; from the consciousness that my Savior "loved me, and gave himself for me," Gal. 2:20.

"Go in this thy might," said the Lord to Gideon, as he cast upon him a look of love and grace. He meant not, O Gideon! that you should subdue the enemy in your own strength. He directed you to His strength, and not your own. It is as if he had said, " Be this your strength, O Gideon! that I have regarded you graciously, and let it encourage you, let it suffice you, that you have found grace in the eyes of the Lord. Go in this thy strength, and conquer."

Oh invaluable assurance! Only possess the assurance, that he is graciously inclined towards you, and you may well be a stranger to fear. Only lay hold of such a testimony, that he is your Beloved, that he is your Friend, and no storms or tempests need dismay you any more; you may laugh at the shaking of the spear; yes, though there were thousands of deaths encompassing you, or thousands of difficulties like mountains surrounding you they will all be surmounted. Do not falter at your own natural weakness, don't be anxious about your own ability. Weak or strong—armed or unarmed—in these respects the race is not here to the swift, nor the battle to the strong. The strength of Emmanuel is yours, his love is like a victorious banner over you; his word is your sword, his salvation your helmet, his righteousness your breastplate; faith in him is your shield and buckler. He is all that you require; his grace is sufficient for you. Wherever he sends you—be it into the fire of temptation, or into the waters of affliction—be it unto domestic embarrassments and necessities, or into severe conflicts and difficult undertakings, nay, were it even into agony and death—yet his having graciously looked upon you, and his having made you sensible of his love, may well induce you to go; yes, go in this you might! You have no cause for fear—none for distrust. Your Savior will accompany and protect you, because he loves you. He whose love is stronger than death, will make all your way plain before you.

Thus was it that Elijah went to the brook Cherith, in the strength of that kindness and favor which he too had received from his Lord. We are now to view him entering upon a new path of duty, equally painful and difficult in itself, but rendered smooth and easy by the strength of which we have been speaking. Yes, it becomes a path of blessing, because the Lord is with him.

1 Kings 17:7-15

> And it came to pass after a while, that the brook dried up because there had been no rain in the land. And the word of the Lord came unto him, saying, Arise, get thee to Zarephath, which belongeth to Zidon, and dwell there: behold, I have commanded a widow woman there to sustain thee. So he arose and went to Zarephath. And when he came to the gate of the city, behold, the widow woman was there gathering sticks: and he called to her, and said, Fetch me, I pray thee, a little water in a vessel, that I may drink. And as she was going to fetch it he called to her, and said, bring me, I pray thee, a morsel of bread in thine hand. And she said, As the Lord thy God liveth, I have not a cake, but an handful of meal in a barrel, and a little oil in a cruse: and, behold, I am gathering two sticks, that I may go in and dress it for me and my son, that we may eat it, and die. And Elijah said unto her, Fear not; go and do as thou hath said: but make me thereof a little cake first, and bring it unto me, and after make for thee and for thy son. For thus saith the Lord God of Israel, The barrel of meal shall not waste, neither shall the cruse of oil fail, until the day that the Lord sendeth rain upon the earth. And she went and did according to the saying of Elijah: and she, and he, and her house, did eat many days. And the barrel of meal wasted not, neither did the cruse of oil fail, according to the word of the Lord, which he spake by Elijah.

We find the prophet still at the brook Cherith. He would not leave his solitude till the Lord bade him move. The howling wilderness was not too dreary for him because God was with him. He was quite content to dwell among the rocks, and to rest upon a couch of

turf; knowing well, that "the Lord will provide." He was regularly supplied with sustenance morning and evening, by his faithful
messengers, whose very cry as they approached him would serve to
awaken his heart to songs of thanksgiving and praise. The little brook
of Cherith, whose very name, in the original language, denotes
drought, as if it were generally more apt to dry up than most other
brooks, had run on till now, and surely by a miracle; but it was only
for an appointed time. For now we behold the scene changing. The
change at its commencement was most unexpected and painful; it
was also in its further development very mysterious; but its result was
as delightful to man, as it was glorious to God.

Three subjects here invite our consideration: I. Elijah's confusion;
II. His departure from Cherith; and, III. Its blessed result.

Elijah's Confusion

I. He had now, during a whole year, been miraculously fed and preserved. But a miracle perpetuated soon ceases to appear a miracle.
And when it begins to be regarded as a matter of course, it fails of its
due impression, and God's hand in it is liable to be overlooked. There
is an eastern story of a boy having challenged his teacher to prove to
him the existence of God by working a miracle. The teacher, who
was a priest, got a large vessel filled with earth, wherein he deposited a kernel, in the boy's presence, and bade him pay attention. In the
place where the kernel was put, a green shoot suddenly appeared, the
shoot became a stem, the stem put forth leaves and branches, which
soon spread over the whole apartment. It then budded with blossoms,
which dropping off left golden fruits in their place, and in the short
space of one hour there stood a noble tree in the place of the little
seed. The youth, overcome with amazement, exclaimed, "Now I
know that there is a God, for I have seen his power!" The priest
smiled at him, and said, "Simple child, do you only now believe?
Does not what you have just beheld take place in innumerable
instances, year after year, only by a slower process? But is it the less
marvelous on that account?"

We are too often like such simple children. Suppose at rising in
the morning we found a loaf added to our provisions, which we could
be certain that neither we nor any human being had put there—we
should then have no difficulty in saying that the Lord had sent it. Yet
we actually find such a loaf every morning added to our provisions,

and it is equally true that God has sent it: but because he has sent it in a less direct and extraordinary manner, (namely, by strengthening our own powers, and blessing our labor to obtain it), and because this is an ordinary case, and what is taking place all the world over, there-fore—how unreasonable such a therefore may be—we find it difficult to realize in it his goodness, his providence, and himself. And let me tell you, that supposing he were to manifest himself in any extraordinary manner, so as to compel us to exclaim, "This is indeed a marvelous interposition of God"; yet let any such manifestation only become continual, and it will be no longer accounted mar-velous; yes, it will be well if it do not cease to be regarded even as Divine. The manna falls once or twice in the wilderness, and it is wondrous in the eyes of all, and the Lord God is praised. But if it falls every day, its coming is a matter of course; and men learn to con-template it as a natural event; they behold the manna, but not the hand that sends it. Water is produced miraculously from the rock; and if it be succeeded by heat and drought, men learn in some mea-sure to give God the glory. But the smitten rock in the wilderness virtually follows the Israelite host; its streams attend them in their daily course; they have no lack of water; and what is the conse-quence? They are ungrateful, and so are we. God is daily working wonders for us also; but in order to learn this, it is good for us some-times to undergo privations.

Not that we mean to affirm this respecting Elijah at the brook Cherith. Far be it from us to think so ill of him. But the apostle James says, "Elias was a man subject to like passions as we are"; and to any one like ourselves, it is very possible for length of time to weaken the impression of what is really wonderful, strengthening to faith, and elevating to the affections; so that Elijah himself might possibly have begun to think, "Ah! this brook flows on only like other rivulets; that is, as long as its spring is supplied!" Thus it is that we children of men are too much disposed to consider things; thus are we apt to put the Divine long-suffering to the trial, and as we account it a small thing to weary men, we go on to weary our God also. But among the many kind offices which our gracious God has taken upon himself, for his children's sake, there is that which he mentions in Isa. 45:4, " Even to old age will I carry you." Indeed, how continually has he some-thing to bear with in our conduct! And as he knows how easily a blessing perpetuated ceases to be a blessing, how wisely does he provide, in his faithful love, that there shall be no lack of changes in our earthly course! Hence he leads us through incessant alternations, as it were, of summer and winter, day and night, rain and sunshine, trouble and help, anguish and deliverance. It is thus that he preserves us in spiritual health, and prevents our wandering from himself. For thus we have always something to transact with him; there is constantly something to be asked of him, or something to thank him for; some deliverance from trouble, or some increased humiliation of spirit, some renewed watchfulness, or some more faithful waiting upon him, is always needed. Doubtless this was one reason why our gracious God led the prophet Elijah in such a circuitous way, and caused him to experience so many trials. How precariously changeful does his life appear! How interwoven with various necessities! Yet, on this very account, it abounded in real and lasting blessings.

Our present text commences with the words, "And it came to pass after a while, that the brook dried up." From this it might be supposed that Elijah was only a short time in the wilderness; but this was not the case. In Genesis 4:3, immediately after the mention of the birth of Cain and Abel, we read, "It came to pass, after a while, that Cain brought of the fruit of the ground as offering unto the Lord." Here the expression "after a while" cannot mean a short time, but must indicate a period of several years. And, in the history before us, the expression, "after a while," denotes at least a whole year; for so long does Elijah appear to have continued in the wilderness. For we learn from the mouth of the Lord Jesus, Luke 4:25, as well as from the apostle James, 5:17, that the drought prevailed during three years and six months. Now we find, from 1 Kings 18:1, that the time when the drought ceased was in the third year of the prophet's residence at Zarephath. Supposing him, therefore, to have been two years and six months at Zarephath, where could he have spent the remaining year, except at the brook Cherith?

That year had now passed over by the help of God, at one time in faith, at another in sight, certainly under many difficulties, but on the whole a thousand times better and more pleasantly than Elijah had probably expected at the commencement. How long he should still remain there he knew not; that he left to God. Perhaps it might be the whole time of the famine. "Well, be it so, if it be the Lord's will!" He had hitherto wanted for nothing. The ravens did their office; the brook continued to flow, and if it had flowed this year, why should it dry up the next? Such were probably the prophet's thoughts at the opening of a new year upon him in the wilderness. But before long the flow of the brook begins to diminish, and Elijah perhaps can scarcely believe what his eyes behold. Did not God say, "Thou shalt drink of the brook," and thus virtually promise that water should not fail him? We may well imagine him now observing the brook more accurately. Yes it is so—the brook is diminishing daily, the bed of the rivulet begins to appear, and soon, where water flowed, all is become dry. "What does this mean?" Even an Elijah might well cast in his mind what manner of providential dealing this should be. At last water was no longer to be found. Oh the depths of God! Oh what peculiar guidance! What a severe trial! "What does this mean?—to be preserved so long, and now apparently forsaken? Such sure promises, yet such a result! Where is the Lord God of Israel? Am I no longer his prophet? Have I sinned against him, that I am now deserted? Does it repent him that he has employed me?" Thus might Elijah have thought; and who can say what other imaginations corrupt nature might have suggested, and how the prophet himself might have begun inwardly to complain? Elijah was evidently in a great strait; for death by thirst seemed imminent; and what is more, the temptation to false notions and hard thoughts of God was near, to which had he yielded, his faith had then dried up, and his confidence had disappeared like the brook.

Yes, it is one of the sorest trials that can possibly befall us, when, having been placed by the kind providence of God in the midst of peculiar comforts, and just beginning to enjoy them with lively gratitude and hope, we are suddenly torn from them, or bereft of all. Our harp is then turned into mourning, and our joy to heaviness. Let us suppose anyone to be under severe domestic affliction or embarrassment, in debt, for instance, and threatened with an arrest in default of immediate payment. You wrestle with God in prayer that he would help you, and his providence sends you the very help you want. Your heart is then melted with thankfulness, and you are disposed to say, "Truly the Lord lives and sees me; he hears and answers prayer!" But suppose that very night your house is broken into, your money stolen, and all your embarrassment returns. Again, suppose that, with much laborious industry, you have acquired the means of renting a small farm; you employ your whole little capital upon it; and you pray God that it would please him to bless your labor with increase, for the support of yourself and your family. And then you behold the seed sprung up, and your fields beautifully verdant. "Thanks be to God," you will say, "I now see his goodness to his creatures." But in a few more weeks, perhaps a dry summer, or a season of excessive rain, disappoints you. What is your language now, in cases of this sort? Do you not call these hard trials, and account them the more severe because they have come upon you in the ordinary way of Providence? Had they been more like Job's afflictions, something out of the common way, you are apt to imagine you could have borne them better; you would then have seen that they came from God, and you are perhaps vain enough to suppose you would have displayed extraordinary patience under them. For instance, had the money which you had so wonderfully received been melted in your safe by a thunderbolt, then you would have said, "The Lord gave, and the Lord hath taken away," Job 1:21. But now, as it has been carried off by thieves, you are apt to think these words of Job inapplicable to your own case; and, as you cannot think it is the Lord who has taken away, you are presently open to another suggestion; "Perhaps it was not the Lord who gave it me, else why should he not have preserved it to me?" In instances like these, it is too easy to imagine that God has well nigh forgotten us, and that we have only been self-deceived in ascribing this and that benefit to his special kindness and love; that they must have been purely accidental, though at the time they appeared marvelous tokens of Divine favor.

In some such manner might Elijah's trial of faith have been aggravated, by the slow and natural exhaustion of the brook Cherith. Had its stream been discontinued supernaturally and at once, there had been no difficulty in seeing the Lord's hand in this event; but in the present case he might have been tempted by the imagination that *nature* was very much left to herself. Indeed, the secondary cause why the brook dried up, is mentioned in the text; for we read, it "dried up because there had been no rain in the land." Perhaps this is added by the inspired penman, to give us a clear idea of the trouble which befell Elijah. We can well suppose that it occasioned him no small trial and conflict, and caused him, upon a severe examination, to suggest many gloomy and hard thoughts of God. But Elijah surmounted them all, kept his faith in exercise, and thus obtained the victory. The word of God was his trust; he had not forgotten who it was that said, "Hide thyself by the brook Cherith that is before Jordan, and thou shalt drink of the brook." He was silent before God in humble faith; in faith he waited; and by faith he crucified the flesh with its affections and lusts.

And you, whom I may address as brethren of Elijah by the brook Cherith, and in the wilderness of this world, you children of God, who are apt enough to sigh when *your* streams dry up, and when *your* resources seem exhausted—Oh, if you did but patiently wait upon the Lord, how strong would you become! If you rested more entirely upon his word, you would see the glory of God! Oh that, instead of indulging the feelings of distrust and discontent, we did but reflect upon God's exceeding great and precious promises in Christ Jesus! Ought the children of faithful Abraham to despond? Ought they who have surnamed themselves by the name of Israel to be faint-hearted?

But the answer to such expostulations too frequently is that "the heart knows its own bitterness," and every one is ready to say, "I am the man who hath seen affliction." Alas, we too impatiently want "that which is crooked" to be made "straight," and that which is rough to be made smooth. Yes, we are apt to think our sufferings are directly contrary to the promises of God. But no, this never is, and never can be, the fact. What happens to us may be contrary enough to our wishes, but can never be contrary to God's word. The truth is, that we have been indulging ideas of our own, concerning the manner in which the Lord is to fulfill his promises; and hence arises our mistake. His promises must ever surely come to pass: they are all Yea and Amen in Christ Jesus, 2 Cor. 1:20. But as to the manner in which they are to come to pass, this we ought entirely to leave to his own wisdom and love; and in the mean-time, to abide patiently in him who will do all things well.

"He who spared not his own Son, but delivered him up for us all, how shall he not with him also freely give us all things?" Rom. 8:32. "Fear not, thou worm Jacob, and ye men of Israel; I will help thee, saith the Lord and thy Redeemer," Isa. 41:14.

The help you are thus taught to expect is such as will always be best for you. It shall be in things temporal, when that is good for you; and it certainly shall always be in things spiritual, which are far better. When, in a spiritual sense, our brook seems to dry, and we are ready to cry, "Where is the blessedness I knew?" when zeal in the cause of Christ abates, and our devotion dies; when we feel no sensible delight in prayer, and the spirit of praise and thanksgiving is gone; when we see nothing around to awaken and encourage us, and the love of many is waxed cold; these exigencies are trying, severely trying. But remember him who has said of his vineyard, "I the Lord do keep it; I will water it every moment; I will even keep it night and day," Isa. 27:3. "No really good thing will he withhold from them that walk uprightly," Psa. 84:11. He will certainly keep his word. Therefore be of good courage. Spiritual drought and barrenness, if you feel it, shall be turned into a blessing. Believe, then, that he will keep his word—and as to how he shall keep it, let not the clay be at strife with the potter. Let him do with you as seems him good; the end of your song will always be, "O Lord, righteousness belongeth unto thee, but unto us confusion of face," Dan. 9:7.

Elijah's Departure

II. Elijah's remaining where he was, for the Lord's sake, who had directed him thither, is a noble example to us. "He that believeth shall not make haste," Isa. 28:16. Elijah waited, and help arrived. But in what manner? with water? with refreshment and consolation? No but with a command, which though it might be acquiesced in by faith, could not possibly be agreeable to flesh and blood. "Arise, get thee to Zarephath, which belongeth to Zidon, and dwell there: behold, I have commanded a widow woman there to sustain thee." Reason was now again constrained to quit the field. Elijah is ordered upon a long and toilsome journey, through a wild and barren country, in a time of general famine and extreme drought. And this into the land of Zidon, beyond the borders of Israel, among a heathen people, enslaved to a vile idolatry, the native country of Jezebel, his bitterest enemy, and the territory of her father, a furious tyrant, also in alliance with Ahab. "And, behold, I have commanded a widow woman there to sustain thee." Strange comfort this to mere natural reason! A woman, who has herself lost her chief earthly sustainer; a Phoenician, who might be a heathen, against whose idols Elijah was so zealous. Besides, amongst so many widows in the land, how is this widow to be found? This, indeed, was "bringing the blind by a way that they knew not," Isa. 42:16. But, "Be still, and know that I am God," Psa. 46:10. His footsteps are not known. Yet most of the paths by which he conducts his servants, though they commence in darkness, or at best in twilight, become brighter as they proceed; by and by the dayspring begins to dawn, and their course shines more and more unto the perfect day.

Zarephath, which was midway between Zidon and Tyre, may signify "a place of smelting furnaces," serving to remind us of the furnace of affliction whereby the Lord tries and purifies his people. The prophet's whole route seemed to be directly toward this furnace. But it was a Divine direction: it was the Lord's will; and, therefore, it was right to go forward in his name. The prophet, perhaps with sorrow, bids a last farewell to his quiet hiding-place where he had experienced such signal tokens of the help of God's countenance; he girds up the loins of his mind, takes his pilgrim-staff of the Divine word in the hand of his faith, and sets out for the heathen land. Rough as was his path, it was a way of holiness; no lion was there, nor any ravenous beast could come up thereon. The Lord was with him all the way that he had to go, even Jehovah, who threshes the mountains, rebukes the winds and waves, and revives the spirit of the humble.

It's Blessed Result

III. We soon find him in the neighborhood of Zarephath, and the Lord, who was there before him, had prepared and arranged all for his reception. He had come near the gate of the city, and lo, the widow woman was there gathering sticks for fuel. The Spirit, perhaps, intimated to him that this was the woman to whom he was directed. Poor as she appeared, by the occupation which now engaged her, his faith could tell him, that if the Lord had appointed her to sustain him, she would have wherewithal to do it. With God, who had fed him a whole year by the ministry of ravens at the brook Cherith, he knew that nothing was impossible. And does not God often take a method of helping us which surpasses all reason and expectation, doing for us exceeding abundantly above whatever we could ask or think and sending us deliverance by means which appeared altogether inadequate; that we might learn to give the praise to him, and that his own name might be glorified. Thoughts like those we have mentioned no doubt passed through Elijah's mind; and while he fully confided in the Lord as the God of the widow and the fatherless, he found no difficulty in regarding their humble home as an appropriate dwelling for himself. "He, therefore, called to her and said, Fetch me, I pray thee, a little water in a vessel, that I may drink." Her readiness to go seems to have encouraged him; for "as she was going to fetch it," he added, "Bring me, I pray thee, a morsel of bread in thine hand." His additional request, however, opened afresh the wounds of this poor widow's heart; she could no longer conceal her feelings. She answered, "As the Lord thy God liveth, I have not even the smallest loaf of bread: all I have is but a handful of flour in a barrel, and a little oil in a cruse; and lo, I have been gathering a stick or two for a fire on my hearth, that I might dress it for myself and for my child, as our last meal in this world, that we might eat it and die!" Oh how affecting and heart-rending was this simple tale! We feel it so, while we read it. But what says Elijah to it? Can he still believe that this is the widow woman whom the Lord has appointed to sustain him? Yes, he is now certain of it. Be it that she is a widow in peculiar distress, having no other companion but her helpless child; all this creates no difficulty in his mind; "Jehovah-jireh, the Lord will provide," Gen. 22:14. And, besides, she seems to know his name, for how has she addressed me? "As the Lord thy God liveth." What an unusual and sweet sound is this, in a strange land, in an idolatrous country! Perhaps she is a secret worshiper of the living God—a rose in the midst of thorns—a hidden dove in the clefts of the rock—a converted soul—one of the few among the heathen whom the word of the Lord has reached. Oh happy thought, to find a brother or a sister in the land of Mesech! "And whence does she know that Jehovah is my God, and that I am his servant? Oh, the marvelous disposal of Divine providence!"

None but those who have felt it, can know how delightful it is, in a strange country, where there are no ways that lead to Zion, or where they lie waste and deserted, to discover unexpectedly among the children of this world, and as it were by the waters of Babylon, some citizen of the Holy Land, some brother or sister in the Lord. Yes, it is an unspeakable delight, and to meet with only one such person makes the desert seem to rejoice and blossom as the rose. At such seasons, we learn by experience, that the children of God are not so deficient in love as they are often supposed to be; we taste the blessedness of that communion in the love of Christ, by which he has enjoined that all men should know we are his true disciples; and occasions of this sort serve to make it manifest. Yes, what we may here suppose to have been Elijah's joy, is still tasted in our world. God be thanked, that in every known region of the earth, and even where wolves abound, and hirelings profess to feed the flock of Christ, the Good Shepherd has his sheep, the Lord has hidden ones who know him, and who follow him. And as sheep that pasture on barren plains often bear the finest fleeces, so is it often with the sheep of Christ; and as they know their Shepherd, or rather are known of him, so it is as wonderful as it is delightful to find how readily they know and acknowledge one another.

Elijah, perceiving that this was the widow of whom God had spoken to him, did not hesitate not to address her in the most encouraging manner. He said unto her, "Fear not; go and do as thou hast said: but make me thereof a little cake first, and bring it unto me, and after make for thee and for thy son. For thus saith the Lord God of Israel, The barrel of meal shall not waste, neither shall the cruse of oil fail, until the day that the Lord sendeth rain upon the earth." And now she evinced that she was indeed the widow whom the Lord God of Elijah had appointed to sustain him for "she went" in faith, "and did according to the saying of Elijah; and she, and he, and her house, did eat many days." How blessed is the way of faith.

Behold, then, this man of God cheerfully sitting down in her solitary cottage. Surely "the voice of rejoicing and salvation is in the tabernacles of the righteous"; for "the right hand of the Lord" on their behalf "doeth valiantly," Psa. 118:15. They rejoice together, not only on account of temporal blessings, but much more on account of those which are spiritual. Israel had lost Elijah, and a poor widow in a heathen land had found him. Thus often does it fare with a people who, though they have been privileged with the most faithful preaching of the gospel, will not turn unto the Lord, with all their heart, and walk uprightly before him. They are cursed with a famine of the word of God; the children's bread is taken from them, and imparted to others whom they account no better than dogs, who however "will receive it," and are languishing for it. Indeed our Lord himself thus applies this part of sacred history to the case of the people of Nazareth, who refused to receive his ministry. "I tell you of a truth, many widows were in Israel in the days of Elias, when the heaven was shut up three years and six months, when great famine was throughout all the land; but unto none of them was Elias sent, save unto Sarepta, a city of Sidon, unto a woman that was a widow," Luke 4:25, 26.

Here then the prophet dwells quite happy under the widow's roof. All distress has disappeared. The meal is not diminished in the barrel, nor fails the oil in the cruse, according to the word of the Lord, which he spake by Elijah. Neither does their spiritual sustenance fail. Well might this poor widow rejoice in the privilege of sitting daily at the feet of this man of God, for instruction in divine things! Can we doubt for a moment that the prophet most gladly opened his mouth in divine wisdom, to impart it to the soul of this simple believing sister? Can we doubt that they prayed together, that they read together out of Moses and the prophets, that they conversed together of the day of Christ, which Abraham saw with gladness? And would they not, think you, occasionally raise a spiritual song to the honor of their Lord and Savior? How swiftly and how pleasantly must the hours have passed with them; and well might the angels of God have rejoiced, as no doubt they did, over this little church in the wilderness! Behold here then, my brethren, the bright egress and happy termination of a path, which commenced in such thick darkness! Only let all the children of God implicitly follow his guidance, and he will assuredly conduct them to a glorious end.

It is a noble testimony which is here borne respecting Elijah, when he was commanded away from his retreat at Cherith. It is said of him, "So he arose and went to Zarephath." Let it then be equally said of you, to whatever duty the Lord may call you away, "He arose and went!" Be the way ever so laborious or dangerous, still arise, like Elijah, and go. Go cheerfully, in faith, keeping your heart quietly dependent on the Lord, and in the end you will assuredly behold and sing of his goodness. Though tossed on a sea of troubles, you may anchor on the firm foundation of God, which stands sure. You have for your security his exceeding great and precious promises, and may say with the psalmist, "Why art thou cast down, O my soul? and why art thou disquieted within me? hope thou in God: for I shall yet praise him, who is the health of my countenance, and my God!" Psa. 42:11.

4

Raising the Widow's Son at Zarephath

The portion of the narrative which we have now to contemplate, is a striking exemplification of that saying of our blessed Lord, "Every branch that beareth fruit, He purgeth that it may bring forth more fruit."

1 Kings 17:17-24.

> And it came to pass after these things that the son of the woman, the mistress of the house, fell sick; and his sickness was so sore, that there was no breath left in him. And she said unto Elijah, What have I to do with thee, O thou man of God? art thou come unto me to call my sin to remembrance, and to slay my son? And he said unto her, Give me thy son. And he took him out of her bosom, and carried him up into a loft, where he abode, and laid him upon his own bed. And he cried unto the Lord, and said, O Lord my God, hast thou also brought evil upon the widow with whom I sojourn, by slaying her son? And he stretched himself upon the child three times, and cried unto the Lord, and said, O Lord my God, I pray thee, let this child's soul come into him again. And the Lord heard the voice of Elijah; and the soul of the child came into him again, and he revived. And Elijah took the child, and brought him down out of the chamber into the house, and delivered him unto his mother: and Elijah said, See, thy son liveth. And the woman said to Elijah, Now by this I know that thou art a man of God, and that the word of the Lord in thy mouth is truth.

Here we have another specimen of God's manner of guidance, and one of those ways which, though wonderfully dark and myste-

rious, lead us ultimately to a clearer experience of the Divine goodness and faithfulness.

Come, and let us behold a remarkable work of the Lord, with its
glorious results. Here is, I. The pruning of a branch that bore fruit; II.
Its bearing more fruit; III. The satisfaction and joy that ensued.

The Pruning of the Branch

I. We still find the prophet Elijah in the peaceful and humble
dwelling of the widow of Zarephath. He has now passed several
months in his quiet retirement. Praise and prayer, holy discourse, and
offices of kindness, contemplation of God's word and works, occupied
his swiftly gliding days; and these were blessed with renewed manifestations of Divine loving-kindness and tender mercy. Now, we are
certain that many among ourselves would be ashamed of what they
would consider such an inactive, quiet sort of life, made up of nothing but receiving and enjoying, so that they would reproach
themselves for it, and seek again, as soon as possible, the scene of
labor and activity. Elijah was not so intent upon laboring for the meat
that perishes. He had long ago renounced, as vain and absurd, the
notion that any value can attach to cares merely human, whether for
laying up treasure upon earth, or for acquiring a treasure in heaven
by our own supposed meritorious services. He knew that all which
men can receive out of God's treasure is a simple and free gift of the
most unconditional favor; and therefore he left it entirely with his
Lord, whether he would appoint him a goodly heritage in the land of
Goshen, under the vine and fig-tree, or station him in the desert, or
in the midst of militant hosts; all he desired was to spend and be
spent in his service.

Thus did Elijah feel cheerfully resigned to spend his appointed
term of quietude at Zarephath, to whatever length it should please
God to protract it. Oh that we all had learned this childlike disposition! Whoever is situated, as it were, like Elijah at Zarephath;
whoever is precluded from outward activity and usefulness in the
world by want of means and opportunities, or of gifts and influence,
or by weakness or age, let him think with Elijah, that it is the Lord's
hand which has thus laid him aside; and instead of inwardly repin-
ing, let him keep the noiseless tenor of his way with thankfulness to
God. And if indeed he lean on the bosom of the Lord Jesus, and can
rejoice in the blessings of God's house, let him sit under his shadow

with great delight, and be only the more thankful for it. Let us not think it necessary to the evidence of our sincerity, that we should be sad and sorrowful, much less gloomy and desponding. Continue at Zarephath, fellow-Christian, as long as God pleases. Rejoice while the Bridegroom is with you; when once he shall be taken from you, then the time of fasting shall come.

Let us pause a moment upon the perpetual miracle experienced in the widow's dwelling. "The barrel of meal wasted not, neither did the cruse of oil fail." By whose care was this? By the care of Him who rules in the armies of heaven, and among the inhabitants of the earth. He it was who replenished the cask and the cruse every morning; and thus blessed his children while they were asleep, and before they could have time to say, "Give us this day our daily bread!" And are not his mercies equally renewed every morning to ourselves? He is the same yesterday, today, and forever. How graciously does he, in every respect, provide for us; and how minutely does his providence condescend to our meanest wants! Yes, he is the Savior of all men, specially of them that believe. What he did at Zarephath, thousands daily experience still, though not just in the same form and manner. And how truly do the children of God experience, in a spiritual way, supplies analogous to those temporal ones which were granted to this widow! However pressingly their necessities may be felt, still the bread of life is not spent, neither does their spiritual refreshment fail. He takes care that your faith fail not. Mark the words—that it fail not. We do not read that whole sacks of meal were brought into the widow's house, nor that her oil-cruse ran over. All we are told is that "the meal wasted not"; she daily received as much as she needed; "neither did the oil fail." So, perhaps, you, Christian, will not receive superabundance of believing joyfulness, so as to be enabled to shout for joy in the furnace of affliction: too much would not be good for you. But rest assured of the faithfulness of God, that he will uphold your faith; this your compassionate High Priest has implored for you, as well as for his apostle Peter; and he will daily supply you with so much patience, by daily renewing it, that although you may occasionally doubt and droop, you never shall despair or perish. A pious writer says, truly and beautifully, "We require just as much patience to wait, as oil is required for our lamps, until the day shall dawn, and the day star arise in our hearts."

Delightful, undoubtedly, was the situation of Elijah at Zarephath. But it is not usually good that a man's life should continue flowing on in one and the same easy manner. A long period of prosperity might lead his corrupt nature to become presumptuous, and forgetful of its meanness and poverty. Perpetual quietude serves to nourish a false spirit of independence. Long seasons of rest, for sacred musings, are too much open to the intrusion of self-complacency; and therefore generally, a condition subject to interpretations or changes, is not good for us. Our gracious God, knowing this, appoints vicissitudes of some kind or other for his children, and pours them, as it has been said, out of one vessel into another, that they may not settle on their lees. A change of this sort now awaited the favored family at Zarephath. The immediate reason of it is known to God alone.

Unexpectedly, in the midst of cheering blessings, a heavy cloud darkened the peaceful cottage. Alas! the widow's son, her only child, doubly dear to her in consequence of his wonderful preservation from imminent death by famine, "fell sick." The sickness increased every hour, and the distress of the poor mother was extreme; but her tears prevailed not. Her delight and hope, the dearest object she had on earth, lay extended in the arms of death. How hard! How severe, according to outward appearance! And yet there was nothing but mercy in this event. Our gracious God intended that this bitter medicine should produce the most salutary effects. It is true, that "no chastening for the present seemeth to be joyous, but grievous: nevertheless afterward it yieldeth the peaceable fruit of righteousness unto them that are exercised thereby," Heb. 12:11.

Its Bearing More Fruit

II. For what purpose, then, was this painful visitation sent? We may ask such a question, though we must never pry too minutely into the reason of everything that befalls us; for now we can know but in part. We cannot interpret all God's dealings at present. His way is in the sea, and his path in the great waters. Clouds and darkness to us are round about him. But of this we may be assured, that "all his works are truth, and his ways judgment," or righteousness; and we shall see this more clearly in a better world. At present, we must simply believe and trust in our faithful God, in the midst of our obscurity and darkness. Yet, in this visitation at Zarephath, his gracious intentions may be guessed at. The widow, we may well believe, was a person of real piety; but then, as it would seem only in the manner of Lydia, before the Lord opened her heart; or like Cornelius the centurion, and some others. They were acquainted with God in a partial and too superficial manner: they held communion with him, but not enough upon the true foundation. They served the Lord, but more in the way of Martha than in that of Mary. They knew something of God's loving-kindness, but not enough of his grace; not being sufficiently convinced of their own sinfulness, the corruption of their own hearts, and of the immensity of that grace which the Lord had bestowed upon them. Their religious feelings were probably more natural than spiritual; yet they possibly regarded such feelings with too much confidence, as a proof of their piety. And when we do this, we are hindered in self-knowledge, we deceive ourselves, and remain injuriously ignorant of the relation in which we stand to the God of all grace. In short, they were well affected to godliness in general, but still too far off from God, ignorant of a Mediator and Intercessor, and not enough broken and contrite in heart.

Now, it is a mercy not to be suffered to remain in this condition, for it partakes more of self-deception than of truth. In order therefore that this good widow might enter fully into the kingdom of God, it was necessary that the Holy Spirit, who had prepared her heart already, should enable her further to see that God's love is grace—unmerited grace, for the sake of another's work—another's merits. But how could this salutary and humbling self-knowledge be conveyed to her heart; and how could it be formed into a vital principle? Two invisible guests break in upon her: the Lord and the Spirit. The one visits the widow's house; the other her soul. The one inflicts the blow; the other expounds it. The one slays her son; and the other makes her sensible of the reason why; namely, that she may know more of herself. Hence her language to Elijah, "O thou man of God! art thou come to call my sin to remembrance, and to slay my son?" See what an overthrow takes place in her spirit. "Thou art come unto me, that my sin might be remembered." It seemed to her as if God had now for the first time looked into her heart. And indeed it is good to be sensible of his discernment of our inmost souls: to be sensible how entirely all things belonging to us are naked, opened, and laid bare to the eyes of him with whom we have to do. But many a one, alas, when convinced of this, will still endeavor to make the best of himself in his own eyes. And if he succeed not in so doing, yet he will seek to escape from self-reflection amid the diversions of surrounding vanities: still, however, he finds no true repose of mind. Thus affliction upon affliction is often necessary for bringing sin to remembrance, that sinners may be effectually awakened, and made alive unto God.

That something of this kind was seen necessary by the God of all grace for the poor widow at Zarephath, seems pretty evident from her exclamation under his chastening hand: "What have I to do with thee, O thou man of God? Art thou come unto me to call my sin to remembrance, and to slay my son?" This is certainly strange language; but as the language of her heart and feelings, it is very significant. Is it not as if she had said, "Why didst thou come to me? I have reaped this from thy visit, that my sins are brought to remembrance, and a sense of them overwhelms me. Thou art such a holy man, that neither I nor my house were worthy to entertain thee. Hence God has seen it necessary to punish me for being so bold, and for acting so familiarly with thee, as if we had been thy equals. Surely it is thy coming that has brought all this upon me. A merciful God would not have scrutinized so strictly a poor woman and an insignificant worm like myself, if he had not found me in thy society; if thy abiding with me had not drawn his attention upon me. Ah, why should you have come unto me? Surely the Lord would not have approached so near to such a poor sinner as I am, if you had not brought his awful presence into my house; for He is always with thee." She intended to express something of this kind. Alas, what absurd ideas. And yet, with all this foolishness, what genuine feeling—what self-annihilation—what humility! The object of the stroke is gained.

The Joy that Resulted

III. And now behold the bereaved parent, bowed down with grief, and sitting with the dead child at her bosom, as if she would again warm its stiffened limbs at her throbbing heart. She weeps at one time for her bereavement, and at another for the multitude of her sins, and knows not which of these distresses her most. Pitiable indeed is her condition! And the prophet we may be sure is touched with heartfelt compassion and sympathy. He probably perceived the design of this visitation, and perceiving also the good effect of it, he delayed not to make preparations for allaying her anguish. He said unto her, "Give me thy son." This composure on the part of the prophet must have been impressive to the distressed widow. Surely a ray of hope must have gleamed within her. But will

Elijah be able to gratify the hopes he is exciting? The prophet is sure of the thing in his own mind. He takes the little corpse from the mother's bosom, hastens with it up into his bedchamber, which no doubt was also his closet for retirement and prayer, lays it upon his own bed, shuts the door, falls on his knees, and applies himself to prayer and communion with Jehovah

And now, listen! What a prayer it is which he pours forth! It is a prayer that certainly would not pass uncensured by us—that certainly would not escape the criticism and the condemnation of our wisdom, had we heard it from the mouth of any other than such a one as Elijah. "O Lord my God," cries he, "hast thou also brought evil upon the widow with whom I sojourn, by slaying her son?" What! does Elijah speak before the living God, of bringing evil; does he venture to approach Jehovah's throne with such a question, and with such a complaint? Yes, he speaks as his heart dictates; and if he speaks fool-ishly—he does it in simplicity, and in faith; and if he pleads too familiarly with God—he does so, encouraged by the blood of the Lamb and the promises of God. It is not for us to censure him, for his prayer was accepted of the Lord. And what was its purport? "Lord, did you care to slay this child? Impossible! Your purpose was to lead the mother through affliction to repentance. This, O Lord, having been accomplished, must the child continue dead? Look, O blessed God, upon this widow graciously, and remember that I am her guest. She has shown much kindness to me. I would gladly recompense her. Do you recompense her, for I am poor and have nothing. And oh remember also, that I am your prophet. I am reproached; you are reproached also. Therefore that your name may be hallowed, and your praise magnified upon earth, now, O Lord, hear my prayer." And having thus expostulated as it were with Jehovah, he arose, threw himself upon the dead child, and stretched himself upon it three times, as though he would say, "I will not leave the child, but will await God's answer to my prayer"; and he cried unto Jehovah and said," O Jehovah my God I pray thee let this child's soul come into him again." A prayer you perceive quite positive and unconditional. And what followed upon this holy boldness in prayer?

"The Lord heard the voice of Elijah, and the soul of the child came into him again, and he revived."

But how does this agree with all our notions and maxims concerning acceptable prayer? Here we have, as I have said, an

unconditional prayer—a prayer too for something temporal—a prayer
for a miracle—a prayer without limitations; yet the Lord heard and
answered it. Yet, our gracious God does not bind himself to our maxims, nor suffer himself to be limited by our rules. This event in the
life of Elijah at Zarephath, is similar to one recorded of Luther at
Wittemberg. His friend Myconius lay on his deathbed, and wrote him
a farewell letter. Luther, after reading the letter, immediately fell on
his knees and began to pray. "O Lord my God; no! Thou must not
yet take our brother Myconius to thyself; thy cause will not prosper
without him. Amen!" And, after praying this, he rose up, and wrote
to his sick brother, "There is no cause for fear, dear Myconius; the
Lord will not let me hear that thou art dead. You shall not and must
not die. Amen." These words made a powerful impression on the
heart of the dying Myconius, and aroused him in such a manner that
the ulcer in his lungs discharged itself, and he recovered. "I wrote to
you that it would be so," answered Luther to the letter which
announced the recovery of his friend.

Another little incident here occurs to me, which I can hardly
withhold, on account of its simplicity and beauty. The mother of a
little girl only four years of age had been for some time most dan-
gerously ill. The physicians had given her up. When the little girl
heard this, she went into an adjoining room, knelt down and said,
"Dear Lord Jesus, O make my mother well again!" and after she had
thus prayed, she said, as though in God's name, with as deep a voice
as she could, "Yes, my dear child, I will do it gladly." This was the little girl's Amen. She rose up joyfully, ran to her mother's bed and said,
"Mother, you will get well." And she recovered, and is in health to
this day. Is it then ever permitted for me to pray thus unconditi-
ally respecting temporal concerns? No, you must not venture to do
so, because you can still ask and doubt. But should you ever be
inclined by God's Spirit to pray thus, without doubt or scruple, in a
filial temper, and with simplicity of heart, resting on the true foundation, and in genuine faith—then pray thus, by all means! No one
dare censure you—God will accept it.

"O Lord my God!" cried Elijah, in his upper chamber, "let this
child's soul come into him again!" "I will" was virtually the answer he
received. And the soul of the child came back; the child began to
breathe, and lifted itself up and left the couch of death. And Elijah—
with what feelings you may readily imagine—took the child down

from his chamber, and delivered him to his mother, and in one sentence short and sweet said, "See, thy son liveth!" He left it to the Holy Spirit to say to her the rest. But how shall I attempt to describe the feelings of the poor widow? She sees heaven as it were opened to her, and this not merely in the restoration of the child, who was now alive again in her arms, but also quite in another way. Indeed she cannot yet speak of her child. "Now by this I know," she exclaimed, "that thou art a man of God, and that the word of the Lord in thy mouth is truth." The word of the Lord! What word of the Lord was it that Elijah had spoken to her? This may we easily conjecture. We find here at the close of the narrative a new key to the whole. It would seem that Elijah had said something to her, during their acquaintance, which she had hitherto been unable to comprehend or believe. It is not difficult to suppose what it may have been. Elijah had probably soon perceived that the woman, with all her piety, was still not resting upon the true foundation; and he had doubtless availed himself of the peaceful days at Zarephath to make her acquainted with the counsel of God for the salvation of sinners—with the doctrine of the promised Messiah—with the merit of his redemption, which he should one day accomplish with the necessity of faith in him, and with other matters of holy living and conversation connected with it. These were, it would seem, strange things to her ears, which she did not know how to appreciate, because she as yet felt no need of them. A sense of this need of a Mediator, and of all atonement, was now powerfully awakened in her heart, after she had become, through sanctified afflictions, convinced of her sinful and guilty condition; and Elijah's word concerning the atonement, and pardon extended to sinners through the merits of the promised. Surety, had now, by this renewed testimony to Elijah's prophetic commission, become unquestionably assured as Divine truth to her soul; so that she could heartily yield herself up to it, and rejoice and be glad in it. And this new faith, confidence, joy, and blissful hope she expressed in the words, "Now I know that thou art a man of God, and that the word of the Lord in my mouth is truth." "I know, I feel, see, taste the true and faithful saying." Henceforth she stood upon other ground. From being a devout person, she was now evinced to be a daughter of Abraham's faith. And at the moment when Elijah said to her, "See, thy son liveth!" her heart was ready to say something greater still—"I know that my Redeemer liveth!" Here was repose after a storm.

5

Elijah and Obadiah

He must increase, but I must decrease," said John the Baptist to his disciples, when he perceived with regret that their mistaken partiality would have placed him above Jesus, whom John had preceded only as a harbinger and herald, proclaiming repentance. He assured them that he himself was only the friend of the bridegroom; that his office was only to awaken the attention of the spiritual bride to the coming of her Beloved, and that having done this, his work was ended. He added, "The friend of the bridegroom, who standeth and heareth him, rejoiceth greatly because of the bridegroom's voice: this my joy therefore is fulfilled. He must increase, but I must decrease," John 3:29, 30. The Baptist, in using these two last expressions, compares his Lord to the great luminary of day; but himself to its harbinger or morning star, whose light gradually decreases as the sun arises, till at length it vanishes altogether. Nor has he a wish to be anything more. He would gladly see himself forsaken by his own disciples, if they will only betake themselves to the Chief Shepherd, to participate in that salvation which is to be found only with him. "He must increase, but I must decrease." The Baptist meant, that he must decrease, not only in personal reputation but also in office. His own office was only to bring men to Christ, by ushering in the sweet sound of the gospel.

That the Blessing would come with help and salvation to sinners, John's disciples knew; but some of them seemed erroneously to imagine that the repentance in which they were exercised, and the life of poverty and austerity which they led, that their fastings, self-denials, and prayers, if they did not possess some atoning power, had in them, at least, something which was to outweigh sin, and the curse belonging to it. Rigid followers, as they were, of John the Baptist, they had not yet been baptized unto Jesus Christ; baptized unto his death. But John, their master, would teach them that they must die more completely, that they must plunge themselves deeper into free grace. "I," said he, "must decrease." "All that I have enjoined upon your repentance, self-denial, fasting, and prayer—must lose all credit with you as any ground of God's reconciliation to you. You must seek this in Jesus alone." "He must increase."

Now in this declaration of the Baptist is comprised the whole mystery of practical religion. Does anyone ask what he must do to be saved? The answer is, "Thou must decrease, and Christ must increase"; comply with this, and you will be saved. Does anyone inquire wherein consists the Christian's sanctification? It consists in this, that Christ increases in us, and we decrease. Does anyone desire to know whether he is advancing in the way of salvation? Observe whether Christ increases, while you decrease, in your own estimation. By nature *we* are great—Jesus little; *we* are strong—Jesus weak. We cannot allow Jesus to be the only Savior, the Alpha and Omega. The excellency of the power is ours—not his; we take carnal reasoning for our guide, instead of the simple word and Spirit of God; salvation is looked for in self-love, not in the Savior alone. But when the word of the truth of the gospel effectually penetrates the darkness of our understandings and the blindness of our hearts, the case is reversed. The "strong man armed" is now become weak; and what appeared so weak before, is felt to be strong, yea, irresistible. The Sun of righteousness now arises upon us with healing in his wings, and we learn more and more to rejoice in his light alone. Our own strength, virtue, and excellency, are things we can no longer bear to hear of. We love to lie humbled before the throne of grace, and to wait for a renewed sense of Divine love, even as "they that watch for the morning." We now decrease, and Jesus has increased with us.

It would be natural to suppose that those who have been thoroughly humbled in repentance and faith, are not likely any more to be puffed up with self-righteousness and vanity. But experience shows that this is a mistaken notion. For the "old Adam" is never entirely dead; though dying as a crucified malefactor, he can still revive and do unutterable mischief. Yea, many a one, even after his conversion, has built anew the things which had been destroyed; he has permitted himself to increase, and Christ to decrease. To mention only a few examples of this falling away, one increases by his ascetic exercises; another, by the enlargement of his knowledge; another, in self-complacency, borrowed from his own influential popularity, or the extent of his beneficent exertions; another thinks much of his own devotional feelings, and of I know not what besides. In such things a man insensibly grows so pious and holy in his own eyes, that these things become gain to him, and are no longer accounted loss for Christ.

Are we not, then, to increase in sanctification? Yes! Grow as the palm tree; but in self-estimation we must ever be only as the hyssop on the wall; we must daily become less and less, weaker and weaker in our own eyes, feeling more and more in want of the Lord's staff for our support; otherwise we have set out in a wrong direction. Children of God must "grow up into him in all things who is the Head, even Christ." The beloved of the Lord, those who are really led by the Spirit of God, are ever gradually descending in self-humiliation. An exemplification of these introductory remarks will be found in the portion of Elijah's history which we now proceed to consider.

1 Kings 18:1-16

And it came to pass after many days, that the word of the Lord came to Elijah in the third year, saying, 'Go, shew thyself unto Ahab; and I will send rain upon the earth.' And Elijah went to shew himself unto Ahab. And there was a sore famine in Samaria. And Ahab called Obadiah, which was the governor of his house. (Now Obadiah feared the Lord greatly: for it was so, when Jezebel cut off the prophets of the Lord, that Obadiah took an hundred prophets, and hid them by fifty in a cave, and fed them with bread and water.) And Ahab said unto Obadiah, 'Go unto the land, unto all fountains of water, and unto all brooks: peradventure we may find grass to save the horses and mules alive, that we lose not all the beasts.' So they divided the land between them to pass throughout it: Ahab went one way by himself, and Obadiah went another way by himself. And as Obadiah was in the way, behold, Elijah met him: and he knew him, and fell on his face, and said, 'Art thou that my lord Elijah?' And he answered him, 'I am: Go, tell thy lord, Elijah is here.' And he said, 'What have I sinned, that thou wouldst deliver thy servant into the hand of Ahab, to slay me? As the Lord thy God liveth, there is no nation or kingdom, whither my lord hath not sent to seek thee: and when they said, He is not there; he took an oath of the kingdom and nation, that they found thee not. And now thou sayest, Go, tell thy lord, Behold, Elijah is here. And it shall come to pass, as soon as I am gone from thee; that the Spirit of the Lord shall carry thee whither I know not; and so when I come and tell Ahab, and he cannot find thee, he shall slay me: but I thy servant fear the Lord from my youth. Was it not told my lord what I did when Jezebel slew the prophets of the Lord, hid an hundred men of the Lord's prophets by fifty in a cave, and fed them with bread and water? And now thou sayest, 'Go, tell thy lord, Behold, Elijah is here: and he shall slay me.' And Elijah said, 'As the Lord of hosts liveth, before whom I stand, I will surely shew myself unto him today.' So Obadiah went to meet Ahab, and told him: and Ahab went to meet Elijah.

Having dwelt for a while with our prophet under the vine and the fig-tree, we have now to accompany him once more into the stormy theater of public life. I. We find him, at the commandment of Jehovah, departing from Zarephath; II. We learn what was happening at this time in the court of Samaria and, III. We have the meeting of Elijah and Obadiah.

His Departure

I. The prophet had been two years and some months at Zarephath. The text expresses the time as "many days," though they seemed perhaps to Elijah but a few. But when we consider how rapidly storms and troubles have generally succeeded each other, in the life of God's most eminent servants, it was a long time for Elijah to have a serene sky, with the exception of some fleeting clouds, for more than two years together. This was a length of tranquillity with which not many of the active servants of God have been privileged.

In such a season of spiritual as well as natural dearth, Elijah must surely have felt as we should do, in having to quit, perhaps forever, this peaceful abode of a pious friend. For the cloud of adversity had burst in blessings on that humble dwelling. The widow, as we have seen, had become to him a real sister in the Lord, of one mind with him, in the truest and holiest acceptation; they enjoyed mutual fellowship in God, and in his word of salvation; and, who shall say that Divine grace had not already begun to appear in the widow's child, restored as he had now been from death itself? From that moment,

perhaps, he had begun to live indeed. "The word of the Lord," however, came to Elijah in the third year, saying, "Go, shew thyself to
Ahab." Thus things may be frequently contrary to our natural inclinations; but these inclinations are as often but of little worth. Our
gracious God has better intentions concerning us, than we can have
for ourselves. We should therefore follow the leadings of his providence at every step, and confide in God as all-wise and good, that he
will not and cannot deceive us. "He is a rock, his work is perfect; all
his ways are judgment," Deut. 32:4.

"Go, shew thyself unto Ahab." Had Elijah now conferred with
flesh, and blood, this would have seemed to him like a command to
plunge into the raging waves of the sea, or to walk into a lion's den.
He had to present himself to a wicked and idolatrous king, a tyrant
armed with despotic power, whose personal enmity against him had
been increasing for at least three years and a half, and had been doubly aggravated by the distress of the country, of which Elijah was
reputed to be the author. During all this time Ahab had been intent
upon apprehending him; had used every effort to trace out his residence; had searched through his own, as well as all the neighboring
states, and had taken an oath from the different tribes and govern-
ments, that they had not found him: and yet all his efforts had been
unavailing. How vexatious to himself, and what a reflection upon his
royal power! If the wrath of a king be as messengers of death, what
had Elijah to expect from such a king as Ahab! And yet he receives
the brief and positive direction, "Go, shew thyself unto him!" But let
no one suppose that the Lord ever expects what is above human
nature from any of his children, without imparting, at the same time,
sufficient grace and strength for the purpose. Let no one, therefore,
imagine that he requires us to fight a fight of faith, without giving us
faith to do so; or that he will lead us into any difficulty and trial,
without making provision for our support and encouragement. Yes,
even should there be forced from us the agonizing cry, "Why hast
thou forsaken me!" he will enable us to prefix it by appropriating
faith, "My God! my God!" which will be enough to keep us from
sinking. He leads none of his children into the valley of the shadow
of death without becoming to them their rod and staff. Besides, however thick the darkness may be, it is always relieved by some little ray
of light. The support he gave to Abraham on his gloomy way to
mount Moriah, was not only by the general belief that whatever God

does, he does well; but by the particular turn given to Abraham's faith, that God would restore his Isaac again to life. This sweetened his three days journey not a little. To Job was given a peculiarly clear and joyful expectation of the final result of his sufferings and of the day of resurrection: "I know," said he, "that my Redeemer liveth, and though after my skin worms destroy this body, yet in my flesh shall I see God." And thus Elijah, on this arduous path of faith, which directed him to Ahab, was supported by the promise, "I will send rain upon the earth." He could therefore thank God, and take courage. He could depart from Zarephath as a messenger of joy, and carry a blessing with him. Yes, though the horrors of drought and famine, though faces emaciated with hunger and thirst, might well have made him shudder on the way; though the thought of Ahab's deadly resentment, and perhaps of an infuriated populace, might well have forced its way upon his mind, he could be cheered by the assurance of his commission to announce the return of rain, and by the hope that many would at length give up their hateful idolatry, and humble themselves before the God of their fathers. Such hopes and prospects we can easily imagine would at least have rendered his painful duty more tolerable.

"Show thyself unto Ahab, and I will send rain upon the earth." Jehovah had condescendingly commissioned his prophet to announce the chastisement of drought upon the land, and even to say, "As the Lord God of Israel liveth, there shall not be dew nor rain these years but according to my word:" and now, therefore, it was to be at Elijah's word that the dew and rain should return. Had these blessings returned without Elijah's mediation, it would have been concluded that Elijah was a false prophet and a boaster; the priests of Baal would have attributed the deliverance to their idol, and would have praised Baal as triumphant over Jehovah in order, therefore, not to miss the sole object of this grievous visitation, and that Baal might be confounded, and Jehovah glorified, it was necessary that Elijah, by a public word, should remove the drought, as a complete proof that his Lord was the true and the living God. Consequently, it was now said, "Go, shew thyself unto Ahab, and I will send rain upon the earth."

"And Elijah went to shew himself unto Ahab." We see, then, the man of God again entering with firm step on His public career of faith, surrounded by a thousand dangers and difficulties, having been

proscribed as a outlaw throughout the nation, yea, as a troubler of
Israel; nevertheless, he went at the commandment of the Lord, and
the power of the Lord was with him.

Happenings in the Samaritan Court
   II. While Elijah was on his way from Zarephath, king Ahab at
Samaria was also setting out on a journey through the land.
Elijah's errand was for the honor of the Lord his God; that of Ahab
was for his cattle, particularly for his horses and mules. This occasion
makes us acquainted with another very pleasing and interesting character; namely, with Obadiah, a man of high rank, holding the office
of chamberlain or steward of the king's household. Hence what is
here written of him is the more remarkable, that "he feared the Lord
greatly."
   If our discovery of a devout widow in a heathen land, between
Tyre and Zidon, excites in us grateful admiration, how much more
pleasing is our surprise to find a real servant of the Lord in one of the
most scandalously corrupt courts ever noticed in history! Here we see
that godliness is not a plant, which, as many suppose, must necessarily be reared in the conservatories of human education,
admonition, and good example; how then could a godly man have
existed in Samaria? The children of God are not the mere creatures
of circumstances; the state of things in Samaria was just adapted to
form Obadiah and everyone else into a child of the devil. Jehovah
"forms a people for himself, to shew forth his praise," when and
where it pleases him, Isa. 43:18-21. As "He hath mercy on whom he
will have mercy," and is gracious to whom he will be gracious; so,
whoever really desires to be as Obadiah, the Lord's servant, cannot
be prevented by unfavorable circumstances from becoming so. Thus
the fear of God, faith, and adoption are the good part that cannot be
taken away by thieves that break through and steal, neither
devoured by moth and rust, nor merged and lost in the iniquities of
the country we live in. Obadiah was enabled to keep that good thing
which was committed to him, though in an earthen vessel, safely
amidst all these dangers.
   It was *greatly* that he feared the Lord. This is indeed a noble tes-
timonial concerning him. For truly it was something great to fear the
Lord with all his heart, at a time, and in a country, wherein the true
worshippers of Jehovah were exposed to public scorn and derision. It

was also something great to adhere faithfully to the Lord, when surrounded by persons bitterly prejudiced against real godliness, and by religious and political institutions set up in direct opposition to the true worship and service of Jehovah. To abide in the faith at a court, where the god of this world had blinded the eyes of the powerful, and had provided every possible temptation to follow the vicious fashions of the day—to keep himself unspotted from the world in a post of honor and responsibility, with the eyes of the public fixed upon him, and all his prosperity depending on the favor of the king—to hold on his course in a situation in which he had frequently to communicate with the most profligate among the great—to fear God, not by halves, but fully—to be no time-server, but to serve the Lord and him alone—this was surely something great in Obadiah. But who then is to be praised for this? The great Obadiah? Far from it—To God and his omnipotent grace be all the glory!

Let this picture of Obadiah be held up to the consideration of those who are so ready to object that their situation and circumstances prevent them from faithfully serving God. This wretched excuse has no other origin than the blindness and deceitfulness of the human heart. Under any circumstances, however favorable, true piety is not indebted to these, but to the grace of God alone; and those who seek and partake of this, serve God in all situations; for what should hinder them? Did our objectors complain that they cannot serve God, because of the corruption of their own hearts, this were a complaint that we might listen to. But thus to complain of outward circumstances is a fearful sign of spiritual death. True Divine life in the soul has a fire in it that burns up this stubble of circumstances. There is a necessity in the case; a necessity which is not to be restrained or checked, much less overpowered, by worldly circumstances.

One signal instance of Obadiah's substantial piety is here recorded. Jezebel had endeavored to remove from the land every prophet of Jehovah, and had already caused many of them to be slain. On this perilous occasion Obadiah was not inactive, but his efforts were employed in the rescue of as many men of the Lord's prophets as possible, and he saved a hundred of them from the iron grip of Jezebel. He "hid them by fifties in a cave, and fed them with bread and water." The hazard or expense of his undertaking proved no obstacle with him; his love of the brethren constrained him. And does not our blessed Savior say, "By this shall all men know that ye are my disciples?" Go, then, brethren, and do likewise, whenever it is necessary. The prince of this world, who was a murderer from the beginning, is still awake, and is exciting, in various places, rancorous opposition to the truth of the gospel. Spiritual wickedness is in many high places, as well as in many humble dwellings. Many a preacher may be forced to resign his pulpit, many a teacher his chair, many a mechanic his employment, and many a servant his situation, because he is a true believer in Christ, and a sincere follower of his example. Therefore, forsake not the assembling of yourselves together, children of God, for mutual edification and succor. Remember Obadiah. If God continues to spare us, whatever blessings of his goodness we enjoy, let them be shared by our distressed brethren, for they are fellow-heirs with us of our Redeemer's kingdom.

We return to the narrative. "And Ahab called Obadiah," and commissioned him upon a business to be executed in concert with himself. How extraordinary, that a man like Obadiah should be in such favor with a wicked man, and with an Ahab! for it could not have been unknown to the king, or to his court, that Obadiah "feared Jehovah greatly." And this Scripture testimony concerning him is utterly irreconcilable with the supposition that he could dissemble either with the tyrant himself, or with anyone else. We can therefore only account for this by supposing that his integrity, activity, and firmness were things Divinely overruled to restrain the most arrogant and rancorous foes and scoffers within the bounds of a certain respect and reverence. Ahab probably had discernment enough to perceive that, among all his courtiers, there was no other equal to Obadiah; and those courtiers too might have been conscious that there was no one of themselves in whom such confidence could be placed, as in this Israelite of the ancient school; and though the king might laugh at his religion, he felt that he could not do without him. And is there not something in every true Christian that exhorts at least a tacit acknowledgment from the bitterest enemies; a "light" to which, though it "doth make manifest" their darkness, they are unable to refuse a portion of their esteem and admiration? Yes, it has often happened that eminently pious men have been singularly honored for their conduct by those who could not understand its principles, and whose own lives were often directly contrary to them.

"Go into the country," said Ahab to Obadiah, "unto all fountains of water, and unto all brooks; peradventure, we may find grass to save the horses and mules alive, that we lose not all the beasts." Lo, the only effect of this long continued chastisement of the Almighty was an anxiety for the preservation of his stud! To such obduracy can the heart of man be brought. Neither afflictions, nor miracles, nor admonitions, nor temporal mercies, are sufficient of themselves to restore the spiritually dead to life. How often are we apt to think concerning persons under some peculiar visitation, that surely now they will be changed and softened, and brought to reflection! We make inquiries, we take pains to ascertain the result; and alas! where we hoped at length to find some serious thoughts about God and eternity, only cares similar to those of Ahab engage their minds ; and, instead of the holy emotions for which we sought, instead of sighs, prayers, and serious thoughts of eternity, we see only a multitude of low desires and cares, bearing them down the stream of life into the boundless invisible ocean: "Though thou shouldest bray a fool in a mortar among wheat with a pestle, yet will not his foolishness depart from him," Prov. 27:22 May Almighty grace have compassion upon us!

Obadiah readily enters upon the business to which his sovereign had commissioned him, and which he could do most conscientiously. Yet—again the question recurs to our mind—how could Obadiah bear to continue in the service of such a ruler, and among the vile and wicked men of which the court was composed? He must have mourned many an hour in secret over the wicked, and must have often sighed in solitude, "Woe is he, that I am constrained to sojourn in Mesech, and to dwell in the tents of Kedar." "In the world ye shall have tribulation"; and Obadiah doubtless experienced this tribulation of God's children, resident as he was amongst those who were strangers to the true God of Israel. But Obadiah could not adopt the convenient maxim, which enjoins flight from our calling, when abiding in it is disagreeable. "My God," he would consider has placed me here for reasons best known to himself; and "it is an easy thing for him to preserve me, though my soul be among lions." Here therefore he remained, for the Lord's sake. And what can be done better by you, who may find yourselves in a similar situation? However much evil you are obliged to be eye-witnesses of, whatever annoyance you may experience, and however you may be ridiculed or oppressed, let such be no reasons for removing of your own accord from the post which God's providence has assigned you. Endure for the Lord's sake, until he himself by his providence deliver you. If you are thrust out, or if circumstances and connections necessarily produce a change in your situation, then remove with an easy conscience, for the Lord has called you. But, until then, endure, and flourish as a lily among the thorns; be as the salt of the earth to a corrupt mass, and as a lighthouse to benighted mariners; for, through Divine grace, you may thus serve to direct many passengers through the hidden rocks and quicksands of this troublesome world, to the haven of rest. And how much soever the raging waves of the sea may foam around you, "He that keepeth Israel will neither slumber nor sleep, and the angel of the Lord is about them that fear him. His faithfulness and truth is their shield and buckler. Blessed are those who put their trust under the shadow of his wings!"

Elijah Meets Obadiah

III. Ahab and Obadiah had now "divided the land between them to pass throughout it"; and "Ahab went one way by himself," while "Obadiah went another way by himself." It was of the Lord's peculiar providence that the king thus went in person, as he was thus made to witness something of the extent of misery and horror which the country at that time presented, if peradventure it might lead his unfeeling heart to feel some salutary emotions. But we know that it quite failed of producing this effect, and instead of returning as a subdued and humbled sinner, we find him only as a wild bull in a net, an infuriated being, whose rage is turned against him that smites him, a man fighting against God.

But let us turn our attention to his pious servant Obadiah. Behold him on the solitary and deserted road, bearing the woes of Israel on his compassionate heart; meeting everywhere with desolations and miseries, which he cannot remedy! The country around him, wherever he advances, once a fruitful field, is now changed to a parched desert; and its whole appearance seemed to say, "Who can stand before thee, when thou art angry?" But that which must have affected him most, and pierced his heart the most deeply, must have been the thought of apostate Israel, who could yet as with a forehead of brass stand insensible to the lightning of Jehovah's power, and the thunder of his judgments; for he sees them continuing to live as

before, in the most unpardonable obduracy. How must it have afflicted him! How could he possibly refrain from holy indignation! God's
children are in this, as well as in other respects, conformed to the
image of their Savior. They bear in a sense the sins of the world upon
their hearts, and like him they have to become repairers of the
breach which the ungodly have made; restorers of paths which others have destroyed. But happy are such persons, they are numbered
among those to whom the man clothed in linen, with an inkhorn at
his side, was directed, in the prophecy of Ezekiel, to "go through the
city of Jerusalem, and set a mark upon the foreheads of the men who
sighed and cried for all the abominations that were done in the midst
thereof."

While Obadiah is thus on his way, absorbed in melancholy reflections, he is met by a solitary and venerable personage girded as a
traveler, and covered with a mantle, whom he immediately recognizes as Elijah, and prostrates himself in profound respect before him.
"Art thou that my lord Elijah?" he asks. Is it possible? Nothing having for a long time been seen or heard of him, he, with many others,
might have supposed that the Lord had secretly taken him to his rest.
The prophet replies briefly in his own manner, "I am, go tell thy lord,
Behold, Elijah is here!" This reply, however, was too brief for the worthy Obadiah, and, indeed, was like an arrow to his heart. He felt that
he was now but a poor, weak, desponding child of man. And all the
children of God must have their trying seasons of personal danger for
the trial and increase of their faith. What "treasure we have is in
earthen vessels," (easily broken) "that the excellency of the power
may be of God, and not of us." This lesson Obadiah had now more
perfectly to learn by the instrumentality of Elijah. And it evidently
cost him considerable conflict with himself. "What have I sinned,"
says he, "that thou wouldest deliver thy servant into the hand of
Ahab, to slay me? As the Lord thy God liveth, there is no nation or
kingdom, whither my lord hath not sent to seek thee: and when they
said, He is not there; he took an oath of the kingdom and nation,
that they found thee not. And now thou sayest, Go, tell thy lord,
Behold, Elijah is here! And it shall come to pass, as soon as I am
gone from thee, that the Spirit of the Lord shall carry thee whither
I know not; and so when I come and tell Ahab, and he cannot find
thee, he shall slay me." These many words are not the language of
tranquil faith, but of human fear and despondency. His imagination

pictured to him dreadful forebodings; that, while he is gone to carry
to Ahab Elijah's message, the latter might be caught away by the
Spirit of the Lord to some unknown region; as had happened, pehaps,
to other saints of God. In the Acts of the Apostles, we have such an
event related, concerning Philip the evangelist. Hence Obadiah
apprehended Ahab's sorest displeasure at his disappointment in los-
ing the prophet Elijah. Ahab would consider himself mocked by
Obadiah; or, at least, would be enraged that Obadiah had not secured
the detention of the prophet; thus Obadiah would lose both his office
and his life. Such were his fearful apprehensions. Natural however as
they were, still they were only thoughts of flesh and blood. He
looked, as Peter afterwards did, at the wind and the waves, but had
lost sight of his Lord.

But, further; he begins to speak of his piety. "I thy servant fear the
Lord from my youth. Was it not told my lord what I did when Jezebel
slew the prophets of the Lord, how I hid an hundred men of the
Lord's prophets by fifty in a cave, and fed them with bread and water?
And now thou sayest, Go, tell thy lord, Behold, Elijah is here: and
he shall slay me." "I am a pious man," he means to say; "you must not
be misled by my court dress, and the office I fill; I am none of the
rebellious children; I have continued faithful to the Lord. Can you
find in your heart to expose a believing brother to the most dreadful
danger?" And truly Obadiah was a pious man, notwithstanding all his
weakness. Who could be offended with him for speaking of his piety,
and recounting his good deeds, on such an occasion! For it was neither presumption nor vainglory that led him to do so, but simply, fear
and dread. Here, however, let us be reminded that our salvation is
built not upon works of righteousness that we have done, but upon
God's mercy; not upon what we are to him, but upon what he is to
us. All our worlds of righteousness together are but a poor foundation
to rest upon.

It was salutary then for Obadiah, and it is salutary also for us, to be
thus taught by providential experience our own weakness, that we
may habitually learn to build more exclusively on that only sure
foundation, Jesus Christ, the foundation which alone can stand for
ever. Our only refuge and consolation, in life and in death, are the
blood and righteousness of the Lamb of God and, that we may
depend upon him and abide in him alone, our gracious God allows
us continually to feel in one way or another our sin and weakness,

that our own utter inability may never be lost sight of. Are we ready to value ourselves upon our courage? His providence unexpectedly suspends over us some danger or threatening storm, and we experience that we are but as a reed shaken with the wind. Do we feel complacency in the strength of our faith? A test of it is presently given us, and we are made conscious that we only dreamed of possessing its genuine power. Are we rich as we think in pious feelings? Soon, very soon, alas! by some apparently trifling accident, do we find our whole stock of goodness exhausted; and we are obliged to confess that out of Christ's fullness alone do we receive. If we imagine that death is no terror to us, and that we shall be able to show the world how men ought to die; a slight glimpse of the king of terrors will easily dissolve our heroic courage. Are we become spiritually proud, thinking of the high advances we have made in holiness? We are soon made to learn the truth of the case. All our boasting now is at an end, and nothing remains for us but to cry, like every other child of God, "God be merciful to me a sinner!" "If I wash myself with snow-water," said Job, "and make my hands never so clean, yet shalt thou plunge me in the ditch, and mine own clothes shall abhor me." And why does this happen to us, but that we may decrease, and Christ increase? The discipline, indeed, is painful to our fallen nature, but the consequences are most salutary.

"The end of the Lord" was now attained in this instance of Obadiah. Self-humiliation had been effected in him, and the light was again suffered to shine upon him. Elijah said, "As the Lord of hosts liveth, before whom I stand, I will surely show myself unto Ahab today." This composed the fears of his troubled heart; so Obadiah went to meet Ahab, and he had now sufficient boldness to tell the tyrant, "Behold, Elijah is here."

6

Deliverance from the Mouth of the Lion

Take heed that thou speak not to Jacob either good or bad," was the injunction of Jehovah to Laban the Syrian, when he "so hotly pursued after" Jacob, as if he mediated revenge, Gen. 31:24. His tongue was immediately tied, his hands bound, and his heart turned back again.

Happy are they who have the God of Jacob for their protector, who "hath cut Rahab and wounded the dragon, who shutteth up the sea with doors and bars, saying, Hitherto shalt thou come, but no further; who stilleth the raging of the sea and the noise of his waves, and the madness of the people." A proof of this will be seen in that part of the history of our prophet which we are now about to consider.

1 Kings 18:17-20

> And it came to pass, when Ahab saw Elijah, that Ahab said unto him, Art thou he that troubleth Israel? And he answered, I have not troubled Israel; but thou, and thy father's house, in that ye have forsaken the commandment of the Lord, and thou hast followed Baalim. Now therefore send, and gather to me all Israel unto Mount Carmel, and the prophets of Baal four hundred and fifthy, and the prophets of the groves four hundred, which eat at Jezebel's table. So Ahab sent unto to all the children of Israel, and gathered the prophets together unto Mount Carmel.

Here is, I. The wonderful protection of the prophet; II. The unjust accusation brought against him; III. The bold language he uses; and, IV. The secret power he exercises.

74

The Protection of the Prophet

I. Obadiah had gone at Elijah's bidding, and sought out the king, informed him, that he had met with Elijah, and that he was still continuing at the place where Obadiah had found him. Ahab accordingly, with what feelings we may better imagine than express, went to meet Elijah. Instead, however, of any of that manifestation of royal anger which is as the roaring of a lion, not a stroke falls, not an arrow flies; nothing ensues but the feeble question: "Art thou he that troubleth Israel?" Here is not even an outrageous curse or menace; just as if the volcano had been suddenly exhausted, and only emitted a little smoke. Thus, the Lord our God can stop the mouths of lions, and enable his people to tread on serpents and scorpions, so that nothing shall by any means hurt them, when they are upon his errands. Yes: the same God who was thus a wall of fire around Elijah, defeating the resentment of Ahab and Jezebel; who delivered Daniel and his three companions; who released Peter from prison; who also, in the case of Luther, the poor Augustinian monk of Wittemberg, put to shame the power of the pope, and of other numerous and mighty persecutors—the same God still lives in the great Head of the church, Christ Jesus; and he is with his people always, even to the end of the world; he is their succor and defense. Depend on it, Christians, you would not pass your days and nights so quietly as you do, were it not for his continual interposition against those who would molest you. The enmity of the prince of this world, and of his servants the children of disobedience, is still unabated. Many an arm of strength, both in the higher and lower walks of life, would be stretched out against you, but that he stays it. For as many as have their heavenly Father's name written in their foreheads, as many as profess Christ sincerely and faithfully before men, as many as will live godly in Christ Jesus, must suffer molestation on that very account in this present world. And that we live so peacefully and quietly in our dwellings, and that our lives are so safe, though in the midst of dangers, is altogether owing to the protection of our almighty Savior, who neither slumbers nor sleeps; who never remits his vigilance over us day or night; who with his mighty angels encamps about his people, and is himself their bulwark. In eternity we shall discover, to our great astonishment, how many enemies Jehovah prevented from injuring us, and from how many of the hands of men he has delivered us. "The name of the Lord is a strong tower; the righteous runneth into it, and is safe." Oh how safe, in such a tower of refuge! Thus Elijah experienced, and thus may we.

The Unjust Accusation

II. The protection which Elijah experienced was of the same kind as that which all the servants of God are wont to experience, and in like manner the accusation charged upon him, as if it were he who troubled Israel, was only another characteristic of the people of God. "Art thou he that troubleth Israel?" said the wrathful monarch, and thus cast upon the prophet the whole blame of God's heavy judgments upon the land. But, from the beginning of the world, this crying injustice on the part of men is one of those afflictions of the cross which believers are called to bear after their Lord and Redeemer. Painful as this must ever be found to flesh and blood, it is one salutary means for purifying us from the remains of in-dwelling sin.

It indeed often appears as if faithful ministers were the stormbirds and messengers of misfortune, the disturbers of peace, and such as "turn the world upside down"; just as Elijah seemed to be, when, at his word, the season of famine overspread Samaria. Religion enters a family, and instead of peace comes division, unanimity is banished from the circle. A believing son or daughter may, to their great grief, excite against themselves their unbelieving parents; and a preacher in like manner, by his faithfulness, may offend the most influential of his congregation, and these may stir up a majority against him, in order to get rid of him. Faithful preaching of the gospel may sometimes be like the sinking of a burning mountain in the sea. Sleepers awake, and the dry bones are stirred. On such occasions, the thoughts of many hearts are revealed. Drunkards become sober, and the sober drunken. On what divisions of heart may we then witness! Congregations splitting, and parties forming! Then also, as in the apostle's time, it is always the case that the faithful and awakening preachers of the gospel are regarded as the offending parties, "the men who have turned the world upside down"; whereas the whole blame rests with those whose hearts are alienated from the life of God, through the ignorance that is in them, and who "love darkness rather than light, because their deeds are evil." Nevertheless, we must be content to bear the blame of being the troublers of Israel. "The disciple is not above his Master, nor the servant above his Lord. It is enough that the disciple be as his Master, and the servant as his Lord.

If they have called the Master of the house Beelzebub, how much more them of his household! Therefore fear them not; for there is nothing hidden that shall not be revealed, nor secret that shall not be known."

We are called to be the salt of the earth, by our life as well as by our testimony, our word and confession to be the salt amidst the corruption of the present age, everyone in his own station, believing parents among their children, masters among their servants, and friends in their friendship. Now if all things remain as smooth and quiet as they were before, among the unconverted, with whom we live, this is an evil sign, and we have reason to inquire whether the salt itself have not lost its savor, But if there is great stir around us, one inquiring, "Sirs, what shall I do," or another crying in his wrath, "Ye are the troublers of Israel," then this may be a good sign to us that we are indeed the salt of the earth, which has not lost its savor.

Elijah was accused of troubling Israel, and certainly he was God's instrument for chastising that idolatrous and wicked kingdom. The children of God, though they are not of the world, even as Christ is not of the world, and though the world overlooks or despises them, have very much to do with the turn of its affairs; they are of no small account in the sublunary disposals of Providence. How many a potent adversary has been felled to the ground, how many a community has dwindled and decayed, because of their opposition to the people of God, who are continually praying, "Thy kingdom come!" How many a blaspheming tongue has been laid silent in the grave, because of that universal prayer of the church, "Hallowed be thy name."

Yes, if our adversaries knew how many things take place in the world on our account, whether for the strengthening of our faith, for our succor, or for the crowning of our prayers—if they knew what influence "the quiet of the land" exercise even here below, upon the fate, both of individuals and nations, and how often it is given into their hands to open heaven or to close it, to bring blessings upon a place or to take them away, to bind the arm of the mighty, and to bring to naught the counsels of the prudent if they rightly understood in what sense the Prince of the host, whose banner we follow, has made us, not only priests but also "kings unto our God"—their rage would exceed all bounds: and how would they then cry out, "Ye are they that trouble Israel!"

His Bold Answer

III. Let us now consider Elijah's answer to Ahab. The prophet stands before a mortal enemy, who is the despotic ruler of the land; and how does he meet his false accusation? Does he excuse himself and cry for mercy? Does he have recourse to flattery or artifice? Does he, in order to save himself, begin to "prophesy smooth things"? Does he conceal from him the true cause of God's judgments upon the land? Does he even endeavor to moderate the king's displeasure, by announcing to him the good news of approaching rain? No; Elijah is a man only for the truth, and for such truth as the occasion calls for. His great and only concern was that the tyrant, together with his people, should judge themselves, humble themselves before the living God, and give him the glory. This was of more importance to him than his life. He knew where he was going, and death had no terrors for him. His answer therefore is, "I have not troubled Israel but thou, and thy father's house, in that ye have forsaken the commandments of the Lord, and thou hast followed Baalim."

Such language as this is seldom heard upon earth. The world is full of flatterers and dissemblers, and such characters abound not only in palaces, but also in ordinary society; but faithful servants of God, who are dead to self-interest, who so love their brethren as to be unwilling to suffer sin upon them— such men are rare indeed. O ye ministers of Christ, among high and low, let us not complain of the little fruit of our labors till we have first complained of our own too great love of the praise of men.

We should see greater things, were not the salutary and awful, "Thou art the man!" so entirely unknown among us. It is not enough that we deal in general truths concerning human corruption, openly acknowledged in our church confessions. How far is all this below the faithfulness of prophets and apostles. If Elijah, or Paul, or John the Baptist, were here, you would hear the trumpet give a very different sound. To how many an Ahab of the present day would it then be said, "I have not troubled Israel; but thou, and thy father's house, in that ye have forsaken the commandments of the Lord." How many a Jezebel would then be told to her face, "The unclean shall not inherit the kingdom of God." How many a publican, "Demand no more than is thy due." How many a Herod, "It is not lawful for thee to have thy brother's wife." How many a Felix, how many a Drusilla, who at present hear only smooth words would then be forced to submit to one closet sermon after another from plain and unsparing lips, upon righteousness, temperance, and judgment to come!

You may well pray that it may be given to you ministers, to make a better use of the liberty which is thus divinely committed to them as an awful and most responsible trust, "to reprove, rebuke, exhort, with all long-suffering and doctrine." And what is the nature of our commission? We have a heaven to promise, and a hell to threaten. We stand forth as messengers in Christ's stead, as the stewards of the mysteries of God. We speak not from ourselves, but that which One who is greater than all commands us to speak. We go forward, surrounded by a cloud of witnesses, as the ambassadors of the King of all kings, and have the right to announce our message to sinners in the name of God, with "Thus saith the Lord!" Oh the dignity or our calling! the holiness of our office! Oh that it more thoroughly pervaded us, and that we were more like Elijah, or Nathan or the Baptist, or the apostle Paul. And were it so, that by the unpleasant sound of truth, we lost a whole squadron of worldly friends, we should soon perhaps find the loss made good by others collected by the gospel trumpet from among publicans and sinners. No, were the measure of our trouble and reproach doubled, the fruit of our labor in God's field might be doubled likewise. We may well humble ourselves one and all, for our insincerity and men-pleasing, in allowing ourselves to cry, "Peace, peace, when there is no peace." This is not tenderness, though it assumes that name; it is the want of true love to our neighbor, and the indulgence of our own indolence and ease. May the Lord kindle a purer flame in our souls, and give us a better love, a love which, where truth, the honor of God, and the salvation of our brethren require it, can speak and act disinterestedly and self-denyingly; yet so that no strange fire mingle with that which is holy, nor we ourselves, as is too often the case, break to pieces, in our zeal, both tables of the law.

"I have not troubled Israel; but thou, and thy father's house, in that ye have forsaken the commandments of the Lord, and thou hast followed Baalim." What was the special sin which Elijah here holds up to view as the chief cause of the whole calamity? Is it the intemperance, or the covetousness, or the frivolity, or the unchaste life of Ahab, and of his father's house? No; it is their departure from God's word and statutes. O brethren! if sins of this sort be the greatest of all sins; if God has visited nations, countries, and cities with fire and sword on account of them; what must be his displeasure in these times, when infidelity is becoming the very fashion in so many circles everywhere; when the forsaking of the statutes of the Lord, and the following of a heathenish rationalism, has found its way even into the home and the workshop; when the declaration, "We will not have this man to reign over us!" virtually becomes more and more general, and the very voice of Baal is, in this sense, to be heard from many a pulpit, many a professor's chair, and many a schoolmaster's desk! when true religion, the belief of the forgiveness of sins through the blood of the Lamb, is not only slighted, but even branded as fanaticism; and the true life in the Holy Spirit, the life of love to Christ, and the following of his steps, is so often declaimed against as pietism and enthusiasm! How will it at length fare with such a generation, if we do not fall down weeping before the lifted rod of the great Preserver of men! And what kind of days have we to expect, sooner or later, in a country, where more than one Noah preaches the righteousness of God; where more than one Jonah calls to repentance; where more than one of Zion's watchmen sounds the trumpet louder and louder, because he sees the sword approaching; and still but a small band is gathered of those who faithfully adhere to and take up the cross; while thousands upon thousands treat the blood of the covenant as an unholy thing, scoff at the word of the Lord, presumptuously turn with disgust from the precepts of Christ, bow the knee to any or every shameful lust, and thus virtually bring their offerings to the abominations of the Moabites and the Amorites! What vials of wrath must at length be poured out upon this favored region! Will it have sufficed, that the Lord has afflicted us with lack of employment and want, with a stoppage of trade and business, and visited us with plague and pestilence? Will he not see it necessary to come with still severer judgments? "Woe unto thee, Chorazin! woe unto thee, Bethsaida! for if the mighty works which were done in you, had been done in Tyre and Sidon, they would have repented long ago in sackcloth and in ashes. But I say unto you, It shall be more tolerable for Tyre and Sidon at the day of judgment, than for you. And thou, Capernaum, which art exalted unto heaven, shalt be brought down to hell." Oh that my people would turn from their evil ways, that the Lord God might repent of the evil concerning us, and turn from the fierceness of his anger, that we perish not!

His Secret Power

IV. Elijah, having thus faithfully delivered his message, now begins to make preparations for a scene which has not its like in sacred history. Jehovah is about to show, by signs and wonders, and mighty deeds, that he is God and none else; and Baal is to be overthrown in one day. "Now therefore," said Elijah, authoritatively, like a representative of God; "Now therefore, O king! send, and gather to me all Israel unto Mount Carmel, and the prophets of Baal four hundred and fifty, and the prophets of the groves four hundred, which eat at Jezebel's table." He speaks the word, and Ahab obeys, and collects the prophets unto Mount Carmel. "Behold how matters are reversed!" the subject prescribes, and the king, yes, such a king, complies! "The thing is of the Lord." The hearts of all are in his hands! The servants of God have, through faith, "out of weakness been made strong, subdued kingdoms, wrought righteousness, obtained promises. If we, as lambs, are sent in the midst of wolves, yet we are clothed with a Divine panoply, and often with a Divine influence upon others, if we are Christ's faithful servants.

We have not, and we need not, any carnal weapons, offensive or defensive. When despised or reviled, we must neither despise nor revile again, much less must we have recourse to the swords with which the world is wont to fight. Instead of all this, there is something else given to the servants of God. "This is the victory which overcometh the world, even our faith." True faith is always accompanied by the illuminating light of the Holy Spirit, whose temples we are, and who always manifests himself as the Spirit of the mighty God. Here is a Divine something that can do wonders. With this something can babes and sucklings still the enemy and the avenger; and defenseless sheep have often with it disarmed their most violent persecutors. This is the true star of honor which gleams through the clothing of humility. As it is better than all the wisdom of the wise, and the cunning of the prudent, so it is of more value than all the honor of the noble, than all the power of the mighty. With it the most simple may remain steadfast against the most seductive subtleties of false philosophy, and put to shame the whole array of abused talents and learning. This secret something, which Christians carry about with them; this unction from the Holy One, which pervades their whole being; this sign of the Son of man, and seal of the Lamb upon their foreheads, is the supernatural armor in which the servants of God do exploits, carry on their conflict with the world, the flesh, and the devil, and, like their Savior, "bring forth judgment unto victory."

Yet let them beware of being exalted above measure. Our safety lies in being ever lowly at the feet of Jesus, and the spirit of his precept to his disciples may well apply to us: "Rejoice not that the spirits are subject unto you; but rather rejoice because your names are written in heaven." All other joy, even the joy at the victories we gain, tends to darken the inward eye, and remove our poverty and dependence from our view. But if the prize of our high calling be continually kept before the eye of faith, its brightness will make us see our own unworthiness. Joy in our present gifts and endowments is mutable and evanescent, for they may be wholly or in part withdrawn from us; but the joy of our fellowship with the Father, and with his Son Jesus Christ, is permanent; for we know that the foundation of God stands sure, having this seal—"The Lord knoweth them that are his, and he abideth faithful—he cannot deny himself." Oh happy they whose names are written in the book of life; and doubly happy they who rejoice in this, above their chief joy! Amen.

7

Elijah and the People on Mount Carmel

It was a remarkable but wise decision that Solomon made in an extremely difficult case, which was once brought before him. Two women came to him with an infant, to which they each asserted a mother's claim: the one stating that the child of the other woman having died, she had taken hers from her before she was awake, and laid her own dead child in its place; whilst the other asserted that the contrary was the truth, saying, "The dead child is hers, and the living is mine"; they therefore besought the king to determine the matter. But how was it to be done? The king called for a sword, and on its being brought he said, "Divide the living child in two, and give half to the one, and half to the other. Then spake the woman whose the living child was unto the king, for her bowels yearned over her son, and she said, O my lord, give her the living child, and in no wise slay it! But the other said, Let it be neither mine nor thine, but divide it." You are aware how the king, from these expressions of the two women, settled the dispute and decided the case, 1 Kings 3:24-27.

A better compassion than that of a woman for her sucking child has God for His dear children. He too will have them entirely as a whole living sacrifice, or not at all. He will not consent to our being divided between himself and the world. The love he requires is that of all the heart, all the soul, all the mind, all the strength. Such likewise is the requirement of our Lord Jesus Christ. "He that loveth father or mother more than me is not worthy of me; and he that loveth son or daughter more than me is not worthy of me." We must

83

be wholly the Lord's. Such was Elijah himself and such he taught others to be; as we shall see by attending to the portion of his history which is now to be considered.

1 Kings 18:21-24

And Elijah came unto all the people, and said, How long halt ye between two opinions? if the Lord be God, follow him: but if Baal, then follow him. And the people answered him not a word. Then said Elijah unto the people, I, even I only, remain a prophet of the Lord; but Baal's prophets are four hundred and fifty men. Let them therefore give us two bullocks; and let them choose one bullock for themselves, and cut it in pieces, and lay it on wood, and put no fire under: and I will dress the other bullock, and lay it on wood, and put no fire under: and call ye on the name of your gods, and I will call on the name of the Lord: and the God that answereth by fire, let him be God. And all the people answered and said, It is well spoken.

A great and ever memorable scene is here to be unfolded. The ancient controversy, whether Jehovah be the one only and true God, is now to be decided by himself. The passage before us, however, shows only the preparation for this astonishing decision.

Here we have, I. Elijah's exhortation; II. His challenge; and, III. His confidence of faith.

Elijah's Exhortation

I. We are to transport our thoughts to the summit of mount Carmel. Below on one side roars the sea, and bounds the view on the other, the eye stretches over the brook Kishon into the spacious plain of Esdraelon, where mount Tabor is seen in the distance, and still nearer the little town of Nazareth, while the lake of Gennesaret glimmers farther beyond in the blue horizon; to the north we behold the mountains of Lebanon with their cloud-capped summits. On the magnificent height of Carmel, so renowned of old for its fertility, there is at present a Christian monastery, and a Turkish mosque, beside many subterranean chapels, caverns, and grottoes, appropriated to religion. Hither, every year, on the supposed anniversary of the memorable day recorded in the text, multitudes of Mohammedans and Christians assemble, to pay a common religious homage to Elijah. How would Elijah himself deal again with these priests of Baal, if he could once more return to the ancient scene of his zeal and his conflict! You are to behold him then at present on the heights of Carmel, surrounded by the four hundred and fifty priests of Baal, the four hundred prophets of the groves, who ate at Jezebel's table, a lewd and profligate race, by the idolatrous king and his pompous court, and by multitudes of the poor, perishing, seduced people, awaiting with anxious curiosity the transactions about to transpire.

These being assembled, Elijah appears before them upon the rising ground, conspicuous to all—a plain man covered with a mantle. He looks around him with a cheerful and undaunted countenance, while all are silent to listen to His address. He then cries aloud to the whole assembly, "How long halt ye between two opinions? If Jehovah be God, follow him; but if Baal, follow him." The effect of this bold and serious address was a dead silence on the part of the assembled multitude. They seem to have felt the power of his expostulation. With the court and the priesthood the case was different; they were decided idolaters, who had sold themselves to work wickedness in the service of Baal. But the people perhaps had not been able entirely to forget what great things Jehovah had done for their forefathers. They could not bring themselves to renounce entirely all allegiance to him; therefore many of them probably sought to persuade themselves that they were not idolaters in reality, but worshippers of the true God, under the name of Baal. They confounded Jehovah and Baal together, and invented a religion, in which they gave themselves up to all the lusts and abominations of heathenism, but retained the self-complacent notion that they still walked in the way of their fathers; and that though the form of their worship might be a little different from that of their ancestors, the substance was the same. What awful self-delusion, what pitiful double-mindedness. Such were the people to whom Elijah addressed his remonstrance.

But if Elijah were now preaching amongst ourselves, would he not still have to deliver many a severe animadversion upon halting, wavering, and instability? Surely he would not long endure the double-mindedness and indecision which prevails among professed Christians. Certainly we see some decided characters on the one side, and on the other—on the path of death as well as on that of light and life and as to the former sort, there is a decided sentence against them already pronounced in the word of God. They prefer the golden calf of the lusts and honor of this world to the Lamb of God suffering and dying; they offer incense to Satan, and yield entire obedience to the flesh. These are decided characters, who know what they are doing; they do not halt—no, they walk straightway toward the worm that never dies, and into the fire that is never quenched. And there is a great multitude of such, both old and young, and in all ranks and conditions of life, vessels of wrath, reserved for the manifestation of the justice of God on the great day. But will it eventually fare better with those who may be called borderers, who halt between two opinions, who practically at least doubt which master they shall serve. And oh that the generation of these halting ones did not constitute the majority among us! But, alas! is it not so? Decided living unto God is surely no common thing.

Supreme happiness is to enjoy fellowship with the Father and with his Son Jesus Christ. This is the one thing needful. Let the Lord be your treasure; let him be your supreme love. "Love not the world, neither the things that are in the world" until it can be demonstrated that these are your supreme good, that these can save and make you happy; that these can redeem and comfort you. Could they indeed do so, then the time you spend on religion would be entirely lost time. Make sure therefore of your choice, and be decided as to how you mean to live and die. Oh woe unto you, halting and lukewarm generation! Do you think you can divide your love between God and the world, between Jesus and Belial? Be not deceived, God is not mocked. Who is the supreme good? is it the Lord? Why then is he not also your supreme love? What means this accursed hunting after things that perish? what this idolatrous desire of vain honor and earthly glory? what this anxious care for riches and comforts and worldly pleasures, this heathenish mourning for temporal losses? If human existence be confined to this present life merely, and if we have nothing beyond it to look for, then "let us eat and drink, for tomorrow we die!" Then "walk in the ways of thine heart, and in the sight of thine eyes"; for why should we then lose time upon an imaginary thing, a nullity? But if this is not our rest; if there be a world to come, an eternity hereafter; what means our loitering upon the way; our settling down in the land of our pilgrimage? Be therefore pilgrims and strangers decidedly; lay aside every sin, everything which would impede your progress; esteem all such things as dross and dung, that you may enter in at the strait gate, and that the word "Eternity" may not at last be a word of thunder to you.

Surely it is well worthwhile to sacrifice all other cares to this one—of escaping eternal punishment, and becoming partakers of everlasting happiness. To act half as children of time and half as children of eternity, brings with it entire death. If the word of God be true, submit yourselves to it in all things, even in those which are ever so opposed to our corrupt nature and wayward desires. Believe it heartily, both in its promises and its threatenings, both when it speaks of the glad tidings of salvation, and when it says that we must all appear before the judgment-seat of Christ, and that except a man be born again, he cannot enter into the kingdom of God. But if you are wiser than God, then show it decidedly; only do not halt, for that is irrational and absurd, and do not mix light and darkness together.

Neither attempt to compromise between God and the world. If Christanity be of God, decide for it with body and soul: embrace the cross; be willing to suffer affliction with the despised people of God; forsake the pomps, pleasures, and vanities of the world, and employ all your efforts to promote the kingdom and glory of Christ. Again, do not halt and waver between the righteousness of Christ and your own. Which of the two will avail you in the judgment? If it be only the righteousness of Christ, then value yourselves no longer on your own supposed virtues, as many do, with whom we cannot be long in company without hearing of the good works they have done and are doing, both of humanity and religion. Neither be undecided as to the choice of your friends and associates: for "he that is not with me," says Christ, "is against me; and he that gathers not with me, scattereth." And the Holy Ghost by his apostle says, "Be ye not unequally yoked together with unbelievers: for what fellowship hath righteousness with unrighteousness? and what communion hath light with darkness? and what concord hath Christ with Belial? or what part hath he that believeth with an infidel? And what agreement hath the temple of God with idols? for ye are the temple of the living God; as God hath said, I will dwell in them, and walk in them; and I will be their God, and they shall be my people. Wherefore come out from among them, and be ye separate, saith the Lord, and

88 Elijah the Tishbite

touch not the unclean thing; and I will receive you, and will be a
Father unto you, and ye shall be my sons and daughters, saith the
Lord Almighty," 2 Cor. 6:14-18.

"And the people," it is said, "answered Elijah not a word"; they
perceived, no doubt, that his remonstrance was well-founded, and his
expostulation just. And does not our remonstrance, made to you
upon it, commend itself to your consciences?

Elijah's Challenge

II. Whether Jehovah be God, or Baal be God, rests not now with
Elijah to determine. Jehovah himself will answer that question. Elijah
proceeds, "I, even I only, remain a prophet of Jehovah; but Baal's
prophets are four hundred and fifty men!" God be thanked that he
was not the only man of God then living in Israel; he however was
the only one at that time who stood up publicly to maintain
Jehovah's cause against his adversaries; the rest were either slain, or
banished, or concealed in dens and caves of the earth. Imagine then
Elijah's situation at this time. Among the whole concourse at Carmel
he knew not a single brother in the land, except Obadiah; not one
besides, who was like-minded with himself, not one who made common cause with him, or kept him in countenance. Think what it
must be for a man thus to stand alone in the midst of a host of
strangers. What an overwhelming power is there in the sight of such
a multitude of opponents to abash and discourage! But our prophet
blooms in this moral desert, like the rose. The peace of God is within him; his heart is at ease; he breathes freely; his tongue does not
falter. He is cheerfully bold to testify the name of Jehovah his God
before this intractable and deluded multitude, because he is zealous
only for the honor of God, and simply devoted to that one thing. We
should not be so easily daunted and confounded in our confession of
Christ before men were we simply and unreservedly devoted to him,
and not secretly concerned also for our own credit and reputation.
But, alas, we have too little love to the God of our life, to the God
of all grace, who has "called us unto his eternal glory by Christ Jesus."
Were we but wholly given up to the simplicity of love, we should
prove invincible; for "many waters cannot quench love; neither can
the floods drown it."

"Baal's prophets are four hundred and fifty men." You are aware,
brethren, how much there is in the feeling of being overpowered by

numbers, to inject the doubt, "Am I then the only person in the right, and all these in the wrong?" How easily are we thus induced to make the gate of the kingdom of heaven somewhat wider, and the narrow way somewhat broader; to give up this or that particular portion of the truth, and not to be so very precise and exact in the cause of the gospel. But Elijah was above the influence and operation of circumstances like these. He was sure of the justice of his cause, and though the whole world had thought differently from himself, he had no mind to compromise, or to give place; no, not for an hour; and why? Because he was able to say, "I know in whom I have believed." He was an experimental believer, whose faith was interwoven with his existence and happiness.

"Baal's prophets are four hundred and fifty men." As if he would say, "This makes no differance to me; no, nor even though they were as many thousands; for we shall soon decide the point with them." He had faith to behold more engaged for him than all that could be against him. And we, my brethren, might also enjoy this holy boldness, if we had more faith and confidence in God. If He is for us, who can be against us? We may rejoice and say, with St. Paul, "O death, where is thy sting? O grave, where is thy victory? Thanks be to God, who giveth us the victory, through Jesus Christ our Lord."

Elijah's Confidence

III. The people on mount Carmel are all on the full stretch of expectation, while Elijah addresses them upon the preparations to be made, and the purpose to be answered by them. "Let them therefore give us," he added, "two bullocks; and let them choose one bullock for themselves, and cut it in pieces, and lay it on wood, and put no fire under: and I will dress the other bullock and lay it on wood, and put no fire under; and call ye on the name of your gods, and I will call on the name of Jehovah: and the God that answereth by fire, let him be God. And all the people answered and said, It is well spoken." They agreed to the proposal; some from curiosity, to see what would happen; others, in the hope that Baal would gain the victory; but some few, perhaps, from a real desire to be certain whether Jehovah was the true God. What a hazardous proposal this appears on the part of Elijah! He ventured the whole credit of Jehovah's worship upon the issue of it. But he acted really at no hazard; he was assured that his gracious God would not leave nor forsake him.

The world has already received more than one answer by fire, so that it ought not to require another: but one more such answer awaits this evil world; "the earth and the works that are therein shall be burned up," 2 Pet. 3:10. God answered by fire the first transgressions, when cherubim and a flaming sword were planted at the gate of Paradise. God answered Sodom and Gomorrah by fire, and the shores of the Dead sea retain the traces of it to this day. By a fiery vision he confirmed his promises to Abraham, when a smoking furnace and a burning lamp passed between the pieces of the sacrifice. From the flame of fire in the bush God spoke unto Moses; and out of the fire, clouds, and thick darkness, he spoke to Israel on mount Sinai. By fire He answered the transgression of Nadab and Abihu, the two elder sons of Aaron, who in their priestly capacity offered strange fire unto the Lord; for "there went out fire from Jehovah, and devoured them, and they died before the Lord." By fire as well as earthquake, God answered Israel in the matter of Korah; for "there came out a fire from the Lord, and consumed the two hundred and fifty men that offered incense." By fire God answered Solomon's prayer at the dedication of the temple; for the fire came down and the glory of the Lord filled the house, 2 Chron. 7:2, 3. God likewise answered the waiting apostles at Pentecost, by cloven tongues as of fire.

"And the God that answereth by fire, let him be God." Let us spiritually apply this to ourselves. The fire of the Holy Spirit, with which Messiah baptizes every true believer, is the witness of God in every such believer. This fire consumes the dross of his corruptions, and warms, cheers, and enlightens his soul. He that is insensible to the testimony of this witness, is still dead in trespasses and sins. Let us show them that our hearts burn within us, by the spirit of our life and conversation before God and man. May the Lord thus inscribe his name on our hearts in the flaming letters of his love, that he may not see it necessary to write it in our ashes in the eternally glowing characters of his just displeasure. For he will answer and declare his name to the adversaries, by the fire that is prepared for the devil and his angels; in order that every creature, either with the voice of rejoicing or in the language of self-condemnation, may give him the glory. Jehovah, he is God, and his name endures or ever. Amen!

8

The Decision at Mount Carmel

Today if ye will hear his voice, harden not your hearts." So spoke the Holy Ghost, by the mouth of David, to the thousands of Israel, Psa. 95:7, 8; and again, by the apostle, to the Christian church, Heb 3:15; and let us seriously take these words to heart.

What is this hardening of the heart? It is having minds unconcerned about God's testimonies; it is allowing ourselves to live in practical unbelief. Judicial hardness arises from resisting one divine and gracious call after another, and overcoming one holy influence after another, through unbelief. The more favored we are with means and ordinances, the more danger there is of becoming hardened. The greatest numbers of hardened, as well as of converted persons, are generally found under the most faithful preaching of the gospel.

There are those among us, who do not cleave with full purpose of heart unto the Lord. They have already succeeded in resisting many a gracious call which was made to them, and in again shaking off many a conviction which had fastened on them. Oh that the demonstration of the Spirit and of power may be now vouchsafed unto us, that we may become as surely convinced that Jehovah is our God, as the Israelites at Carmel, whose further circumstances we are now about to consider, were convinced by the answer of fire from heaven that "Jehovah, he is the God!"

1 Kings 18:25-40

And Elijah said unto the prophets of Baal, Choose you one bullock for yourselves, and dress it first; for ye are many; and call on the name of your gods, but put no fire under. And they took the bullock which was given them, and they dressed it, and called on the name of Baal from morning even until noon, saying, O Baal, hear us. But there was no voice, nor any that answered. And they leaped upon the altar which was made. And it came to pass at noon, that Elijah mocked them, and said, Cry aloud: for he is a god; either he is talking, or he is pursuing or he is on a journey, or peradventure he sleepeth, and must be awaked. And they cried aloud, and cut themselves after their manner with knives and lancets, till the blood gushed out upon them. And it came to pass, when midday was past, and they prophesied until the time of the offering of the evening sacrifice, that there was neither voice, nor any to answer, nor any that regarded. And Elijah said unto all the people, Come near unto me. And all the people came near unto him. And he repaired the altar of the Lord that was broken down. And Elijah took twelve stones, according to the number of the tribes of the sons of Jacob, unto whom the word of the Lord came, saying, Israel shall be thy name: and with the stones he built an altar in the name of the Lord: and he made a trench about the altar, as great as would contain two measures of seed. And he put the wood in order, and cut the bullock in pieces, and laid him in the wood, and said, Fill four barrels with water, and pour it on the burnt sacrifice, and on the wood. And he said, Do it the second time. And they did it the second time and he said, Do it the third time. And they did it the third time. And the water ran round about the altar; and he filled the trench also with water. And it came to pass at the time of the offering of the evening sacrifice, that Elijah the prophet came near, and said, Lord God of Abraham, Isaac, and of Israel, let it be known this day that thou art God in Israel, and that I am thy servant, and that I have done all these things at thy word. Hear me, 0 Lord, hear me, that this people may know that thou art the Lord God, and that thou hast turned their heart back again. Then the fire of the Lord fell, and consumed the burnt sacrifice, and the wood, and the stones, and the dust, and licked up the water that was in the trench. And when all the people saw it, they fell on their faces: and they said, The Lord, he is the God; the Lord, he is the God. And Elijah said unto them, take the prophets of Baal; let not one of them escape. And they took them: and Elijah brought them down to the brook Kishon, and slew them there.

What are our reflections after reading this wonderful narrative of sacred history? Is not the answer of Jehovah powerful and full of majesty? Yes, the voice of Jehovah divides the flames of fire, the voice of the Lord shakes the wilderness. May we really feel its power and majesty! Here we see, I. The god of the ignorant and infatuated world; and II. The God of Abraham, of Isaac, and of Jacob.

The God of the World

I. How poor a god is that of the ignorant and infatuated world! Elijah had made his proposal—Both parties were to sacrifice a bullock; and each was to call on the name of his God.

"And the God," said Elijah, "that answereth by fire, let him be God." And all the people agreed to it. "It is well spoken," cried they, as with one voice; and thus the important moment was now come, which should once for all decide whether there is a God in heaven, and who he is. Elijah lost no time. He said unto the prophets of Baal, "Choose you one bullock for yourselves, and dress it first; for ye are many; and call on the name of your gods." He gives them the precedence, on account of their numbers; "ye are many"; you have the majority on your side.

This has always been the case in the present evil world, that the majority have taken the wrong side; and they so outnumber the little flock of Christ on earth, that they could as it were swallow them up, if the safety of the latter depended on their numbers. "Ye are many!" Yes, indeed; numerous as the weeds of an uncultivated field; vessels of wrath every where; all Israel, except seven thousand; a remnant only preserved; all the rest in Samaria, and her towns and villages, alienated from the life of God. And is it not just the same in many Christian countries at present? True it is, in this world they have the upper land, and not without reason; for the prince of this world is their monarch. Hence, they are honored and looked up to; and we are the off scouring of the people; they are the great and the wise, and we the fools. They are the party that have the judgment of the public in their favor; and the voice of the greatest geniuses, and of the most brilliant talents, and the applause of the public journals and we?—ah, if any one takes our part, he thinks he is doing a most condescending work of benevolence. We stand as a sort of criminals before the great public, and have no advocate but Him, who was in the form of a servant, and who, instead of defending our cause before the world, tells us that "his kingdom is not of this world"; and bids us look to the future for our consolation. What wonder is it, that we appear utterly wretched and ridiculous to the world, when the very Judge to whom we appeal is one whom they have long ago crucified. Well, be it so, you children of the father of lies! be the first, and have the superiority; for you are many. The Lord is at hand!

But to return to the narrative. The priests of Baal make preparation for the sacrifice. This they were obliged to do on account of the people. Probably they would rather have let it alone. If they taught the people to worship Baal against their own better knowledge, how wretched must they now have felt while they cut up and dressed their bullock so that they would have been glad to be themselves placed in the victim's stead, to escape the shame and disgrace which they were now bringing upon themselves. But such a season of the most horrible confusion in the face of their own congregations, shall eventually seize upon all hypocritical and lying priests, however they may now deceive and mislead the people at their altars or from their pulpits. The sacrifice being prepared, they begin to cry aloud, another begins and cries, "Baal, hear us!" and if his confidence fail him, a third rallies his drooping spirits and shrieks out, "Baal, hear us!" One fixes his eyes on the clouds; a second looks down unto the depths, to see whether the longed-for flame will not burst forth; and another hearkens intently to hear it rumble in the ground beneath him. But though they wait with desponding countenances, from morning until noon, and from noon until the time of the offering of the evening sacrifice, it is all in vain. The cry of their frenzy dies in the echoes of the mountains. There was neither voice, nor any to answer, nor any that regarded. There lies the sacrifice on Baal's altar, still unconsumed! At last they begin to be desperate, and to act like madmen. They leap upon the sacrifice, as if to provoke Baal to anger, and to call forth fire from him in consequence of it. Or else the meaning is, that they perform a frantic religious dance about the altar, after the manner of Baal's orgies. Be this as it may, there is no notice preternaturally signified of it, either in heaven or on earth.

A miserable deity indeed—a mere nonentity was their idol; for an idol is nothing in the world. And does the favorite deity of this enlightened age deserve any better name? Is the god of the Bible-hating and froward generation of the present day—is the god of most of our philosophers and poets, of our politicians and journalists—is the god of many of our seminaries and universities, professors and students—is the god of our modern scientific institutions—is the god of our polished circles and of our fashionable assemblies, in which it is regarded as disreputable to have even the appearance of adhering to the God of the Bible—is such a god any better, anything more real than the deity of Baal of old?

What mean those fashionable expressions which we hear everywhere substituted for the name of God, the revealed Jehovah? I mean the expressions "heaven, fortune," and such like. How came these expressions to be so in use, except as a flimsy veil to hide the aversion men have to the name and the word of God? How do they hate to hear of anything like Divine communication and manifestation, of answers to prayer, of Divine influence on the heart, of communion with God, of experience of his presence. These are mere fabulous and absurd notions to them; these they esteem as mere delusion—proof enough that, with their god there is neither voice, nor answer, nor attention—proof enough that what they call heaven, and fortune, and fate, denotes a mere nonentity. And is this indeed the god of our rationalists, and so many of our literary men and illuminated dreamers? It is; and the belief of no better a god than this spreads from them through all ranks; and no marvel; for a god such as this, that cannot concern himself about the affairs of men, of course will suffer a thousand sins and excesses to take place without being offended. And this is the very thing they want: that the service of the flesh may be a thing allowed; that falsehood, deceit, and flattery may stand as commendable prudence, and the most voluptuous dance be regarded as an innocent amusement; they wish for a god, to whom it is indifferent what a man thinks and believes—a god, by whose name any one may with impunity swear falsely; a god, in whose presence a man need not be ashamed of any loose discourse nor blush at any impure jest. Behold, such is the god of this perverse generation! I speak not of all, but of the majority. Such is their universal father, as they would gladly conceive him to be; yes, vain, conceited, Bible-hating, and falsely rational generation. Woe unto you for what will you do in the end thereof, in that day when your fear cometh, "then distress and anguish cometh upon you?" Then your cry will be no better than that of Baal, hear us and such will your pretended prayers to God be found to have been all your life long. For the god whom you now profess to serve is no God, but only an imagination of your own.

For true is that which the Holy Ghost says by the apostle John, "He that abideth not in the doctrine of Christ, hath not God," 2 John 9. Tremble at this word of the Lord, all ye who have not the God of the Bible, who have not God in Christ; for you are "without hope, and without God in the world"; you are practical atheists.

But to return to Carmel. There is no end, at present, to the out-cry and idolatrous noise. Elijah stands by, and surveys the tumult. How must his heart have been ready to break with compassion; yet what a holy indignation must he have felt within him; then again, how foolish and ludicrous must the scene have appeared! And it came to pass at noon, that Elijah mocked them, and said, "Cry aloud: forasmuch as he is a god; either he is talking, or he is pursuing, or he is on a journey, or peradventure he sleepeth and must be awaked." Perhaps he has his head and his hands so full, that he neither hears nor sees you. Perhaps he is engaged in meditating on some under-taking; or arranging the thunder and lightning; or else he is not at home, but engaged in the chase; or perhaps he has laid himself down a little, and is asleep; cry aloud, and awake him!

Yes, just as there are doubts, which must be expelled, not by rea-sons and arguments, but, as one of the primitive fathers says, peremptorily with such an expression as "fie, fie," which we should use to children; and just as there are cares which are best removed by a smile; so there are absurdities and errors, to which a little well-timed irony is the best reply. Where reason no longer avails, and where proofs are no longer acknowledged, such irony may occa-sionally serve a useful purpose. Something like it is met with in the 44th chapter of Isaiah; and there, also, it is leveled at the sottishness of idolatry. What can be done with obstinate, self-conceited people, who, perhaps, do not once give themselves the trouble to read the gospel, and examine it? Why should we contend long with such about the truth, seeing that all men have not faith; nor is it com-municable, like an article of merchandise? Perhaps it is better to advise such persons to "stay at Jericho till their beards are grown"; and to say no more. Human nature, in the obstinate, ignorant, and self-conceited, is sometimes more caught hold of by brevity like this, than by ever so long and serious an address. Are you disposed to blame Elijah for being able to mock and use irony during such a momentous scene? If so, you are wrong. He discovers here a free and unruffled state of mind; an inward confidence and cheerfulness about the truth and justice of his cause; a certainty of success, and that the true and living God will not forsake him. If there had been the smallest doubt, the least uncertainty in his soul, he would certainly have indulged no disposition to irony.

But what is the effect of it upon Baal's prophets and votaries? It excites their vexation and impatience to the highest degree. Baal must hear now—he must come forth, whether he will or no. Their cry to Baal is now intense; they draw out their knives and lancets, and lacerate their bodies, according to heathen custom, until they stream with blood; as if they had still retained some remnant of the ancient maxim, that without shedding of blood there is none. With their sinful blood they think to induce Baal to hear and answer them; and then they begin to prophesy—that is, to make all kinds of enthusiastic motions, and to rave and mutter forth horrible incantations. But there was no voice, nor any that answered, nor any that regarded—all was in vain. And even with the living God himself such excitements of spirit, and forced ecstasies and devotions, are not the way to gain an answer to our prayers. However much you may excite yourselves, Jehovah has no pleasure in such sacrifices. Mere solemnity of countenance, bowing down our bodies, praying ourselves hoarse, spending whole hours in mere will worship, are not the things to propitiate God; and as long as you think them to be so, you receive no answer from him.

The God of Abraham, Isaac, and Jacob

II. This unavailing cry of the idolaters was continued from the morning until the time of the evening sacrifice. Then Elijah stood forth in simplicity and uprightness, without pomp and show, with a tranquil countenance and a firm deportment; so that every one might well presume that he was a prophet of the true God. "And Elijah said unto all the people, Come near unto me. And all the people came near unto him." On the top of Carmel lay the ruins of an altar, here called the altar of Jehovah. It had probably been built there in better times, and had been thrown down by the idolaters. This altar Elijah now repaired; as if he meant to say, "May God restore thee, O Israel may God restore thee, thou mournfully dilapidated sanctuary of the Lord!" For what Elijah now did had a significant meaning. He took twelve stones, according to the number of the twelve tribes of Israel, in order to rebuild with them the altar in the name of the

Lord. This was figuratively to say, "God will perform his promise to Jacob, and will keep his covenant with him whom he surnamed by the name of Israel." About the altar Elijah cast a trench—and then prepared the wood, dressed the bullock, and laid it upon it and might he who afterwards spoke of Christ's decease, which he should accomplish at Jerusalem, now have sighed, "Oh that thou wouldest soon prepare thy sacrifice, thou Priest of God, that offering which perfects forever them that are sanctified!" He commanded that water should be poured on the wood, and on the sacrifice, in order that the miracle might be the more unquestionable, and no one be able to object, as if fire had been secretly applied.

"Fill four barrels with water," said he, "and pour it on the burnt sacrifice, and on the wood. And he said, Do it the second time. And they did it the second time. And he said, Do it the third time. And they did it the third time. And the water ran round about the altar; and he filled the trench also with water."

The preparations are now completed. A secret awe thrills through the assembled multitude: deep silence prevails. "And it came to pass at the time of the offering of the evening sacrifice," (which is with us about three o'clock in the afternoon, a solemn and important hour, the ninth hour, as it is called in the evangelists,) "That Elijah the prophet came near, (to the altar,) and said, Lord God of Abraham, Isaac, and of Israel, let it be known this day that thou art God in Israel, and that I am thy servant, and that I have done all these things at thy word. Hear me, O Lord, hear me, that this people may know that thou art the Lord God, and that thou has turned their heart back again!" Elijah calls God by his name, Jehovah God, which he had given himself in the beginning, to denote his condescending and compassionate love to fallen man; he calls him, "the God of Abraham, Isaac, and of Israel," that he might excite in the hearts of this backslidden people a humbling remembrance of all the good which Jehovah had shown to them and to their fathers from ancient times, by his own free grace. Elijah prays, "Let it be known this day that thou art God in Israel, and that I am thy servant, and that I have done all these things at thy word." The honor of God is his supreme desire. He would also have his own mission confirmed in the eyes of the people, and he added, "Hear me, O Lord, hear me"; expressive of the fervency and earnestness of his spirit, "that this people may know that thou art the Lord God, and that thou hast turned their heart back again." The glory of God, and the salvation of the people—these two things formed the entire object of all that the prophet did and said. And what shall we admire the most in this prayer—the prophet's zeal for God's glory, or the ardor of his love for the degraded house of Israel—his boldness in asking such great things, or his firm confidence in not doubting that God would testify to his own cause? No: we wonder most at the unspeakable grace of God, which teaches a handful of dust and ashes, as man is, thus to believe, love, and pray. To him be the glory!

And now, what happens? Mysterious moment. The whole revelation of God is at stake. If no answer follows, the whole fabric falls in, and the ground of our hope is gone. Then all that Elijah has testified—all that the prophets have spoken before him, and which Elijah has confirmed, will be accounted a delusion; and the God of Abraham, of Isaac, and of Israel, will be no longer regarded! The prayer is uttered. The silence of death reigns in the assembly—every heart beats high; in every face is the extreme of expectation; when, lo! the answer comes; the Amen is given; the fire of heaven descends in the sight of everyone, directly upon the altar, consumes the burnt offering, the wood, the stones, and the earth, and licks up the water in the trench. "And when all the people saw it, they fell on their faces: and they said, Jehovah, he is the God; Jehovah, he is the God." Elijah's faith is crowned, the foolish priests are put to shame; and all the gods, which are not the God of the Bible, are confounded and annihilated.

Ah, what has not the merciful God, the God of Abraham, of Isaac, and of Israel performed, to bring us to the knowledge of himself, and to faith in him! Has he not spoken to us without end, in nature and in the Scriptures; by creation, providence, and revelation; by arguments and figures; by prophets, apostles, and ministers; by signs and wonders of every kind, in the most intelligible manner, condescending to our weak capacities as a most merciful Father; and yet, how few are there who really know him! How few give him the glory! O untoward and perverse generation of this world, come near—come, near! Behold not only the testimony by which the Lord answered Elijah upon Carmel, but likewise all the testimonies in which Jehovah has made himself known. We will place some of them before you, so that you may once more see and remember them. He has given living testimonies of himself, by thousands; and that which he gave in these last days, when he spake unto us by his Son, was not the last. Look at the altar of his church built upon himself as its pillar and basis, and on the twelve living stones of the apostles. Look at the sanctuary of God, its stability, its age, its extent, where the life and light of the Holy Spirit, that fire of the Lord, never goes out day or night; is not this spiritual temple an abiding proof that Jehovah lives? Look at every stone of this building—every converted sinner. Here was a ruined altar, but see, it is restored; here was also a surrounding trench of thousandfold sins, enticements, connections, and obstacles, which closed the entrance against the Lord; but lo! his fire has penetrated. Here were also stones—a hard heart and an unteachable mind; here was also wood and earth—deadness, carnality, and darkness; but the flame of Jehovah has consumed the earth, the wood, and the stone, and dried up the floods of ungodliness; and the desolated ruin is become a memorial of the glory of God. Yet how few believe our report; and to how few is the arm of the Lord thus revealed in the present day! Nevertheless, whether men believe it or not, they shall be surrounded with the testimonies of Israel as with a wall, so that only two things will remain to them— either to cry, "The Lord he is the God!" or, as real children of Belial, to declare that they will have nothing to do with Jehovah. It will thus at least come to a decision. Whosoever this day returns home from mount Carmel, without caring to have it said in his heart, "The Lord, he is the God!" let him hesitate no longer to take his place in the ranks of those who are of their father the devil, the god of this world, who blinds the eyes of those who believe not.

The people on mount Carmel gave glory to the God of Israel; but the priests having hardened their hearts from his fear, and remaining still prophets of Baal, they were therefore ripe for destruction. And Elijah said unto the people, "Take the prophets of Baal; let not one of them escape." The people are ready enough to do it; for they now perceive the abominable deception which these destroyers of souls had practiced upon them. They fall upon them, drag them down, at Elijah's command, to the brook Kishon, and assist the man of God in destroying them. However painful this execution must have been to the tender and compassionate heart of the prophet, and how many thousand times soever he would have preferred being God's instrument of these men's conversion rather than of their destruction, yet, because the honor of God demanded it, he could deny his human feelings, and be obedient, notwithstanding natural tenderness and gracious compassion. I say, obedient; for in the law of God, given by Moses, Deut. 13:6, 9, it is expressly said, "If any one will entice thee secretly, saying, Let us go and serve other gods, which thou hast not known, thou, nor thy fathers, thou shalt surely kill him; thine hand shall be first upon him to put him to death, and afterwards the hand of all the people." This express command of Jehovah the prophet was obliged unhesitatingly to obey, however much his feelings might rise against it; for he was appointed of God to contend zealously for the law, to reestablish the statutes of Jehovah in Israel, and to restore the tables of mount Sinai to their ancient honor. And it is not fit that a servant of the Lord should in such a case confer with flesh and blood. "Speak, Lord, for thy servant heareth," is the language of the obedient spirit.

Christ has introduced another dispensation under the New Testament; and the summary punishments of the Old Testament have been exchanged for long-suffering. Hence the righteous and the wicked grow on together until the harvest; but were the same mode of procedure adopted now as in the days of Moses and Elijah, there would be no end of the slaughter; so numerous are the votaries of Baal, even in the midst of a church which is called protestant and evangelical. But the woe pronounced against them will surely come, it will not tarry "beyond the appointed time." He who comes from Bozrah, traveling in the greatness of his strength, who is red in his apparel, will come, and put in motion the wine-press of his wrath. His glittering sword is bathed in heaven, he has bent his bow and made it ready, for the overthrow and destruction of all seducers.

Go on, hirelings and wolves, in your thousand places of concourse, and persuade your poor flocks to sacrifice unto other gods than Him whom Abraham called his Lord, and whose goings were heard on the mountains of Israel. Go on, corrupters of youth, blind leaders of the blind, and amidst the plaudits of the ignorant and ungodly, despise the sovereignty of the Ancient of days, that you may imagine on his throne a being of your own defining, that you may dream the Almighty to be such a one as yourselves. Go on, you people of rank and fashion, and proudly sneer at the true incarnate Jehovah of the Bible, and pay your worship to the wisdom of the day! Alas! the angel is already flying through the midst of heaven, and crying, "Woe! Woe! Woe to the inhabitants of the earth!" The sword is already drawn, to slay you, the pile of Tophet ordained of old is already erected, on which, forsaken by your imaginary gods, you will become flaming monuments forever of the Divine justice, and of all holy vengeance. Oh it is fearful indeed to fall into the hands of the living God; for he is a consuming fire. I beseech you to lay it to heart; he is a jealous God, and a consuming fire!

But thou, Israel, take the harp, rejoice and be glad! thy God liveth! Carmel and Golgotha, heaven and earth, vie with each other, in showing forth, "Thy God liveth!" Join in the song, O Israel! and cry aloud as with the voice of a trumpet, laying one hand on your heart, and lifting up the other on high, "My Lord, he is the God!" The everlasting King! This shall be known in all the earth! Amen.

9

The Prayer on Mount Carmel

We have already had three remarkable instances, in Elijah's history, of the efficacy of the fervent prayer of a righteous man. First, "he prayed earnestly that it might not rain, and it rained not on the earth by the space of three years and six months." Second, he prayed for the restoration of the widow's son, and the child was restored to life. Third, he prayed for the answer by fire to consume the sacrifice, and to decide the controversy with Baal and his priests. Now we have him praying again, and the heaven gives rain, and the land once more brings forth her fruit. Let us this day learn the blessing of walking with God, and conversing with the Keeper of Israel by continual prayer.

1 Kings 13:41-46

And Elijah said unto Ahab, Get thee up, eat and drink; for there is a sound of abundance of rain. So Ahab went up to eat and to drink. And Elijah went up to the top of Carmel; and he cast himself down upon the earth, and put his face between his knees, and said to his servant, Go up now, look toward the sea. And he went up, and looked, and said, There is nothing. And he said, Go again seven times and it came to pass at the seventh time, that he said, behold, there ariseth a little cloud out of the sea, like a man's hand. And he said, Go up, say unto Ahab, Prepare thy chariot, and get thee down, that the rain stop thee not. And it came to pass in the meanwhile, that the heaven was black with clouds and wind, and there was a great rain. And Ahab rode, and

went to Jezreel. And the hand of the Lord was on Elijah; and he girded up his loins, and ran before Ahab to the entrance of Jezreel.

The fire has borne its testimony; the waters now speak. In how
many and various ways does our gracious God testify of himself, that
he is the living God of providence. This, also, is done in answer to
the prayer of Elijah. Here is I. The preparation for prayer; II. The prayer itself, and, III.
The answer to it.

The Preparation for Prayer

I. We are to imagine ourselves at the foot of mount Carmel, in the
plain below, where the prophets of Baal were slain. Those idolatrous
priests have fallen by the hand of Elijah and his new followers, and
their blood is mingled with the brook Kishon; and praise redounds
to God, who is holy in all his ways, and who is glorified by the overthrow of his enemies, as well as by the hallelujahs of his friends.

Three years and a half had the heavens been shut up from yielding a drop of water to the thirsty land of Israel. What an appearance
must the face of the country now have presented! All vegetation
parched and burnt up; man and beast reduced to skeletons; and all
flesh faded like the grass. They who had now become believers in
God must have been filled with unusual terror. They had attained to
the knowledge of him amidst the thunders of his judgments; he had
appeared as in flames of fire. Therefore for the sake of these poor
trembling sheep, our prophet was heartily desirous that his Lord and
God should again show his goodness and loving-kindness. He longed
earnestly, that for the glory of God, and the people's good, the brazen
skies should now dissolve in abundance of rain, and the season of
famine and distress terminate. For this purpose it was necessary that
Elijah should speak to God. The prayer of faith was to him what the
staff was to Moses, with which he divided the Red sea, and struck
water from the flinty rock.

Ahab appears to have remained with the people by the brook
Kishon, and to have witnessed everything, even the slaying of his
priests not without a partial assent, for Ahab was evidently a weak,
capricious tyrant, destitute of character, and governed and molded by
present circumstances. The miracle on Carmel, and the enthusiastic cry of the people, "The Lord, he is the God!" had made a

momentary impression upon him; so that he might have even thought at the time, "Be it so, Jehovah is God!" But his heart was not changed; no true faith had taken possession of it. Many a one may receive impressions from what is taking place around him, so as to be moved by them for a time; but soon recover his former state of mind, and go on afterwards just as if nothing had happened. Such was the case with Ahab, and others, at the fiery testimony on Carmel.

Elijah, about to retire for prayer, wished to be relieved from the company of Ahab and his attendants, and he said unto him, "Get thee up eat and drink; for there is a sound of abundance of rain." In these words we cannot help discerning a well merited reproof to the wretched monarch. It looks as if he had said, "Thy carnal ease is thy principal care; now take it; it will not much longer be disturbed by drought and famine." It implied also that the king's presence was not wanted; especially while Elijah was about to converse with his God. And does it not convey a touching reproof to any of us, if the children of God are obliged to become mute and monosyllabic on our entering their company, and immediately turn the discourse upon the weather, politics, or the news of the day? Is it not a Divine admonition to us, when we cannot help feeling that we are burdensome to them, that we interrupt them, and when it is gently hinted to us that we do not perhaps feel ourselves quite at home, that we are rather out of our element? Yes, to be thus sent away from Christian society, and banished as it were from the sanctuary of God, is surely a foretaste of future judgments. And how many among us must daily swallow the bitter pill of being told, in one way or another, "Get thee up, eat and drink; we should be glad to be without you; we cannot go on comfortably while you are present."

"Get thee up," said Elijah; and added, "for there is sound of abundance of rain"; a sound of a rustling, as is usual before an approaching storm, in the tops of the trees, and upon the waters. Whether he heard it only in faith, with the ear of the spirit, or whether God rendered his bodily hearing so acute that he really heard it from afar in the elements, or in the higher regions of the air, we need not inquire. It is enough that he heard it, and it sounded to him like the tolling of the bell for prayer, even as a forerunning Amen, to the aspirations for which he was preparing himself: and it strengthened him in the hope, that his will, in desiring rain, was one with the will of God, who would now send rain.

We sometimes hear such a sound also; and whenever we do, let it be to us what it was to Elijah—a summons to prayer. It ought to be so to us according to God's intention. When, at any time, the preaching of the truth is blessed to a church, and the word reaches the soul when a movement appears in a congregation, and a general excitement prevails—when tears of emotion flow, and people meet together and say, "What a powerful, impressive sermon!" there is then a rustling, and it is then time, children of God, to lift up your hands and pray, that after the sound, the rain may come. Again, when some judgment has occurred in the neighborhood; when a barren fig tree has been unexpectedly cut down before our eyes; when a scorner has been evidently smitten by Providence that the simple may beware; or whatever it be, when the whole neighborhood is alarmed, and unbelievers themselves are obliged to confess that the hand of God is visible—then pray that it may not stop there.

When you are informed that one individual is desiring the sincere milk of the gospel, and that another has risen up from the seat of the scornful, and shows an inclination to come among the people of God; or, when you perceive that amongst the members of your household there is an inquiry after eternal things, and that your children begin to hear gladly of the Lord Jesus; then the sound reaches your ears; then it is time to lift up your heart in prayer. Yes; be watchful, children of God! never fall asleep on the walls of Zion, keep your ears attentive, and listen in every direction—in the church and in your houses, among your friends and relatives; and when you hear the rustling, even if but faintly and as at a distance, go immediately to your closet, fall down at God's footstool, stretch out your hand and cry, "O Lord, we will not let you go, unless you pour upon us the gracious rain of thine inheritance." And the same course should be pursued when there begins to be a rustling, not merely among others, but in your own selves; when it thunders and lightens in your own darkness; when a word strikes you, and a ray of light comes into your souls; when the glory of Christ is more clearly manifested to your mind, and your soul enjoys a foretaste of his grace—then, give the more diligence to make your calling and election sure. The rustling is not the rain itself; but the forerunner of the rain, as a Divine summons to prayer. O regard it as such!

While Elijah was thus employed, Ahab, we are told, went up to eat and to drink. Miserable man after all the great and heart-affecting scenes of the day, he felt just as if he had witnessed an interesting, though somewhat tedious comedy, after which refreshment is welcome, and food is relished. Would that such characters were not too common even at present.

Many among us are not a whit better than Ahab. But a fearful woe awaits those who suffer the most convincing testimonies, the loudest calls to repentance, and the most affecting works of God to pass before them, like a shadow or a dream. They please themselves with such things for a while, as with a pleasant song, or a beautiful painting; but carry nothing away with them from our churches and meetings, except perhaps a feeling of the length of the service, or some topic for conversational display, together with a good appetite for the next carnal meal. Yes, this is all; though perhaps in the morning the Lord by His Spirit has answered as with fire before their eyes and ears. However, we will not detain them; "let them go, eat, and drink!"

The Prayer Itself

II. When Ahab was gone, Elijah went up to the top of Carmel; in spirit however, we find him descending into the valley of humiliation. On Carmel's summit, where all was calm and still, as in a solitary closet, no unbidden guests followed him; here he could converse uninterruptedly with the Lord. On the top of Carmel, too, he could the sooner perceive if his prayer was heard, and he stood there, as on a lofty watch-tower, from whence he could widely survey both sea and land. However, he does not seem to have made much use of this commanding view; for, on reaching the summit, he kneels down, closes his eyes, bends his head forward toward his knees, and in this posture he begins to address the Lord, and to pray for rain. Behold him! Would it be supposed that this is the man, who a short time before stood upon Carmel as a vicegerent of God, seemingly empowered with a command over the elements? Yet he now humbles himself in the dust, under the feeling of his own poverty and weakness. What does his whole demeanor express but abasement, and consciousness of his littleness and unworthiness! But it was the will of God that we should for once behold his great prophet in such a situation, and overhear him in his closet, in order to teach us where his strength really lay; to show us that it has been God's rule, from ancient times, to work with weak instruments, and to do wonders by bruised reeds, in order that we might see whence even an Elijah derived his greatness; and not be tempted to place the honor and glory upon the head of man, instead of laying it at the feet of him to whom it belongs; and that we might feel the force of that encouraging sentence of the apostle James, "Elias was a man subject to like passions as we are." When he stood before the people, he was God's ambassador, and as such had to speak and to act in virtue of his high commission; but when he stood before God, he was a poor sinner and a worm, who was only able to live by mercy, and had nothing to demand but everything to beg at a throne of grace. On the summit of Carmel the feeling of his unworthiness seems to have quite overwhelmed him. How could it be otherwise, when he looked back upon the events of that day, and upon the whole course of his life to that moment! What success had been granted him, in the fulfillment of his desires and prayers! What succor, what preservation, what answers had he experienced! And who was he? We hardly dare to say it; but he will have it confessed before God and men, how unworthy he is of the least of all these mercies; how much he regards himself as the chief of sinners. And, in this consciousness, he appears before the Lord, entreating again a new wonder, although the altar is still smoking from the fiery testimony, which the Lord, at his request, had so recently given.

When Elijah had wrestled awhile with God in the depth of self-abasement and poverty of spirit, in a manner which perhaps few of us know from experience for all believers do not tread in a path of such a deep and thorough humiliation—he said unto his servant, "Go up now," that is, to the declivity of the mountain, "and look towards the sea!" He placed him as it were on the watch-tower, to look out and inform him when his prayer was beginning to be answered by a sign of rain becoming visible in the distant horizon. For he was certain of a favorable answer, in faith on the word and truth of Him who had said to him at Zarephath, "Go, show thyself to Ahab, and I will send rain upon the earth!" The servant went, looked out in the distance, and cast his eyes about on all sides; but the sky was as clear as crystal—not a cloud to be seen. He came back, and said, "I see nothing." But it is a matter of daily experience, that help does not appear at the first cry, nor is the harvest reaped the moment after the sowing time of prayer. This is certainly not agreeable to flesh and blood; but, spiritually considered, it is very salutary. What would be the consequence, if God's treasures were always opened at our first knocking? Should we not then seem to be rulers and commanders in the city of God, and forget our dependent condition? Should we not be in danger of making an idol of our prayer, as the Israelites made of the brazen serpent, and think it is our prayer that effects all; that in it we possess a secret charm, a divining rod, or a legal claim upon the bounty of God? We should soon become self-sufficient. Therefore our gracious God does not always appear to hearken to this first cry; but lets us stand awhile at the door, so that once and again we are obliged to say, "I see nothing." We ought then to reflect a little, and become deeply conscious that we have, in reality, nothing to claim, but that all is mere unmerited favor. If we make our first approach to his footstool in the character of just persons, he keeps us back until we feel that we are poor sinners, unworthy petitioners; and are ready to say, "Truth, Lord: let the dogs eat of the crumbs which fall from their master's table." Such is his method.

"There is nothing," said the servant. But our praying Elijah does not despair. The reason why we generally so easily grow weary, and so soon cease from praying, is, because we are not sufficiently earnest for the blessing we implore. This, however, was not the case with Elijah. He therefore bids the servant to go again seven times. But why precisely seven times? Does it only mean several times, or is there here any particular emphasis in the number of seven? And why was the servant to go thus again and again? What would it avail him to hear every time, "There is nothing"? Doubtless it stimulated the prophet's ardor; it animated him to wrestle the more earnestly with God; it made him still less and less in his own eyes, and drew forth deeper and deeper sighs from his contrite soul. How would his fervor in prayer thus augment from one minute to another? To obtain a speedy hearing is much more agreeable to our natural feelings, but waiting long far more beneficial for us. Those are the most blessed spots on the face of the earth where prayer is wont to be made with the greatest fervency and perseverance. During this process of persevering prayer, our corrupt nature receives the most deadly blows; then is the heart thoroughly broken up, and prepared for the good seed of the word; the remains of self-love are demolished; the chambers of imagery are cleansed, the foundation of truth in the soul is laid deep, and when at length the answer comes, how great is the joy!

The Answer

III. The servant returns the seventh time, and says, "Behold, there
ariseth a little cloud out of the sea, like a man's hand." Elijah's prayer
is answered! It is true, it is only a little cloud, at first hardly visible.
But, when God gives the first-fruits, he always gives the harvest in
due time. If you have received a little grace, rejoice! you have hereby a pledge that you shall receive more. If there be something of his
Spirit in you, know that abundance of grace is in reserve for you.
Forgiveness is a pledge of adoption, and renewal of spirit commenced
will be carried on unto the day of Christ. Therefore let every sincere
Christian rejoice, who sees in himself or others a little of Divine
grace. Let him but continue instant in prayer, and the blessing shall
increase abundantly.

And the prophet said unto his servant, "Go up, say unto Ahab,
Prepare thy chariot, and get thee down, that the rain stop thee not."
Thus was literally fulfilled what Elijah had said: "There shall not be
dew nor rain these years, but according to my word." Therefore the
Lord did not let the full shower come all at once; but, first of all, a little cloud that was scarcely visible, that Elijah might have time to
announce the approaching rain to the king, that the rain might come
at the word of the prophet; and that it might be fully apparent that
Jehovah, the God of Elijah, was the Governor of the world. The servant comes to the king, who perhaps was stationed in a pavilion
upon the mountain, while the sky is still clear, and seems to promise
anything but rain. "Prepare thy chariot," was the message; "get thee
down, that the rain stop thee not!" "Rain!" would the astonished
guests exclaim; "Rain!" would the people cry full of joyful hope; and
scarcely had they lifted up their eyes, when every region of the sky
seemed to reply, "Yea, and amen; abundance of rain!" Dark thunder-
clouds ascend out of the sea, one after the other; the heavens become
black, the wind sets all the sea in motion, roars through the forest,
and a violent storm pours down upon the land. O welcome
streams! refreshing floods! The face of the earth is renewed, and all
nature rejoices. A breath of life breathes over the fields, wood and
meadow are clothed with new verdure, the birds resume their music
in the branches, and man, and beast, and everything seems as if
resuscitated. The voice of rejoicing is heard in the dwellings of the
righteous, and joy fills the hearts of the godly. Ahab is already seat-
ed in his chariot, and on his way to his royal seat in Jezreel. But "the

hand of the Lord was upon Elijah." Jehovah invigorated him with supernatural bodily powers, so that the prophet, girding up his loins, ran before Ahab's chariot, which doubtless was at full speed, on account of the deluging rain. The prophet was now a living memorial to the king, to remind him of all the great things which the God of Israel had brought to pass by his prophet; that Ahab might not easily forget them, but carry the fresh impression of them to Jezebel. Elijah therefore outran the chariot before his eyes, through all the torrents of rain and tempest, till he came to the entrance of Jezreel.

"And Elijah," says the apostle James, "was a man like as we are, and he prayed earnestly that it might not rain: and it rained not on the earth by the space of three years and six months. And he prayed again, and the heaven gave rain, and the earth brought forth her fruit." And why does the apostle notice this? He adduces this instance of Elijah's success in prayer as an encouragement to us to persevere in prayer, and to believe that we also shall not fail of being answered, if we only pray in faith; because, "the effectual fervent prayer of a righteous man availeth much," James 5:16. And indeed, who can recount all the wondrous instances in which the truth of this declaration has been realized! Through prayer, Moses turned away the fierce wrath of the Almighty from Israel; and with outstretched arms he smote the host of Amalek. Manoah, by the voice of his cry, drew down a visible manifestation of the Divine presence in human form, Judg. 13:8. Through prayer at Mizpah, the prophet Samuel smote the army of the Philistines, and caused the thunder of terror to roll over Israel's foes, 1 Sam. 7:9-12. Through prayer, Josiah the prince died in peace, 2 Kings 22:19, 20. Through prayer, fifteen years were added to Hezekiah's life; the three men were preserved in the burning fiery furnace; and to Daniel it was said by Gabriel, "I am come because of thy words." At the prayer of the brethren on the day of Pentecost, the heavens were opened; and, another time, after they had prayed, the place where they were assembled was shaken, and all were filled with the Holy Ghost, Acts 4:31. Prayer burst the fetters of Peter, and broke open the doors of his prison. Prayer rebuked storms, healed the sick, and brought back the dead to life. And what shall I say more of the power, the wonders, and the performance of prayer? The whole Scripture is full of them. And our church, also, would be full of them—all Christendom would be full of them—were there more prayer in our churches and more of this incense on our public, family, and private altar. But prayer sleeps among us, for what we pray—morning and evening, according to custom—is sleepy, dull, and heartless repetition of devotional language. It does not deserve the name of prayer. Keep these ceremonious compliments to yourselves, the Lord does not want such service. The confessions of the broken and contrite heart, the cry of the humble, the expression of real godly sorrow, the opening of our ears to our heavenly Father, the breathings of grateful love, the acknowledgment of dependence on the name of Jesus—these are the things which constitute true prayer.

Brethren, pray that the Spirit of grace and supplication may be poured out upon us; and then ask what you will and it shall be done for you. "He that cannot lie" has promised it. Only ask in His name, as the children of God, by faith in Christ Jesus, trusting in God's faithfulness to his promises, and you will certainly succeed at last. If six times the answer should be, "There is nothing" yet wait the seventh time, which is the proper and the Lord's time. He will give the answer you need. Too often we omit to notice God's answer to our own prayers; otherwise how frequently should we find, to our glad astonishment, that, as in the case of Daniel, at the time of our supplication the commandment had gone forth to help us. Therefore let the call to prayer be ever regarded by us as the invitation to an unspeakable privilege. "Continue instant in prayer." Pray in the Spirit, in the Holy Ghost, and not in your own self-sufficiency; and you will pray with power. Pray for yourselves, pray for all, and pray with faith and expectation; for in the immutable word, that word which must survive both heaven and earth, it stands recorded, "Verily, verily, I say unto you, Whatsoever ye shall ask the Father in my name, he will give it you," John 16:23. Amen.

10

Flight into the Wilderness

He that cometh from heaven, is above all," was the testimony of the Baptist to Him whose shoe's latchet he deemed himself unworthy to unloose. And the whole course of our Lord's ministry confirms this testimony. It is the glorious manifestation of one who is "above all," and wherever we see the Savior appearing and acting, in the narrative of the Gospels, the impression irresistibly forces itself upon us: here is one, greater than Moses and all the prophets and apostles—here is one, who is separate from sinners, and above every creature—one, who came down for a short time to our world, as into a strange country, but whose peculiar residence is on the throne of glory and majesty. We are convinced that no mere man could have acted as he did, however divinely commissioned. Miracles as great as his were wrought by the apostles and prophets; but the manner in which they were wrought by him, and by them, exhibits an immense distinction between the one and the other. They, with all their derived powers, show themselves to be but men, and while they perform their miraculous works, they seem treading, as it were, on strange and unknown ground. When they divide the seas, it is with trembling hands; the dead, who awake on their call, are received by them with much astonishment. The surrounding anxious preparations, which generally precede their miracles, show clearly that they are of themselves but poor worms, invested but for a moment with a power not their own, the gigantic weight of which well nigh overwhelms them.

But how different is the impression which forces itself upon us in contemplating the miracles of Jesus! When he arises to pacify the tumult of the elements, or approaches the tombs to reanimate the dust, we feel at once that He is above all. He evidently acts by his own independent power and authority, and performs his miracles by his own sovereign will. In him we see no long and anxious preparations; nothing of that internal conflict, which a Moses experienced at the Red sea, or of that trembling earnestness with which an Elijah raised the dead at Zarephath. He bears no staff in his hand, nor any other mark of dependence. With simple dignity he stretches out his hand; and the blind see, the sick and the palsied arise and walk. He needs no appeal to the power of another, but says, "I will; be thou clean," and the leper is cleansed. He beckons, and the winds and waves are rebuked; he commands, and the dead arise from the grave of corruption. Glory and majesty surround him in all his doings, and unfold unto us the fullness of the Godhead. Who ever spake as He spake, whose very prayers were expressions of his will? Who ever comforted his people as He did, who loved them and gave himself for them? Thus we see him on every occasion as the Holy One of God, entirely distinct from all created beings; one who is higher than the heavens, and who is entitled to all praise and adoration; and his whole appearance places in him a glory, majesty, and greatness, which fills heaven and earth, and which would have overwhelmed us had it not been a glory full of grace and truth. Yes, he is above all: and great as was the prophet Elijah, his infirmities, as we shall presently have occasion to notice them, will serve to remind us how infinitely inferior every one is to the all-perfect Prophet, Priest, and King, our Lord Jesus Christ.

1 Kings 19:1-4

> And Ahab told Jezebel all that Elijah had done, and withal how he had slain all the prophets with the sword. Then Jezebel sent a messenger unto Elijah, saying, So let the gods do in me, and more also, if I make not thy life as the life of one of them by tomorrow about this time. And when he saw that, he arose, and went for his life, and came to Beersheba, which belongeth to Judah, and left his servant there. But he himself went a day's journey into the wilderness, and came and sat down under a juniper tree: and he requested for himself that he might die; and said, It is enough; now, O Lord, take away my life; for I am not better than my fathers.

The man of God is again called away from public activity and reformation and his path loses itself once more in the solitudes of a wilderness. What now befell him served for spiritual exercise to himself. The torch is shaken, that it may afterwards glow the brighter, and the refiner of Israel must himself undergo further trial and purification. We have here to notice, I. Elijah's persecution; II. His flight; and, III. His dejection.

Elijah's Persecution

I. Our imagination can picture Ahab now arrived at his palace at Jezreel, which appears to have been his summer residence, on account of its agreeable situation. We are certain that Jezebel, his queen, could not have been indifferent as to the issue of the great contest at Carmel, and we may well suppose that she was expecting, with impatience, the return of the king. We have seen that he returned at full speed, in a violent rain, and it is easy to imagine him hastily alighting from his chariot before the palace, and hurrying into the apartments of his imperious consort, to announce to her the wonderful occurrences he had just witnessed. Elijah, meanwhile, remains in the neighborhood, awaiting the issue of the great events which had been brought to pass. His hopes were probably at this time raised high; perhaps he even promised himself an immediate return both of prince and of people to the God of their fathers.

Ahab, full of the tidings of these strange events, told Jezebel all that Elijah had done, and how he had slain all the prophets with the sword. We can imagine with what emotions he would enter her apartment, and say, "The Tishbite has triumphed! Fire from heaven has confirmed his word. Upon his prayer, I beheld with my own eyes flames fall from the skies, consume the burnt-offering, the wood, the stones, and lick up the water in the trench. All the people can bear witness to it. They fell on their faces, and cried out, as with one voice, that Jehovah is God. The priests of Baal are slain; Elijah and the people have destroyed them, and their blood is flowing in the brook Kishon. They were laughed at as liars and impotent deceivers. Their authority and their worship is gone forever. There is universal enthusiasm for Elijah. He is a prophet of the living God. The miracle on Carmel has placed it beyond a doubt, and these heavy rains completely confirm it. At his command; they fall; he closed heaven, and he has now opened it again."

In some such manner as this, we may suppose the king communicated the tidings to Jezebel, and then breaking off in the midst of his narrative, as if he had been thunder-struck. On what account? Alas, he sees the features of his queen gather blackness like a storm. The weak king, "as one whom Jezebel his wife stirred up," for thus the sacred historian speaks of him, is evidently completely under her influence, and when he perceives the effect his narrative has upon her, his opinion is quite changed; he begins to take another view of the wonders at Carmel, as also of Elijah himself. Jezebel resolves to gratify her bloodthirsty revenge, and she is the adored mistress of Ahab's affections. The deluded monarch appears not to have dared to think differently from Jezebel his wife. He appears as a lamentable instance of one, who, though not totally insensible to the voice of truth, continues a wretched slave to the father of lies. His heart was given to Jezebel, and her affection is the price to which everything else was to be sacrificed. On her behavior to him was all the happiness of his life suspended. He was the sport of her tempers, and she exercised over him unlimited control. Pliant, like clay on the potter's wheel, and capable of taking any form, he was always ready to be what she was pleased to make of him. Sold, by affection, under her influence, he soon lost the last remains of manly steadfastness, and before he was aware, his own individuality was so much sunk in that of his proud and imperious mistress, that he heard only with her ears, saw with her eyes, and felt and thought only with her.

A great many persons, in every age, are thus led blindfold by human influence. The chains with which the prince of darkness binds mankind, yoke and banner, are not always the grosser vices and lusts; he secures thousands of souls to himself and to hell by attaching them with the silken cords of a tender affection to persons who have taken a decided part with the enemies of the cross of Christ. Now, whatever the bond may be, whether paternal, filial, conjugal, or social, the effect is the same. The influential person or persons rule with irresistible power, and the poor captive soul thinks not for itself, has no firmness or independence; friends and party govern it altogether, and this in spite of the most distressing convictions. Nor is it by perverted human affection alone that men are kept back from the truth. There are others, and not a few, who are equally far from the kingdom of God, by reason of the homage they pay to human intellect, either in themselves or others. The corrective of all these different sorts of error would be a heartfelt belief of those plainest declarations of the gospel: "Ye are not your own, for ye are bought with a price: therefore glorify God in your body, and in your spirit, which are God's," 1 Cor. 4:19, 20. "He that cometh from heaven is above all," John 3:31. "I am the light of the world: he that followeth me shall not walk in darkness, but shall have the light of life," John 8:12. And again, "I am the way, the truth, and the life," John 14:6. And you who exercise influence over others, take heed that you prove not, in this respect, the agents of the great enemy of souls; for if through you any "weak brother perish," "his blood will be required at your hands." Remember, that whoever destroys a soul, "him will God destroy."

Woe then unto those men of talent and acquirements, who, with revolting ingratitude, transmute the gifts and abilities, with which God has blessed them, into weapons of darkness; who, under the influence of the great deceiver, assault the most sacred things of God. Woe unto those much-admired rulers of literature, who, in wicked self-deification, use the power they possess over the minds of men, to rivet more firmly the bonds of infidelity and hostility to Christ upon the neck of the present generation, and who exert their genius in preparing those intoxicating notions and antichristian systems which delude themselves and others to their destruction! Woe to those laurel-crowned heads that cover the kingdom of sin with fantastic enchantments, and overturning every sacred restraint, implant the horrible delusion in the mind, that he does not sin who only contrives to sin poetically and elegantly! Woe to those whose voices give the tone to the world, who have sufficient talents for becoming the Ezras and Nehemiahs of their time, but who are a pestilence to the age they live in, by darting forth their wit in seductive and blasphemous falsehoods, and abuse the weak understandings of those who hang in admiration upon their lips, in order, imperceptibly, under the pretense of superior light, to scatter sparks of rebellion against Jehovah and his anointed! Woe, woe unto these betrayers of mankind! Their part will soon be acted. A time is coming, when, from the very lips that now satiate them with their plaudits, only the dreadful thunder of furious execrations will meet their ears; and when the very hands, which now crown them with laurel, will be extended toward heaven against them, to draw down upon them the lightning of an eternal curse. Be not deceived! mistake not the present course of things for the final decision. That decision will be pronounced by Him, whose eyes are as a flame of fire, and who weighs with other scales than those of the deluded world, which only pays homage to external glitter. Your glory has its season and its period, like the flower of the grass. "All flesh is grass, and all the goodliness of man as the flower of grass. The grass withereth, and the flower thereof falleth away," 1 Pet. 1:24.

But to return to Jezebel. The fire of hell is kindled within her, James 3:6; she thirsts to avenge the blood of the priests of Baal. In her judgment, better would it have been that the whole nation had perished with hunger and drought, than that such a triumph should have been prepared for the prophet and his God. The showers of blessing that now returned to soften the clods of the field, cannot soften her obdurate spirit. Well would it be for the world, if no such characters still remained in it but consider in how many places the triumph of the gospel increases the opposition of unbelievers. What scoffing and ridicule at the outpouring of the Spirit, and what contempt of piety and conversion to God, are vented by many in their writings and discourse! The voice of Jezebel is virtually regarded by many as the voice of truth; and this in our accredited newspapers, in our refined circles and assemblies, in our poetry and philosophy, even in the chairs of divinity professors, and in many, very many of our pulpits. But woe unto the spirit of Jezebel in every age! That woe has been pronounced by Christ himself, and is recorded in the last book of the sacred volume. "Behold, I will cast that woman Jezebel into a bed, and them that commit adultery with her into great tribulation, and I will kill her children with death," Rev. 2:22, 23. This is their end.

Jezebel, the wife of Ahab, has now sworn by her gods that Elijah shall die. But Jehovah, who can bind the unicorn with his hand, and put a hook into the jaws of the leviathan, will now interpose to preserve Elijah. "He who taketh the wise in their own craftiness," and "infatuates the counsel of princes," has only to leave Jezebel to the madness of her own evil passions, and lo, she so imprudently forgets herself, as to send and apprise the prophet of her murderous intention against him. This was, of course, the very way to defeat it. "Jezebel sent a messenger to Elijah, saying, So let the gods do to me, and more also, if I make not thy life as the life of one of them by tomorrow about this time!" Elijah hears the message. What does it mean? Does it mean, indeed, that all his labors and conflicts are to result in his own disappointment and death? Is this the conversion of Jezebel, and Ahab, and of Israel, which he had hoped for? Alas, what a bitter draught for the soul of this man of God! Who shall comfort him at this lamentable turn of events? Certainly he had never received a more painful stroke upon his spirit than this; and if his faith steers clear amid such rocks without shipwreck, it must be owing to the support and guidance of an Almighty hand. But does the Lord take any pleasure in frustrating our hopes, and leading us to despondency and doubt? O no; far be it from Him! "He will fulfill the desire of them that fear him." The hopes he raises in us he will fulfill; only we must not think to prescribe to him the time or the manner in which he shall do it. He will never suffer his servants really to "spend their strength for naught and in vain." When therefore they seem to be frustrated for a time, it is only that they may learn that their success is not "of him that willeth nor of him that runneth." He finishes all his works and crowns them all, but he does it in his own mysterious way. He allows discouragements and impediments to arise, that his wisdom and power may be hereby the more manifest, and that the creature may learn that this is the Lord's doing. Nothing, therefore, which we engage in for his glory, shall be eventually unsuccessful; but then the Lord alone must be exalted.

Behold, such are the ways of God! Set then your minds at rest respecting all present difficulties; only do your duty, and commit yourselves to God. He will be able, at the proper time, to solve every difficulty. Reserve your judgment for the final issue, and remember that "The beauty of a thing," as a primitive father observes, "appears at the moment of its maturity, which God waits for. He that tastes the blossom instead of the fruit, will pass a wrong judgment upon it. That would limit his idea of the beauties of vegetation to their appearance in the winter season, would judge very blindly." Yet how often do we conclude thus hastily as to the ends of God's providential government and disposal of human affairs!

Elijah's Flight

II. Let us now follow Elijah in his proceedings upon receiving this alarming message. "When he saw that, he arose, and went for his life, and came to Beersheba, which belongeth to Judah." In this instance, Elijah's faith appears in some measure to have failed him. The very words of the sacred narrative seem to give us a significant hint as to his state of mind at this period. For the words are, "When he saw that." What did Elijah see? Not God's promises, and, power, and faithfulness; these at least only dawned upon him in the background, with broken and feeble rays. But in the foreground very different things appeared; the infuriated Jezebel threatening his life, and all the horrors of a cruel death. Instead of soaring above these as on eagles' wings, and looking down upon them with sublime composure, as on former occasions, the pressure of human terror seems to have been too strong for his mind, especially as backed by the disappointment of his hopes on Israel's account. "He arose, and went on his life"; or, as others have rendered it, "he arose and went whither he would"; which serves further to intimate the obscurity of his course and the uncertainty of his steps. He had at this time no express Divine direction, as to whither he should go. Hitherto his way had always been marked out for him most distinctly by his Lord; but not so now. There was no particular Divine word to serve him for a staff on this journey; no distinct commission shining before him like a lamp, giving wings to his feet, and firmness to his steps. He went forth into the wide world in uncertainty, distracted by doubts, and unaccompanied by the consoling consciousness that he was taking this road for God; since he went it only for himself, and for the sake of his own life; and verily this thought was not at all calculated to relieve his oppressed mind.

How pleasant and comfortable is it to pursue those paths, however rough and thorny, in which we feel assured the Lord has commanded us to walk! How joyfully is everything undertaken, begun, and accomplished, that comes to our hearts as a Divine commission! We then run, and are not weary; we walk, and are not faint. But to have put to sea without knowing if we had not better have remained at home—how painful is the thought!

The mind of the prophet appears to have been in this painful state, when, perplexed about the ways of God, and grievously disappointed at present appearances, he left Jezreel without any consciousness of the Lord's direction. The strange circumstance that the queen had thus imprudently disclosed to him her murderous intentions, might indeed have led him to conclude that the Lord thus warned him to flee for his life; but this was only a human inference, and no clear Divine declaration; but though the Lord may thus permit us, like Elijah, to go whither we will, without giving us any plain intimation by his providence, yet this is only a procedure of his wise and tender love. For hereby we come the better to learn what a blessed thing it is to know we are in the service of our God, and to walk at all times in the light of his guidance; like Israel, resting at his word, and at his word striking our tents and advancing. And the more we learn to appreciate this happy state by experience of its contrary, the easier to us is the petition, "Thy will be done!" and the more earnestly shall we hearken to what the Lord God will say concerning us, and ask beforehand his counsel and direction in everything. Again, though God's children seem to go "whither they will," in uncertainty and doubt whether the Lord is pleased with them or not, still their faithful God accompanies them as before, even while he often keeps himself long concealed. He never leaves them, but he leads them, though by secret guidance, always to a happy end. This Elijah experienced. The Lord was with him on the way, however little the prophet was conscious of it. Let us only have patience, and before we are aware, the clouds will pass away, and it will be seen, as in the case of Elijah, that we have not gone in every respect whither we would, but that God has all along been leading us.

After Elijah had traveled for many days, and gone through a great part of Samaria and the whole of the land of Judea, he came at length to Beersheba, as it were by chance; for he had as little to do at Beersheba as at any other place. Here however he could not remain; his spirit was too afflicted for common society. Even the company of his faithful servant was burdensome to him. What could the servant do for him? He could not enlighten the darkness of his afflicted spirit, nor explain the mysterious providence which had disquieted it. Therefore, leaving him at Beersheba, he went alone into the solitary wilderness, into the very heart of it, a whole day's journey, until the sun went down. He then threw himself upon the heath under a juniper tree, and sank down under the load of his melancholy thoughts.

Elijah's Dejection

III. Thick darkness hung over the prophet's soul. This is shown by his whole conduct—a close reserve, his desire for solitude, his planless wandering into the gloomy wilderness, all indicate a discouraged and dejected state of mind. Perplexed with regard to his vocation—even with respect to God and his government—his soul lies in the midst of a thousand doubts and distressing thoughts. It seems tossed on a sea of troubles, without bottom or shore; and there appears but one step between him and utter despair. There he sits, like an exile in the midst of the fearful solitude, as if cast out by God and the world; with his eyes fixed; full of gloomy and painful thoughts. His spirit lies in the land of Israel, and in the midst of idolaters, the children of better forefathers. Oh the melancholy images which pass before him! The heart-rending scenes which are portrayed upon the tablet of his memory! He sees the people reeling on mount Carmel in their idolatrous orgies; in Samaria one idol temple rises up before him after another; the streets of Jezreel resound with blasphemies against the living God and his servants; and Jezebel is drunk with the blood of the few believers who fell victims to her revenge. Such are the images which vividly and dreadfully present themselves to his mind. And wherever he turns his eyes amidst the horrible scene, there is no herald of God; no voice of a single prophet is lifted up against it. Perhaps now he thinks, "Why did I not remain? Why did I flee, and forsake my poor people?" And if the distress of his spirit had not been already excited to the utmost, surely such thoughts as these must have tended to that effect.

The pious servant of God has had enough of this vale of tears. He is heartily weary of painful conflicts and fruitless labors; his soul longs for its rest. "It is enough!" sighs he to Heaven, his eyes glistening with tears. "It is now enough, O Lord! Take away my life; for I am not better than my fathers." Ah! Who could have thought that Elijah could ever have become so weak and faint-hearted; the man, who seemed invincible in the armor of his faith, and superior to every storm! But to us it is consoling, that even such a one as Elijah sat under the juniper tree, and thought in his despondency that he was unable any longer to bear the burden of life. "It is enough, O Lord! Why should I remain longer in this land of travail? My existence is useless. If my labors in Israel, in the midst of so many signs and wonders, have missed their aim, where shall they be of any service? It is enough! Why should I remain here any longer to witness the decline of thy kingdom? Therefore take now, O Lord, my poor and troubled soul from me; for I am not better than my fathers. Certainly I hoped to see what many kings and prophets have desired to see; but I too have been disappointed. But who am I, that I should venture to desire such great things at thy hand; who am I, that with presumptuous hope,

could promise myself a preference, for which saints, whose shoes I am
not worthy to bear, have longed in vain? It is enough; now, O Lord,
take away my life!"

Thus spoke Elijah, distressingly excited in mind. It was from a
strange mixture of feelings that his prayer arose. His soul was not in
a state of harmony; and yet, in the midst of the discord, the sweetest
tones arose which could be breathed from a human soul. His prayer
was not like the peaceful and cheerful language of Simeon, "Now
lettest thou thy servant depart in peace!" nor like that clear, con-
siderate, and calm expression of Paul, "I have a desire to depart and
to be with Christ!" But yet it was not the same as that of Jeremiah,
"Cursed be the day in which I was born!" nor as that of Job, "Let that
day perish; let not God regard it from above, neither let the light
shine upon it!" Elijah's state of mind was more subdued, and gentle,
and therefore not so wretched as theirs. The discordant groans of
vexation at fruitless labor and disappointed hopes, certainly sound
too audibly through his sighs; but at the same time his words breathe
an affectionate sorrow for the poor people, and a holy grief at the
apparent decline of the kingdom of God.

It must be confessed that there is something in his prayer that
looks like a complaint against the Lord himself; but, at the same
time, tears of regret are already pouring out to quench it in his heart,
and the very moment when the complaint escapes him he feels the
sinfulness of it, and on this very account is filled with grief. It cannot be denied, that in the expression, "It is enough!" we behold the
anguish of a soul which, disappointed in its fairest expectations,
seems to despair of God and of the world, and is impatient and weary
of the cross; a soul which, like Jonah, is dissatisfied with the dealings
of the Almighty, and by desiring death, seeks, as it were, to give him
to understand, that it is come to such an extremity, that nothing is
left but the melancholy wish to escape by death from its sufferings.
Nevertheless a Divine and believing longing accompanied even this
carnal excitement in the soul of Elijah, which, thirsting after God,
struck its pinions upwards to the eternal light; yes, the key-note of
this mournful lamentation was the filial thought that the heart of his
Father in heaven would be moved toward him, that his merciful God
would again shine forth upon his darkness, and comfort the soul of
his servant. Thus we see, in the prayer of our prophet, the elements
of the natural and of the spiritual life fermenting together in strange

intermixture. The sparks of nature and of grace, mutually opposing each other, blaze up together in one flame. The metal is in the furnace, the heat of which brings impurity to light; but who does not forget the scum and the dross at the sight of the fine gold? "Lord, it is enough!" Ah, this little prayer is known also amongst us! How many a workshop, how many a chamber and bed of sorrow do I know, from whence this aspiration is almost incessantly ascending to heaven, in the midst of many tears and pangs! Many of these supplicants are mistaken, just as Elijah was. It is not enough yet. Many a faithful laborer has yet to learn that his labor is by no means in vain in the Lord, although he thinks it is. Many a righteous one shall yet see the light arise here below, which, contrary to the express promises of God, he thinks is forever extinguished. Many a broken instrument will the Lord raise again for his work, before he takes it away into the land of rest; and many a troubled sufferer, before he departs, shall again take his harp from the willows, and sing thanksgivings to him, whose counsel is wonderful and his ways mysterious, but who does all things well. And then it will indeed be "enough." Ah, who is warranted yet in saying, "It is enough!" It is only enough, when the Lord says it. And if you have still to remain for years in the ravage of affliction, be assured that you will eventually acknowledge, with joyful acclamations in heaven, that then only was it enough, and not a moment earlier, when the Lord stripped you of the garments of your pilgrimage, and took you unto himself.

One word more. If at any time you feel disposed again to say, "It is enough," and that you can bear the burden of life no longer, do as Elijah did, flee into the silence of solitude, and sit under—not the juniper tree—but under that tree whereon the Incarnate Son of God was made a curse for you. Here your soul will assuredly find sweet refreshment from Christ's acceptable offering to God. He is a hiding-place from the storm, a covert from the tempest, a shadow from the heat, as rivers of water in a dry place, as the shadow of a great rock in a weary land. Whether it be true or not which is related of the juniper tree, that no serpent ventures near it, we can say this in a better sense of that "tree of life," under which we encourage you to take refuge. Here the viper of discontent will not fasten upon you, nor the " old serpent" inject the poison of murmuring against God into your soul. At the sight of the cross, you will no longer think of complaining of the greatness of your suffering; for here you behold sufferings, in comparison with which yours must be accounted a light affliction, which is but for a moment; here the righteous suffers for you—the just for the unjust. In the view of the cross, you will soon forget your distresses; for the love of God in Christ Jesus, to you a poor sinner, will absorb all your thoughts. Under the cross you are prevented from supposing that some strange thing is happening unto you; "the disciple is not above his Master, nor the servant above his Lord"; and as the kingdom has been bestowed upon the Head, so will it also be upon the members. At the foot of the cross you are preserved from impatience; for you cannot but rejoice exceedingly that what you are enduring is only a temporal suffering, and not the curse which fell so dreadfully upon your Surety. At the foot of the cross, your grief will soon be lost in that joy and peace of God, which drops from this tree of life into the ground of your heart, and the foretaste you will here obtain of heaven will sweeten the troubles of this life as with the breath of the morning, and before you are aware, will bring over you, as over Elijah, the feelings of a heavenly repose; yes, the cross itself will be transformed into such a medium between heaven and earth, that the most comforting thoughts shall descend into your soul, and the most grateful thoughts shall ascend from your soul to heaven like those angels of God seen in a vision on the plains of Bethel by the solitary and benighted patriarch Jacob.

11

Visit Under the Juniper Tree

Jerusalem is the city of the great King," saith the Lord, Matt. 5:35. Where is Jerusalem? Where the eye overflows with tears of mourning after God; where the knee and the heart are bowed at the throne of grace; where the hands of faith are lifted to the cross, and lips of sincerity utter their prayers and praise—there is Jerusalem.

Jerusalem, O thou lovely city of God, on whose towering heights the banner of the cross waves; thou art the joy of the earth, and thou alone. There is nothing beautiful, nothing noble, nothing worthy of regard but Jerusalem. Who would like to dwell in the wilderness of this world, if Jerusalem with its peaceful tabernacles did not stand in the midst of it? What is it makes this life of banishment tolerable, yea delightful? It is Jerusalem!

Jerusalem! O it is good to be within its walls, to sit together as fellow-citizens, according to the privilege of the new birth; to sing together in the ways of the Lord, that great is the glory of the Lord in the midst of us; to speak often one with another upon faith's bright prospects that lie before us, to number up our joys with which the "stranger intermeddleth not," or to place ourselves at the windows toward the east, and breathe the morning air of everlasting day, and refresh ourselves with thoughts of the blissful futurity that awaits us. "O Jerusalem, if I forget thee, let my right hand forget her cunning!"

Where are the treasures of God displayed, and the jewels of heaven exhibited? Where burn the torches of eternal light? and where springs up the fountain of peace and joy, which is inexhaustible? Where does the soul look into the opened books of life? Where does

126

the true Israelite obtain the oil of joy from the flinty rocks? Where drops the balm which heals every wound? Where, but in Jerusalem! They shall prosper that love thee, O Jerusalem! They shall go from strength to strength who set their heart upon the ways of Zion!

But if all this is true of the spiritual Jerusalem on earth, what shall I say of the Jerusalem which is above, which lies on the other side of the river of death, where the everlasting palm trees grow, and the still waters flow from the eternal hills, and the angels sing to their golden harps among the trees of paradise? Thither we are journeying, we happy pilgrims, from Jerusalem to Jerusalem. While you who love the world, and the things that are in the world, are on your way to Tophet, to the valley of destruction, to everlasting night, we are going to full and cheerful day, and on our staff is inscribed, "The citizenship of heaven." And if we sometimes appear to you as those that dream, and you see our eyes glistening with tears while looking at the far blue distance, it is because of our longing for home and all you can say is, "They are weeping after Jerusalem."

And who has built us the city, and who has made it so beautiful for us! Jerusalem is the city of the great King. "Here is my rest for ever; here will I dwell!" says he. He dwells there, and the city rests peacefully under the wings of his love. We are traveling to Jerusalem.

1 Kings 19:5-8

> And as he lay and slept under a juniper tree, behold, then an angel touched him, and said unto him, Arise and eat. And he looked, and, behold, there was a cake baken on the coals, and a cruse of water at his head. And he did eat and drink, and laid him down again. And the angel of the Lord came again the second time, and touched him, and said, Arise and eat; because the journey is too great for thee. And he arose, and did eat and drink, and went in the strength of that meat forty days and forty nights unto Horeb the mount of God.

This narrative belongs to the children of God, especially to the afflicted amongst them. The Lord's faithful care over his servants, especially in a dark and cloudy season, is here displayed in the most heart-refreshing manner. This Divine and gracious protection is made apparent, I. In the answer to prayer, which the prophet receives; II. In the appearance of an angel, whom the Lord sends to him; III. In the miraculous refreshments of which he partakes; IV. In the delightful prospect which God opens before him; and, V. In the supernatural strength given him for his journey through the desert. Let us devoutly meditate on these delightful manifestations of the paternal love of our God.

The Answer to Prayer

I. Elijah had wished for death, after being obliged to give up the hope of the regeneration of his beloved Israel. Life had no longer any attractions for him. The love of life can bear up under the privation of many earthly endearments, but it cannot survive the absence of hope. When he sees this flower fading, he sinks, and is weary of his existence. And if he had not been a man of God—ah! who knows into what still more dreadful abyss than that of impatience and despondency he might have fallen!

It appeared as if the Lord had suddenly given up his work, and his prophet with it. The Divine superintendence was concealed too deeply in the disguise of second causes for a mortal eye to penetrate through it. No, it seemed to have been withdrawn, and to have left room for human vicissitudes; at least it seemed so to the prophet. He was unable, in such an unexpected turn of affairs, to discover the intentions of God. He found himself, as it were, in a dark labyrinth, without any candle of the Lord to shine upon his faith, or any clue to conduct him through it. And if we consider how such situations of the godly are always taken advantage of by the powers of darkness, and how the tempter doubtless assaulted the fugitive under the juniper tree with the fiery darts of distressing doubts and horrible suggestions, we can easily comprehend how even such a champion as Elijah could thus despond; and, in the deepest dejection and anguish of soul, cry to Heaven, and say, "Lord, it is enough! take now my life from me, for I am not better than my fathers!"

Such prayers, however, which ascend toward heaven rather in the wild bursts of carnal passion, than in the sacred fire of Divine love, and which are not borne upward to God upon the wings of faith and hope, but upon the gusts of natural excitement—such prayers the Lord is not wont to answer; yet he does hear, so merciful is he, the breathings of the pious soul, ascending through all this clamor of carnal feeling, and in spite of it. Experience shows that he is not willing to let his children finish their course in vexation and sadness.

However violently the storms may rage around that spiritual life which is in them, he suffers it not to be swallowed up and drowned in the commotion. Their sky generally becomes serene again before they reach the harbor if not temporally, yet spiritually. Listen, wounded and sorrowful souls! your hour of removal will not arrive till the Lord has first reconciled you to his providential government and gracious discipline, and compelled you cheerfully to acknowledge that "He doeth all things well!" A calm will succeed the storms and tempests of your life, although it may not be till the evening of your pilgrimage; and you shall be enabled to say, "Lord, now lettest thou thy servant depart in peace!" Yes, you shall become willing to bear, even still longer, the cross after him, if it be the Lord's pleasure. Your course will terminate not tumultuously—no, but in the cheerful serenity of a sabbatical dawn; and in the midst of a radiance, beaming from the heavenly Zion, will your Divine Friend translate you to the joy of the eternal hills, that his guidance may be extolled not only above, but even here below, and his grace and faithfulness be glorified in the sight of your surviving brethren, and of an ungodly world.

This sabbatical morning had not yet dawned upon Elijah. It was now one of the darkest moments of his life, in which he seemed like a man who had fallen out both with God and with the world. The request which, in time of weakness and gloomy despondency, he had ventured to bring before God, was denied him. His life was not taken from him. He must yet live to see glorious things, and learn again to praise the faithfulness of Him whose promises are Yea and Amen; he must yet be brought to feel humbled and astonished at his former doubts and anxieties; to find the most pleasing solution of every apparent difficulty and contradiction in God's dealings with him, and to be placed in such a sunshine of Divine favor, as he had never before enjoyed. And then would be the time to say, "It is enough"; and the hour would come, when—not under a solitary tree in the dreary wilderness—no, but in splendid triumph, he should be carried directly over the dark valley into the land of everlasting rest.

Oh that we were not so impatient, when our gracious God occasionally denies our requests! How kind it is, with respect to our real and best interests, that the Lord gives us according to his will, and not according to our own; and that he condescends so graciously to guard us against the attainment of our poor and often foolish wishes! We may rest assured, that whenever we pray without success, that which we desire is not only not best for us, but would rather be injurious, or is at least inferior to what he really intends for us. How many a faithful minister would never have experienced the Lord's faithfulness crowning the labors of his servants, had he been called away from this life at the time when, in gloomy despondency, he desired it! How many a Christian pilgrim would never have seen anything of the spiritual manna, and of the spiritual streams from the rocks, had God listened to him when, with fear and trembling, he begged him not to lead him into a desert! How many a brother would this day be unable to rejoice that the power of Christ has so rested upon him, if the thorn in his flesh, the messenger of Satan, had been removed at the time he entreated such relief with many cries and tears! Take courage, therefore, my brethren! Believe that the denial which the Lord occasionally puts upon our requests will eventually yield us an abundant cause for praise, as the assent with which he at other times graciously crowns them. Do not think the time too long which you have to wait. You may be ready to exclaim, "O Lord, make it all end; it is enough!" But no, you must first travel, like Elijah, through a desert unto Horeb, that you may there hear the still small voice of peace. There must first come things which shall compel us to exclaim, "O Lord, righteousness belongeth unto thee, but unto us confusion of face!" And after that, the end; then the pilgrim's staff is dropped and the longed for "Now" of good old Simeon is arrived.

Elijah did not die—his hour was not yet come. So far his petition remained unanswered, yet not entirely so. The prophet longed for rest. Rest he was to have, not however by the stroke of death, but by that of natural sleep. He lay down and slept under the juniper tree. It was indifferent to him where he lay; whether on a silken couch or upon the heath; under a thornbush, or in a royal pavilion. The burden of life was alleviated, the juniper tree lent him its refreshing shade, the inward tempest of his soul subsided, grief and uneasiness departed, tormenting thoughts gave place to sweet and spiritual rest, body and mind became completely renovated. Such intervals of rest fall to the lot of all who bear the cross. Even in the midst of the desert our gracious God is able to provide for us a place of repose; the storm does not rage incessantly; peaceful hours intervene unawares, and the burden upon our shoulders becomes for a while a resting pillow to our heads, upon which we insensibly gather recruited strength. At one time the Keeper of Israel sends us bodily slumber in the midst of our sorrows and what a welcome guest may it not prove to us, particularly when spiritual conflicts threaten to confuse the senses and absorb the spirits. At another, pleasant dreams perform to us the ministry of angels; poor Lazarus is in thought translated into Abraham's bosom, and lonely Jacob is borne aloft from his stone pillow into the opened heavens. At another season, a sympathizing Jonathan visits me in my outcast condition, and by his affectionate conversation, imperceptibly removes my depression. At other times, some consoling truth of revelation is by a text or hymn suggested to my mind, and hope diffuses its mild and cheering light in the midst of my darkness. In short, the very days of storm and tempest have their hours of repose and mercy. Therefore let no one be anxious, however steep and thorny his path, however dreary and rough his road. When his weary knees are ready to sink, God will know how to provide him a resting-place, and he shall be able to say, "I laid me down and slept; I awaked, for the Lord sustained me." And although these may be only short pauses, still they remind us how easily he could, if he pleased, at any moment deliver us out of every trouble. And a believing assurance of this is sufficient to overcome every anxiety and fear.

The Angel's Appearance

II. The man of God lay and slept under the juniper tree, to all outward appearance as one forsaken, and, like the disciples in Gethsemane, "sleeping for sorrow." Yet a Divine watch is kept over him. Grace, mercy, and peace are with him. Here we have a sensible demonstration given of the ministry of the elect angels about them that fear God, sent forth to minister to the heirs of salvation. An angel "touched him, and said unto him, Arise and eat." Here is one instance, among several which are given in the Holy Scriptures, of the pleasure enjoyed by angels in ministering to God's saints on earth. Behold then, in this gloomy wilderness, the ministry of an angel of God, who finds an addition to his happiness in preparing help and refreshment for a servant of God in his distress and sorrow! O Israel, a people saved by the Lord, what people is like unto you in this world, wherever you are scattered and dispersed, or in whatever age you live! What glorious attendants minister unto you, even to the least heir of salvation among you! Solitary as any one of you may seem in many a path of duty, that is the very situation where he is attended by company of the best and noblest kind. Thus was Jacob attended at Mahanaim. And indeed it may be adopted as a general mark, that where the world closes against any servant of God, there heaven opens to him—a wonderful mixture is there of poverty and dignity in the condition of the children of God, even as there was in that of Christ himself upon earth, to whose image and likeness all his people are conformed! And if I asked you for the most venerable places upon earth, where would you direct me? Perhaps to some stately palace, or well fortified castle, or magnificent cathedral; perhaps to the halls of learning and science, or to those edifices where all the glories of riches and art are collected! But I would rather point out to you the place where a Magdalene lies weeping at the feet of Jesus, or a poor sinner is rejoicing in the mercy he has obtained; where a Lazarus dwells, or a Martha and Mary. Though the walls be but of clay, and the roof of straw, yet here in Bethel, here is no less than the house of God. Here dwells a royal priesthood, clad in the beauty of the Most High. High and invisible guests are their companions, and eternal love overshadows them with her wings.

The action of the angel in waking the prophet and bidding him "Arise and eat," may be spiritually applied to many a one among ourselves. Though the weary pilgrim stood in great need of bodily refreshment, he does not appear to have felt the want of it, and required first to be incited externally to make use of it. So an afflicted soul may often need nothing so much as the food of the word of God, and yet by brooding over his troubles may go on for some time insensible of this want. Though he opens the Bible, he may feel no attraction toward the truths it contains, nor any desire for the benefit of Divine ordinances, and may be ready to ask, "What good will these things do me?" This is a pitiable and melancholy condition; but the help of God arrives to relieve it, either by a suggestion immediately from his Spirit, or by the medium of a Christian friend, or of some apparently accidental, but in reality providential occurrence, that he should "arise and eat"; should take up and read, or go and hear the word of life. Then he finds a spiritual appetite returned, and his soul is strengthened by the word of God.

Miraculous Food Provided

III. "Arise and eat." Thus said the angel; and Elijah awoke, "and as he looked around, behold, there was a cake baken on the coals, and a cruse of water at his head. And he did eat and drink, and laid him down again."

Thus he appears to have been so well lodged and provided for here in the wilderness, as to leave him nothing more to wish for. Oh the tender compassion of God: for "so, he giveth to his beloved sleeping," Psa. 127:2. (Luther's version.) Yet how few learn to cast all their care and anxiety about temporal provision on Him who cares for them! What a serious and difficult thing does it seem to many of us to practice that instruction of the inspired apostle, "Be careful for nothing; but in everything, by prayer and supplication, with thanksgiving, let your requests be made known unto God." To "cast all our care on Him who careth for us," appears to blind natural reason, a perilous method of proceeding. But is not our reluctance to follow this direction a reason why we experience, in our own lives, so little of his aid, who orders all things both in heaven and earth, and who has the hearts of all in his hand? His remarkable interpositions in behalf of Elijah we are too apt to regard as prodigies of a golden age long since gone by; hence almost the only sounds at present heard even in the tabernacles of the righteous, are sighs and lamentations for embarrassments, disappointed prospects, and unsuccessful undertakings.

The bread and the water with which God nourishes souls in the wilderness, are the doctrines and promises of his word. But as the cake was baked on the coals for Elijah, and the water placed at his head in a cruse, so we need to have the truths of God's word prepared for us by his Spirit, and set before us by his providence, that we may take the benefit of them for our spiritual refreshment and nourishment. And how refreshing and strengthening do we find those truths, when God has again spread his table for us, and we again feed on the bread of life, by faith in our hearts, with thanksgiving, and refresh ourselves, with the Divine promises, and rejoice with renewed confidence in the Divine favor! Then do we thank God for the season of hunger and sorrow through which we have passed. It then seems to us as if we had never before feasted at such a passover, and we become more sensible than ever of the value of that bread of life, which our gracious God has prepared for us.

Elijah, apparently more asleep than awake, stretched out his hand, ate of the bread, drank of the water, and sank down again, weak and weary, and fell asleep. For that he fell asleep may be supposed from the angel's touching him a second time. We, however, should have thought that his surprise would have been so excited, and his thoughts so set in motion, as to have rendered it impossible for him to fall asleep again immediately. But here is no appearance of surprise expressed. He partakes of the refreshment, not as if he were lying in a desolate uninhabited wilderness, but as if he were at home in his own dwelling. If he was not in a half-awakened state, he must have been absorbed, like Mary Magdalene at her visit to the sepulchre, in higher thoughts. This is no unsupposable case; and, spiritually applied, it is a very common one. Persons of weak faith, and under strong spiritual temptation, may hear the word of consolation, and receive it; but taking only a hasty draught of the living waters of promise, the enjoyment is soon gone again. It is however not without its use. If it effect nothing more, it serves to revive and confirm the persuasion that He who can thus cast a ray of comfort into the benighted soul, is able at any moment to send into it the full sunshine of peace.

The sleep of Elijah serves also to remind us of those who are for the most part spiritually asleep, and have never yet been thoroughly awakened. They eat and drink, or, in other words, they hear much that is good, they read the Bible, and are regular in attending the worship of God; yet everything seems lost upon them, and not the smallest decided proof of spiritual life is discoverable in them. Yet let no one venture to say, before their course is ended, that such persons have eaten and drunken in vain. They may suddenly one day prove the contrary to your surprise. The food they have received may unawares be found effectually to have nourished them. Let all diligently use the means of grace.

A Delightful Prospect

IV. "The angel of the Lord" then "came again the second time, and touched him, and said, Arise and eat; because the journey is too great for thee." Though God may allow his servants to be tried beyond their own inherent strength, he never suffers them to be tried beyond what he himself enables them to undergo. He prepares and strengthens them before he leads them to any conflict, before he lays his cross upon them. When we enjoy days of special refreshment in spirit, it is generally a sign that new trials of faith await us, for which, through this refreshment, we must make vigilant preparation.

Elijah now "arose, and did eat and drink," and his slumber and weariness disappeared. The word of the angel seems to have quickened his soul as much as the food had refreshed his body. The angel had spoken to him of a further "journey" which the prophet had now to undertake: which was the same as telling him that God had a new commission for him, and that he was still on a career of which he had not yet seen the end even at a distance. It had seemed to him as if his own heart had "devised his way" into this wilderness; he now finds that "the Lord had directed his steps," and was still directing them. He is again persuaded that God is present with him, and he springs up as a young roe, and no longer goes "whither he would," but in the name of his gracious God, he again sets out on his way. Oh how blessed is it, after going on for a season in uncertainty and darkness, sighing with David, "I am sorrowful and forsaken," unexpectedly to discover some indubitable proof of the Divine presence with us, some Scriptural evidence that things are really different from what we supposed, and that we are really walking in a path which God has marked out for us!

Strength for the Journey

V. Elijah is now himself again; he has found God to be the lifter up of his head. "And he went in the strength of that meat forty days and forty nights unto Horeb the mount of God." He travels through the sandy desert alone yet not alone, for God is with him. He is not anxious as to whither the Lord is directing him, or about the purpose intended by this strange journey. Forty days and nights he travels on, without rest or intermission, through the silent wilderness—a miraculous journey, which was performed in the strength of the food with which God by his angel had refreshed him. To help by many means or by few, or with no means at all, is one and the same thing to Him, who upholds all by the word of his power. He, who multiplied the loaves and the fishes at his pleasure, could give to a little all the virtue of much. In short, Elijah had no need, during the whole journey, of either refreshment or rest. The hot wind during the day did not exhaust him, nor the difficulties of the night fatigue him. Thus he bore about with him, in the renewed courage of his spirit, and in the unexhausted strength of his limbs, an abiding seal and pledge that the Lord was with him, and that the hand of the Almighty sustained him.

The desert, over which Elijah traveled forty days and nights, was the same through which the tribes of Israel traveled during forty years, under the convoy of the cloudy and fiery pillar. Surely this, if any, was holy ground. It had been traversed by the feet of the mighty, it was rich with the most stupendous associations of thought, and with the most interesting recollections. Here the whole miraculous history of the ancient fathers would revive before him in the liveliest colors. Fresh images and scenes from that age of wonders would recur to his mind at every step, and the very profound silence around him would assist in the consideration of the sublime things, of which these spots had been once the theater. As often as he descended into a green and palmy vale, he alighted in spirit upon some resting-place of his fathers. As often as the shade of an overhanging rock received him, it was as if the incense of the sanctuary breathed around him; for the prayers of the pilgrims of God had hallowed these shades. Here or there, he would think, perhaps Moses had rested and taken counsel in the sacred circle of his elders; and the leader of Israel would still seem kneeling before the Lord, and speaking to him, "as a man talketh with his friend." Thus one heart-elating thought would follow another.

The history of the forty years' journey would attain a form and a vitality beyond what he had hitherto realized. At one time he would seem to be gathering the manna with the ancient fathers; at another to be standing with the wounded before the brazen image of the serpent, and feeling with them the return of health. Presently he would be in spirit at the altar which Moses built, and called it "Jehovah- Nissi," the Lord my banner; and then again he would hear the desert resound with loud thanksgivings and solemn hymns of praise to the faithfulness and truth of Jehovah. Every new scene on which he entered would bring before him some new event and feature of those journeyings which were irradiated with the glory of God; and whatever consolation and encouragement is comprised in these histories, would rush upon him with sublime and overwhelming wonder, to exhilarate him with a spring of hope and joy, that seemed to give wings to his feet, and banish the last remains of fear and care from his spirit. Assured that he was pursuing his way under the shadow of the same Almighty hand which once covered the whole host of Israel, he would cheerfully pursue his journey, not doubting that he was led by the right hand of Him who under the juniper tree had given him the direction to depart, and had endued his feeble frame with a strength which no fatigue of the journey was able to diminish, and that as soon as the end was attained, he should be bidden to rest and lay down his traveling staff in peace and safety.

O faith, faith! blessed companion of the children of God! Its wondrous power deprives the wilderness of its horrors, and the deepest solitude ceases to be solitary under its guidance! All that earth and heaven possess of beauty and treasure belongs to God's children. That which is distant is brought near; faith develops hidden things, and awakens past events to new life. Faith merges the gloom of the present into the bliss of the future, and paints the sky of many a departing sun with the dawning radiance of a better world. In the midst of sublunary changes, faith anticipates a peaceful paradise. It peoples our bereaved family circles with holy and heavenly company; it associates both worlds in close connection, and unites things past, present, and to come. In its light the sacred narratives seem acted over again, and our own personal history becomes a sacred record of Providence. It has the power of realizing the dead as if they were alive; the patriarchs are our contemporaries, although their ashes repose in the sepulchre of near six thousand years. By its voice they still converse with us, although to human ears they speak no more; by faith's realizing aid they visit us in our darkness with kindness and consolation; by its light we see a cloud of them as witnesses encamped around us; and whatever grace they experienced is, through faith, appropriated to ourselves. Faith nourishes us with the promises made to Abraham, sustaines us with the strong consolation of the oath divinely sworn unto Isaac; it gives us the staff of Jacob to support our steps; it enables us with Moses' rod to divide the sea, and with David to leap over the wall and rampart! O faith, faith! doorkeeper of every sanctuary, master over all the treasures of God! may He who is your Author draw near unto us; and He who is your Finisher bend down himself toward us!

12

Arrival at Mount Horeb

Many a true Christian has enjoyed luminous intervals in his life, which may be called his moments on Tabor. Such an interval was that experienced by Moses, when, overpowered by holy zeal for the honor of God, and carried away by the ardor of a superhuman love, forgetting himself, he broke out in the astonishing words: "Yet now if thou wilt forgive them their sin; and if not, blot me, I pray thee, out of thy book!" And such, if we follow the common translation of the passage, Rom. 9:3, appears to have been the case with the apostle Paul, when he said, he could wish that himself were accursed from Christ for his brethren, his kinsmen according to the flesh. If our cool, sober, calculating people of the present day are unable to comprehend ecstatic expressions like these, it is no wonder, neither is it any proof that holier men were not sincere in their wonderful desires. An infant is incompetent to enter into the ideas of a valiant warrior; still there were such men as Gideon and David. Even Moses or Paul themselves, after the Divine ecstasy of the moment was over, might feel astonished at the elevation to which their souls had been raised. For in such moments they were transported far above their ordinary feelings.

You know, besides Paul and Moses, a third who was all along actuated thus; who said, "I have a baptism to be baptized with, and how am I straitened till it be accomplished! He actually carried his desire into effect; "He was willingly made a curse for us." Many who call themselves Christians shake their heads at this truth; they do not believe that the love of the Lord Jesus went so far as to undergo the penalty belonging to the sins of the world. Were these adversaries of the atonement in the right, it would follow, that the disciples, Moses and Paul, were above their Master in love to mankind. Therefore, from this very love on the part of his disciples, we can show that they are in the wrong. For, from whom did those disciples derive their fervor of love? Was it from themselves? Certainly not! It was from their Savior's fountain of love. Out of his fullness did they receive. As then the stream is, such must the fountain be; and what we perceive in the copy, must be found in the original. Had there not been in the heart of Jesus a love which could desire to become an anathema for sinners, how could it ever have been found in his disciples?

The recollection however of such love as this, in Moses or in Paul, is not altogether advantageous to the prophet Elijah, in comparing the scene of his life which we are now about to contemplate; for it presents a striking contrast to the conduct of those two saints.

1 Kings 19:9-11

> And he came thither unto a cave, and lodged there; and, behold, the word of the Lord came to him, and he said unto him, What doest thou here, Elijah? And he said, I have been very jealous for the Lord God of hosts: for the children of Israel have forsaken thy covenant, thrown down thine altars, and slain thy prophets with the sword; and I, even I only, am left; and they seek my life, to take it away. And he said, Go forth, and stand upon the mount before the Lord.

Here we have the man of God again before us, in circumstances which are overruled to increase his humility and experience of the life of God in his soul. The particulars which his portion of Elijah's history brings before us are well worth our attentive consideration.

Here is, I. The night's lodging in the cave; II. The Divine reproof; III. The prophet's complaint; and, IV. The direction to appear before the Lord.

In the Cave

I. The prophet's efforts to restore Israel to the faith of their fathers had apparently failed. The mighty miracle on Carmel seemed to have produced no other fruit than redoubled hatred on the part of the idolaters; Jezebel's murderous intentions had been brought to ripeness by this event. Having been informed of this, the prophet fled without Divine direction. "He went whither he would, to save his life." His distress increased with every step, and reached its height

upon his arrival in the wilderness. He thought himself forsaken of
God, and having become weary of life, he prayed for death; where-
upon God, by an angel, sent him refreshment in body and spirit. He
learned that he was still conducted of God, and that the Divine
thoughts toward him were thoughts of peace and not of evil, to give
him an expected end, Jer. 29:11. In the strength of the food of which
partaken, and of the joyfully surprising angelic message, he entered
upon the "hard journey," and traversed the desert for forty days and
nights, with high expectations of the result in which these solitary
wanderings should terminate.

Now, when the forty days are drawing to a close, he sees in the
azure distance a rocky mountain glistening before him, which soon
becomes better known to him by its peculiar appearance and
remarkable summits. It was mount Sinai, towering like a magnificent
temple. Another height near it appeared like its antechamber; it was
lower than the former, but as boldly formed, and as wild and rocky.
This was Horeb. What must have been the sensations of Elijah at
first beholding these sacred and ever-memorable heights! What elevating thoughts and delightful hopes must have engaged his mind!
Here, he might suppose, God would again meet him in all the glory
of his benignity, and unfold to him truths respecting the restoration
of Israel which would change his mourning into rejoicing, and gird
him with gladness. As it was on Horeb that the Lord appeared to
Moses in the burning bush, Elijah would in a lively manner be
reminded of the good will of Him that dwelt in the bush, and would
be expecting it for himself. As it was the smitten rock of Horeb that
yielded a miraculous supply of water to the hosts of Israel, Elijah
would here think of a water which would refresh and invigorate his
soul. As it was on Horeb that the uplifted hand of the man of God
prostrated the hostile strength of Amalek, and gave Joshua his glorious victory over the armies of the aliens, Elijah perhaps might
reckon upon hearing from Horeb that sentence upon Ahab and
Jezebel which would put down blasphemy and the destruction of
souls in Israel! On Horeb, God renewed his gracious covenant with
his people after he had delivered them from the iron furnace of
Egypt; and Elijah might expect fresh assurances and promises
respecting his work of reformation.

Elijah being arrived at the mount of God, we may further imagine
him climbing the rocky ridges to its summit with feelings of pro-

foundest veneration. It is evening. His feet stand upon Horeb, and doubtless his spirit prays in fervent expectation of further communications from the Lord. He would naturally experience alternations of hope and fear. He cannot but think that the Lord has conducted him to Horeb, yet he knows not wherefore. He is in an almost indescribable solitude. Nothing but rugged layers of stone, one above another, around him, and tangled thickets, with here and there a melancholy cypress or a gloomy tamarisk. Alas, the devout wanderer might be at a loss what to think of his situation, and feel as if he were banished from the whole world! No trace of any human being is to be perceived. The honor of this lonely forsaken situation would be augmented by the approach of night. Ought he to travel on?

He cannot do it. He feels the limit of his journey to be assigned him here. The strength which bore him through the desert, perhaps, has forsaken him; and, no less so, the cheerful spirit and the courage to proceed, and therefore nothing is left him but to seek out some retreat, which may shelter him from wild beasts and poisonous serpents. He wraps his mantle around him, creeps into a gloomy cave, of which there are many on this rocky mountain, and lies down, in order to pass the night in this melancholy lodging. This was, probably, one of the most anxious nights of his life; for instead of enjoying the cheering manifestations of the Divine presence, or realizing any of the high expectations he might have indulged on his miraculous journey to Horeb, he was obliged, in most comfortless outward circumstances, to bury himself in the horrors of a desolate cavern. It may be easily supposed that no sleep could close the good man's eyes that melancholy night. Satan, too, would not be inactive in his attempts against so decided an enemy but would summon all his strength to overthrow the faith of the hard-tried prophet, and to wound him with his fiery darts. For the circumstances in which Elijah was now placed would give to the father of lies great advantage, in tempting him to doubt and distrust the love, and word, and promises of God; as if the Keeper of Israel himself could sleep, or, if not, could delight in chastising and trying his servants. "Where is now thy God?" might be suggested to Elijah. "Where is now thy boasted happiness in his service?" And who knows whether the prophet was still ready for the conflict, or took the field fully armed, with cheerful courage, to resist such crafty wiliness of Satan! This at least we know, that if the invisible arms had not held him which were wont to uphold him, especially when he was least aware of it, the temptation of despair would have swallowed him up.

The Divine Reproof

II. Elijah takes up his abode in the cave, and thus further experiences that God's ways with his servants lead to self-mortification and total self-denial. What his feelings were, no tongue can adequately tell. Silently and mournfully he contemplates the decay, as he fancied it, of his last and fondest hopes, when, lo! a voice reaches his ear amid the deep silence of his solitary abode. "And behold the word of the Lord came to him, and said unto him, What dost thou here, Elijah?" Elijah at once recognizes the voice of the Almighty. But what an unexpected question was this! What a contrast to the expectations he had probably carried with him to Horeb! Perhaps he had thought that the whole journey from Samaria hither had been a Divine path, and that the Lord himself had called him to Horeb, in order to bestow upon him there peculiar blessings. And now such a salutation, or rather such an alarming inquiry. It must however have served to undeceive him, and to lead him to consider the state of his heart. It placed before him the arbitrariness of his flight from Jezreel. It reminded him especially of the weakness of his faith; it must have made him ashamed, and have incited him to the profoundest humiliation.

When troubles come upon us, and we are disposed to lament over disappointed hopes and undertakings, God is gracious in making known to us our sins and infirmities, which are in one way or another the occasion of every disquietude. Unless this is done, we are in danger of misunderstanding his dealings with us, and of distrusting his love and faithfulness. A sense of our own guilt and unworthiness is the best preservative against those pangs of heart of which Asaph speaks, Psa. 73:21. As it serves to explain many apparently severe parts of the Divine conduct toward us, so it prevents the peevish and complaining thoughts which would often arise within us, respecting the hardships of our condition. How satisfied do we then become, nay, how heartily glad and thankful, when only a glimpse of forgiveness, a single ray of undeserved favor, shines once more into our hearts! We seem as if needing nothing more to make us happy; we submit humbly and serenely under the Divine will, and all murmurings are exchanged for contrite and thankful confessions. "O

Lord, righteousness belongeth unto thee, but unto us confusion of face, because we have sinned against thee," Dan. 9:7, 8.

"What dost thou here?" By an inquiry of this sort, divinely applied to the conscience, many a one has been shaken out of carnal security for the rest of his life. Painful indeed has been the experience of many a sinner, when thus overtaken on the paths which lead to death. But this has sometimes ended in the most happy result; for men have thus, like the prodigal son, "come to themselves," and returned to their Father's house and found a happy welcome there. But we may be even associated with the children of God, and yet the same question may surprise and alarm the conscience: "What doest thou here?"—suggesting that we do not really belong to such society as we have mingled with, and may thus produce great distress and perplexity in the soul; leading it however to deep self-examination. It has also been the means of awakening sleepers in Zion, who are hereby aroused to spiritual conflict; and the unwatchful and careless are prevented from going further astray. Thus it acts as a means of separating them more entirely from the spirit and ways of this vain world, and of attaching them more firmly to the service of the Lord Jesus. But, alas, how many among us are there, of whom, although they bear the Christian name, it is to be feared that they are wandering in the wilderness, out of the way of God! Oh that the Almighty may this day meet them with the inquiry, "What doest thou here?" May it bring them to their right minds, and guide them into that way of peace, which hitherto they have not known.

The Prophet's Complaint

III. The prophet at this question recollects himself, and answers, "I have been very jealous for the Lord God of hosts." This indeed was true, and he could say with the psalmist, "The zeal of thine house hath eaten me up." Alas, in the Laodicean character of the present day, how little is there of this spirit! Men can see and hear much that is contrary to God, with an indifference that speaks but too plainly how lukewarm they are in his service, how unconcerned they are for his glory. Where, alas, do we see that fervor with which the ancient saints, the prophets, apostles, martyrs, and confessors testified to the truth in their days? How earnestly did they cry day and night to God, that he would exalt himself in his own strength among the nations! Where is that self-devotedness which Moses showed, when he prayed, "Yet if now thou wilt forgive their sin—and if not, blot me I pray thee out of thy book"; where do we now find such fervent intercession for others? O pray, pray, that the spirit of ancient wisdom, love, and zeal may again be poured out with awakening and reviving energy upon us!

"The children of Israel," continues Elijah, "have forsaken thy covenant, thrown down thine altars, and slain thy prophets with the sword." Now if this be a sufficient cause for being zealous for the honor of God, how is it that we continue so unmoved? Why do we not glow with zeal for the Lord of hosts? Are not the banners of rebellion against God waving openly enough around us? and are there not enough blasphemers and despisers, who have forsaken the covenant, in the midst of us? Must the name of God be still more openly profaned than it is already, in word and in deed, among us? and must the measure of iniquity become still more full, before we will wrestle with God, that he may exalt himself in the earth, and fill it with his glory? Is not this the reason of our lukewarmness; that we do not keep our own hearts with all diligence, out of which are the issues of life? Personal and practical piety, real spiritual-mindedness, is a thing too little kept up by the diligent use of secret prayer. Is not this the true state of the case? Do we indeed give ourselves time to allow the fire of devotional love to kindle in our hearts; or do we not suffer ourselves, after some few superficial performances in private, to be led away to other pursuits? How then is it ever likely that, in such a state of mind, we should be truly zealous for the Lord of hosts, and for the spiritual interests of our brethren; or be able to say, with Jeremiah, "I am pained at my very heart"; or, "It was in my heart as a burning fire shut up in my bones, and I was weary with forbearing, and was unable to restrain myself," Jer. 4:19; 20:9.

Elijah says further, "I, even I only, am left." The only one, he means, on the field of battle; for he was not the only child of God in Israel: but the others had fled, or were hidden in the rocks and caves. "And they seek my life, to take it away." He does not disguise it, that to save his own life he had left Samaria, and fled to the wilderness, but relates the matter with all sincerity and candor. God is gracious to those who open their whole hearts to him, however it may reflect upon themselves. But however candid this confession of Elijah may be, it does not sound becomingly. However much holy indignation it expresses at the general contempt put upon the name of Jehovah, there is human chagrin and vexation mixed with it, and it betrays an undue excitement of natural feeling. Moses, when he placed himself in the breach for his idolatrous people, and entreated the Lord to blot him out of his book, if he would not forgive them, and Paul, when he, in holy zeal, uttered the wish to become accursed for his brethren, appear much greater than Elijah does in this instance. For he seems to accuse his people, with some natural vexation and vehemence, and even to plead against them before the Lord. Even more his saying to God, how very jealous he had been for him, and then laying before him the fruitlessness of this jealousy and the unexpected and grievous result of his activity, seems to imply some complaint against God himself, as if he had said, "Lord, why have you done this to me? How could you leave your servant to be treated thus? How so forsake the work of your own hands?" The Lord however purposes answering these accusations himself; and vouchsafes him such a reply, as will preserve him all his life after from similar mistakes.

The Divine Command

IV. "And he said, Go forth, and stand upon the mount before the Lord." This Divine injunction, I could wish, in a certain sense, that you would also lay to heart. It has reference to all who are situated in some respects as Elijah. The cave, from which he was bidden to go forth, may remind us of the darkness and perplexity in which our own hearts have involved us. Happy he who perceives it, and whose eyes are opened to see the spiritual darkness and corruption generated from his own bosom! But he must not think to bury himself in this. It would be perverse and injurious to do so. Many among us however have often done so; they have imprisoned themselves in the mere thoughts of their own hearts, and we hear nothing from some, but complainings of the deadness, depravity, poverty, and helplessness of their souls: truths, all good and salutary in themselves, but wretchedly misapplied to paralyze every spiritual and benevolent exertion. O go ye forth from such a cavern of darkness, and stand upon the mount before the Lord! You will find neither life, light, nor peace in your own hearts. Go forth, in spirit, from your gloomy cell to the mount: behold the Lamb of God: look up to him who was suspended on the cross for the ungodly; contemplate his spirit, his love, his merits! It is this which makes the believer courageous, joyful, and strong; and imparts new life to his spirit.

The same may be said to those who are troubled with evil thoughts, and incited to evil actions. He who busies himself in the painful consideration of such things, who lingers amidst the dark horrors of these temptations, looking only at the fiery darts which crowd upon him; he who stays in such a cavern as this, is liable to be swallowed up in despair. But let us go forth out of the cave! Let us stand upon the mount before the Lord, where Jesus presents himself, having been in all points tempted like as we are, yet without sin, and we shall find him in all points able also to succor them that are tempted. In the mount, the Lord shall be seen as having "spoiled principalities and powers, and made a show of them openly," and as "ascended on high, having led captivity captive, and received gifts for men." Contemplate this mighty conqueror in whom you have also overcome; bring all your wretchedness before him, roll your burden upon him, and he shall sustain you; courage and strength shall be given to you; you shall have victory and triumph over the world, the devil, and the flesh.

The same may be said to all who suffer under the pressure of temporal trouble, sorrow, need, sickness, disgrace, or any other adversity. Do the waves of this world thus toss you? Look not with Peter at the storm, instead of looking to Him who can rebuke it. Look not with Martha to the grave of corruption, instead of to Him who is the resurrection and the life: this is only to imprison ourselves spiritually in our own gloomy cave. There can be neither joy nor peace in doing this. Go forth go forth! stretch out the hand of faith toward the mighty and outstretched arm of Divine love; spread the wings of hope; stand forth upon the mount whereon is laid the sure foundation of Zion. Hereby you will learn something of the paternal heart of Him, who, though his ways are mysterious, nevertheless does all things well; and you will gain a prospect of that better country where "they shall hunger no more, neither thirst any more, neither shall the sun light on them, nor any heat; for the Lamb that is in the midst of the throne shall feed them, and shall lead them unto living fountains of waters; and God shall wipe away all tears from their eyes." Whatever our circumstances may be, to place ourselves on every occasion before the Lord, with an open heart, without reserve or guile, is the grand secret of happiness and peace while we continue in this world. Yes, and when the outward man itself perishes, and the eye grows dim in the shadow of death, the soul shall hear a voice behind it, saying, "Go forth, and stand on the heavenly mount before the Lord!"

13

Manifestation on Mount Horeb

The children of God in this world are in close and wonderful connection with Christ their Head, and with each other. This connection consists not merely in the unity of their sentiments, faith, and conduct; the communion of saints is a deep and blessed mystery, and is very properly placed in the creed as one of the articles of the Christian faith.

Our blessed Lord speaks of believers as one, even as He and the Father are one. In various places of Scripture they are represented is composing one body, united to their glorious Head, Christ Jesus. Thus St. Paul says, 1 Cor. 12:26, 27, "Ye are the body of Christ, and members in particular." "If one member suffer, all the members suffer with it; or if one member be honored, all the members rejoice with it." He also extends this representation further still, and calls the union among them a mystery.

Now those, to whom this mystery is in any measure unfolded, find it a great, an invaluable treasure. Oh it is one of the most consoling, one of the most refreshing truths of the whole gospel, that, all who believe are one. But it may be asked, in what degree are they one? We occasionally hear persons complain and say, "I cannot certainly deny that God has drawn me to himself; but still I dare not apply to myself this or that particular consolation, or promise. It may belong to others, but not to me." These are foolish ideas, my friends. They go upon this supposition, that every Christian stands alone; and that one has no participation in what another possesses. Whereas, according to the Scriptures, every Christian is an inseparable part of the whole body. The gracious promises of God are given to his church as a body. Therefore, the question is not, "Am I a beginner in religion, or an advanced and experienced pilgrim? Am I strong in the inward man, or weak and infirm?"

The Divine inheritance does not depend upon the measure of our strength, or the degree of sanctification we have attained. Only ask whether you may number yourself with the poor and despised house of Israel; and, if you can answer in the affirmative, then, whether you are the greatest in the kingdom of heaven, or the least—the last or the first—you have equally a right to apply to yourself whatever good has been announced to the people of God in any part of the Bible. If you read, for instance, that the Lord declares concerning his church, that "the gates of hell shall not prevail against it" include yourself in this promise, and say, "I am invincible!" for what is said to the whole, has reference also to yourself who are a part. If you read of the city of God, that "God is in the midst of her, she shall not be moved; God shall help her, and that right early"; think, "God is with me, I shall not be moved, he will help me early"; for you are as much a part of the city of God as Abraham, John, and Paul were. It is thus we must learn to regard ourselves—not as insulated individuals, standing alone; but as parts of one whole, and members of one body. And, when one brother receives some blessing from the Lord, we must not say to ourselves, "This has happened to such a one, but he is quite unconnected with me." No, we must then rejoice, and think, "This benefit has accrued at the same time to me; the Lord has also been thus kind and gracious to me; I have also received, in what has been bestowed upon my brother, a new seal and pledge of the loving-kindness of my God toward me: for I and my brother are one; we belong to one and the same glorious body, and if one member be honored, all the members rejoice with it."

You see, my friends, what abounding consolation is contained in that single truth—that we are all one body; and what a new and delightful meaning the histories of all the saints of God must gain by it, with reference to ourselves! Let the consciousness, therefore, of this mysterious unity and fellowship accompany us to the scene which we are now about to contemplate, and lead us to rejoice in the glorious and gracious manifestation of God granted to the prophet Elijah upon mount Horeb, as an exhibition of kindness vouchsafed not to him alone, but to us also, as members with him of one body in Christ.

1 Kings 19:11-13

> And, behold, the Lord passed by, and a great and strong wind rent the
> mountains, and brake in pieces the rocks before the Lord; but the Lord
> was not in the wind: and after the wind an earthquake; but the Lord
> was not in the earthquake: and after the earthquake a fire; but the Lord
> was not in the fire: and after the fire a still small voice. And it was
> when Elijah heard it that he wrapped his face in his mantle, and went
> out, and stood in the entering in of the cave.

Need I point out that it is a majestic scene to which we are now
approaching? It is an event as richly significant and as abundantly
consolatory, as any we meet with in the annals of God's servants.

Let us, I. Consider it in its historical course; and then, II. Inquire
into its immediate object.

A Lesson in History

I. "Go forth," it had been said to Elijah, "and stand upon the
mount before the Lord." The prophet hears it, and leaves his cave:
and no sooner is he gone forth, than signs occur, which announce to
him the approach of the Almighty. The sacred historian here, indeed,
depicts in simple language a most sublime scene. The first sign was
a tremendous wind. Just before, probably, the deepest silence had prevailed throughout this dreary wilderness. Suddenly all is in the most
dreadful uproar about him. The mountain-tempest breaks forth, and
the bursting rocks thunder as if the four winds, having been confined
there, had in an instant broken from their prisons to fight together.
The clouds are driven about in the sky like squadrons of combatants
rushing to conflict. The sandy desert is like a raging sea tossing its
curling billows to the sky. Sinai is agitated, as if the terrors of the law-
giving were renewing around it. The prophet feels the majesty of
Jehovah; it is awful and appalling. It is not a feeling of peace, and of
the Lord's blissful nearness, which possesses Elijah's soul in this
tremendous scene; it is rather a feeling of distressing distance; "a
strong wind went before the Lord, but the Lord was not in the wind."

The terrors of an earthquake next ensue. The very foundations of
the hills shake and are removed. The mountains and the rocks,
which were rent by the mighty wind, threaten now to fall upon one
another. Hills sink down and valleys rise; chasms yawn and horrible
depths unfold, as if the earth was removed out of its place. The

prophet, surrounded by the ruins of nature, feels still more of that Divine majesty which "looketh upon the earth, and it trembleth." But he still remains without any gracious communication of Jehovah in the inner man. The earthquake was only a second herald of the Deity. It went before the Lord, "but the Lord was not in the earthquake."

When this had ceased, an awful fire passes by. As the winds had done before, so now the flames come upon him from every side, and the deepest shades of night are turned into the light of day. Elijah, lost in adoring astonishment, beholds the awfully sublime spectacle, and the inmost sensation of his heart must have been that of surprise and dread; but he enjoys as yet no delightful sense of the Divine presence, "The Lord was not in the fire."

The fire disappears, and tranquillity, like the stillness of the sanctuary, spreads gradually over all nature; and it seems as if every hill and dale, yes, the whole earth and skies, lay in silent homage at the footstool of eternal Majesty. The very mountains seem to worship; the whole scene is hushed to profound peace: and now, he hears "a still small voice. And it was so, when Elijah heard it, that he wrapped his face in his mantle," in token of reverential awe and adoring wonder, and went forth, "and stood at the entrance of the cave."

Its Peculiar Purpose

II. If, now, we inquire into the peculiar signification and primary intention of this Divine manifestation at Horeb, we can hardly remain long in doubt about it. It seems that the Lord intended thus to lead the prophet out of a variety of doubts and sorrows, in which he had lost himself. Outward events had appeared to him quite enigmatical; and his inward thoughts were very confused and painful. He had lost his clue to Providence, in the unexpected turn of events which the kingdom or God in Israel had suddenly taken. It was in God's name, and by his commission, that he had forsaken his native mountains of Gilead, and had gone to Samaria to recover backsliding Israel to the faith of their forefathers. The means for such a work had been placed in his hands by God himself. It was given him to shut heaven, and to open it again. He had performed signs and wonders, such as had not been done in Israel for centuries, and had labored as abundantly as any saint before him. From such exertions Elijah expected to witness effects produced; and he probably hoped for nothing less than a penitent return of the whole people to the service of Jehovah. The fervent man of God, however, erred in his calculation. The result of his faithful labors corresponded not with his hopes, but proved just the opposite to them. At the very moment when he had hoped to lead back the regenerated people, with psalms and hymns of rejoicing, to the altar of the living God, he sees himself exposed to danger in every direction; and his labor appears to have been in vain. Such things were too mysterious for him, and he could not reconcile them with his present ideas of God.

This doubting state of mind had been augmented in the solitary cave at Horeb, and had now attained its height; when the majestic sign—the wind that rent the mountains, the earthquake, and the fire—passed before him, but the Lord was not in them, nor in any one of them, Elijah did not derive from them those spiritual blessings which are mentioned by St. Paul, 1 Cor. 10:1-4, as having been given to the fathers who "were baptized in the cloud and in the sea; who did all eat the same spiritual meat; and did all drink the same spiritual drink: for they drank of that spiritual rock which followed them: and that rock was Christ." None of these blessings was typically expressed, or conveyed in the tremendous manifestations given to Elijah. He did not, nor was it intended that he should, obtain from them a single crumb of that spiritual food, or a single drop of that spiritual drink. They were not the means of any delightful union between his soul and his God, or of any gracious communication. He only felt himself overwhelmed in an awful manner, by the greatness and majesty of God, and by the sense of his own infinite distance from him; and all this wrought neither love nor peace in his spirit, but served rather to make it shrink into bondage, and to produce that state of mind which Isaiah and Job felt, when the former said, "Woe is me! I am undone; because I am a man of unclean lips"; and the latter, "Thine eyes are upon me, and I am not."

But how very differently did the prophet feel, when, after this tumult of the elements, he heard that still small voice which gave to his terrified spirit a taste of the gracious loving-kindness of his God! His experience surely must then have been like that of the seventy elders, who saw the God of Israel in the very same desert, and the same place, Exod. 24:10, 11, and on whom "he laid not his hand." His presence did not destroy or consume them, but only refreshed and delighted them. A happiness so ineffable seems now to have been given to Elijah. The Lord now "loosed his bands"; his oppressed heart was set at liberty. All within him rejoiced at God's gracious nearness; he felt the tender mercy of Jehovah; he covered his face with his mantle, and was willing to lay himself down at the feet of his God, and to give himself up more unreservedly than ever to him.

He had heard in the strong and mighty wind, an echo, as it were, of the dreadful reproofs and words of thunder, with which he had struck the consciences of the people of Israel. The earthquake represented the plagues and judgments which he had inflicted upon the country. The fire would remind him of the flames of Carmel, and of the bloody execution of which it had been the signal. In this way Elijah had appeared as another Moses, with the burning torch of the law—a herald of the just and holy God, who is not to be mocked. But the zealous prophet was mistaken in promising himself, from this procedure, results which never accompany the thunders of the law, but are only wont to be coupled with the still small voice of the gospel. What had he expected? Nothing less than an immediate penitent return of all Israel to the God of their fathers. In this hope he went too far. He was not justified in cherishing such expectations; and it was this that was to be brought to his mind, in a convincing manner, on Horeb. Amidst the terrible phenomena which passed before him, he was to be taught in a lively manner, that the manifestation merely of the power and majesty of God, where its burning brilliance was not tempered by grace, might indeed inspire the sinner with anxiety and terror, but could not really humble and convert him. He was to become conscious that the demonstration of infinite holiness, unassociated with "the kindness and love of God our Savior," can only overawe and repel; but is by no means adapted to produce contrition, or penitential confession, or to incline the heart to the Lord with fervent affection. Now he was to experience in his own heart that grace alone can really soften, melt, and convert the heart; and that the blessed results, which he had anticipated from the thunders of the law and the Divine judgments, can only be produced by the loving-kindness and tender mercy of Jehovah.

In the significant occurrences on Horeb the pleasing prospect was further to be unfolded to him, that the Lord, who had not yet finished his work of reformation in Israel, would, in due time, after the earthquake, storm, and fire, come also with the voice of the gentle whisper, which the hearts of men would then be unable to resist, and which would bow down the mighty; and with what joy must Elijah have apprehended this promise! But was his labor in Israel then a lost labor? Had it been superfluous and useless? By no means! The prophet was to learn that just as the terrible signs he had seen on Horeb had not been unavailing to himself, but had made him more susceptible to the gracious and gentle whisper that followed them, and increased his desire for the manifestation of the loving-kindness of God; so, in like manner, the Lord would point out to him, that his prophetic exertions in Israel had not been without salutary consequences. They had prepared the hearts of the people for impressions of another kind; and thus he was taught that his peculiar vocation, generally speaking, consisted in ploughing up the hardened soil of their backsliding minds; in presenting the forgotten law in all its majesty before their eyes; in awakening the sleepers and terrifying the secure with the thunders of the law, and thereby exciting among them an earnest desire for the gospel, and a hunger and thirst after the righteousness which is by faith that it might be by grace.

Thus Elijah had his difficulties cleared up; and in what a wonderful and glorious manner! By this single Divine act, the ways of God were fully justified to his mind; the mystery of his own life was satisfactorily explained; he was brought, in a gentle but most convincing manner, to a sense of his mistakes; and while on the one hand the honor of God was gloriously vindicated, the prophet on the other hand was deeply humbled, and constrained with all his heart to confess, "Thou, Lord, art righteous, but unto me belongeth confusion of face!" And though Elijah, soon after, repeated the complaint, it was then in a totally different spirit from that in which he uttered it before. It proceeded then from a contrite, humbled mind. The gloomy vexation, the disturbed temper, the inward strife and murmuring, had all disappeared. The jarring discords of his beclouded mind were dissolved, and harmony was restored in his soul.

Thus I have endeavored to give you some explanation of those mysterious events which took place on Horeb; at least with respect to their immediate meaning and object. That this history has remained enigmatical to so many readers may probably arise from the excessive, or rather let me say, improper ideas they formed of the sanctity of our prophet. They viewed him as a being who was no longer subject to human errors, and incapable of deviating from the path of Divine simplicity, and of humble, filial, and unreserved submission to his Lord. But Elijah was a man "subject to like passions as we are." He was also not yet entirely free from what we all inherit from Adam; and we have the key to the wonderful conduct of the Lord toward him on Horeb, not in the prophet's perfection, but in his infirmity. Yet, after all, how great must Elijah have been, that for his reproof and instruction, heaven and earth, as it were, are moved; the rocks rend, and the mountains fall; and how must the mighty God have loved him, to make him an object of such condescension!

Thus we find here a trace, and a beautiful one it is, of evangelical instruction in Horeb, in the vicinity of mount Sinai itself. Though the office of Elijah was rather secondary to that of Moses, than (like that of his illustrious antitype John the Baptist) precursive of Christ, still it comprised the elements "of good things to come." And could this holy prophet have unbosomed himself fully, according to the tenor of that evangelical character which shines through the veil of his awful severity, and according to the tenor of that "still small voice" which he heard: doubtless he had enough within him to have cheered the hearts of thousands. But the time for such things was not arrived. The people among whom he lived were not ripe for such disclosures; hence he had to keep his faith almost to himself before God, and to merge the office of an evangelist in that of a terrible reprover.

Here then we leave Horeb, and I trust not without refreshment and blessing. May Jehovah, who is good and gracious, faithful and ready to forgive, visit us all with the still small voice, and may our whole life be in one sense like the standing of Elijah before him with his face wrapped in his mantle! Amen.

14

Renewed Mission

One of the most affecting narratives of the Old Testament is that of the wonderful preservation of Moses in his infancy, Exod. 2:1-10. Lo, at the brink of the Nile, among the reeds, there floats a small ark or basket, made of bulrushes, and carefully secured from leaking by cement of slime and pitch! For a treasure indeed lies concealed in it—a beautiful infant acceptable to God, and dear and precious to its mother above everything in this world. She has therefore thus secured it, that in its floating cradle it may, if possible, escape the destruction which Pharaoh's cruel sentence has denounced upon all the new-born males of Israel. A mother's love has prepared this infant's couch, with many silent tears and unspeakable anxiety; and while it lies there, in peril on the waters, the sisterly love of Miriam fixes her within sight of it, to watch its fate. The providence of God brings to the banks of the river the daughter of Pharaoh, who, noticing the strange object, sends one of her maidens to fetch it. "And when she had opened it, she saw the child: and, behold, the babe wept. And she had compassion on him and said, This is one of the Hebrew's children." Then said his sister to Pharaoh's daughter: "Shall I go and call to thee a nurse of the Hebrew women, that she may nurse the child for thee?" And she said, "Go." And the maid went and called the child's mother. And Pharaoh's daughter said unto her, "Take this child away, and nurse it for me, and I will give thee thy wages." Thus, by the Divine disposal, were the mother and the child again brought together.

Much spiritual comfort may be derived from this narrative. As many of us as belong to Christ, are hidden as it were in an ark, which cruelty cannot penetrate, nor the floods of the ungodly submerge; this ark is his heart and his love. But many of us, like the infant Moses, who lay in the ark and wept, know not how safely we are thus preserved. Many of us float upon the waves of this troublesome world, in the region of the leviathan and the piercing serpent, amid many anxieties and terrific apprehensions. But be not afraid; remember who watches over you! If you perish, the eternal love of God must perish too: for into that ark have you been received, and none shall pluck you out of the Savior's hand. Nor shall you float upon the waters for ever. Be of good cheer: though you see nothing but darkness and death before you, the providence of God, the Keeper of Israel, is near you to watch over you, as over all the Israel of God. The portion of sacred history now to be considered will show how needless are all our distracting cares and anxieties.

1 Kings 19:1-11.

> And, behold, there came a voice unto him, and said, What doest thou here, Elijah? And he said, I have been very jealous for the Lord God of hosts: because the children of Israel have forsaken thy covenant, thrown down thine altars, and slain thy prophets with the sword; and I, even I only, am left; and they seek my life, to take it away. And the Lord said unto him, Go, return on thy way to the wilderness of Damascus: and when thou comest, anoint Hazael to be king over Syria: and Jehu the son of Nimshi shalt thou anoint to be king over Israel: and Elisha the son of Shaphat of Ahel-meholah shalt thou anoint to be prophet in thy room. And it shall come to pass, that him that escapeth the sword of Hazael shall Jehu slay and him that escapeth from the sword of Jehu shall Elisha slay.

This part of the narrative presents at first sight much that is strange, when viewed in connection with the great event just before related. Who, for instance, would have expected that the prophet should renew his former complaint, or that the Lord should dismiss him with commissions and disclosures like these? Yet it only requires a closer consideration of the matter, to elucidate most satisfactorily what thus is doubtful and obscure.

Let us, I. Take another glance at the Divine manifestation on Horeb; then, II. Listen to the prophet's complaint; after which we shall, III. Pause and consider the instructions he receives; and lastly, Inquire into the nature of those commissions with which the Lord dismisses him.

Another Look at Horeb

I. The majestic scene of wonders on Horeb has already passed before us, and its meaning has been in some degree developed. It depicted the character of the Old Testament dispensation, and the office of the law as our schoolmaster, to bring us to Christ; while, in the "still small voice," we discern the gentle whisper of gospel grace. Thus we are enabled to see these grand occurrences as taking place not for Elijah's sake only, but for ours also; and we must not leave them without a glance at their rich import.

The Lord often comes to those to whom he graciously reveals himself, as he came to Elijah on Horeb. Has your own experience furnished nothing similar? Do you know nothing of the storm which he sends before him, as it were, rending the mountains; of the earthquake, which subverts everything within us and casts down imaginations; of a fire of terror and dread preceding the Lord of glory? Are your rocks still unbroken? Have your heights not yet been cast down, or the deceitful ground of self-righteousness and self-sufficiency removed from under you? And yet you imagine you have heard the gentle voice of grace? You are not perhaps aware that the father of lies approaches men sometimes as an angel of light, and whispers smooth things in their ears. This destroyer is able to pervert the promises of God into the snares of death, and he considers those secured as his prisoners, who suffer themselves to be caught by his false assurances of Divine favor! Oh tremble at the artifices of the old serpent; and remember, that the comforter who seeks to quiet your conscience without mortifying your flesh, is not the Lord, but the wicked one! For Jesus does not draw near with his still small voice, without first overthrowing every high thing that exalts itself against him, and subverting the power of the old man within us. "Strait is the gate, and narrow is the way, which leadeth unto life." "Many shall seek to enter in, and shall not be able." Seeking is not sufficient here—there must be striving. The new creation within us rises upon the ruins of the old and corrupt nature. Wherever grace builds, it first pulls down, and it is by bringing to naught things that are, that God makes out of us what we by nature are not.

There was, some years ago, a very gifted preacher, who for several years preached with great earnestness and success the doctrine of the cross; and who, on that very account, was violently opposed. One of his opponents, a well-informed person, who had for a long time absented himself from the church, thought, one Sunday morning, that he would go and hear the gloomy man once more, to see whether his preaching might be more tolerable to him than it had been before. He went; and that morning the preacher was speaking of "the narrow way," which he did not make either narrower or broader than the word of God describes it. "A new creature in Christ, or eternal condemnation," was the theme of his discourse; and he spoke with power, and not as a mere learned reasoner. During the sermon, the question forced itself upon this hearer's conscience, "How is it with myself? Does this man declare the real truth? If he does, what must be the inevitable consequence?" This thought took such a hold upon him, that he could not get rid of it, amid any of his engagements or amusements. But it became from day to day more and more troublesome, more and more penetrating, and threatened to embitter every joy of his life; so that at last he thought he would go to the preacher himself, and ask him, upon his conscience, if he were really convinced of the truth of that which he had lately preached.

He went to the preacher. "Sir," said he to him, with great earnestness, "I was one of your hearers, when you spoke, a short time since, of the only way of salvation. I confess to you, that you have disturbed my peace of mind, and I cannot refrain from asking you solemnly before God, and upon your conscience, if you can prove what you asserted, or whether it was an unfounded alarm." The preacher, not a little surprised at this address, replied with convincing certainty that what he had spoken was the word of God, and, consequently, infallible truth. "What then is to become of us!" replied the visitor. His last word startled the preacher; but he rallied his thoughts, and began to explain the plan of salvation to the inquirer, and to exhort him to repent and believe. But the latter, as though he had not heard one syllable of what the preacher said, interrupted him in the midst of it, and repeated, with increasing emotion, the anxious exclamation, "If it be truth, sir, I beseech you, what are we to do?" Terrified, the preacher staggered back. "We" thinks he, "what means this we?" and, endeavoring to stifle his inward uneasiness and embarrassment, he resumed his exhortations and advice. Tears came into the eyes of the visitor; he smote his hands together like one in despair, and exclaimed in accents which might have moved a heart of stone, "Sir, if it be truth, we are lost and undone!" The preacher stood pale, trembling, and speechless. Then overwhelmed with astonishment, with downcast eyes, and convulsive sobbings, he exclaimed, "Friend, down on your knees, let us pray and cry for mercy!" They knelt down, and prayed; and shortly afterward the visitor took his leave. The preacher shut himself up in his closet. Next Sunday, word was sent that the minister was unwell, and could not preach. The same thing happened the Sunday following. On the third Sunday, he made his appearance before his congregation, worn with his inward conflict, and pale, but his eyes beaming with joy, and commenced his discourse with the surprising and affecting declaration that he had now, for the first time, passed through the strait gate. You will ask what had occurred to him in his chamber, during the interval which had elapsed. A storm passed over before him—but the Lord was not in the storm; an earthquake—but the Lord was not in the earthquake; a fire—but the Lord was not in the fire. Then came a still small voice; on which the man enveloped his face in his mantle, and from that time knew what was the gospel, and what was grace.

No sooner was Elijah favored with the still small voice, than he wrapped his face in his mantle. This is an emblem of the Christian's state of mind, who veils his face with humility and self-abasement before God. The law fills him with apprehension; the knowledge of sin casts him down to the ground; but the holy shame, the deep and silent contrition, which is so pleasing to God, begins to be felt when the Lord has come with his still small voice. "Behold," it is said in Ezekiel 16:62, 63, "I will establish my covenant with thee; and thou shalt know that I am the Lord; that thou mayest remember, and be confounded, and never open thy mouth any more because of thy shame, when I am pacified towards thee for all that thou hast done, saith the Lord God." Yes, when such a whisper of the most unmerited mercy breathes upon us, our high looks are lowered—our lips are silent—we are overwhelmed with shame. But it is shame without distress; it is a trembling without slavish fear; it is a humiliation replete with love and blessedness. Oh how well-pleasing is it to the Lord! We have already seen the prophet in various positions. We have seen him clothed with strength and intrepidity, contending like a lion with God's enemies; we have seen him in the tempest, with undaunted front, like a rock in the sea, unmoved by the winds and waves—but surely he never appeared more noble and amiable than here on Horeb, when at the still small voice of the Divine peace, he bowed his mighty spirit, and, trembling with confusion and delight, wrapped his face in his mantle.

The Prophet's Complaint

II. We further read, that he then went forth and stood at the entrance of the cave. He does not yet appear to have fully understood the meaning of these wonderful manifestations. And, while he stood there, "behold, there came a voice unto him, and said, What doest thou here, Elijah?" This question, repeated the second time, seemed to direct him back to the scene of activity. We should suppose that he would not have needed to be thus aroused again, but would, after such a gracious experience as had just before been given him, have hastened back, with winged feet, to the work of reformation. But instead of this, he breaks out again, to our astonishment, into his former complaint, as if the wonders God had shown him had been forgotten. "I have been very jealous," he answered, "for the Lord God of hosts; the children of Israel have forsaken thy covenant, thrown down thine altars, and slain thy prophets with the sword; and I, even I only, am left; and they seek my life, to take it away."

The manifestations of God's grace to Elijah had been suited to convince him that his labors in Israel had not been in vain; but though he might now be ready to say, "Lord, I believe," he had still reason to complain and cry, "Help thou mine unbelief!" His anxious spirit would still gain further satisfaction, as to the manner how, the time when, and the means whereby the Lord's intimation would be fulfilled: and no sooner do his thoughts recur to the grievous and desperate state of things in Israel than a feeling of gloom returns, and he pours out his complaint as before.

Believing in darkness, on God's bare word, where nothing like a fulfillment of the promise is to be seen, is certainly a great and glorious thing by which God is honored; and oh that such a faith were more frequently found amongst us! Alas, even where true faith really exists, it is but too generally in a state of conflict, and seldom triumphant and perfected! You find yourself, for instance, in a critical situation; the cares of this life and domestic embarrassments press you down; you can see no outlet—every human prospect of help is vanished. You now get an insight into the promises of God: "I will never leave thee, nor forsake thee. Fear thou not, I am with thee. Behold, I have graven thee upon the palms of my hands!" You know that He who thus speaks addresses you, and that his word is truth. You take the word, and a staff in your hand, you hope the best where, to all outward appearance, there is nothing to hope; you believe in the dark. This is believing on the word of God. But have we generally such a faith as this? O that we had! But is not our faith generally like a bark on the stormy ocean, which, but for the kind providence of God, would soon be dashed to pieces? And if at any time we are enabled to rejoice, and to say, "The Lord will do all things well," do we not too soon resume our doubting inquiry, "Alas, how shall it be performed?"—or if we can exclaim with confidence, "Lord, let me come to you on the sea," yet no sooner do the wind and the waves rise against us, than our confidence is gone, and we begin to cry, "Lord, save me, I perish." Thus our faith is in continual conflict. Let us therefore watch and pray, lest we enter into temptation.

The Instructions He Is Given

III. Elijah is told to depart in faith: "Go, return on thy way to the wilderness of Damascus!"

He receives a threefold commission from the Lord, and with it strength to his faith, and provision for his journey. "When thou comest, anoint Hazael to be king over Syria." This is a reply to Elijah's first complaint, "The children of Israel have forsaken thy covenant." "I will appoint them a rod of correction," is the Divine answer. "Hazael, the servant of the Syrian king, shall go through the briers and thorns for me. Go, and anoint him to be king over Syria!" Hazael afterwards became king, and a severe scourge to the children of Israel. He burned their fortified towns, slew their young men, and barbarously treated those whom nature in its most savage state might have pitied. He served the Lord as the staff of his indignation, and was one of the storms which were to go before Jehovah, overturning the mountains, and rending the rocks; and, when he had finished his work, he was laid aside. Thus the Lord knows how to make use of the vessels of wrath; if one time as channels, through which he pours forth his indignation upon those who have not known him, and upon the kingdoms that have not called upon his name; at other times, he uses them as shepherds' dogs, that serve to keep his flock together, and to bring back the wandering sheep.

Who knows what our own churches have still to experience? We are at present evidently under Divine forbearance; can any one of us say how long it will last? It cannot be expressed, how much mercy has already been expended upon us. Yet how many are there who really thank God, and are heartily devoted to his service? Suppose the Lord were suddenly to remove all his true children from the midst of us, and leave the impenitent to themselves—would our population suffer a very perceptible decrease? Or is it not the case with ourselves as it is everywhere else; that the little flock of Israel among the Canaanites is like a drop in the ocean, and like the little stars, which, in a tempestuous night, twinkle only here and there among the black and stormy clouds? Are not a great part of our people dead, though many of them hear the sound of the word of life? This is very awful! For years together they have assembled in our congregations, but they seem only less and less sensible to the value of revealed truth. They have no hunger and thirst after it. Neither the thunder of the law; nor the sound of its trumpet, has any effect upon them; nor does the sweet melody of Divine grace, and of the promises of God, melt their hardened and worldly hearts. Many of our people are lukewarm—neither for nor against, neither cold nor hot; they hear the words of Christ, but they do them not.

Surely, if they continue in this state, he will reject them with abhorrence. A great part of our people praise Christ and the world with the same breath; they bow themselves before God and mammon in the same ceremony. They desire to be merry with the children of this world, and to be blessed with the children of God; they wish to possess Christ, but will not, for his sake, part with the world. Such is by far the majority of persons among us; whether high or low, rich or poor. What will be the consequence of all this? May the Lord have mercy upon us! For, if we go on in this way, nothing but evil can be prophesied concerning us! The patience of God has an object, but we are defeating it. Who knows whether it may not soon be said to some angel in heaven, "Go now, and appoint this or that man for an Hazael; and let this deceiver, or that son of deceit, be placed over such and such a church!" Who knows whether the preachers, who now stand in your pulpits, may not be the last who shall ever offer the gospel of peace to our unthankful churches, and whether the

destroyers are not already training under the hand of Satan, and only
wait for our departure to take possession of our places with the torch
of the false prophet in their hand, kindled from the bottomless pit!
Perhaps, in a few years, all faithful preaching among you will be at an
end; the people will have become foolish and dissolute; the Lord's
flock will be taken away, and his fire extinguished to the very last
spark. And when the righteous are removed from among us, and no
holy hands bear up the ark any longer, its overthrow and ruin must
be the result. "Oh that thou hadst known, even thou in this thy day,
the things which belong unto thy peace!" Yet forty years, and perhaps
our Ninevehs will be overthrown; and wherever the carcass is, "there
will the eagles be gathered together!" Awake, therefore, and sit down
in sackcloth and in ashes; let everyone turn himself from his evil way,
and from the iniquity of his hands. Who can tell if God will not turn
and repent, and turn away from his fierce anger that we perish not!

Elijah was to anoint Hazael, a stranger and foreigner, to be king
over Syria, that he might become a scourge to Israel. This was his
first commission; and the second was to anoint Jehu the son of
Nimshi, to be king over Israel. This was an answer to the prophet's
second complaint, "They have thrown down thine altars, and slain
thy prophets." As if God had said, "I will vindicate mine own glory;
the house of Ahab shall be desolate, and Jehu shall be the axe to its
roots!" And so it came to pass. Jehu was the man who rooted out the
house of Ahab from the earth, so that neither stump nor stalk was
left. He caused Jezebel to be thrown from the window of her palace,
and suffered her carcass to be trodden down as mire in the streets. He
slew the seventy sons of Ahab in one day, caused their heads to be
displayed in two heaps at the gates of the town of Jezreel, destroyed
the priests of Baal in their own temple, cast the holy vessels belonging to it into the flames, and made an end of the worship of Baal in
Israel.

Such was the end of Ahab's house; and similar instances have
been seen in modern times. Even in our days, there is no want of
examples of the rooting out of entire houses and families, because
they hardened their hearts against the Lord, and bitterly opposed his
children and servants. Though these ungodly men may flourish for
a season, like a green bay tree, and though they be permitted for a
while to gratify their enmity against the people of God, who have
done them no harm; yet, before they are aware, the scene is reversed,

some destroyer brandishes the sword of vengeance. One fails in business, and comes to poverty, with his whole house. Another, given up to the will of his flesh, sinks miserably into the filth of sin. One must flee away branded with ignominy; and another is brought, by degenerate children, with sorrow to the grave. One is smitten with madness; another is delivered unto Satan for the destruction of the flesh, or, overwhelmed with despair, with his impious right hand destroys himself. The babel of worldly prosperity cracks to its very foundations; and, where the Lord breaks down, there is no building up. An evil impenitent death—that awful finishing of temporal judgments—is only the first step to that sequence of terrors, upon which no grave can close. The castaways go with Judas to their place, and their names are mentioned no more upon earth, or mentioned only with abhorrence. Has anything of this kind ever happened among us? Answer this question for yourselves! One thing I know, that still many a house of Jezebel exists among us, which must one day have to give an account for their mockery at true piety, and their opposition to the children of God: and that, except they repent, they will in that day judge it better for them to have been bound to a millstone, and drowned in the depths of the sea, than thus to have offended the little ones of Christ's flock.

The third commission, which was given to Elijah, must have been to him the most pleasing of all. It contained the answer to his third complaint, that he was left alone, and they sought his life; and it was as if God had said, "Be not cast down, Elijah, you are not the only one who is left; and, if you were the only one on the field of battle, do you not think that I can raise up prophets, when I need them? Go, and anoint Elisha the son of Shaphat, of Abel-meholah, to be prophet in your place. And it shall come to pass, that he who escapes from the sword of Hazael shall Jehu slay: and he who escapes from the sword of Jehu shall Elisha slay." Thus, a great and strong wind, that should rend the mountains and break in pieces the rocks before the Lord, is announced against backsliding Israel in the person of Hazael; an earthquake in the person of Jehu; and, in the person of Elisha, a fire of the wrath as well as of the love of Jehovah. Elijah now sees that the Keeper of Israel has not forsaken his vineyard. This instruction invigorates him in body and soul; and when, in addition to this, he hears from the Lord's mouth the surprising information that there are still seven thousand who had not bowed their knees to

Baal, the gloomy cloud on his mind is entirely dissipated, and nothing prevents him from joyfully setting out in faith to give glory to God.

If a sword of the Lord is to pass through this congregation—and a sword will surely come—oh that it may not be Hazael's or Jehu's sword, but the sword of Elisha—the two-edged sword of the Spirit, which is the word of the living God! This good sword, with which he takes the prey from the mighty, may the Lord sharpen more and more, that it may better do its office among us, and pierce, and divide, and penetrate in a greater degree than it has hitherto done! May it cast down the proud into the dust—drive the carnally secure from their refuges of lies—cut away self-righteousness, and so wound them that are whole, that they may resort only to Jesus for healing!

"Gird thy sword upon thy thigh, O Most Mighty, with thy glory and thy majesty; and in thy majesty ride prosperously because of truth and meekness and righteousness; and by thine arrows let the people fall under thee!" Psalm 45. "And may the people which are left of the sword find grace in the wilderness; even Israel, when thou goest to cause him to rest!" Amen. Jer. 31:2.

15

The Hidden Church

I will rejoice in Jerusalem, and joy in my people"; says the Lord by the prophet Isaiah, 65:19. These words give us insight into the paternal love of God, which ought to draw us toward himself. We here behold the close relation which subsists between God and his people; of which indeed we should entertain conceptions far too mean, were we to compare it merely to the relation exsisting between a gracious sovereign and his pardoned criminal subjects, or between a condescending and forbearing master and his servants. We are not only objects of his sparing and pardoning mercy, we are incomparably more than this. The Lord rejoices over his people; he delights in them that fear him and trust in his mercy. He beholds them—not as they are in themselves, but as clothed with the righteousness of their surety, and beautified with his spirit of holiness. He loves those who are renewed by his grace, even as he loves the express image of his person. For those whom he thus loves are conformed to the image of his Son.

It has been said by someone, suppose the sun in the heavens, which enlightens, warms, and fructifies everything, were a rational being that could see everything within the reach of its beams, it would then behold its own image in every sea, in every river, in every lake, and in every brook—nay, it would even see itself reflected on the loftiest mountains of ice; and would it not, in the abundance of its joy at such glorious radiance, forgetting itself, embrace all these oceans, seas, and rivers—nay, the very glaciers, in its arms, and delight over them? Thus Jesus Christ, the Sun of righteousness, beholds his image and divine work in every renewed soul as in a polished mirror. Thus seeming to forget himself, in the abun-

166

dance of the joy that was set before him, he could condescend to
wash the feet of his disciples; thus it was that he exclaimed to the
Syrophenician woman "O woman, great is thy faith!"

Thus our Eternal Father beholds in his children the beauty of his
Son, Jesus Christ, with a complacency greater than we are able to
express. He embraces them with the arms of his love and he loves the
image of himself in which he has renewed them.

Happy are the people who are in such a case; yes, blessed are the
people who have the Lord for their God! Some of them are spoken
of in the portion of the history now before us; and such, in all ages,
may be called the hidden church.

1 Kings 19:18.

> Yet I have left me seven thousand in Israel, all the knees which have
> not bowed unto Baal, and every mouth which hath not kissed him.

These words conclude the Lord's address to Elijah at Horeb. After
announcing the heavy judgments which were to come upon backsliding Samaria by means of Hazael, Jehu, and Elisha, this pleasing
communication follows, like the still small voice. The last shadow of
anxiety was now dispelled from the prophet's mind.

This announcement of God, respecting the seven thousand faithful worshippers reserved in idolatrous Israel, may lead us, I. To
consider that God has ever a hidden church; and, II. To reflect upon
the promises made to it.

God Has a Hidden Church

I. "O Lord! thy name is forgotten, and the last pillars of thy temple are shaking; and I, even I only, am left; and they seek my life, to
take it away." Such were Elijah's complaints, and they were correct
enough for human knowledge. The days indeed were evil; the age of
Noah seemed to have returned; all was dark, dead, ruined, and desolate; and the vintage of God seemed gathered from the earth, with
the exception of two or three on the topmost bough. Painful in the
extreme must all this have been to such a spirit as Elijah's; but, suddenly, he receives from God himself the astonishing tidings that
seven thousand were still reserved, who had not bowed the knee to
Baal, nor kissed him. How astonished must the prophet have been at
this disclosure! How ready to recall his words, "even I only, am left

alone!" and with what renewed courage must his new commission have been undertaken!

And what could be more delightful, in this our day, than to be surprised by similar intelligence? Certainly, our own age seems greatly superior to that of Elijah; but there is much that is only exterior show, which can hardly be mistaken. If all that appears to be divine life were really such; and if all were evangelists, who in modern times are preaching, not for the truth, but against it; if they were men of God, led and gifted by the Spirit of God, and bowed the knee in truth to the exalted Redeemer in all the multitudes, who in every place crowd into the places of worship, really said in their hearts, "Come, let us return to the Lord"; if the thousands, who, in Bible and missionary associations, labor in building the ark, all came into this ark themselves—nay, if even all whom we see uniting for meetings of edification and prayer, could be regarded as true worshippers, then might we indeed say something good of our times, though much would still remain to be wished for. But of what use is it to deceive ourselves? Things are far from being what their appearance would indicate. Alas, many things which, from a distance, look beautiful, are found, when more closely examined, to be full of deformities, if not mere phantoms of what they seemed to be.

Yet, supposing we could regard all who have the show of piety as real Christians, how few would even these be, compared with the number of those all around us, who openly show themselves to be unbelievers! The prevailing spirit of our times is that of infidelity and apostasy—a spirit of pretended illumination, but, in reality, of the blindest presumption—a spirit of opposition to the plain word of God and of arbitrary determination upon good and evil—a spirit of idolatrous exaltation of mere natural reason above the revealed wisdom of God. Among the great mass of nominal Christians, both of the learned sort and of the illiterate, it has long been taken for granted, that the doctrine of our native corruption is a gloomy fancy, and that of salvation by the blood and righteousness of Christ an antiquated and by-gone notion. It is held that the miserable tinsel of exterior decorum, the mere flimsy garniture of selfishness, is quite sufficient to satisfy God; and that a Divine Mediator is not at all necessary to the salvation of men. Many have long been agreed, that the dogmas of a few conceited philosophers, so called, are more to be trusted than the truth of God delivered by Christ and his apostles; and that such faith as that of Paul, Peter, or John, is insufferable in the present day, as being absurd, mystical, and unworthy of any maturely instructed mind yea, that it ought to be banished from the earth, even by persecution, if no other means will suffice.

Such is the prevailing spirit of our modern Christendom, which, with some, is disguised by a Christian profession; while with others it has shamelessly cast off all disguise. It is found in every district, and in all ranks of society, and is taught in by far the greater part of our schools. Millions of men baptized in the name of Christ, lie at the feet of this impious lying Spirit. If you travel through the country, in whatever direction, you find it discovering itself in every company, at public tables, and in private families. Go from one church to another, and you will almost everywhere find that this spirit or seduction is the preacher and expositor. Inspect a multitude of our modern hymn books and catechisms, and instead of the Spirit of God, this spirit of darkness in the garb of religion will confront you; yes, and in a very large number of our places of education, this spirit is the Moloch to which our youth and children are sacrificed. Yes, a review of the Christian world, in the present day, is enough to make every pious spirit shudder. The spirit of antichrist is prevailing in the world to such an extent as it has never done heretofore; and it is almost time to join in with the complaint of the psalmist, "Help, Lord! for the godly man ceaseth; for the faithful fail from the children of men!" Psa. 12:1.

Surely then many think far too favorably of the present times. But do not others think far too gloomily of them? We are willing to believe they do, and the experience which Elijah had, who thought that he only was left, and afterwards heard, to his surprise, that there were seven thousand in Israel who had not bowed the knee to Baal, may help to confirm us in this belief. Assuredly the Lord has many servants with whom we are unacquainted, he has hidden ones whom we may never hear of in this world; and many a country, and many a city, would perhaps long ago have been as Sodom and Gomorrah, had not a small remnant of such been left in those places. "The kingdom of God cometh not with observation;" for, behold, "the kingdom of God is within you." We do not sufficiently consider this, even as Elijah did not; and therefore we may be often mistaken with reference to this kingdom.

It is not unfrequently the case, my brethren, that we measure the temple of God with a very incorrect measuring line, and therefore deceive ourselves as to its breadth and extent. For instance, we are apt to take it for granted that where there are no enlightened preachers, there can be no true Christians. But we forget that God has promised, where the shepherds are corrupt, to take charge of the flock himself! Where has he made the regeneration of his chosen entirely dependent on human instrumentality? Lo! in the midst of the desert, he often plants, with His own hand, the loveliest roses; and from the rudest copse we often hear the sweetest notes of the nightingale. We are also apt to think, that where nothing is heard of awakenings, no awakenings take place. But must there be always a sound when it rains, and cannot children be born to the Lord as dew from the womb of the morning—silently and secretly, before daybreak, and while multitudes are asleep? We are apt to take it for granted, that where there is no opposition to the gospel, there must be a dearth of decided Christians. Certainly, the words still hold good, "I am not come to send peace, but the sword!" and this is commonly shown to be the case. Still there may be real Christians, who, without living under the fear of man, go on in such a quiet, retired, and gentle way, as not to be so exposed to the rancor of the children of this world; and if the Lord say to Laban, "Take heed that thou speak not to Jacob either good or bad," can Laban act otherwise? It is generally taken for granted, that in certain connections, stations, and companies, for instance, in the courts of infidel or worldly minded princes, a child of God cannot possibly be found; but do we not see, in the example of a Joseph, an Obadiah, and a Daniel, that even this may be the case? Obadiah seems even to have possessed the confidence and regard of such a man as Ahab.

The state of Christianity is also frequently estimated by the religious meetings convened in any place, and by the numbers who attend them; but is this estimation always correct? May it not be possible, that in a place where no such meetings are held, there still may be many children of God, who are restrained from coming together only by timidity and reserve—for such things may be found even in true believers—and who are obliged to secrete themselves, like the seven thousand in Elijah's days? And is it not a part of the providential guidance of many souls, to be directed rather to secret and retired intercourse with God, than to much open conference with their brethren? Hence it may follow, that possibly in those places where no sympathy or activity exists for religious institutions, as for Missionary and Bible Societies, perhaps nothing is wanting but information respecting such institutions, for the excitement of such an interest; or some sincere servants of God may have still so much to do with their own spiritual concerns, that they hardly know how to turn their attention to public efforts of this kind. All this is possible. But it may be asked, can there be any ground for supposing a people of God to exist, where no works of pious writers are read; where there is no information found respecting the progress of the kingdom of God in the world; where scarcely an evangelical sermon or book is ever read or heard of? I answer, we are not sure that in such places there are no people of God. I know some whom you would all acknowledge to be holy persons, were I to name them, who, nevertheless, read nothing in the world but their Bibles and hymn book, and daily wipe their eyes for joy, that they are so rich, with these two books, and think that in these they possess a library which, in their whole life, they will never be able to exhaust, and that they can find nothing so beautiful anywhere as in the Bible! Who can blame them? Now, there may be many such persons in the world, who are very little known.

Moreover, we are apt to make the number of the faithful smaller than it is, by defining too arbitrarily and narrowly the characteristics of a state of grace. We, for instance, lay down a certain process as always observed in the Holy Spirit's work of conversion, whereas He is free as the wind that blows where it pleases. Infinite wisdom is seen in an endless variety of processes in the visible creation; and, as uniformity is not its rule in the kingdom of nature, so neither is it in the kingdom of grace; but the same object is attained here also by variety. A gracious change of mind may be as truly wrought by one process as by another. If you have had long to sigh and groan in spirit before your sins were forgiven you, still grudge not him whose way has been made to prosper more rapidly, and to whom the Lord has earlier shown his loving-kindness. "It is the Lord; let him do what seemeth him good." Or, if it be given you to gain spiritual strength more easily, while another is day and night troubled with "a thorn in the flesh," and cast down again and again—is he, on that account, no child of God? If it be to have much knowledge and experience, must it necessarily be given you necessarily to another also; and can there be no retired and reserved children of God and if you are active and zealous in awakening others, efficient in preaching, exhortation, while others are not so, nor are able to be so, are you therefore to question the genuineness of their piety? We must never measure others by ourselves. If we seek more after the chief and essential matter, namely the contrite spirit and the genuine love of Christ and of the brethren, we shall perhaps be led to number many as belonging to the flock of Christ, whom at present we are apt to overlook.

Elijah, as we find, received an express revelation concerning the faithful in Israel, and their number. The Lord unveiled to him the hidden church, and it may be supposed how great was the astonishment of this man of God, at learning that among the very people he had so severely accused, there were so many as seven thousand, who had not bowed the knee unto Baal. He had regarded himself as the only light in the darkness of Samaria; and now behold! a whole firmament of chosen souls is disclosed to his view.

We have to be thankful that even still the church is sometimes refreshed by such pleasing discoveries. Often, on the very spot where we expected to find only thorns and briers, we find a cultivation like the garden of the Lord, and sweeter flowers than are wont to bloom in the more frequented parts of Christendom. Thus lately, in a village in France, in the cottage of a notorious fortune-teller, was discovered a goodly group of the lambs of Christ's flock, transformed into that character from its very opposite. So likewise there was very recently found, in one of the most dissipated cities in the world, a spiritual plantation of Divine grace, which we should never have looked for in such a moral desert; and yet it had secretly flourished there for several years, known only to the heavenly Husbandman, who planted and kept it. In another quarter, where the voice of preaching had long been entirely silent, there was found a considerable company of thriving children of grace, secretly sprung up without any apparently efficient means, of whom the church might be ready to say, "Whence came they? and who hath begotten me these?" And, in another place, we unexpectedly beheld, through the intervention of a pious emperor, three hundred saints, of whom almost no one knew anything, lately coming forth from the prisons of malefactors—three hundred, who had not bowed the knee to Baal, and who, for that very reason, had lain in irons without the emperor's knowledge. God sometimes shows us (it was a happiness frequently enjoyed in my former parish) some old mariner in the midst of a rude and ungovernable crew, who has grown grey in the midst of the most brutal associates; but behold, he is steering toward Jerusalem, and his guiding star is the star of Bethlehem; or some rough barge-man or sailor, who has grown up in the seat of the scorners; but lo through his rude exterior glistens the pure brightness of a genuine Christian character, and beneath his rough leather shirt beats a heart moored by that anchor, which enters into that which is within the veil. And again, as has frequently happened to us, we enter a house to preach repentance to some whom we suppose to be spiritually dead, and we are sweetly surprised by the greeting Christian smile of one or more in the family, betraying a secret acquaintance with the peace of God, and perhaps more deep experience in Christ than we ourselves possess. Such discoveries serve to shame our timidity, to strengthen our faith, and enlarge our hearts; they also teach us to be more prudent and gentle in judging of others, and to take a brighter and more hopeful survey of the world at large. When I think of these possibilities, I feel like one who is passing through the shaft of a mine, where one stroke of the mattock to the right or the left, may possibly discover to him a new vein of precious metal.

Yes, however low may be the present state of the church, we have reason to conclude that it is not so poor and destitute of persons influenced by Divine grace as we are ready to imagine. I believe, that if it pleased God to lift the veil, we might be surprised with the discovery of such numbers as would seem like a resurrection scene. We doubt not but the Prince of the host has still many an ambush of reserve in this world, and that he needs only to sound the trumpet, as he will do, in due time, according to Zech. 10:8, and then we shall be surprised at beholding troops of Christians about us, as Elisha's servant was surprised at beholding troops of angels covering the mount of Dothan, 2 Kings 6:17. How often has it happened, that in a church where, for many years, the word of God had been seldom heard, and of which it was a matter of doubt whether such a church contained in it one real believer, a single occasional discourse, delivered from its pulpit by a stranger, has proved the signal for calling forth, all at once, numbers of timid sheep from their state of concealment! And may not such occurrences give us reason to hope that there are yet many more of the Lord's "hidden ones," with whom we are unacquainted?

How surprised shall we be in eternity, when the veil shall be removed, to find there, from quarters where we least looked for them, among the multitude whom no man can number, standing before the throne, many who were never known as the Lord's people in this world; whom circumstances, or local situation, or their outward defects and infirmities, or their retiring humility and modesty, had concealed from our view! And not only in eternity, but also in this world, such a joyfully surprising disclosure of the hidden church awaits us—and who knows how near its time may be—that the prophetic language, in Song of Sol. 6:10, will resound as then fulfilled, "Who is she that looketh forth as the morning, fair as the moon, clear as the sun, and terrible as an army with banners?"

Promises to the Hidden Church

II. If we look in the daytime toward heaven, we cannot see the stars of God. They are there fixed in the firmament, but the eye cannot perceive them. Wait until evening. The night invites their rays from concealment, and in the dark you behold again their gentle luster. Thus it is with the church. In the sunshine of worldly prosperity they are scarcely perceptible, and the difference between them and the better sort of the children of this world is sometimes hardly discernible. But in this case, also, have patience until evening, and their glory will light up before you. As doubtless, at the time when Hazael the Syrian broke in upon the land with fire and sword, these seven thousand in Israel were made manifest; so also, on the day of the mighty sifting, which awaits the Christian world, we shall be better able rightly to measure the Lord's temple upon earth.

Those days of purification are hastening on with rapid flight. There is no want of signs of the most diversified kind, which, like the petrel before the hurricane, announce to us the nearness of that period in which the Lord will manifest that his fan is in his hand, and will thoroughly purge his floor. Predictions hasten to their fulfillment; and the days are approaching, in whose wild perplexity even the elect, were it possible, might be deceived. Then, if a time should come, when the mark of the beast shall be obtruded on our foreheads at the point of the sword or bayonet, when nothing can save us from torture or a bloody death but a renunciation of Christ and his gospel, the gold will be separated from the dross in the church, and it will be made apparent where the substance of godliness existed, and where only the appearance and tinsel of it. Alas, how many a star, respecting which we have at present no such presentiment, will then fall from the firmament of the church; and what clouds of chaff shall we then see borne away on the wind, even from places where our eyes at present perceive nothing but rich floors of wheat! For everything that is not from the Spirit of the Lord, will not survive the ordeal of that day; and everything which now assumes to itself the ornaments of the sanctuary, but is not clothed with them by the Lord's hand, will be seen in the shame of its own nakedness.

At the very same period, when trees "without fruit" shall fall, when multitudes of false brethren shall be severed and distinguished from the true; thousands, of whom at present we know nothing, shall then throw aside the veil, and with cries of "Hosannah!" shall range under the banner of martyrs. When no other choice will be left but between Christ and Belial, then will those who heretofore have been reserved and timid declare themselves openly for Christ and his cause. Thousands, who in the days of comparative quiet seemed to hang down their heads, will rise like young eagles in the beclouded heavens; and the most weak and bashful in the church will be as David. Thus, one joyful phenomenon after another will surprise us in those days. The deeper the night becomes, the more richly studded and brilliant will be the firmament. The elect shall be gathered from the four winds, and come forth like a new and blooming creation; and we shall seem "like unto them that dream, when the Lord shall thus turn again the captivity of Zion," Psa. 126:1, 2, and when we shall hear hosannahs resounding ten thousand thousandfold from all the ends of the earth, Isa. 52:10.

But what will most joyfully surprise us at that time, if we live to see it, is that it will be given even to us poor timid sheep, who are now so weak in faith, to descend cheerfully, if need be, into any tribulation, for Jesus' sake, and glorify God even in the fires. What the Lord says of the seven thousand in our text, will then have reference to us: "I have reserved them to me," and no one who belongs to the Lord will have any cause to fear. Children of God are preserved, into whatever trials they may fall. Satan may sorely harass them; but they shall come off more than conquerors. The world may oppose and distress them, but this is all it can do. They are "reserved," and "preserved for ever." "In the world ye shall have tribulation: but be of good cheer; I have overcome the world," says the Lord, John 16:33. Thus, however weak in themselves, they survive, when the overflowing

scourge shall pass through the earth, and in the last times of temptation, when the fan is purging Jehovah's floor. Be of good cheer,
therefore, whoever of you are sincerely following Christ. Whatever
may happen, the seed of Jacob shall be delivered, for the Almighty
himself is their rock: and his church stands so firm, that the gates of
hell shall not prevail against it! Let the clouds then gather and fore-
bode the storm—let Hazael and Jehu gird on their weapons! "Yet,"
says the Lord, "have I left me seven thousand in Israel, all the knees
which have not bowed unto Baal, and every mouth which hath not
kissed him."

Let us then open our hearts to the consoling hope, that not only
we ourselves shall certainly be preserved, though thousands may fall
at our right hand, and ten thousands at our left, but that in the great
tribulation which shall come upon the whole earth, a church shall
discover itself around us, of which as yet, we, in the weakness of our
faith, have scarcely dreamed. For thus says the Lord, Zech. 10:9, "I
will sow them among the people: and they shall remember me in far
countries; and they shall live with their children, and turn again."
Yes, he has scattered them like grains of wheat, in all the world, that
from them, under the dew of the Divine blessing, a wondrous harvest
might spring. Therefore every place and every family, where such living seed is deposited, though it be only a single grain, may, on that
account, be already counted happy. Who knows to what increase
such a single grain may yet arrive! Certainly, it often fares with this
seed, as our Lord says, "Except a corn of wheat fall into the
ground and die, it abideth alone," John 12:24. It is true that believing parents, friends, or teachers, must often themselves previously
descend into the grave, and then it is that their prayer is found to
have been heard; their example is remembered with powerful
influence, and their admonitions recalled and laid to heart; it is only
from their ashes that vigorous plants spring forth, and it is on their
tombs that the first penitential tears fall of those they leave
behind. Their labor is never in vain in the Lord, but sooner or later
its fruit is found. "They that were sown, saith the Lord, shall live with
their children; and turn again," they shall increase and be multiplied.

We may well rejoice at such a prospect. Let us give up all narrow
notions of the kingdom of God. Moreover, as the Lord knows them
that are his, and we do not always know them, let us not presume to
judge of their number by our own knowledge. They may not be made

and fashioned according to our own preconceived pattern; they may not wear the garb and cut of our own preference, and yet they may be citizens of heaven. Only let it be remembered, that the seal to which every such citizen is conformed, is this: "Let every one that nameth the name of Christ depart from iniquity." Wherefore lay apart all gloomy and dejected thoughts that would discourage you from being "steadfast, unmovable, always abounding in the work of the Lord." The everlasting preservation, final victory, and future glory of every true member of Christ's holy church should fill us with joy and rejoicing. "God hath set his King upon his holy hill of Zion." The Lord Jesus Christ shall receive the nations for his inheritance, and the uttermost parts of the earth for his possession. "Behold, the Lord God will come with strong hand, and his arm shall rule for him. He shall build the temple of the Lord, and give himself no rest, until he has made Jerusalem a praise in the earth. The earth shall be full of the knowledge of the glory of the Lord, as the waters cover the sea; and they shall come from the east and from the west, and sit down in the kingdom of God," Isa. 40:10; 62:7; 11:9; Matt. 7:11. Seeing then that we know these things, we rejoice greatly, and look upon the world, not in the gloomy coloring of our own pessimism, but in the dawning light of the sun of revelation. Christ must reign, and the "mountain of the Lord's house shall be exalted above the hills, and all nations flee unto it," Isa. 2:2. Let not, then, our eyes be dimmed, nor our hearts be distressed by the mists of the present day. Faith already plants the standard of victory upon the scene of conflict; for it has respect to "the time of the end"; and, although the trophies of Satan be exalted on high, still faith is not daunted. It sings of the triumph of the Lord; and bears inscribed on its banner that mighty word of the Almighty: "I have sworn by myself, the word is gone out of my mouth in righteousness, and shall not return. That unto me every knee shall bow, every tongue shall swear, and say, in the Lord have I righteousness and strength," Isa. 45:23, 24. Amen.

16

The Calling of Elisha

The manifold wisdom of our blessed Savior appears perhaps no where more admirable and striking, than in his approach to sinners; the consideration he showed for different shades of character, and the peculiar readiness and propriety with which he met every one's disposition and situation, are sufficient of themselves to show from whence he came. We have striking instances of this in Luke 9:54-62. In this passage we have the four principal temperaments of the human mind before us: the choleric, the sanguine, the phlegmatic, and the melancholy: and we behold Christ treating each of them with consummate wisdom. The inhabitants of a Samaritan village, where Jesus on his journey to Jerusalem intended to sojourn, refused to receive him. When his disciples, James and John, heard this, they were filled with indignation, and said to their Master, "Lord, wilt thou that we command fire to come down from heaven and consume them, even as Elias did?" Here we have a choleric disposition. And the Lord, in the most admirable manner, turned and rebuked them, and said, "Ye know not what manner of spirit ye are of." He presents his own spirit as a contrast to theirs, and unfolds to them a humbling insight into his love to sinners, and his compassionate intention in coming into the world. The Son of man, he says, is not come to destroy, but to save them. Nothing could have been more appropriate to allay the irritation of their feelings, and to give them an entirely different tone, than these gracious and gentle words of the most compassionate Friend of sinners.

Shortly after this, a man comes up to him on the road, saying to him, "Lord, I will follow thee, whithersoever thou goest!" Here was a sanguine disposition. The man appears to have been carried away with the brilliant actions and Divine loving-kindness of Jesus; and it was necessary that this flighty and enthusiastic mind should be brought to sit down and count the cost. Hence, the answer of the great Master, "Foxes have holes, and the birds of the air have nests, but the Son of man hath not where to lay his head."

Another comes to our Lord, and thus addresses him, "Lord, suffer me first to go and bury my father"; by which he appears to mean, "Allow me to remain in the house of my parents till my father dies; I will then reflect further on the subject." This man then was of a phlegmatic temperament; a person slowly excited, quiet, even, and inclined to indifference. Our Lord again treats this person in a wonderful manner, entirely appropriate to such a disposition. He speaks strongly, seriously, and awakingly, in order to produce an immediate and firm resolution in this procrastinating spirit, and says, "Let the dead bury their dead; but go thou and preach the kingdom of God."

The Lord meets with a fourth, whom he had anticipated by saying to him, "Follow me." But he replied, "Lord, I will follow thee, but let me first go bid them farewell which are at home at my house." Can we doubt what is the temperament of this individual? It is the melancholy, the slowly roused, but deeply and durably susceptible; which is seldom taken by sudden surprise, but is oftener stolen upon by slow but strong affections; which is more inclined to care and sorrow, than to mirth and joy; which does not shun labor, but is wont to pursue its objects energetically. These characteristics are conspicuous in his very language to our Lord. The thing which first presents itself to his mind is the dark and fearful consequences of following Christ. Therefore he desires to embrace his family once more, and perhaps, as it seems to him, for the last time. To meet such a disposition there was need of encouraging and firm language, which might disperse the clouds of melancholy, and give the resolution to break through a host of cares. The man needed an arousing call to the standard, and such a call the Lord addresses to him, "No man, having put his hand to the plough, and looking back, is fit for the kingdom of God." Here then we may well admire the penetrating eye of the Searcher of hearts; the skill of the great Physician; the infinite condescension of the Prince of peace.

In the last of these occurrences, a scene of Old Testament history seems evidently referred to. What the person whom Jesus called here requests for himself, is the same which Elisha requested of Elijah before he undertook to follow him: and our Lord, in the words, "He that putteth his hand to the plough," appears to have intended to refer the man to the example of Elisha, in order to excite him to a quick and cheerful determination. This example is about to come under our consideration, in the portion of Elijah's history at which we are now arrived.

1 Kings 19:19-21.

> So he departed thence, and found Elisha the son of Shaphat, who was plowing with twelve yoke of oxen before him, and he with the twelfth: and Elijah passed by him, and cast his mantle upon him. And he left the oxen and ran after Elijah, and said, Let me, I pray thee, kiss my father and my mother, and then I will follow thee. And he said unto him, Go back again: for what have I done to thee? And he returned back from him, and took a yoke of oxen, and slew them, and boiled their flesh with the instruments of the oxen, and gave unto the people, and they did eat. Then he arose, and went after Elijah, and ministered unto him.

We find Elijah, after he had departed from Horeb, arrived at Abel-meholah, in Palestine, near the river Jordan, on the estate of Elisha the son of Shaphat, commencing the accomplishment of what the Lord had commissioned him to do. He calls Elisha, and Elisha obeys the call; these are the two points which require our attention for the present.

Elijah Calls Elisha

I. From the solitary desert of mount Sinai, we are now to follow the prophet back to the smiling low-lands of Jordan, and to walk upon the fruitful plains which surround the little town of Abel-meholah. We there meet with twelve husbandmen behind their ploughs; eleven of them are servants, but the twelfth is the son of a substantial landed proprietor. He is called Elisha, and his father Shaphat. He does not esteem it beneath his dignity to put his own hand to the work; he drives, in the sweat of his brow, his yoke of oxen before him, in the company of his servants. The plentiful rains, which had lately descended, had made it delightful to be out in the fields, and to follow the plough. The blessing of God sensibly perfumed the air; and the fields, which for three years and had been a barren wilderness, seemed now, after the refreshing showers, impatient for the seed-time, to unfold their newly derived powers. How often, perhaps, had this husbandman, as he broke up the furrows, conversed with his servants of the mighty wonders with which Jehovah had of late visited their native land! How often, perhaps, was the name of Elijah mentioned, and the fiery sign on Carmel made the subject of discussion! For they had probably been eyewitnesses of that miracle; and might belong to those seven thousand who had not bowed the knee to Baal. Perhaps it was at the very time when they were thus conversing of those wonderful days, that behold! a man draws near to them, of venerable aspect, covered with a mantle, and having his loins girded as a traveler; and, as he comes nearer, the oxen stand still, and the husbandmen look at each other, as if they would say, "Who can this stranger be, and what brings him here?" But who shall describe their joyful surprise, as they recognize in the solitary traveler now approaching with quicker steps towards the son of Shaphat, the very man whose name and deeds had resounded through the whole country—Elijah the Tishbite.

The sacred historian says that he found Elisha; whether this implies that he knew him before, or whether he was enabled thus to find him, by special Divine direction given him for the purpose, we are not informed. But of this we may be certain, that Elijah had not for a long time found a more gratifying acquaintance than this. Elisha was the first child of God, whom, after a long period of solitude, he had the happiness to meet; he found in the person of the son of Shaphat, the first and the chief of the seven thousand, and the first seal of the promise granted him at Horeb on behalf of his people. The simple and pious Elisha was the man in whose sphere of action the still small voice of God's tender mercy and love would be heard by the children of Israel, so as to turn them to the Lord their God. He was the first messenger of Jehovah, who should sow the fruit of righteousness in peace upon the land, which his predecessor had broken up by judgments; yea, who should bind up the hearts that were broken. Even his name expresses the character of his Divine commission. It signifies, "My God is salvation"; and the history of his ministry is given, as it were, in this one word. His labors, compared with those of his predecessor, appear upon the whole peculiarly evangelical. He goes about in meekness, and his peaceful course is marked with benefits and blessings; nor is it accompanied by the dreadful majesty of divine and burning jealousy, but by the mild and amiable light of Jehovah's condescending love. He stretches out his right hand, not to close heaven, but to bring down its showers of blessing. His office is evidently that of a deliverer, sent to announce that "the Lord is gracious." A new period was therefore to commence with Elisha's mission; a season of Divine loving-kindness, after the days of judicial punishment; a time of the still small voice. Elijah seemed to be aware of this; and it may be easily imagined with what delight he must have embraced Elisha, as the man who was to be instrumental in fulfilling his best hopes for Israel.

Elijah found him behind the plough. It is not without meaning that this is mentioned in the history. Here then we have a pleasing picture of a man, who, notwithstanding the gifts with which he was endowed, continued lowly in his own eyes, and led a humble and unassuming life. How many, gifted like him, would have thought themselves too good for the plough, and born to a sphere of life above that of a simple farmer; would have persuaded themselves that they must not withhold their talents from mankind, that they must go forth into the field of public labor, to enlighten and guide the world. But such thoughts did not enter the mind of Elisha. His pretensions went not beyond his plough and his husbandry; he saw his vocation in these quiet and rural occupations, and well satisfied with this, he "minded not high things." How much more amiable and beautiful is such a disposition than the opposite one, which is now so frequently met with among Christians! "Labor for the kingdom of God," is become the watchword of the day; we certainly rejoice at it, but with very mingled feelings. There is too much vanity and self-complacent pushing forward, which, alas! may be seen on this field of activity. No sooner does anyone imagine he has found himself possessed of talents and gifts ever so small, than he hesitates not to regard himself as a pillar of the church of God. The condition and calling in which he has hitherto been is no longer the proper one for him. He immediately begins to think, if not to talk, of a higher station, to which he imagines himself born. We ought undoubtedly to let our light shine before men; but then everyone should do so in the situation in which Providence has placed him. Nor does God intend, by this command to let our light shine before men, to refer simply to the office of the ministry, or to any official teaching in his church. It is not merely your lips, Christian, but your life, which is to be the lamp. It is your general character and conduct which are to edify your brother and glorify God. He intends that all your thoughts, words, and works, should silently testify that you are born of God, and that the peace of God dwells in your heart. Then it is that you throw around you that gracious radiance which the Savior means when he bids you let your light shine before men; then it is that you preach the gospel, as the power of God unto salvation, more effectually, than can be done by words. And remember that those spiritual lights have the purest radiance which are the least conscious of their own brightness; and that those divine flowers diffuse the sweetest fragrance which make the least display.

That excessive pressing of religious men into public notice, which characterizes the present day, is only another sign of the spiritual poverty of the times. There is a great dearth of truly great and noble spirits in our modern Christendom. No eagle pinions at present soar in our firmament; hence the smaller birds, the minds of inferior case having no living standard by which to discern their own littleness, are emboldened to regard their own modicum of talents and endowments as an evidence of a divine vocation to great and exalted things. Happy would it be for Zion were that vain activity, which is not of God but of the world, confined to the world itself, and not obtruded within her sacred enclosures! Happy would it be for her people, were there not so mournfully prevalent among them an idolatry of worldly instrumentality, and mere human talents! Why is it that God so frequently calls home his most excellent servants and evangelists, in the bloom of life, from their useful labors, but—as one purpose at least—to secure them from the peril of that idolatrous admiration with which these mortals are too often extolled in what are called the religious periodicals; and to let the survivors know that the pillars of His temple are not flesh; that wisdom does not die with any creature; and that none but Himself is the basis, the support, and the builder up of his kingdom.

When Elijah has found Elisha, he takes his prophet's mantle from his own shoulders, and throws it over those of the son of Shaphat. What must have been the feelings of the plain and unassuming husbandman upon this occasion! for he well understood this significant action, and could view it as nothing less than a consecration to the prophetic office, and a call to be the assistant, follower, and representative of the Tishbite. It is to be lamented, that, in the present

day, the Christian ministry is too exclusively and systematically confined to persons who have undergone a certain mode of education;
which was never the case with the church in its purest times. May
God raise up and put forth among us more of those who are taught
rather by the unction of the Spirit of God, than by the mere external apparatus of scientific institutions! Not that these are to be
despised or neglected; far from it! but they furnish, after all, only the
exterior of a Christian minister's qualifications.

Elisha Obeys the Call

II. After Elijah had cast his mantle over his successor, he went
away without uttering a word; and this he appears to have done to
render more impressive the meaning of his symbolical action. Elisha
well understood it. He lays the reins on the necks of his oxen, leaves
them standing with the plough in the midst of the field, and hastens
after the man of God. We do not find that he either resisted the call
with a variety of objections, or made many words about the too great
honor done him, or about his own incapacity for the office; no, the
matter was briefly and speedily settled. He thought not about himself but about the heavenly Caller, and his power and grace. He
leaves in God's hands the dignity and burden of his office; and
receives the prophetic commission with the same equanimity as he
had taken in hand the plough or the mattock. Oh lovely simplicity,
and serenity of a humble and childlike spirit!

Elisha, however, had more to leave than his team and field. His
father and mother were living, and them he felt bound, first of all, to
inform of his high calling, and to desire their prayers and parental
blessing. Accordingly he runs after Elijah, and requests of him a short
interval, saying, "Let me, I pray thee, kiss my father and my mother,
and then I will follow thee." How very differently does the son of
Shaphat begin his prophetic career from what is related of Elijah!
Him we find descending from the mountains of Gilead, as if he had
come from another world; and his first prophetic utterance is that of
a delegate of Omnipotence: "As the Lord, the God of Israel,
liveth, before whom I stand, there shall be neither dew nor rain these
years, but according to my word." His family connections are concealed from us. Not a word is mentioned of his father and his mother,
nor is there anywhere an allusion to his genealogy or relationship.
The softer feelings of human tenderness and domestic alliances seem

unknown to his elevated soul, and he steps forth gigantically conspicuous above his age and generation. There is an imposing majesty in his whole character, which keeps everything about him, as it were, at a distance; he resembles mount Sinai itself in his relation to the Israelites.

Elisha's character is quite of another kind, and in the circumstances of his coming forth into public notice, he appears as any other man. The sacred history conducts us to his house and family. We are made acquainted with his occupation and connections. We behold him at his plough as a common husbandman, as one whose feelings and experience are the same as our own; who participates in all our relative circumstances; who, like ourselves, is closely allied by blood, affection, and tenderness, to the circle in which he lives; who is a stranger to none of the sensibilities of our common nature; who can feel the pain of separation and taking leave of friends; and in whose bosom beats, in every respect, the heart of an ordinary member of the family circle. We can venture familiarly to approach him, and we feel our hearts drawn to him in so doing. Now, all this was suited to the official character which Elisha was to sustain in Israel. While Elijah was as another Moses, a vindicator of the Divine holiness, and an ambassador of Divine wrath against all who violate his law, and therefore appeared as he did; Elisha, on the other hand, was appointed as an evangelist and representative of Jehovah's lovingkindness, and was to shine before men in a very different light, not to threaten and terrify, but to allure, persuade, and convert. Hence God sent him to the tabernacles of his brethren as one of themselves, and stationed him as a friend, in whom the most timid might feel confidence, and whose humane and affable personality might operate benignly on the minds of men.

Elisha shows himself to have been a beloved and affectionate son; and we at once feel our hearts drawn out toward anyone in whom we perceive such features of character. Partings in some respect like that which Elisha had now to undergo, but far more bitter and painful, are those which take place when a love to Christ in one part of a family, and an opposite feeling in the other, divides and causes variance between parent and child, brother and brother, friend and friend. What is every real conversion to God, but a virtual taking leave of worldly connections hastening away out of their moral atmosphere, a withdrawing from the jurisdiction of their thoughts, opinions, and influence, into a totally different, and, to them, strange and distant province? Though such a separation is a most felicitous one for those who renounce the course of this world, still it has its pain and bitterness; for alas, it is uncertain whether he who forsakes all for Christ, may not now have become separated forever from those who are dear to him by nature's ties, and may have to miss them in heaven; and what can be more painful than this! He who has never experienced such parting pangs, either does not naturally love his worldly connections, or else he is not yet effectually separated from them; and though in his exterior religious habits he may be different from them, he is not really so in the dispositions of his heart.

It happens occasionally, that this spiritual parting takes place with much anger and strife; not only on the part of those that remain behind—who can be surprised at this?—but even of those who, as they say, are desirous of leaving the world. It seems to me, however, that it is it comparably more in accordance with the nature of a true conversion, that the separation take place on the part of the converted, with affectionate regrets, as in Elisha's case; and, I confess, that where I see anything else, it wounds me like an arrow, and so contracts my heart toward a new brother, that I cannot ardently welcome him. I have seen many a soul turn from the world and come to the Lord; but oh! what separations were they, when the persons were in true earnest about their conversion! It was just as if their first love now filled their hearts to the very brim: "Oh that my dear father or my dear mother, would but accompany me! Oh that my brother, or my friend, would choose the same good part!" How tenderly did they entreat them to be reconciled unto God! What anxiety to perceive any traces of the work of grace in their dear relatives. What inward sighs and supplications, "O Lord, be merciful to them also, and save their souls, as thou hast done mine!" Everyone must be counted happy, whom the hand of mercy leads forth from the multitudes of the blind and dead into the kingdom of light; but more happy is he, who when God awakens him, needs not to bid farewell to his dearest friends on earth, but can say to them, "You went before me; and now, by God's grace, I am following after you. My name is with yours in the same book of life, and your Lord and Master is now mine!" Oh what a blessed welcoming and embracing then commences! They were once divided, but are now united forever! O converted parents of unconverted children, believing children of unbelieving fathers or mothers, oh that such a joyful day may soon dawn upon your dwellings!

Elijah had no objection to Elisha's request. "Go," said he, "and return again, for what have I done to thee?" The natural endearments of his paternal roof would not be found any temptation to him; for the Lord himself had stirred in him; and what had Elijah done to him, except to communicate the outward and visible sign? Family connections have often stood in the way of many a converted person; but Elisha's father and mother evidently appear to have been no such hindrance to him. They were probably devout persons. And though it required no little self-denial to give up a faithful and affectionate son, perhaps their only son, the joy and prop of their old age, especially with considerable danger of his falling a sacrifice to the idolatrous hand of power, still they readily complied, and doubtless said, "The will of the Lord be done!"

While Elijah was proceeding on his way toward the wilderness of Damascus, Elisha went and took a yoke of oxen, probably those he had been accustomed to drive, and slew them, and boiled their flesh with the instruments of the oxen, and gave unto the people, and they did eat. This action appears signficant, as if Elisha hereby meant to seal his covenant with the Lord, to take a solemn leave of his previous station, life, and occupation, and to testify his entire and voluntary resignation and dedication of himself to God, who had called him to his office. A similar procedure must spiritually take place in our houses and in our hearts, if we desire to enter into life. "He that forsaketh not all that he hath," says Jesus, "cannot be my disciple." Whatever you love out of Him, or more than him, must be given up. Is mammon your idol? Renounce it, otherwise Satan holds you by a golden chain. Is it credit and reputation among men? Away with it, and seek the honor which comes from God only. Is it wisdom and understanding? Renounce them, and become a fool for Christ's sake. Is it a life of ease, fashion, or pleasure? Burst these silken but slavish bonds, and crucify the flesh with its affections and lusts. We cannot be God's people unless we are so entirely, with all that we have and are. But this is not all. The very instruments of the oxen must be given up, the very garments spotted by the flesh must be hated; every weight, every besetting encumbrance must be laid aside and hewn in pieces. A whole and entire sacrifice is what the Lord desires for his altar; and his watchmen cry, "Depart, depart ye, go ye out from thence, touch no unclean thing; go ye out of the midst of her; be ye clean that bear the vessels of the Lord!"

The parting meal with which Elisha now entertained the people, while on the one hand it was hospitable and cheerful, had in it on the other hand something solemn and sacred. Elisha, as the ruler of the feast, seems willing to leave with them his parting blessing, in a manner best suited to give them a cheerful idea of the Lord's service. It may be imagined how Elisha felt upon this occasion. The mysterious memento, which Elijah had left with him, and his own consciousness of the prophetic call, had put his mind upon the stretch. However dear to him were his beloved parents and connections, he embraces them, and leaves them. As to his future provision for this world, he casts all his care upon the God who feeds the ravens, and clothes the lilies of the field. Thus he sets out with a light heart and a cheerful countenance. "He arose and went after Elijah, and ministered unto him."

In like manner must we all be ready to follow the Lord Jesus. He has cast upon us his mantle. If we are his disciples indeed, our hearts are so touched and animated by his Spirit, that we can prefer nothing in the world before him, nor can we suffer any other object to rival him in our hearts. Oh may God grant that we may all realize him as our God and our Savior; may the wings of his mercy be spread around us, that we may finally enter into an eternal and sabbatical rest!

17

Naboth's Vineyard

A woman of Canaan is mentioned, in the New Testament, as remarkable for her humble acknowledgment of unworthiness, and for the greatness of her faith in Christ, Matt. 15:21-28. She said, "Truth, Lord: yet the dogs eat of the crumbs which fall from their master's table." By these words she surmounted the last obstacle, which Jesus had placed before her as a trial of her faith. And as the brightness of the sun is reflected in a dewdrop, so the whole glory of the gospel and the inmost state of all true Christians shines forth in these words of the woman of Canaan.

"Truth, Lord," said the woman; and how much is implied in this one word, "truth." You know that the Savior had been just speaking of "dogs," which he placed in contrast to the children of the house. The woman answers, "Truth, Lord," and thus confesses herself liable to the Lord's accusation. But she adds, "yet," and indeed, in these few words the glory of the gospel shines forth in all its brightness. Though the two words stand in close connection here, yet we shall find, on closer consideration, that there lies much between them. A cross is between them, surrounded by all the terrors of Divine wrath; an altar, streaming with the most precious blood that ever flowed on earth; a Lamb, that takes away the sins of the world; and a Surety, who has taken upon himself the punishment which was due unto us. Yes, blessed by God! though "of a truth" we deserve the Divine wrath and indignation, and are in danger of the judgment and the council, "yet" a throne of grace has been erected, and an eternal redemption has been obtained. Help has appeared for the miserable, life for the dead, grace for rebels, and righteousness for sinners. Such are the feelings of all who are indeed of the fold of the good

Shepherd. A deep sense of their own misery, accompanied by a sure confidence in God's mercy through Christ Jesus, is the characteristic of all true believers; and thus it is the glory of the blessed gospel, that to the humbling and self-condemning "truth, Lord," we can add a joyful "yet."

Do you inquire, why I have commenced this discourse with these reflections on the conduct of the woman of Canaan? I have done so partly to diffuse at least one cheering sunbeam over the awful nightmare which we are about to consider, and partly to enable you to form a better judgment of that other woman of Canaan, whose character will be depicted in the history before us. There too, in the case of Ahab, we shall also hear of a "truth, Lord," but entirely different from that of the firstling of the gentiles at the coast of Sidon; for it is not accompanied by a humble and believing "yet," it does not lead the sinner to the cross of his Savior.

1 Kings 21:17-21

And the word of the Lord came to Elijah the Tishbite, saying, Arise, go down to meet Ahab king of Israel, which is in Samaria; behold, he is in the vineyard of Naboth, whither he is gone down to possess it. And thou shalt speak unto him, saying, Thus saith the Lord, Hast thou killed, and also taken possession? And thou shalt speak unto him, saying, Thus saith the Lord, In the place where dogs licked the blood of Naboth shall dogs lick thy blood, even thine. And Ahab said to Elijah, Hast thou found me, O mine enemy? And he answered, I have found thee: because thou hast sold thyself to work evil in the sight of the Lord. Behold, I will bring evil upon thee, and will take away thy posterity.

About the time when Elijah called Elisha from the plough, and consecrated him to be a prophet, a terrible war broke out between Syria and Israel. The Syrian king, Benhadad, with an enormous host, which was aided by thirty-two tributary allies, took the field, quite unexpectedly, against Ahab, but by God's help he was defeated and compelled to terms of peace. Where Elijah abode, during these tumultuous time, we are not informed. It is only after the disturbances are over that we find him reappearing in the narrative, and this as an ambassador of God. He was sent to Samaria to reprove king Ahab for his sin. This mission of Elijah is the subject of our present consideration. We will notice, I. Its occasion; II. Its object; and III. Its immediate consequences.

The Occasion

I. "The word of the Lord came to Elijah the Tishbite, saying, Arise, go down to meet Ahab king of Israel, which is in Samaria: behold, he is in the vineyard of Naboth, whither he is gone down to possess it." The crime Ahab had committed against Naboth was the occasion of the prophet's present mission to him. We are already acquainted with king Ahab, the weak instrument of others, who always allowed himself to be governed by circumstances, and just what these made of him such was he. Thus at one time he could show himself even kind and generous—as in his behavior to the vanquished Syrian monarch, so that a prophet was even commissioned to reprove him for his ill-timed lenience: "Because thou hast let go out of thy hand a man whom I appointed to utter destruction, therefore thy life shall go for his life, and thy people for his people," 1 Kings 20:42. He could also, the very next moment, according as he was externally wrought upon, perpetrate the most infamous cruelties, especially when it could be done without endangering his person.

Under better influence, Ahab would probably have been a better king: but, led as he was by such a woman as Jezebel, and by such a host of sycophants as his composed court, he necessarily became the very tool of iniquity. As he was very effeminate and loved luxury, he left the affairs of his government, in a great measure, to Jezebel his wife, and was glad when he could pursue his pleasures with undisturbed ease. After the war was finished he had retired to his country residence at Jezreel. To pass away the time, he amused himself with beautifying and enlarging his sumptuous palace and gardens. Adjoining the latter was a vineyard, which belonged to the paternal inheritance of Naboth the Jezreelite. Ahab having thought that his grounds would be much improved by the addition of this piece of land, set his heart on obtaining it. Accordingly he sent for the proprietor, told him his wishes, and offered him either an exchange of land, or the value of it in money. But Naboth could not properly part with his vineyard, because, by the law of Moses, no Israelite was permitted to sell his inheritance. All land was to be considered as the Lord's property, and held only as a fief under him. It was indeed allowed to be exchanged, but even then it was to be restored in the year of jubilee. This was the Divine command, and Naboth would not deviate from it, nor would he make an exchange, because he foresaw that the idolatrous king would pay no regard to the year of jubilee, or the laws respecting it. Therefore he answered, "The Lord forbid it me, that I should give the inheritance of my fathers unto thee." He was not afraid of confronting the idolatrous monarch as a worshipper of the God of Abraham; and we rejoice to see here another individual of that seven thousand, who had not bowed the knee to Baal.

The king was not prepared for such a refusal as this. He could not endure the frustation of his favorite plans, and especially by one who doggedly, as it seemed to him, and in despite of his royal authority, adhered to the ancient law, and refused homage to the Sidonian idol. Wounded in his pride and dignity by this supposed insult, he hastens to his palace, behaves like a spoiled child whose will has been resisted, throws himself upon his bed, turns his face to the wall, and refuses to eat. Jezebel, astonished at finding him in this disconsolate condition, inquires what has happened, and learns from him the whole affair. Her reply to him is that of a resolutely unprincipled, despotic, and abandoned woman: "Dost thou now govern the kingdom of Israel? arise, and eat bread, and let thine heart be merry: I will give thee the vineyard of Naboth the Jezreelite." It is as if she had said, "Is this all that troubles you? We will soon finish this matter. What kind of a government would it be in Israel, if such things were permitted!" Thus, partly to revenge the insult which the king's majesty had sustained, and partly to attach her husband still more closely to herself, she takes measures immediately to procure the vineyard at any price. She writes letters in Ahab's name, to which she misapplies the royal seal; she orders the elders and nobles of the town to proclaim a fast, which was usually done when any great calamity had occurred, or any dreadful crime committed. She requires them to assemble the people, to put Naboth upon a mock trial before them, and to suborn two villains to give false evidence against him, and accuse him of having uttered blasphemies and curses against God and the king. This being done, Naboth was condemned unheard, dragged out of the town, and cruelly stoned to death. And when the bloody execution was accomplished, Jezebel went triumphantly to Ahab, and said, "Arise, take possession of the vineyard of Naboth the Jezreelite, which he refused to give thee for money: for Naboth is not alive, but dead." When Ahab heard that Naboth was dead, the miserable man rose up from his melancholy and chagrin, "to go down to the vineyard of Naboth the Jezreelite, to take possession of it." Such was the atrocious crime, primarily, of Jezebel; but Ahab equally participated in it, since he heartily approved of the infamous deed, and readily seized the property. Indeed he would probably have contrived and perpetrated the deed itself, had he been possessed of that resolution and cunning for which his wife was so remarkable. They were both of them the murderers of Naboth, both defiled with his blood, both guilty, and equally deserving punishment.

This atrocity was the more horrible and shameful, because it was certainly not obstinacy which induced the unfortunate man to reject the king's offer, but faith in the God of his fathers and obedience to his holy ordinances. But there is no doubt, as we have already observed, that this very circumstance exasperated the murderers still more, even enraged them to the highest degree. Worldlings can least of all bear to have anything refused them upon grounds of piety and faith. Thus an unbelieving master has often required a pious servant, or laborer, to join in some dishonest plan in trade or business; and when the latter has refused, the thing would often have been taken no notice of, if the servant had only assigned some worldly reason for his refusal, such as the danger of adulterating goods in such a manner, or the injury it might cause to the master, and the like. But when persons in this situation have referred to the will of their Savior, and mentioned the law of God as the reason for their refusal, cursing and reviling have been the consequence, and they have been threatened with dismissal from their service, or a discontinuance of employment; and though matters were not carried to the length of a stoning to death, yet virtually and in principle, Ahab and Jezebel were there on the one side, and Naboth on the other.

The Object

II. Ahab's wicked pleasure at taking possession of Naboth's estate was not of long duration. However secretly the murderers had acted their part and devised their infernal plan, One, of whose presence they thought not, had seen and noticed all. This secret witness was no other than He whose eyes are as a flame of fire; the Keeper of Israel who neither slumbers nor sleeps; the Discerner of the thoughts and intents of the heart, who understands its thought afar off; who is about our path, and about our bed, and spies out all our ways. Surely he had seen it, and had "prepared for them the instruments of death, and ordained his arrows against the persecutors."

But why, when the Almighty saw the impious deed devising, did he not interpose to prevent it? Why did he not rescue innocent Naboth, who was his servant and his child, and brought into peril by his faith and obedience? For replies to such questions as these, the Scripture refers us to the world to come. Till then, we must silently and resignedly submit to the many mysterious disposals which occur in God's government of the world. We must often, in opposition to appearances and short-sighted reason, rely solely on the sure word of prophecy, by faith give God the glory, and acknowledge that even what appears to the carnal mind foolishness, is in reality adorable wisdom; and that what is apparently contadictory in the Divine government, is part of an economy and plan which will eventually call forth our profoundest admiration. God's thoughts are not our thoughts, and his ways are infinitely higher than our ways. "We do not understand his mode of government," says an enlightened writer, "and are always liable to run into mistakes, both when we commend and when we find fault with it." God has infinite complacency in his own designs, and is infinitely above all the opinions of men. "It is really absurd," says the same author, "to wish for a hair more or less than we possess; and it is certainly better to be Elisha than Absalom, better to be as Lazarus at the rich man's gate, full of sores, than to be the rich man himself." Let the earth be what it will to us; provided God reign in it, or rather in our own hearts, his ways will ever be good in our estimation.

It is true that the permission of such an event as the death of an innocent man like Naboth, under circumstances of the most despotic cruelty, is sufficient to exercise our faith, and to stagger the judgment of natural reason. But events of this description will all be satisfactorily explained in eternity. Let us leave them to the Lord: he will solve every such difficulty hereafter, to his own glory and his people's happiness. We may be quite sure that it was with no discontent or complaint against Divine providence that Naboth, just after he had closed his eyes upon this world, amid volleys of stones, opened them before the throne of God. And doubtless his cruel death is, to this moment, a subject of praise with his spirit; and could he now converse with us, any dissatisfaction on our part at God's providence toward him would give him pain, and he would call upon us to join him in adoring that providence as full of wisdom and love.

This you may allow to be true; but still you are ready to ask, what becomes of the promises of God, when it can fare so ill with such a man as Naboth? I answer, The promises of God are still what they ever were: "They are all yea and amen in Christ Jesus." God has promised, to those who love him, that all things shall work together for their good: and so it really happens. He has promised to be with them in fire and water; and he *is* with them. But you seem to assume that the promise is, that neither fire nor water shall come nigh them, nor any pain or mishap befall them; but this is not correct. It is, on the contrary, expressly said that the way to the kingdom of God is "through much tribulation"; and the Savior does not conceal it from his friends, that he appoints unto them the kingdom, *even as* his Father hath appointed it to him, Luke 22:29. "But if this be so," you may be tempted to say, "we must be in continual anxiety, and cannot be certain of escaping any danger. If we travel in a lonely place, we are not certain that robbers and murderers will not attack us. If we cross a river, or the sea, we have no certaintly that we shall not be drowned. If we are deprived of work or wages, we have nothing to assure us that God will preserve us and our families from starvation. If the pestilence rage around us, we have no assurance that the destroying angel will pass over our houses. There are, then, no promises to secure our preservation from calamities; so that, though we are God's children, we must be subject to the same apprehensions as those who are strangers to the covenant of promise!"

Such conclusions are erroneous! Though it is not unconditionally promised us that we shall escape every danger and misfortune; yet "he that believes shall see the salvation of the Lord"; and "all things are possible to him." You know that great assurances are given us—assurances of unlimited extent—promises which leave us lacking nothing. Whatever may be the distress by which we are threatened, we need only "call upon the name of the Lord," according to his express declaration, and we shall be delivered. The Savior has said, in John 15:7, that inasmuch as we abide in him, we may ask what we will, and it shall be granted us. But what is it to abide in Jesus? It is indeed a great and important matter, which is pointed out to us by this expression. For if I really abide in Christ, then I forget myself; I behold myself in Christ, and the evil conscience of sin is lost in that of his merits. I count myself as dead with him, risen with him, and exalted with him above the world, sin, and death. I rejoice in his righteousness as my own. I feel assured that God neither can nor will deny me, since I am his child, and well-pleasing to him is the son of his love, anything that is good for me; hence nothing prevents me from joyfully casting myself, with all my concerns, upon the tender and paternal heart of God. Thus, there may certainly be a life free from care and fear, even in the midst of a thousand dangers; there is a state of mind, in which we have in our hands a key to all the treasures of God, and a shield against every danger both of body and soul. Only learn the happy art of being in Christ, and of asking in his name, then ask what you will; and, while praying, you have your petition.

But to return to our history. The black deed at Jezreel has been perpetrated. Naboth lies buried under the earth; but the voice of his blood cries to Heaven for vengeance. The great Advocate and blood-avenger of his church hears it, and prepares for judgment. He gives to his servant, the Tishbite, a commission to king Ahab; "Arise, go down to meet Ahab king of Israel, which is in Samaria: behold, he is in the vineyard of Naboth, whither he is gone down to possess it. And thou shalt speak unto him, saying, Thus saith the Lord, In the place where dogs licked the blood of Naboth, shall dogs lick thy blood, even thine." Dreadful message! One would think Elijah himself would have shuddered at such a knowledge as he had of the righteous judgments of God, had he known nothing of the grace of the gospel. But he knew much of this, by his own experience, as is evident by attentively considering his history and character; and this rendered him undaunted and of good courage.

The Immediate Consequences

III. The king of Samaria is gratifying the lusts of his heart in the vineyard of Naboth. He exults over the valuable plunder, and is considering how this acquisition may be turned to the best advantage, and united with his grounds. But suddenly he hears footsteps behind him, and turning about, beholds, to his amazement, a man approaching him, in whose stead he would rather have seen a whole army marching against him, and who had never come upon him more unseasonably than just at this moment. It was Elijah the

Tishbite. The prophet had sent no one before him to announce his approach, or inquire whether it is the king's pleasure to admit him into his presence. He assumes his rightful prerogative of speaking in the name of Jehovah, and makes no scruple of surprising the monarch in the midst of his pleasure-grounds and gardens. Dreadful must such a meeting have been to Ahab. He had probably vainly hoped that Jezebel had frightened away this unwelcome guest for ever. He had thought him far away beyond the mountains; if not, which he would have greatly preferred, in his grave. But lo, he stands before him like an apparition from another world; no, like the ghost of the murdered Naboth. Anticipating but too truly his message, he exclaims, before a word is uttered from Elijah, "Hast thou found me, O mine enemy?" Thus his own fury and malignity betray him, and become his own accusers.

How commonly is it the lot of our ministers to be treated like Elijah, when they succeed in finding out sinners in the church; or rather, when, by their instrumentality, sinners are found of God! Yes, when our arrows hit the mark—when one and another of our hearers is compelled, against his will, to see his moral deformities in the mirror we place before his eyes—then it is immediately said to us, in the hearts of those who are thus smitten, "Hast thou found me, O my enemy?" We are then regarded as disturbers of men's peace, and as taking a malicious pleasure in distressing their minds. As for charity, we are accused as strangers to it, and gloomy views of enthusiasm are the things we are charged with preaching and teaching. Our sermons are denounced as unsound and extravagant. Such are the heavy charges which we are obliged to put up with; but sometimes mere hard words are not deemed sufficient, and the criticism becomes of a more active kind. These individuals seek to repay us for venturing to promote, in the only right way, their peace of mind, by resolving never to hear us again, but to go in future elsewhere. Go, then, such people, wherever it pleases you. It is not we who have "found" you, but it is *God* who has found you by our means, and from him you cannot escape. His word has pierced to the joints and marrow, and no endeavors of your own will avail to get rid of it, until the same Almighty hand which pierced you shall heal the wound. If he is leading you to repentance, spare yourselves the fruitless labor of kicking against the pricks. No means you resort to of this world's devising will be effectual to heal the wound that is rankling in your conscience.

The burning in your heart will only increase from day to day, till it is quenched in the blood of the Lamb. Oh that we might but "find" you effectually, we would gladly submit for a while to be treated by you as enemies. "I have found thee!" said Elijah, serene and undaunted. How must the criminal have felt at these words! Confused and oppressed by the dreadful accusations of his conscience, he saw himself utterly unable to offer the smallest defense against the denunciation of the prophet. And it came upon him with still greater force, since it had found him in Naboth's vineyard itself, where the prophet could appeal to the very stones of the vineyard to cry out and awaken the king's conscience. Truly it was a pitiable position which the king of Samaria occupied at this moment. He had, probably, never before experienced such a disgraceful defeat. The glory of his regal crown has vanished in an instant. He stands before the messenger of God as a poor perplexed delinquent, out of whose hands every weapon had been wrested; nothing now was left him but his own stifled and impotent rage; and it must have been painful to the Tishbite himself, to see his sovereign thus overpowered, confused, and abased before him. Thus the Lord is able with a word to bring down the pride of the haughty.

Who can resist the appaling power of that word, "I have found thee," when it comes as the language of the holy law, by which is the knowledge of sin, but not of mercy? May everyone of us feel it, if we have not felt it hitherto; but may it be accompanied by the gracious tidings of forgiveness and justification by faith in the atonement of the Son of God! Yes: with the dreadful sentence, "Cursed is every one that continueth not in all things that are written in the book of the law to do them," may the blessed announcement be heard in our inmost souls that Christ is "the end of the law for righteousness to every one that believeth"; and that "whosoever believeth in him hath eternal life." If we hear believingly the one announcement, "Depart, ye cursed, into everlasting fire"; may we hear believingly the other announcement, "Come unto me, all ye that labor and are heavy laden, and I will give you rest!" Then shall the "fearful look-ing-for of judgment" be exchanged for that "godly sorrow which worketh repentance unto salvation not to be repented of"; and the terrors of the law will give way to that inward contrition, which not only God will not despise, but which is the work of his own hands, the first sign of a new and endless life. It is not the terror of the Divine holiness, but the manifestation of the love of God toward us in Christ Jesus, which softens the heart and renews the soul.

By this the believer is more and more divested of self, becomes the willing servant of the Lord, and finds in his service perfect freedom. He now loves God, and serves him; not in the slavish bondage of fear, much less in the vain endeavor of serving two masters; but from the constraining influence of gratitude; even as St. Paul could say, "The love of Christ constraineth us." He performs that which is good, as it were spontaneously, from a vital principle within. Here is an instance wherein, as we may say, liberty and necessity are closely allied to each other. The true believer becomes a captive of love, and yet in this captivity he enjoys the only true liberty. Such are the happy effects of the gospel of peace. The law works no such wonders as these. Only where love and grace reign, are the true springs of life and salvation to be found. Only yield yourselves up to the influence of this grace and love, and you will inhale, with every breath, the powers of the world to come, and will be elevated in spirit above the love of the world, and of the things of the world, as if a thousand hands were conducting and welcoming you into the heavenly places!

18

Ahab's Repentance

The Scripture repeatedly speaks of A BOOK OF LIFE; and St. Paul notices, Phil. 4:3, the names of his fellow-laborer Clement and others, as inscribed in that book. It is, as its title imports, a book of life. No judgments are written in it; no sentences of death are recorded. It is full of the promise of life eternal; and they whose names are written in it never die; they have already passed from death into life; everlasting youth awaits them beyond the grave; and thrones of never-fading glory and joy stand prepared for them in heaven. This book is, in other words, the paternal heart of our almighty and most merciful Father. In this book a number of names are inscribed; that is, a great multitude, which no man can number, are all individually and continually remembered before him; and every one of them is infinitely dear to him, and eternally beloved. They are the names of his people, his chosen, his children, his heirs, being joint heirs with Christ; and redeemed to himself by the blood of the Lamb. By a mystical union with Christ their Surety, they are bound up in the bundle of life with the Lord their God. In him, the Beloved, are they made accepted and glorious; and because he lives, they also live forever and ever. The book of life is open in heaven. There it is read again and again, and they who read it are never weary of so doing. The Son of Man himself sees in it the "travail of his soul, and is satisfied." This book indicates to the Shepherd his sheep, to the Bridegroom his bride, to the High Priest his redeemed, and to the Prince of peace the people in whose heart is his law. Even to the holy angels is this book opened. They are sent forth to minister unto them who shall be heirs of salvation; for which purpose they must know the names that are written in this book. And continually are they becoming more and more acquainted with it, and increasingly wonder and adore the God of all grace, as they behold the names of those whose sins have been many, and are forgiven.

Now, if there be any one object in the world more worthy of our curiosity than another, I think we shall all agree in saying what it is: surely it is the sight of our own names inscribed there. On the fact whether our names shall be found there or not, is suspended our peace and happiness throughout eternity. If they are, then Hallelujah! from henceforth all generations shall call us blessed; if they are not, then woe is unto us, for we are undone! But can this fact be ascertained here on earth? I answer, that even here on earth we may know from Scripture the characteristics of those whose names are in the book of life. The chief of these is a contrite heart, longing after God. It must never be forgotten that there are two ways of crying for mercy, and it is not every kind of humiliation before the Lord which will justify us in concluding that our names are inscribed in his book. Therefore deceive not your ownselves! But if you seriously desire to know what it is which distinguishes true and gracious humiliation from that which is only the working of natural feelings, you may learn it from the portion of sacred history which we are now about to consider.

1 Kings 21:21-29

> And I will cut off from Ahab every male, and him that is shut up and left in Israel, and will make thine house like the house of Jeroboam the son of Nebat, and like the house of Baasha the son of Ahijah, for the provocation wherewith thou hast provoked me to anger, and made Israel to sin. And of Jezebel also spake the Lord, saying, The dogs shall eat Jezebel by the wall of Jezreel. Him that dieth of Ahab in the city the dogs shall eat; and him that dieth in the field shall the fowls of the air eat. But there was none like unto Ahab, which did sell himself to work wickedness in the sight of the Lord, whom Jezebel his wife stirred up. And he did very abominably in following idols, according to all things as did the Amorites, whom the Lord cast out before the children of Israel. And it came to pass, when Ahab heard those words, that he rent his clothes, and put sackcloth upon his flesh, and fasted, and lay in sackcloth, and went softly. And the word of the Lord came to Elijah the Tishbite, saying, seest thou how Ahab humbleth himself before me?

because he humbleth himself before me, I will not bring the evil in his days: but in his son's days will I bring the evil upon his house.

The prophet delivers his message in Naboth's vineyard, and announces to the trembling tyrant, with all boldness, the dreadful punishments which should come upon himself and his family. Here then let us consider the impression which this announcement made upon the guilty monarch; noticing, I. How Ahab's repentance was called forth; II. What kind of repentance it was; and, III. What were its consequences.

How Ahab's Repentance Came

I. Elijah's address evidently produced unusual terror in Ahab's mind, and induced him to humble himself in some degree before God. Nor does this surprise us: for it contained not only an awful accusation which Ahab could not deny, but likewise an awful sentence upon himself and his posterity, pronounced, as from the mouth of God himself, with singular impressiveness and power.

A threefold crime is here laid to the charge of the king of Israel; that he had provoked God to anger—that he had made Israel to sin—and that he had sold himself to work wickedness in the sight of the Lord. It was for this cause that the sword of the Almighty had been whetted for the destruction of himself and his house.

Observe, then, how Jehovah is represented in the first part of the accusation, as a God who may be so provoked by continued insults and rebellions, that his long-suffering is like a bended bow, which needs only to be drawn to a certain tension in order to break. This certainly sounds very human; but faith is far from stumbling at such language; for it stands in need of such representations of God. We need to be told of God in an intelligible manner, and to be addressed by him in the language of our nature; in expressions of mercy, sympathy, and displeasure; as caring for us; as taking cognizance of our very thoughts; as loving us; not as inaccessible to us, or unconcerned about us. Now just such is the God of the Scriptures.

Ahab is further accused of having made Israel to sin. This he had done by his impious example, and by those infamous decrees which had made the worship of Baal the religion of the state, and exposed the true worshippers of Jehovah to the most cruel persecutions. Woe unto those, who, like Ahab, not satisfied with destroying themselves, seek to infect others with their pestilential errors, and to carry them along with them in their own fall! Such men will not only have to bear the burden of their own iniquity, but the guilt besides of all those unhappy victims who were led away by them, and who will pursue them forever with their vindictive curses. Such men will have hereafter the horrid distinction which their lives seem to be aiming at in this world—the distinction of being more like their father the devil, in whose works they have been so preeminent.

The remaining point of guilt which Elijah alleged against Ahab was that he had sold himself "to work evil in the sight of the Lord." And "there was none," says the sacred historian, in another place, "like unto Ahab, who did sell himself to work wickedness in the sight of the Lord, whom Jezebel his wife, stirred up." "Sold himself to work evil!" What a dreadful charge! Yet it is as true as it is dreadful, not only concerning Ahab, but concerning every unconverted man. "I am carnal," said St. Paul, in reference to his natural condition; "sold under sin; for what I would, that do I not; but what I hate, that do I." Try an experiment only for one day, with the law of God; labor to keep, fully, any one single command of God; and however it may grieve you, depend on it that, before evening, you will be obliged to take up for yourself the same humiliating confession with the great apostle.

It is a common proverb that "Every man has his price"; that there is something for which everyone will be found willing to sell himself. These are words of awful import, and yet they are but too true concerning every natural man. The children of this world, proud as they are of themselves, may always be bought with one temptation or another: honors, profits, pleasures of one class or another, will induce them to debase themselves more and more. The idol to which Ahab sacrificed was his affection for Jezebel. His own will, his honor, his peace of conscience, the salvation of his soul, the favor of God—all that he had or hoped for, was laid at this idol's feet. Would that he were alone in such infatuation; or only one of a few! But alas, it is common in every age. Let anyone ask himself, why he is an unbeliever; why he despises the people of God; why he serves the world and the devil, and endeavors to stifle every good conviction. By what influence is he constrained thus to act? Ask him, and he will tell you that he feels the influence of custom and example, and of his own natural inclinations; that his connections, the favor of men, or the attachment by which he is bound to other persons and other things, are the causes which indispose him to the serious care of his immortal soul. But what impious constraints are these! What an accursed alliance, though it be under the sacred name of friendship itself, must that be, which is connected with enmity against God! Whoever of us has hitherto walked in these human chains, let him separate himself from them without delay. "If any man love the world, the love of the Father is not in him." "He that loveth father, or mother, or son, or daughter, more than me, is not worthy of me." Forget not the blessing of Moses upon Levi: "Who said unto his father and to his mother, I have not seen him; neither did he acknowledge his brethren, nor knew his own children: for they have observed thy word, and kept thy covenant: they shall teach Jacob thy judgments, and Israel thy law; they shall put incense before thee, and whole burnt-sacrifices upon thine altar," Deut. 33:9, 10. "Ye are bought with a price," says the apostle; "therefore be ye not the servants of men!"

The heavy accusations which Elijah, in Jehovah's name, brought against the king of Israel in the vineyard of Naboth, must have been the more terrific on account of those dreadful denunciations with which they were followed. The first of these was, "In the place where dogs licked the blood of Naboth shall dogs lick thy blood, even thine!" And so it came to pass, as is most strikingly shown in the subsequent history. For soon afterwards Ahab proclaimed a war against the Syrians, contrary to the express command of the Lord and in spite of the warning of the prophet Micaiah: "If thou return at all in peace, the Lord hath not spoken by me." And he returned not. For in the very first battle he was slain. "A certain man drew a bow at a venture, and smote the king of Israel between the joints of the harness. Wherefore he said unto the driver of his chariot, Turn thine hand and carry me out of the host; for I am wounded." And so it was done; and the king died at even; and the blood of his wound ran into the midst of the royal chariot, which was afterwards washed in the pool of Samaria, the very place were Naboth was murdered; and there they washed his armor, and the dogs licked up his blood. Verily there is a God that judgeth! Have mercy upon us, O Lord Jesus!

The next "curse of the Lord" was "upon the house of" Ahab. "Behold, I will bring evil upon thee, and will take away thy posterity, and will cut off from Ahab every male, and him that is shut up and left in Israel, and will make thine house like the house of Jeroboam the son of Nebat, and like the house of Baasha the son of Ahijah. Him that dieth of Ahab in the city the dogs shall eat; and him that dieth in the field the fowls of the air shall eat." How awful is it, when the iniquities of fathers are visited upon their children to the third and fourth generation! Nor did any part of the threatening fail of its accomplishment, as you may see by consulting 2 Kings 9 and 10. Jehu was raised up by Providence to put the Divine sentence in execution. Him God caused, by a prophet, to be anointed king over Israel, and Jehu lost no time in bringing the kingdom under his authority, but directed his first march to Jezreel, where king Joram the son of Ahab resided. Joram, perceiving his approach, went out in his chariot to meet him; and, having met him in the portion of Naboth the Jezreelite, he asked, "Is it peace?" To whom Jehu replied, "What peace, so long as the whoredoms of thy mother Jezebel and her witchcrafts are so many?" Joram, hearing this, endeavored to escape; but Jehu drew a bow with all his strength, and smote Joram between his arms, so that the arrow went out at his heart, and he sank down in his chariot.

Then said Jehu to Bidkar his captain, "Take him up, and cast him in the portion of the field of Naboth the Jezreelite, according to the word of the Lord." And it was done. There Ahab's blood flowed, according to the letter of the Divine threatening, from the veins of his son, upon the same ground which had been polluted by the blood of the innocent Naboth. In the same manner were Joram's sons and all the relatives of Ahab destroyed by the sword, so that neither root nor branch remained of that idolatrous house. The idol priests met with the same fate. In one day they were all slain by the sword; the images, together with the temple of Baal in Samaria, were broken to pieces, and idolatry, for a season, was banished out of Israel.

The third judgment which Elijah announced to Ahab was to fall upon Jezebel. "The dogs," said he, "shall eat Jezebel by the wall of Jezreel." And so it came to pass. For when Jehu entered the city of Jezreel, the queen, having "painted her face, and tired her head, looked out at a window." But the infamous woman did not succeed this time with her meretricious arts; the heart of the rude captain remained unmoved and impenetrable as a rock. He lifted up his eyes, and called to the chamberlains who stood near her, to throw her down; and they threw her down, so that the wall and the horses were sprinkled with her blood, and she was trodden under foot, like the mire in the street. And it was not till after Jehu had gone into the city, and had eaten and drunk, that he said, "Go, see now this cursed woman, and bury her: for she is a king's daughter. And they went to bury her, but they found no more of her than the skull, and the feet, and the palms of her hands." And they that were sent returned to Jehu, and told him; then said he, "This is the word of the Lord which he spake by his servant Elijah the Tishbite, saying, In the suburbs of Jezreel shall dogs eat the flesh of Jezebel: and the carcass of Jezebel shall be as dung upon the face of the field in the suburbs of Jezreel; so that they shall not say, This is Jezebel!"

Behold, my brethren, how the Lord fulfills his word! How ought this thought to strike all impenitent sinners with horror: for he who denounces against them everlasting punishment, is the same God whose name is FAITHFUL AND TRUE; and it is easier for heaven and earth to pass, than for one tittle of his word to fail.

What Kind of Repentance It Was

II. The thunder of Elijah's denunciation produced on this occasion some effect. Ahab knew whom he had before him, and that it was not this man's custom to beat the air, and to utter vain words. The idolatrous monarch is astonished, and deeply affected. He feels the load of guilt which lies upon him. His conscience is alarmed, and his past iniquities rise up in terrific array before him. Doubtless it must have seemed to him as if he saw the spirit of the murdered Naboth standing before him; as if he heard from the graves of the massacred saints a thousandfold cry ascending to heaven for vengeance against him; as if the lightnings of God's fiery jealousy already flashed over his guilty head; and as if he heard behind him the howling of the dogs of Jezreel panting for his blood. The feeling which over-powered him at the fiery sign on Carmel revives in all its liveliness, with a thousand horrors. He is now but too assuredly convinced that Jehovah is God, and that Elijah is his messenger. The poor powerless wretch feels as if he were already at the judgment seat of the Almighty; as if the thunder of the Divine rebuke was rolling over his head; as if the angels of justice were about to drag him to the place of torment. He forgets his crown and his purple, conscious that he is an enormous sinner, and is not ashamed to express this consciousness before God and man. He descends into the dust, rends his clothes in token of the distress and wretchedness of his soul, puts on sackcloth, and falls down before the God of Elijah; appoints a fast, unconcerned whether it may please his heathen consort or not; even during the nights. His penitential exercises are continued; he goes softly and sorrowfully for a time, like a real subject of penitential grief. Joy is mute in the palace, which was ordinarily so full of merriment; the pipe and the viol no longer resound through the glittering rooms; the royal residence is like a house of mourning and death; and the gloom of the king spreads itself like a black cloud over all his attendants.

This mourning of the king of Samaria was real as far as it went. The wretched outward dress in which he appeared was a true expression of his inward temper and state of mind. Still, much was wanting in his repentance to render it a repentance unto life and salvation. It was not a mourning like that of the woman who was a sinner, at the feet of Jesus, like that of the thief on the cross, or that of the poor publican. Ahab's repentance was utterly destitute of love; and it is love which hallows all our acts and deeds, and gives them a real value.

Let us take occasion, from this conduct of Ahab, to learn what is a real and godly repentance. St. Paul describes it, when, in Gal. 2:19, he says, "For I through the law am dead to the law, that I might live unto God." By the law to which he is dead, is to be understood here, the sum of the Divine demands on man, together with the threatenings and curses attached to it. Now, the apostle here tells us, not that he has escaped like a truant from this schoolmaster, or deserted the law like others; but that he is dead to it, lawfully delivered from it, even as a woman is no longer bound to her husband, but may contract a new marriage when her first marriage is terminated by the death of her husband. Every man, whether he knows it or not, is thus, by nature, bound to the covenant of the law. That is to say, if he obey the law perfectly, the law will reward him; if he disobey it, which he always does, he becomes liable to the penalty of its curse. As soon then as the law vindicates its injured majesty in the conscience of any one, the bondage of that curse is felt. Consequently the terrified individual generally undertakes to satisfy the law in the way of obedience, by his own good works; and he thinks he has ability sufficient for the purpose. But here he sets his feet upon a path, from which no one ever brought anything back, but broken bones, a wounded heart, and a troubled conscience. Alas, what does he now experience? Instead of coming forth from the mire of sin, he daily sinks deeper into it; and instead of moving ahead, he hourly retrogrades. His best resolutions are rendered fruitless by his inability; and the mournful consciousness that he is a thousand times more corrupt than he had ever supposed, and the vexation, anger, trouble, and chagrin which the law is wont to cause in every one who ventures to cope with it in his own strength—these are the only and the bitter fruit which he derives from his labor.

What then is to be done? Perfect obedience can be thought of no more; he gives up the idea of it, and seeks to come to an agreement with the law in another manner. But how? He tries to flee from the law—he turns deserter. "Why," thinks he, "should I torment myself any longer upon a path where my sincerest endeavors are perpetually defeated!" And with this desponding thought he returns to his former vain conversation, gives the reins to his flesh, and indulges freely the desires of his heart. But though he forsakes the law, the law does not forsake him. It pursues him, and disturbs him, from time to time, with its awful denunciations; for these are within him, and he cannot flee from them. What is he now to do? One way still stands open to him. He endeavors to capitulate with the law, and to come off with it on amicable terms. He resolves to keep it as well as he is able, and seeks to live according to its requirements, as far as it lies in his power; and thus he hopes it will cease to curse him so dreadfully, and allow him to comfort himself with the mercy of God as to all in which he may still be deficient. But, however reasonable such a proposal may seem, it proves unsuccessful. The law will not be satisfied with any partial fulfillment. It demands a perfect obedience; and however much the sinner may do, as he thinks, to the utmost of his ability, the law does not at all lower its tone of condemnation, but still disquiets the conscience. Hence the poor helpless man finds no resource left, but to plead guilty at once before the tribunal of heaven, confessing that the law is just in its demands and threatenings, declaring his own moral bankruptcy, and crying with the apostle, "O wretched man that I am! who shall deliver me from the body of this death?" Nature, indeed, strives mightily against this condemnation, recoils from pronouncing sentence against herself and trembles at the death she has deserved. But the light shines victoriously into her darkness. The convinced soul sinks, as a man slain in battle, before the foot of the throne of grace, and with dread, distress, and amazement, exclaims, "Woe is me, for I am undone!"

Now, when a sinner has thus, with heartfelt seriousness, pronounced sentence against himself before the throne of God, he has begun to die to the law. For here is an end of his supposed self-righteousness, and of his own supposed ability. But that true repentance, which the Scripture calls a godly sorrow, and a repentance which does not need to be repented of, does not as yet necessarily exist. This is but, as it were, dying before the Divine holiness; as we see was the case of St. Paul, in Rom. 8. "When the commandment came, sin revived, and I died. And the commandment, which was ordained to life, I found to be unto death." Now thus dying under the law, and by the law, does not amount to dying to the law. The sinner, thus alarmed and humbled, is dead to the supposition of his moral excellencies; but the marriage between him and the law is not yet dissolved. On the contrary, this severe husband and schoolmaster still rebukes and chastens him; for the sinner has yet an enmity against the law, as well as against Him who gave it. His whole nature murmurs at it; he is vexed and irritated that the law exists; he does not love it, he would rather see it destroyed, because it robs him of his peace, and puts a restraint upon his sinful flesh. Hence, his repentance is not of the right kind; he is not renewed in the spirit of his mind: and that *dying* to the law, of which the apostle speaks, is still to come.

Now, this glorious and happy death comes by "the law of the Spirit of life in Christ Jesus," Rom. 8:2. And this law is no other than the gospel; whereby alone it is that true, divine, and saving repentance is called forth. Let us, then, consider once more the case of the awakened and alarmed sinner, trembling almost on the verge of despair. His natural disposition is still opposed to the law, and the distress of his conscience forbids him to lift up his eyes to the Lord. But, as the light of the New Testament begins to irradiate the darkness of his mind; the cross appears amid the clouds of his distresses; the glad tidings of the gospel sound in his ears, and reach his understanding and his heart. And now observe what a wonderful change immediately takes place in his whole being. He hears that there is help and redemption for him; he hears that the Father, in order to save him, has sent his only begotten Son into the world; he hears that this Holy One has taken our sins upon himself, and that he has paid the debt, suffered the deserved punishment, endured the wrath of God, in the sinner's stead, and has thereby obtained eternal redemption for him. The sinner hears it, is amazed, scarcely believes for joy, looks at his Surety, beholds his sufferings, his head crowned with thorns, his countenance beaming with infinite love, and his heart, once pierced for sinners, full of compassion and mercy on their behalf. What feelings of gratitude spring up within him under such manifestations of the kindness and love of God his Savior! He bows himself under the scepter of his Divine Deliverer! Filial reverence and godly sorrow take the place of servile fear, and peaceful adoring humility supersedes the terrors of the broken law. His enmity against the law is departed; for how should he hate a law which no longer condemns him? His hatred to it is changed into love, for it is the expression of the Divine will of that same gracious God, to whose mercy he owes all his salvation. Hence, he now delights in the law, and flees from sin as from a serpent. He flees from it; not because of terror and outward constraint; not from fear of punishment; but from love to the Savior, whom he would now gladly obey in every respect, and to whose glory he heartily desires to dedicate his whole life. This is true and godly repentance unto life; a repentance springing from faith and love. A wonderful death has now taken place. The marriage between the law and the sinner is dissolved, and that lawfully. The law now leaves him in peace; for the believer in Christ is made "the righteousness of God in him"; and what the law commands, is now the very fruit which the good tree produces of itself, from the new principle of faith in the Son of God.

But the repentance of Ahab was not of this kind. His enmity against the law was not abolished and slain by faith and love. It was the punishment, and not the sinfulness of sin, that made him tremble. Had no curse followed, his transgressions would have pained him but little. But, because this punishment was delayed, he turned back into the path of destruction, and by so doing, furnished the clearest evidence that his sorrow proceeded only from selfishness, and that the dominion and love of sin still prevailed within him.

The Consequences of His Repentance

III. But though Ahab's repentance was far from genuine, it was nevertheless regarded by the Almighty with some favor. He therefore sent his word to Elijah the Tishbite, and said to him, "Seest thou how

Ahab humbleth himself before me? Because he humbleth himself before me, I will not bring the evil in his days: but in his son's days will I bring the evil upon his house." Here was a delay of execution; but no revocation of the sentence. The curse still rested upon Ahab and his house. Yet even this respect shown to a repentance which had so little intrinsic worth, this exemption of Ahab from personally experiencing those storms which impended over his house, was an instance of great condescension and favor. But why, it may be asked, if Ahab's humiliation was so little worth, was any Divine regard shown toward it? This, we answer, was to show by a living example that self-condemnation and abasement before God is the way to escape his anger, and obtain his favor. Just as a novice in any art or trade may be cheered by words of encouragement at the first favorable attempt which he makes, however imperfect it may be; so the exemption that the Lord made in Ahab's favor on his repenting, was calculated to encourage him to aim at something better. Self-condemnation, self-abasement, and giving God the glory, are the first steps from spiritual death to spiritual life. We are not, therefore, to regard it as any decisive mark of our state of grace, that we at any time experience the forbearance of God upon humbling ourselves before him or that he at any time vouchsafes a notable answer to our cry of distress, and disperses some of the heavy clouds which impend over us. For, all this may be only as an encouragement to true and sincere repentance; it by no means proves that we *are* really restored to true friendship with God.

All history shows that whenever any prince or people have given glory to God and his word, though only by an outward confession, it has been attended with signal blessings of Providence. But to infer from this that such nations and princes were in special favor with God, would be found unsupported by Scripture. We often see persons, whom we dare not regard as truly converted to God, who nevertheless agree to all the statements and confessions of Scripture truth; they are evidently controlled by a certain dread of God's displeasure; but they do not live in obedience to the commandments of Christ. On the contrary, they love the world, and the things of the world; and yet God temporally blesses them and their household, and they enjoy the respect and regard of persons far more piously disposed than themselves; but these external blessings must never be accounted an evidence of their own state of grace; for, if they be so regarded, men may find themselves one day miserably undeceived. God often gives many temporal blessings to such persons, that his goodness may lead them to true repentance. But these temporal favors are no seals of Divine adoption. Let no one, therefore, deceive himself; for, "except ye be born again, ye cannot enter the kingdom of heaven." The best that can be said of all others, is what was here said of Ahab: "Seest thou how they humble themselves before me? Because they humble themselves before me, I will not bring evil upon them in their lifetime; but at length that day shall come upon them as a thief, and they shall hear it said unto them, I know you not; depart from me!"

As many of you as are still "without," are in a situation similar to that of Ahab in the field of Naboth. Dreadful curses are pronounced upon you; awful judgments hang over your guilty heads; snares, fire and brimstone, storm and tempest, all which will one day discharge themselves upon you, O unhappy people! Only one outlet stands open to you and this consists in true self-condemnation and self-abasement. Not that these things have any merit belonging to them; but they imply a hunger and a thirst after righteousness, and that righteousness is to be found in the Lord Jesus Christ. The moment you stretch out the hand of faith to lay hold on this righteousness, the curse is removed, and you are made accepted in the Beloved.

Let Ahab's example ever be a warning to ourselves, lest, notwithstanding the most remarkable visitations of the Almighty, the strongest allurements, the most lively emotions—yea, notwithstanding much penitential conflict, and many answers received to our prayer—still we should fall short at last. Take heed that your repentance exceed the repentance of Ahab, lest it should have to be repented of when it is too late. Yes, when the hour is at hand, in which it is appointed you to die; when you are left alone with the remembrance of your sins, and the gates of eternity are opening before you, you may indeed perform a repentance, which may not be unto life, except you repent now. At such an hour there may be no word of comfort for you that will reach your heart, or heal your wounded spirit. For the repentance of a death-bed is very uncertain; it may contain no true repentance toward God, nor any true faith toward our Lord Jesus Christ. For how often do we see such a repentance unaccompanied by any heartfelt lamentation over the man's spiritual corruption, by any hungering or thirsting after righteousness, by any longing after fellowship with God, or by any desire of love to God! It is nothing more than the mere shudder of nature; it is only that awful dread of the Most High which the evil spirits felt, when they besought Jesus not to command them away into the deep! But may God be gracious to us and fill us now with that "godly sorrow, which worketh repentance unto salvation not to be repented of!" Let our repentance be that of affectionate children, who can have no rest till the kind but justly offended parent again looks complacently upon them; let faith and love be the life and soul of our repentance; let it prove its genuineness by an unfeigned surrender of ourselves into the Lord's hands. Then shall there be joy in heaven over us among the angels of God; then shall we have an indubitable pledge and seal of our adoption into the family of God; and hereafter all tears shall be wiped away from our eyes.

19

The Journey to Ekron

B ut thou hast not called upon me, O Jacob; but thou hast
been weary of me, O Israel!" Isa. 43:22. I scarcely know a
more heart-affecting expression than this. It is the mournful language of a neglected and disregarded friend. And who is this
friend? It is he who is Love itself; it is the Father of mercies, the
Savior of sinners. Alas! who has more cause for such complaint than
himself! If anyone is forgotten, neglected, and mistaken on earth, it
is the compassionate Friend of penitent sinners! Yes, do not men
seem to have conspired to blot out the remembrance of him? The
church, which is called by his name, for the greater part, rejects him.
The larger number of the pastors of his flock will not hear his voice.
The seal of the Lamb, in the present day, is in many places a seal of
reproach. Decorum forbids even his name to be mentioned; social
life has cast out the Lord of glory as a disturber of its peace; science
increasingly disregards him in places very many; art dedicates its colors and its melody to other gods and most of the writings and books,
which are circulated through the world, boldly disclaim any connection or friendship with Him.

There is therefore sufficient reason for the mournful complaint
of the Holy One of Israel: "Thou hast not called upon me: thou hast
been weary of me!" And who can doubt that he has a right to make
this complaint, or that he has the very best claim upon our affectionate remembrance? Behold, he took our nature upon him; he
became a man of unparalleled sorrows; his head was crowned with
thorns; he was crucified for us! Yes, out of free love to sinners, he
yielded up himself, that he might be our Surety and Representative,
standing in our place, and bearing our punishment; and, be

astonished, O ye heavens! regarding as parts of his own mystical body every individual whom he has redeemed. Yes, that he might associate us with himself in his glory, he associated himself with us in his death. He caused our sins to be placed to his account, that he might clothe us with his virtues; he suffered himself to be crushed beneath our curse, that he might raise us to his own glory. Behold, this has he done for us! What do you think then? Does he require too much of us in requiring us to remember him, to call upon him, and not to be weary of him? This requirement he makes of everyone of us. May the heart of everyone be open to receive it, and to comply with it! For, are there none among us to whom it may be said, You no longer wish to remember Him and to be in communion with him, as you once did? You have forgotten your first love. Once you seemed to wait upon him, but now you love the world and the things that are in the world; preferring its husks before the bread of eternal life. Is it not so? "Return, thou back-sliding Israel, saith the Lord." O think upon what he has done for you; how he has preserved you; how he has delivered you. There was a time when you believed that the Lord had done it. But now you have forgotten this, and forgotten even the Lord himself. But his memory is not like yours. Lo! he stands before you, and complains that you have not called upon him, but have been weary of him. O listen to this word of the most condescending mercy and the most astonishing love! The infinitely holy Creator addresses his sinful creature, saying, "Thou hast been weary of me, O Israel!" O smite upon your breast, and say, "God be merciful unto me a sinner." May our meditations on the subject now to be considered serve to impress these thoughts more indelibly upon our hearts!

2 Kings 1:2-4

And Ahaziah fell down through a lattice in his upper chamber that was in Samaria, and was sick: and he sent messengers, and said unto them, Go, inquire of Baal-zebub the God of Ekron whether I shall recover of this disease. But the angel of the Lord said to Elijah the Tishbite, Arise, go up to meet the messengers of the king of Samaria, and say unto them, Is it not because there is not a God in Israel, that ye go to inquire of Baal-zebub the god of Ekron? Now therefore thus saith the Lord, Thou shalt not come down from that bed on which thou art gone up, but shalt surely die. And Elijah departed.

This narrative may serve for a variety of serious reflections. We divide our meditation into three parts, showing; I. The application to Ekron; II. The Divine jealousy; and, III. The paramount claims of Jesus Christ.

The Application to Ekron

I. Israel had now changed its ruler. Ahab had fallen under the hand of the Lord, and the throne was filled by his son Ahaziah, a worthless character, who did only evil in the sight of the Lord, walking in the ways of his father and mother, and causing Israel to sin. He served Baal and worshipped him, and provoked the Lord God of Israel to anger, as his father Ahab had done. The Almighty therefore saw it not good to sheathe the sword of vengeance. The first painful stroke upon Ahaziah was the revolt of the Moabites. This people had for many years been tributary to the kings of Israel; but under Ahaziah, they rebelled, and conquered. We have now before us another visitation, which Ahaziah experienced. Standing one day on a balcony of his palace, the balustrade on which he leaned suddenly gave way. The king was precipitated to the ground, was seriously injured, and "was sick." The Lord not infrequently so arranges it, that his judgments lay hold of the ungodly and profane at the very time when they are most at ease. How often have we heard of men, who, with the cup of festivity in their hands, and the sound of the harp and the violin their ears, have been suddenly struck dead by the Divine hand, have fallen paralyzed to the ground, or been seized by some other catastrophe! The severity of God is then rendered the more apparent by the contrast between their revelry and their woe; and the cry against the vanity of the world, uttered by such judgments, is the more loudly and alarmingly heard, by reason of the sudden reverse.

Ahaziah lies sick; but, alas, we behold in him the same state of mind on his sick bed as we perceive in many others who come within our own observation. Here is only another proof of the melancholy truth, that the severest afflictions are ineffectual in themselves to soften the sinner's heart; and thus we see that the power which converts the soul does not consist in misfortunes or any outward events, but solely in the mercy and grace of God. How much had Ahaziah heard and seen in his father's time, which, humanly speaking, might have led him to repentance! How remarkably had the Almighty revealed himself again in Israel, and what terrific proofs had he given of his severity and jealousy! Though all this must have been fresh in Ahaziah's memory, yet he acts as if such awful realities, with his own father's fearful end, had been only an idle tale, and instead of humbling himself before the living God, his heart still cleaves to idolatry. He sends to the Philistine oracle at Ekron, where men worshipped an idol named Baal-zebub, that is, the lord of flies, probably so named because the plague of flies, which was common in that region, was attributed to his displeasure; or else, because he was honored as a protector from that plague. The idol of Ekron was supposed to give oracular answer, through the medium of its priests, respecting future events ; and it had obtained such general credence, that it was resorted to from a considerable distance. That the predictions there uttered, and the prodigies there exhibited, were not merely the illusions of priestcraft, but were founded upon some reality, and were connected with infernal influence, can hardly be doubted. Pagan idolatry in general seems to be supported and maintained by infernal magic. When, in the Divine judgments upon antichrist and his kingdom, Satan shall suffer that signal defeat which is denounced against him in the word of God, it will be found that it was he who created and maintained the worship of idols, and that it was from his agency that the kingdom of darkness and falsehood received its principal support. And when heathenism shall become bereaved of this satanical support, then will the eyes of the blind world be opened, and men will be astonished how they could have adhered for thousands of years to a mere nonentity, and will come from the east and the west to worship the Lord in Zion.

The idol at Ekron and his oracle was the first remedy that the sick king at Samaria could think of. He assembled his servants about him, and proceeded by their means to an act of impiety as great as could be committed in Israel. "Go," said he, openly and shamelessly, "inquire of Baal-zebub the god of Ekron, whether I shall recover of this disease." Conduct such as this of Ahaziah cannot outwardly be imitated by ourselves, because gross idolatry has long ceased to exist in this part of the globe, and the polite world is too enlightened to consult the devil in person, having long held Satan and hell to be merely the puerile notions of antiquity. Yet after all, we find, upon closer inspection, that even our own philosophic age is full of that heathen leaven, though it is now molded into a more refined form;

and experience shows that disbelief of the "sure word of prophecy" only leads into new superstition. It is true, the presentiment of an invisible world, and the necessity of entering it, is indelibly impressed upon the human mind. But those who scorn to submit this feeling to the rule of Scripture, and to seek satisfaction in the divinely revealed record, are sure to sink under the dominion of darkness and imposture.

As a counterpart to the oracle at Ekron and Endor, we have, in the present day, visionaries and somnambulists; instead of the Delphic tripod and the Dodonian oak, we have pretended prophets and seers, gurus, whose numbers are greater among the people than is generally supposed; and if we are above believing these, still we have our forebodings, our presentiments, and our dreams, of which many are apt to make as much as of the Divine oracles. The place of the ancient heathen mysteries is occupied by a multitude of secret associations, in whose mystic obscurities thousands seek those disclosures which they refuse to accept from the hand of the living God; and though they can smile with scorn at the magicians of antiquity, they do not think it beneath them to have recourse to amulets and charms, to which popular belief ascribe mysterious powers; or to endeavor to cure diseases by what are called sympathetic remedies. But suppose we are free from such superstitions, still when we hear a mother entreating the physician to save her child, and when, upon anyone referring to the blessing of God for success, offense is taken at this reference, is not this the same spirit as we see in Ahaziah? Is not this a running after idols, an idolatry of means? Yet how common is this among us! How many are there who have never seriously thought of applying to the God of Israel—and who seem to know of no other God in their necessities and embarrassments, except the creature—dust and ashes! But woe unto those who give to idols the glory which belongs to God alone! That the Lord does not regard such conduct with indifference, the sequel of this narrative will teach us.

The Divine Jealousy

II. What then became of Ahaziah? He sent to Ekron, to inquire of Baal-zebub; but instead of the lying voice of the idol, he hears the awful words of the living God. The angel of Jehovah directs Elijah the Tishbite to "go up to meet the messengers of the king of Samaria, and to say unto them, Is it not because there is not a God in Israel, that ye go to inquire of Baal-zebub the god of Ekron? Now therefore thus saith the Lord, Thou shalt not come down from that bed on which thou art gone up, but shalt surely die." It is Christ, the Angel Jehovah, who spoke thus to Elijah. Why it was he is not difficult to understand. Jehovah Immanuel had the greatest cause for being displeased at Ahaziah's impiety! He had done everything to gain the hearts of men, and to lead them to the most entire confidence in himself. During a series of ages he had visited his people Israel with manifestations of the most condescending kindness and love. Even in the times of the patriarchs, he had shown how his "delights were with the sons of men," and how ready he was to assist them with his counsel in all their affairs; not only with means ordained by himself, but even without means upon many and various occasions. He had revealed himself as "a very present help" to those who sincerely sought him; and had shown his loving-kindness in such a manner, that it seemed as if he lived for their sakes. Yet Israel revolted from him, and resorted to idols. This was indeed a heinous offense, and justly provoked his displeasure. He therefore appeared himself, to complain of the ingratitude, and with how much reason does he send word to the messengers, saying, "Is it because there is no God in Israel, that ye go to inquire of Baal-zebub, the god of Ekron?"

We can imagine with what difficulty some will be persuaded that it was indeed the eternal God who here appeared to Elijah, and spoke to him as the children of men speak. But we must learn to know him in his deepest humiliation, in the manger and on the cross, and become acquainted with him in that love in which he was willing to become despised, and rejected in the eyes of men, in order to bring us to glory; and in which he devoted himself to death as the Lamb of God, that he might obtain for us eternal redemption by his blood. When we have once become acquainted with him in these profound humiliations, his other condescensions will no longer astonish us. He who has seen that which is greater, ceases to be perplexed at that which is less.

Nor let anyone be offended, because the mighty God appears in this history as *provoked*, at inquiry being made at Ekron, instead of being addressed to Himself. Blessed be his grace! it is because of the greatness of his love that he is not indifferent how we are affected toward him. He wishes to be beloved by his people; and not this only, but with wonderful and most condescending kindness, and with a holy jealousy, he watches over our love to him, and desires to possess it entirely. Yes; his children may well be on their guard against dividing their hearts between God and mammon. He will not suffer it, but will rather use severity even toward those who are as the apple of his eye. He will come with the rod, and chastise them; or he will tear from their arms the objects which rob him of his place in their hearts. For he seeks to possess their whole hearts; and how blessed are we, when He who alone is worthy of our supreme love, has obtained it!

The Paramount Claims of Jesus Christ

III. And as he desires our love, entire and undivided, so it is his will that our confidence for peace and strength should be reposed in himself alone. Immanuel must be *all in all* to us. When Moses said, in the spirit of prophecy, Deut. 33:8, "Let thy thummim and thy urim, O Levi, (let thy light and thy righteousness,) be with thy Holy One, whom thou didst prove at Massah, and with whom thou didst strive at the waters of Meribah"; doubtless he refers to Christ. It is as much as to say, "O Levi, do not seek thy light, and thy perfections or thy righteousness, elsewhere; do not sever thy high priesthood from Messiah; do not go to any other for thine oracles." But how does this apply to us? I answer, Surely a separation of the urim and thummim from the Holy One is effected, when we are no longer satisfied with him alone; when we consult human inventions for our help and comfort, instead of walking in the simplicity of honoring the Lord Christ; when we seek to be our own priests and to atone for ourselves, instead of letting all our light, and righteousness, and perfection rest with our Holy One.

There are no complaints more commonly heard among believers, than of the poor work they make of praying, praising, and thanksgiving. Hence they become painfully afraid, lest their poor utterances should never obtain a hearing. But remember the great Intercessor, who stands day and night before God, to receive the petitions of his people, and to present them before the throne. Remember also that the sufferings and death of Christ, his obedience and righteousness— even the whole sum of his infinite and precious merits—make intercession for you, and, as it were, pray with you. Wherefore, believer, if you can only utter three words before God, if your very voice seems stifled at the foot of his throne, yet remember that he loves you with the same love with which he loved his Son; and, as often as you pray, hold fast this confidence. Remember that your great intercessor prays with you and for you, and that your prayers ascend through his righteousness. This will give unction to your petitions, and whatsoever you ask you will receive of him.

In the breastplate of the high priest were set twelve precious stones, engraved with the names of the twelve tribes of Israel. Thus these names were surrounded with glory and beauty; and as they served to typify the spiritual glory and beauty which, all the Israel of God possess in their true High Priest, Christ Jesus; so they may serve to remind us not to separate our sanctification from Christ; but to let it rest entirely with him. Thus let your urim and thummim be with the Holy One. But alas! in how many ways is this precept forgotten by professed Christians, and how many systems and methods are there which disagree with it! Proud self-sufficient man, in his hereditary depravity, would live without dependence upon Him who is made unto us of God, not only wisdom and righteousness, but sanctification also, 1 Cor. 1:30. How many who call themselves Christians are righteous in their own eyes, and pure in their own sight! And what a system of iniquity has been built up for ages in support of this delusion! Devotees to this system think, by the accomplishment of a certain daily task of religious exercises, to make themselves perfect in the sight of God. Such is the system of popery. There are many who seek their excellence in a variety of outward observances, and would gladly persuade themselves and others that they are purified from every spot of sin. But how little do they know the depth of their own natural corruption, or the infinite holiness of God! Whereas the foundation of all our hope and confidence ought to be only the perfection of our Surety, Christ Jesus. The faith of the heart in his imputed righteousness is the only true spring and principle of all Christian virtue. Its clothing is humility, its fruit is love, its aim is the glory of God.

When counsel was asked of God in Israel, application was made to the High Priest, who, by the urim and thummim, obtained a Divine answer. In like manner let us act, and not make ourselves our own counselors. When we are anxious as to what we shall eat, what we shall drink, and wherewithal we shall be clothed, what are we doing? Is our High Priest dead, and are you constrained to bear the official breastplate yourselves? Cast your cares upon him, and He

will be your Counselor. Don't allow this or that particular event to
confuse or startle you; all will come to pass as the great Prophet of the
church has predicted. Look around you upon this present world from
the strong ground of His word, and you will find firm footing amid
the whirl of daily occurrences: you will understand, in some salutary
measure, the book of providence, and will look forward with joy to
the finishing of the mystery of God. The eye of the Christian looks
over the gloomy foreground into the golden distances which lie
behind, and sees the dawn of jubilee fringing with rosy edges the
clouds of the present scene of things. Lastly, let our whole wisdom be
with Christ. Let us cleave to the sure word of prophecy, so much the
more courageously and faithfully, as the father of lies shall make
greater efforts to seduce us from our citadel, and to strip us of our
Divine armor. Away with that philosophy and science which are
falsely so called; away with the dreams of modern illuminati; away
with all vain pretensions to spiritual gifts, and abide in that which
you have heard from the beginning. "Keep that which is committed
unto you; but shun profane and vain babblings!" Let your light and
your righteousness, your knowledge and your wisdom, rest with the
Holy One, even Christ.

Remember that as the names of the children of Israel were
inscribed on the precious stones of the high priest's breastplate, so our
Savior bears the names of all his children upon his heart; and that as
their names are laid upon him by the Father, so Christ's name is laid
upon them. "As the Father hath loved me, so have I loved you." Let
us rejoice in this for "as he is, so are we in this world." In Him therefore who died for us we can triumph, and say, "Who shall lay any
thing to the charge of God's elect? It is God that justifieth. Who is
he that condemneth? It is Christ that died, yea rather, that is risen
again." In him who is risen again, "who is even at the right hand of
God, who also maketh, intercession for us," we can triumph and say,
"O death, where is thy sting? O grave, where is thy victory?"

Let not unbelief, therefore, let not spiritual barrenness, let not
cold-hearted prayers, or any adverse occurrence, deprive us of the
enjoyment of him, so as to make us doubt his love, and utter the
unbelieving complaint, "The Lord hath forsaken me, and my God
hath forgotten me." Let us assuredly believe in the unchangeableness
of his love, and thus be preserved in cheerful obedience and resignation. Let us become accustomed to regard ourselves as bound to

the heart of our great Mediator; and commit to him who thus bears our names before God the whole care of our safety and happiness. Of all that the Father has given him will he lose nothing.

Let us not, then, burden ourselves with matters which God has as little imposed upon us as we are fitted for them. Let us commit all our affairs to our great Shepherd, Mediator, and Intercessor, and, leaning on his almighty arm, go on our way rejoicing. It is thus he would have us to act, and thus he fulfills in us the blessing of the prophet, "Let thy urim and thy thummim be with thy Holy One!" Remember that he is, and ever shall be, "all and in all." As he is "made of God unto us wisdom, righteousness, sanctification, and redemption"; to look after any other and than that which is prepared for us in him is vile ingratitude, an insult offered him, a crime against his majesty. Cursed, therefore, be the paths that lead to Endor and to Ekron! The feet must fail and be maimed that are found on these roads! There is a God in Israel! who—be astonished, O heavens!— full of salvation, righteousness, and aid, will supply all our need! To whom do we owe all our love and confidence, but to him? O let us be dissolved in tears of joy before our King; and "Let thy urim and thy thummim ever be with thy Holy One, O Levi!" Amen.

20

The Preaching by Fire

The vital energy of the church of God upon earth manifests itself in a threefold activity, directed to the three great objects of self-renovation, union, and extension. Of this threefold operation of the true church Paul speaks, in Eph. 2:20-22.

By self-renovation, we understand the effort of the church to expel from within her every foreign and unscriptural element that may have crept in; to remove errors from her midst; and to build herself up on the true foundation of the prophets' and apostles' doctrine, "Jesus Christ himself being the chief corner stone."

By her endeavors after union, we understand that activity of the true church by which she seeks to combine believers more closely together, and to promote more and more their growing up into him, who is the Head, even Christ; "in whom all the building fitly framed together, groweth unto an holy temple in the Lord."

By missionary activity, the church endeavors to enlarge her boundaries, to recover new provinces from the prince of darkness, to increase the number of her children, whether from the heathen or the nominally Christian world, and to build then together on the same foundation, "for an habitation of God through the Spirit."

Now wherever the true church exists she invariably manifests this threefold vital activity; but sometimes one indication of it predominates over the rest. In some places, for instance, the doctrines of the majority are correct and scriptural, and the church has rather to devote her powers to the growth and union of her children. But, in general, her self-renovating activity is what is most required, and her work is to lay afresh those foundations which the father of lies has subverted.

The prophet Elijah was an eminent reformer of the Old Testament church. The restoration of idolatrous Israel to the faith of their forefathers was the commission entrusted to him; in his time, therefore, the church appears in the activity of self-renovation. We should keep this in view as we meditate upon the events of his life, and thus, we shall better understand the peculiar character of some of those events. That part of his history in particular which is now before us, will hereby become divested of the strangeness of its first appearance.

2 Kings 1:5-17

And when the messengers turned back unto him, he said unto them, Why are ye now turned back? And they said unto him, There came a man up to meet us, and said unto us, Go, turn again unto the king that sent you, and say unto him, Thus saith the Lord, Is it not because in Israel, that thou sendest to inquire of Baal-zebub the god of Ekron? therefore thou shalt not come down from that bed on which thou art gone up, but shalt surely die. And he said unto them, What manner of man was he which came up to meet you, and told you these words? And they answered him, He was an hairy man, and girt with a girdle of leather about his loins. And he said, It is Elijah the Tishbite. Then the king sent unto him a captain of fifty with his fifty. And he went up to him: and, behold, he sat on the top of an hill. And he spake unto him, Thou man of God, the king hath said, Come down. And Elijah answered and said to the captain of fifty, If I be a man of God, then let fire come down from heaven, and consume thee and thy fifty. And there came down fire from heaven, and consumed him and his fifty. Again also he sent unto him another captain of fifty with his fifty. And he answered and said unto him, O man of God, thus hath the king said, Come down quickly. And Elijah answered and said unto them, If I be a man of God, let fire come down from heaven, and consume thee and thy fifty. And the fire of God came down from heaven, and consumed him and his fifty. And the third captain of fifty went up, and came on his knees before Elijah, and besought him, and said unto him, O man of God, I pray thee, let my life, and the life of these fifty thy servants, be precious in thy sight. Behold, there came fire down from heaven, and burnt up the two captains of the former fifties with their fifties: therefore let my life now be precious in thy sight. And the angel of the Lord said unto Elijah, Go down with him: be not afraid of him. And he arose, and went down with him unto the king. And he said unto him, Thus saith the Lord, Forasmuch as thou hast sent messengers to inquire of Baal-zebub the god of Ekron, is it not because there is no God in Israel to inquire of his word? therefore thou shalt not come down off that bed on which thou art gone up, but shalt surely die. So he died according to the word of the Lord which Elijah had spoken.

Thus ends the narrative which commenced with the mission to Ekron. "Our God is a consuming fire!" "God is not mocked!" "It is a fearful thing to fall into the hands of the living God!" Let us pause and consider the marvelous contest here related. Here is, I. Ahaziah's attempt against Elijah II. The prophet's victory; and, III. Ahaziah's awful overthrow.

Ahaziah's Attempt at Elijah

I. The messengers of the king are already on their way to Ekron. Leaving the guilt of their mission with their master's conscience, they proceed with alacrity on their journey, and have already settled in their own minds the time when they shall arrive at Ekron. But the Lord knows the thoughts of man, that they are vain. Another oracle comes forth to meet them, from a quarter quite unlooked for. All at once a living barrier stands in their way. A man suddenly appears before them, of a majestic figure, clothed in a hairy mantle. Here is no troop of angels, nor any mailed band of men; nothing but an individual fellow-man, without armor or weapons. Yet astonishment seizes the courtly messengers at the sight of him, and their train and equipage are obliged to halt. "The Tishbite!" is the word of alarm from one to the other; and, before they have time to inquire and advise together, the venerable stranger confronts them and discharges his Divine commission

"Is it not because there is not a God in Israel, that ye go to inquire of Baal-zebub the god of Ekron? return, and tell your master, Thus saith the Lord, Thou shalt not come down from that bed on which thou art gone up, but shalt surely die!" The stranger, having spoken these words, turned about and went his way. We may well imagine the consternation occasioned by this unexpected encounter; how the men looked fearfully at each other, and knew not what to say. Little had they dreamed of carrying back to their prince such a speedy

answer to his inquiry, and this too without money and without price.
But from whom does it come? Oh they are conscious that it comes
from an oracle who cannot lie. They have no heart to proceed on
their journey to Ekron; they dare not do it. They know too well this
terrible man, the fire-attested messenger of Jehovah's displeasure.
They turn about in haste, as if the least delay were dangerous, and
return with awful apprehensions to Samaria. Verily, it cannot
always be foreseen what may happen on such journeys as those to
Ekron or to Endor. It is a fearful thing to pass by God and his word,
and to turn aside to lying vanities. In courses like these, how many
have met with such disclosures as might well both make their ears
tingle, and their hearts quake? Many a one, by having recourse to
refuges of lies, has forever lost sight of the light of truth, and lived
and died under strong delusions. Let us, therefore, never forget the
exhortation of the apostle: "Little children, abide in him; that, when
he shall appear, we may have confidence, and not be ashamed before
him at his coming," 1 John 2:28.

The Prophet's Victory

II. King Ahaziah, lying upon his couch, supposes his messengers
to be on the road to Ekron. But, lo! unexpectedly the door of his
apartment opens, and the messengers stand before his bed. Almost
before he has time to wonder what this can mean, they begin to
relate to him what has happened to them on the way. "There came
a man up to meet us, and said unto us, Go, turn again unto the king
that sent you, and say unto him, Thus saith the Lord, Is it not
because there is not a God in Israel, that thou sendest to inquire of
Baal-zebub the god of Ekron? therefore thou shalt not come down
from that bed on which thou art gone up, but shalt surely die."
Terrific as was this message, the king collects himself sufficiently to
inquire, "What manner of man was he which came up to meet you,
and told you these words?" "He was an hairy man," answered they,
"and girt with a girdle of leather about his loins." This portrait was
well known to the king. "Yes," says he, with as much composure as
he could assume, "I thought so; it is Elijah the Tishbite!"

The king dismisses his messengers. "Send me hither one of my
captains," cries he, with stifled fury and resentment. The captain
appears in the sick man's chamber, and reads in the features of his
lord the nature of his commission. "Go, with your troop," says

Ahaziah, "seize Elijah the Tishbite, and bring him to me!" The captain bows obediently, and hastens to fulfill the king's orders. Let us reflect a moment on the monstrous presumption which the sick monarch here exhibits! He knows who the man is whom he is about to attack. He has seen the mighty acts with which the Lord had borne testimony to this his own messenger. He knows that God had a second time, in Elijah's case, "hearkened to the voice of a man," and that this redoubted champion of truth has the Almighty himself for his shield; yea, that the thunder and fiery flame of heaven has been at his command. Yet all this does not prevent him from taking the field against the prophet, and thus virtually declaring war against the King of kings. Impiety renders him frantic, and his feverish fury robs him of his understanding. A handful of chaff would now contend with the fire, and a fleeting vapor would combat with the storm. Surely all this is no longer merely natural. Strong satanical delusion has taken possession of this senseless transgressor, and it is evident that he is become judicially blind.

The captain with his fifty departs upon his commission, and it is not long before he meets the enemy. On the summit of a mountain— probably on Carmel—they come in sight of the prophet. There he sits, solitary and silent, immersed in sacred meditations. But he sits there, like a king upon his throne, secure in his God, and surrounded by an invisible guard. He beholds the host approaching him with glittering weapons, and easily imagines who has sent them, and what is their errand. But he is not afraid, in his invisible but impregnable fortress. He is well able to confront them under the banner of his God, and quietly suffers them to come against him. They approach nearer and nearer, to surround him as their prisoner; but something in his appearance, or in their thoughts of him, keeps them still at a respectful distance. It seems as if they had a presentiment of peril, should they venture to seize him. The captain, therefore, contents himself with imperatively declaring His master's order: "Thou man of God, the king hath said, Come down." The prophet feels a holy indignation for the honor of his God. He opens his mouth with a faith which would have removed mount Carmel into the midst of the sea, had it been necessary, and exclaims, "If I be a man of God, then let fire come down from heaven, and consume thee and thy fifty!" No sooner had he uttered the words, than Jehovah heard them; for to prayers which seek only his honor and glory he refuses not his Yea and Amen! The fire descends from heaven, and the captain, with his fifty, lie dead below the prophet's feet.

When this terrible event is notified to the king of Israel, he becomes so infatuated with rage that instead of perceiving what power he was fighting against, he sends forth a second captain with his fifty, seemingly more daring than the first; who finds Elijah still in the same place. He draws near, at the head of his fifty, to the servant of the Lord, and with astonishing presumption, addresses him, in sight of the slain around him, "O man of God, thus hath the king said, Come down quickly." "If I be a man of God," answers Elijah the second time, "let fire come down from heaven, and consume thee and thy fifty!" And the fire of God came down from heaven, and consumed him and his fifty.

One would suppose that the intelligence of this second defeat would have caused a change in Ahaziah's mind, and have induced him to conclude a truce in this impious war; but, no! he is resolved to hold it out to the last. He sends out a third captain with his fifty, for the purpose of bringing the prophet to him as his prisoner. The captain departs with his company of soldiers, and there is a fearful prospect of the wrathful judgment being repeated a third time. Elijah still sits in the same place upon his eminence. He is not afraid of many thousands; for he knows that he has sufficient strength in his God to lay any army in the dust that might come against him. But when the third captain, at the head of his company, arrives at the mount, and beholds the man of God, and the dead bodies of the slain lying below, he is seized with a feeling of reverential dread, which he in vain labors to overcome. He feels that it is bearing arms against the Almighty himself to bear them against his ambassador; and, overpowered by the awe with which the presence of the holy man inspired him, and by the conviction that Elijah's God is the true God, he puts up his sword into the scabbard, approaches the prophet with reverence, falls on his knee before him, and exclaims, "O man of God, I pray thee, let my life and the life of these fifty thy servants, be precious in thy sight. Behold there came fire down from heaven, and burnt up the two captains of the former fifties with their fifties: therefore let my life now be precious in thy sight!"

Oh how must Elijah have rejoiced at this submission to the living God, which saved him from the mournful necessity of vindicating the honor of Jehovah a third time with consuming flames of fire! For he had no pleasure in the death of the wicked; but it was his delight, even as it is the delight of his Lord, that the sinner should turn from his ways and live. Doubtless it caused him no little pain, when he was compelled to call for the sword of the Almighty to be unsheathed, and his fire from heaven to descend. But when this did take place, it was his divine vocation; and the holy object of his mission required it, for the extermination of idolatry, and the re-establishment of that Divine law which had been trodden under foot, and of that faith of the fathers which had become extinct. The weapons of Elijah's warfare were, therefore, not carnal. They were wielded by that queen of passions—an ardent love to God and his cause—and they were brandished in obedience to a holy zeal for the glory of Jehovah's name. It was because the canker of idolatry had eaten so deeply into the heart of the chosen people, that such severe remedies were required for the healing of the people.

In considering such narratives as the present, we should ever remember that the times of the Old Testament were very different from those of the Christian dispensation; and that much which it became Elijah to perform would be far from proper for a subject of the new covenant. Our Savior, in Luke 9:54-56, expresses himself significantly as to the distinction between the old dispensation and the new. When the disciples, James and John, said to him, "Lord, wilt thou that we command fire to fall from heaven, and consume them even as Elias did?" our Lord replied, "Ye know not what manner of spirit ye are of. For the Son of man is not come to destroy men's lives, but to save them!" It seems as if he had intimated that the days of severity were past, and that those of mildness had succeeded them.

The discipline of mount Sinai no longer bears the rule; but patience and love. Elijah was a herald of Divine justice, and therefore he necessarily appeared with lightning and thunder on his lips; but we are messengers of grace, who must gain the hearts of sinners by the gospel of the tender mercy of God; and thus our feet must be "beautiful upon the mountains." And, as the patience wherewith the vessels of wrath are endured, has ever since shown that a hand once pierced sways the scepter of the world's government, and that a Friend of sinners sits on the throne of dominion; so ought the New Testament church to exhibit a faithful likeness of the gentle and patient Lamb of God, in whose blood they have been made clean, and who, through enduring and suffering, entered into glory. The lovely image of the compassionate therefore infinitely more becomes us, as followers of the Lamb. The Son of man ought always to be visible in his members. It is better to pray for the enemies of his righteous cause, than to invoke God's displeasure upon them. It is unspeakably more befitting us, in patience and meekness, to heap coals of fire on the heads of our adversaries, and to overcome them by the power of love, than to call down the wrath of the Almighty upon them. In short, our whole disposition and conduct ought to evince that we are the disciples of Him who "came not to destroy men's lives, but to save them"; and that, by the cross of Christ, a fountain of love has been disclosed, which has taught us to bear all things, to believe all things, and endure all things; a love which many waters cannot quench.

The Awful Overthrow of Ahaziah

III. The captain, having humbly besought Elijah that his soul, and the souls of his fifty, might be precious in his sight, was spared. For God resists only the proud and the perverse; but gives grace to the lowly. The Lord said to Elijah "Go down with him: be not afraid of him." What a command! what a mission! He was now to enter into the very midst of the enemy's camp, and repeat to the enraged king, at Samaria, the judgment of Heaven. But the command and implied promise of his God lifts him up, as on eagle's wings, above every fear. He leaves the lonely hills, and hastens, at the captain's side, to the royal city.

As a conqueror enters the gates of some captured fortress, amid the waving of victorious banners, so did Elijah enter the city of Samaria. He knew that in the assembling crowds around him there were few who were not his adversaries; yet he walks through them with a dignity that curbs the insolence of the boldest blasphemer. The king, perhaps, is impatiently inquiring whether there be any news of the arrival of his prisoner; when, lo! the door of his apartment opens; and who can describe Ahaziah's amazement at beholding the object of his hatred—the man with the hairy mantle and the leathern girdle, himself approaching his couch? Yet Elijah utters no hard word, no triumphant taunt. He knows that in this ungodly man he still beholds his lawful monarch and chief magistrate. Elijah knows that "the powers that be are ordained of God"; and hence, though he is the Lord's prophet, and standing before an apostate and idolatrous king, he in no way trespasses upon the respect due to royal dignity. He adheres strictly and literally to the message entrusted to him by the Lord; and, without adding to it or taking from it, he declares, "Thus saith the Lord, Forasmuch as thou hast sent messengers to inquire of Baal-zebub the god of Ekron; is it not because there is no God in Israel to inquire of his word? therefore thou shalt not come down off that bed on which thou art gone up, but shalt surely die!" Elijah, having thus spoken, departed. But the words he had uttered remained behind. "He died," says the sacred historian, "according to the word of the Lord which Elijah had spoken." The church of God on earth had one destroyer less, and hell one victim more!

"In Judah is God known," sings the sacred psalmist: "his name is great in Israel. In Salem also is his tabernacle, and his dwelling-place in Zion. There brake he the arrows of the bow, the shield, and the sword, and the battle. Selah. Thou art more glorious and excellent than the mountains of prey. The stout-hearted are spoiled, they have slept their sleep: and none of the men of might have found their hands. At thy rebuke, O God of Jacob, both the chariot and horse are cast into a dead sleep. Thou, even thou, art to be feared: and who may stand in thy sight when once thou art angry? Thou didst cause judgment to be heard from heaven; the earth feared, and was still, when God arose to judgment, to save all the meek of the earth. Selah. Surely the wrath of men shall praise thee: the remainder of wrath shalt thou restrain. Vow, and pay unto the Lord your God: let all that be round about him bring presents unto him that ought to be feared. He shall cut off the spirit of princes: he is terrible to the kings of the earth," Psalm 76.

Hallelujah: To him be the glory and the kingdom forever and ever! Amen.

21

The Work-Day Evening

Sacred history may be regarded as a Divine prediction, which is as yet only in part fulfilled. When we are grieved with the present sad and gloomy state of things, we may well resort to these pleasing oracles, which set forth in type as well as in prophecy the representation of future and better times. For with reference to all that formerly took place that was beautiful or glorious, in the land where Israel sojourned, it may be said, "The thing that hath been, it is that which shall be," Eccl. 1:9. From the history of Eden, down to that of the glorious Pentecostal church, every happy event recorded shall ultimately be renewed in a far more glorious manner. May this certainty cheer and animate us as we approach, in the history of Elijah, one of the most glorious events to which Divine grace ever gave birth before the Christian era.

2 Kings 2:1-6

> And it came to pass, when the Lord would take up Elijah into heaven by a whirlwind, that Elijah went with Elisha from Gilgal. And Elijah said unto Elisha, Tarry here, I pray thee; for the Lord hath sent me to Bethel. And Elisha said unto him, As the Lord liveth, and as thy soul liveth, I will not leave thee. So they went down to Beth-el. And the sons of the prophets that were at Beth-el came forth to Elisha, and said unto him, Knowest thou that the Lord will take away thy master from thy head to day? And he said, Yea, I know it; hold ye your peace. And Elijah said unto him, Elisha, tarry here, I pray thee; for the Lord hath sent me to Jericho. And he said, As the Lord liveth, and as thy soul liveth, I will not leave thee. So they came to Jericho. And the sons of the prophets that were at Jericho came to Elisha, and said unto

him, Knowest thou that the Lord will take away thy master from thy head to day? And he answered, Yea, I know it; hold ye your peace. And Elijah said unto him, tarry, I pray thee, here; lo, the Lord hath sent me to Jordan. And he said, As the Lord liveth: and as thy soul liveth, I will not leave thee. And they two went on.

The prophet has finished his work upon earth, and the stormy labors of the day are followed by a beautiful evening, tinged with the golden light of another and a blissful world. He is like the mariner, who, after a long and perilous voyage, is now in sight of his harbor, and joyfully hastens to strike his top-masts and take in his sails. He walks for a few days longer, as if already within hearing of the music of heaven; and can now gratefully recount some of the fruits of his labors, for they begin to manifest themselves more clearly to his view. The events we are now about to consider will form a pleasing contrast to his past history, and will serve to remind us of that happy period when the enigmas of this life will all be explained in the most satisfactory manner, and its temporary discords resolved into the most exquisite harmony.

Three points in the passage before us are especially worthy of our notice: I. Elijah's desire for retirement; II. His visits to the schools of the prophets; and, III. The reception he meets with there.

Elijah's Desire to Retire

I. Elijah had withdrawn from more public notice into the secluded neighborhood of the Jordan. We find him at present in the little town of Gilgal, not far from Jericho, on that memorable spot where Joshua, after the miraculous passage of the river, set up the twelve stones, and dedicated them as a lasting memorial of the Divine mercy and faithfulness; "that all the people of the earth might know the hand of the Lord, that it is mighty." If ever these ancient words had deeply affected Elijah, and inspired his mind with renewed vigor, it must surely have been now; when his own situation, in many respects, so strikingly resembled that of his forefathers. If those massy stones were still remaining, as in all probability they were, how must he have felt at the sight of them! He also might erect his Ebenezer near them, and consecrate it with tears of sweet and humble thankfulness. For how frequently had he himself been led by the hand of the Almighty through an overflowing Jordan!

The prophet has now completed his pilgrimage. He knows it by a Divine revelation. The horses of fire and the flaming chariot stand already prepared behind the clouds to catch him away; nor has the Lord concealed from him the distinguished manner in which he is about to be taken home. He therefore goes from Gilgal to Bethel, to bid a last farewell to his dear children, the sons of the prophets. He hoped to have made this journey alone; but scarcely had he taken his staff, when Elisha appears ready to join him. However much he wished to be alone at this time, he loved his faithful friend too dearly to reject his society at once. They therefore set out together; but they had not gone on long, before Elijah is unable to conceal his desire for solitude. He therefore says to him, "Tarry here, I pray thee; for the Lord hath sent me to Bethel." But no! Elisha cannot this time accede to the wish of his venerable master. "As the Lord liveth, and as thy soul liveth," replied he, "I will not leave thee"; and they proceed together on their way. Twice again at Bethel and at Jericho—Elijah repeats his request with increasing urgency, "Tarry here, I pray thee; for the Lord hath sent me to Jordan." But all such entreaties were of no avail. Elisha persisted in affirming, "I will not leave thee."

This urgent wish of Elijah to be alone is not difficult to explain. He knew what a great distinction the Lord intended for him, such as from the beginning of the world had never been conferred on any saint of God but once; and what was even Enoch's triumph compared with that of the Tishbite? Elijah was not only to be translated into heaven by a way which passed not through the gates of death; but this translation was also to take place visibly, with a glory never before witnessed. A whirlwind was to accompany it; a fiery chariot from another world was provided to fetch the prophet home. He probably knew the day and the hour when this would occur. Only consider this deliberately, and you will be ready to wonder that he did not sink under the weight of such an expectation. How must he have felt, when, lifting up his eyes to the heavens, and looking at the stars in the firmament, he would say to himself, "Behold, in a few days I shall be passing through those heavens, far beyond the Orion and the Pleiades, far beyond the sun and the moon; and then—oh then I shall enter into the very sanctuary of heaven, into the eternal light of day, where the triune Jehovah sits on his throne, where the angels strike their harps, and the patriarchs dwell in their peaceful tabernacle. Then I shall see all the ancient fathers—Noah and Enoch, Methuselah and Melchizedek, and the father of the faithful, and Moses, and the psalmist, the man after God's own heart; and dwell among them forever! I shall hear them speak of the times of their pilgrimage and of a thousand tokens of God's loving-kindness—yea, and I shall behold the King of kings and Lord of lords, even Jehovah himself!" Is it any wonder that in the midst of such thoughts, even the company of his dearest friend was too much for him? Especially when he reflected upon who he was, that the Lord should vouchsafe to him such a distinction, and when, with the exaltation that awaited him, he also remembered his past life, which, though the Lord had enriched it with great glory, was yet but the life of a poor sinner, stained by many sins and defects; how must such reflections have induced him to seek to be alone with his God! He had had much spiritual experience since he had been employed in the Lord's service; but surely never could his thoughts have been so exalted as at present. What wonder was it he should wish to pour out his soul alone with God? The vessel of a human heart was too narrow for it, though it were the heart of a friend. How much had he to reflect upon, to confess, to mourn over; and how much cause too for thanksgiving and praise! Whether Elisha comprehended this, we do not know. He would certainly have done his master an acceptable service had he complied with his request and remained behind. Nothing however could induce him to do so. He was firmly resolved not to leave him.

But there was still something else, which induced Elijah to wish for the absence of his friend; a something, which, if this man of God had not already won our best affections, could not fail to incline our hearts to him. It was humility, which influenced Elijah in wishing to decline the company of his friend. O thou noble Tishbite, how does your greatness cause us to be ashamed of ourselves! Who desires to be nothing, that God may be everything, and trembles at the thought of being taken for anything more than a dim shadow of the glory of Jehovah! Concealing the secret of your approaching triumph within your own bosom, you flee the eye of witnesses, and are anxious to veil your glory, lest anyone should praise and admire, instead of the Sun, the little dewdrop, in which his image is reflected! And yet you had not seen Him who spake: "I am meek and lowly in heart;"—"I seek not my own honor, but His, that sent me." We indeed have seen and known the Beloved of the Father: and yet how much more is there of His image to be seen in you, than in us!—"Tarry here, I pray thee; for the Lord hath sent me to Bethel!"—Yes, we understand your request, and are ashamed for ourselves!

Oh I know not anything more lovely than those Christians, who are thus humble in their own eyes; who are so deeply conscious of their great unworthiness, that they fear, with a holy anxiety, lest what is the fruit of free and unmerited grace be in any wise attributed to themselves and their own godliness! Oh that there were also among us many such truly modest and humble characters! For these find favor even with the unconverted world.

Thrice—at Gilgal, at Bethel, and at Jericho—did Elijah, with increasing importunity, entreat his companion to leave him; the Lord having directed him first to one place and then to another. Thrice does Elijah receive the same decided reply, "As the Lord liveth, and as thy soul liveth, I will not leave thee." Elijah was therefore obliged to yield to the determination of his friend. And doubtless he was the more ready to acquiesce in it, as we might infer, from Elisha's language, that the Lord had revealed to him the secret of his approaching exaltation, and that he had received Divine direction to accompany his departing master to the borders of Jordan, perhaps that he might afterwards be able to bear testimony of this wonder to the world. It appears likely that this was the case, and that it was this which induced him to say, "As the Lord liveth, and as thy soul liveth, I will not leave thee." The great and glorious things which the Lord performs among men must not be hidden in a corner. In dire time they must be published upon the housetops, and contribute to make known the honor of Him who will fill heaven and earth with his glory. Hence it often happens that he places secret witnesses about his children, even where they think themselves unobserved by any human eye. Thus, many a pious spirit enters heaven, supposing that no one knew anything of his life and experience, and even ignorant himself of the glory which God had shed around him. But after such holy persons have left this world, everything comes to light; the Lord removes the veil which concealed their real character, and it is made known to the praise of his grace, as well as for the encouragement of surviving brethren, how mighty the power of God was in their weakness, and how much the Lord had accomplished in them and through them. Hence the memory of the just becomes blessed even on earth, and they live in the affectionate recollections of many.

"Their works do follow them." They leave a sweet savor here below, and cheer, and animate many surviving imitators. Such were the characters of two individuals lately deceased, well known to many of you—the worthy Jaeniké of Berlin, and the faithful Krafft of Cologne. How many admirable things respecting both these persons have come to light since their departure! What a number of the loveliest actions of their lives did we hear for the first time at their graves! Oh, I hope there are still many among us, who, like Abel, will begin to speak loudest when dead; and who at present have the fairest and brightest side of their life "hid with Christ in God."

His Visits to the Schools of the Prophets

II. Elijah and Elisha went on from Gilgal together. Their course was directed first to the little town of Bethel. The sons of the prophets at Bethel went out to meet them; and the same thing happened when they arrived at Jericho. These were remarkable and highly gratifying occurrences, especially at a time when faith seemed almost extinct in Israel, and "the ways of Zion mourned." And who were these sons of the prophets? Let me briefly attempt to answer this inquiry. When Moses, looking upon Israel, exclaimed with delight, "Behold how wise and understanding they are, and a glorious people!" none will be disposed to question the truth of these words, but those who are acquainted with no other education, than what was taught in the schools of Athens, and who do not know any higher standard of judgment, than that which is afforded by the show of heathen wisdom and genius. God had reserved to himself the education and instruction of the people of Israel. In their divinely appointed institutions we see the ground-plans and models, according to which the Almighty, in the jubilee or millennial age of his kingdom, will call into being that grand renovation which awaits the earth and all that is upon it, whether animate or inanimate. And as in the history of this distinguished people all the institutions of human society find their best models, so do those of instruction in particular. Scholastic institutions, according to the modern system, do not appear to have been known in Israel, at least until the Babylonian captivity. But instead of these, home and school were one, and in the place of paid teachers, instruction was poured forth from the tender hearts of father and mother. The child learned to lisp the name of Jehovah under the vine and the fig-tree, before the door of the peaceful dwelling. There the sacred histories of antiquity, recounted with the eloquence of affection, passed before its admiring soul. There the ideas of God and of the great ends of human life were gradually impressed upon the tender mind. There it early learned that which is eternally true and beautiful, and good for the human mind to know; and this was learned, in the animated imagery of sacred historic record, by many an Israelite child, almost before it had become conscious that its years of tuition had arrived. Thus it was pleasantly initiated into Israel's wisdom, hopes, and prospects, and guided into a way of thinking, feeling, and anticpating, which penetrated upward through the clouds of heaven, and forward through the bounds of time. Having enjoyed the benefit of such a popular education in the highest sense of the word, many a young Israelite came forth from the paternal dwelling, vigorous in body and in mind, with an eye open to everything that is worth observing; susceptible, like good ground, of the best cultivation; and carrying in his hand, from his very home, the key of Scripture, of history, and of nature. The stars of heaven, the trees and flowers of the field, preached to him; and the instructive voices of the Levites and prophets, which were constantly heard through the country, found in his mind a ready attention.

Now, if among those youths there was one who was pressed in spirit to penetrate deeper into the mysteries of the kingdom of God, and to search after the wisdom which comes from above, as the vocation of his life, and to become a teacher of Israel; the schools of the prophets, which, since the time of Samuel, appear as the fairest blossoms of Israelite history, were open to receive him. These were a kind of missionary seminaries of a superior order, and owed their origin chiefly to the contrast of a mournful state of ecclesiastical declension and moral disorder. The decrepit character of the superannuated high priest Eli, surrounded by his degenerate sons, too clearly indicates the state of things at that period. Such were the persons who ought to have been the crown of the nation, and the guardians of the sanctuary. A speedy and powerful remedy was therefore requisite, to prevent the moral degeneracy from becoming universal. This remedy God sent in the person of Samuel, who shines as a bright luminary in those gloomy days. With his appearance commences a new epoch in the history of the Old Testament church. He united in himself the offices of judge, prophet, and priest; at a happy moment he put his hand to the helm of the shattered church and state, and was the means of preserving both from destruction. By him those seminaries of the prophets appear to have been first set on foot, which contained the promise of better things in Israel, and served as a security to the well-being of the country, in ministering to that righteousness which exalteth a nation, and probably furnishing it with a succession of able counselors and leaders. For this purpose he appears to have gathered about him companies of pious, intelligent, and studious young men, who were called the sons of the prophets; who also became Israel's brightest ornament, and the repository of her intellectual treasures.

The Scriptures mention four of these interesting seminaries: two in the time of Samuel; one at Kirjath-jearim, where the ark of the covenant was kept at that time, 1 Sam. 10:5, 10; another at Ramah, where Samuel is expressly mentioned as "appointed over them," 1 Sam. 19:18-24; and two more in the time of Elijah and Elisha, at Jericho and at Bethel. There were, probably, other such seminaries established by Elijah at Samaria, Gilgal, and elsewhere. There, or very near these towns, were settled, as little colonies, these servants of the Lord; the unmarried ones, as it should seem, in one household together, and the rest in families apart at their own cottages. The pupils of these establishments had to maintain themselves by their labor, as husbandmen or mechanics. This was not thought strange in Israel, much less contemptible. Indeed, it has ever been the practice of that nation to teach their children some trade, even though they might be destined to learning and sacred offices. Many of their most respected rabbis have been even surnamed according to their civil professions, as "Rabbi Judah, the baker"; "Rabbi Isaac, the smith"; "Rabbi Johanan, the shoemaker," etc. Nor was it ever imputed to Paul or to Aquila, by their enemies, as anything degrading, that, besides their ministerial office, they were tentmakers. That the sons of the prophets carried on such occupations, is evident from 2 Kings 6:4, where we find them with the axe and tools, cheerfully engaged in constructing their dwellings.

The study which chiefly occupied these sons of the prophets was doubtless that of the Divine word; and the tongues of their teachers were as "the pen of a ready writer," who had himself searched into the deep things of God. Their instructions were doubtless something else than what passes for theological learning and knowledge in the present day. Undoubtedly they were employed upon the positive meaning and practical import of Divine revelation. If sacred history were the subject of their discourse, it was for the purpose of tracing in some edifying manner the footsteps of Jehovah; or of concluding from things past upon those which were future. The mysteries of the Aaronic priesthood and of the ceremonial law, we may suppose, formed another subject of instruction in the schools of the prophets. Thus, the bleeding Lamb of God, that was to bear and take away the sins of the world, would be presented to them in the exposition of the sacrificial institutions. They searched in the mines of that "hidden wisdom," of which David speaks in Psalm 51; and before the wondering hearers were aware of it, the hieroglyphics of the tabernacle were beautifully explained and unfolded before their eyes. Moreover, as their religious and civil codes were intermingled, especially under the theocracy, the one would not be studied without the other; neither can we suppose that the cultivation of their own language would be neglected, especially as it was the most sacred tongue in the world. Their studies would also be connected with devotion, very differently from the popular studies of modern days. The spirit would be sought after, and not merely the letter. The depths of true wisdom would be sounded; and thus, treasures of things new and old would be brought forth by sanctified intellects.

The special employments, however, in which the sons of the prophets are exhibited to us in Scripture history are those of prophecy and sacred song. In 1 Sam. 10 we find a whole company of such disciples meeting Saul on the hill of God, near Kirjath-jearim, with "a psaltery, a tabret, a pipe, and a harp," before them; and themselves prophesying. And, in 1 Sam. 19 we see king Saul, on another occasion, at Ramah, meeting an assembly of the sons of the prophets prophesying, with Samuel set over them. It is evident, from both these passages, that the art of sacred melody was diligently cultivated in those retired nurseries of piety; and that this art was devoted, according to its original appointment, to the praise of God and the cheering and beautifying of civil and domestic life. Ancient traditions tell us much of the great attainments of these sons of the prophets in the lovely art of sacred song, and how affectingly they thus poured forth the harmony of their souls. By what is called their prophesying, in 1 Sam. 10 and elsewhere, we understand an outpouring of the language of the heart in song or in prose, under the

special influence of the Holy Spirit; and these effusions we must conclude to have been always of the sublimest and holiest nature.

Now, if the final object of these excellent schools was not precisely
to form prophets and seers—for such, the Lord alone forms and
call—yet the Lord was pleased to have ready such assemblies of his
saints, from which, when he saw good, he might select a messenger
for himself, endowed with all human preparatives, whenever these
were deemed requisite. It is highly probable that most of the prophets
proceeded from these institutions; at least, the shepherd Amos seems
to point out his vocation to the office as an exception to the rule,
when he says, in ch. 7:14, 15, "I was no prophet, neither was I a
prophet's son; but I was an herdman, and a gatherer of sycamore fruit:
and the Lord took me as I followed the flock, and said to me, Go,
prophesy unto my people Israel." At any rate, these institutions provided the country with many enlightened teachers, many worthy,
well-instructed, and faithful heads of families, and judges. And, even
had they not done so, still their very existence answered a high and
holy purpose. They were the depositories of Israelite light and justice;
they shone as luminaries in a crooked and perverse nation; and
reproved apostasy more severely by their example, than could have
been done by the most powerful language. Their quiet but mighty
influence served to oppose the inroads of surrounding heathen darkness. They were also a spiritual asylum, wherein spiritual mourners
might find instruction, comfort, and peace. And who shall say what
streams of living waters, from those fountains of Israel, refreshed and
fertilized the country at large!

O what sorrow fills my heart, upon turning from the picture of
these ancient and piously devoted seminaries back to our own times,
to contemplate the establishments for instruction, which modern wisdom has devised, and of which it boasts. O you sons of Israel, how
much better were you provided for, than most of our youth in the
present day! and yet we are—Christians! Where are institutions at
present to be found, in which another spirit rules than that of the
world and the profane? Where can we behold flourishing seminaries,
in which a Christian's hope for his children would flourish also? Alas,
they do but rarely, very rarely indeed exist; notwithstanding our systems of education, those boast of the age we live in. In what, then,
consists the vaunted perfection of such systems? Is it in those fragments of classical literature which are crammed into our youths; or

in those ornamental accomplishments to which our daughters are made to sacrifice their health and mental cultivation? Or, is it in the almost general separation of modern instruction from the word of truth, the gospel of our salvation? Or, is it in the more popular manner in which individual branches of knowledge are treated, apart from all deeper investigation, apart from their general connection, and above all, apart from the knowledge of God as their chief end and perfection? Or, does the excellence of our modern education consist in purely heathen conceptions of liberty, morality, and justice, as accredited to our youth in many seminaries, by blind leaders, who never study the sacred oracles with half the diligence, zeal, and respect with which they study the classic writers of ancient Greece and Rome? And here I cannot refrain from inserting the remark of an enlightened writer upon the present state of education in Germany. "Education," he says, "is become a system of seduction. Young men, and even school-boys and apprentices, are trained into instruments of faction and rebellion, and are found the most active associates of tumult and revolt in the present day. Yes, the most audacious blasphemies and execrations are uttered in the ears of listening youths, and even of children, against clergy, magistrates, and public institutions, while the minds of the young are thus easily excited, and drink in these iniquities like water. A monstrous ignorance of the word of God, an affecting and deplorable want of Scriptural knowledge, exists far and wide; for, during the last thirty years, our youths have been beguiled of all the blessings of holy things in our public and private seminaries; yes, in our very universities; and those who have most distinguished themselves in perpetrating these spiritual robberies have become the most reputable, popular, and best rewarded. The most vapid and superficial talking passes for religious and moral instruction; and school-books full of subtle omissions, or of the most daring attacks upon religion, are introduced by authority. Instruction in history—that memorial of Divine justice and human sins—is commonly abused to the implanting of national pride, and the dissemination of the most pernicious principles and doctrines."

If we do not yet find this gloomy description fully realized everywhere, we have to ascribe it exclusively to an invisible Watcher, who has hitherto set bounds to the floods of Belial. Let us commend to Him, who still cherishes thoughts of peace toward us and not of evil, our places of tuition, both high and low; may he reform, consecrate, and renew them! It is true that greater importance has been attached in some places to religious instruction, and the hours devoted to it have been doubled. But this alone will not cure the evil. Another spirit is waiting in our schools and seminaries to complete, animate, and sanctify every branch of instruction. We ought, therefore, to pray for the outpouring of the Spirit of Christ; and, God be thanked! we never shall seek it in vain. We have Divine promises in abundance, which encourage us to look forward, in prayer, for better days. Particularly would I refer you to that prophecy of Zechariah, which shall assuredly come to pass: "In that day shall there be upon the bells of the horses, HOLINESS UNTO THE LORD; and the pots in the Lord's house shall be like the bowls before the altar. Yea, every pot in Jerusalem and in Judah shall be holiness unto the Lord of hosts: and all they that sacrifice shall come and take of them, and seethe therein: and in that day there shall be no more the Canaanite in the house of the Lord of hosts," chap. 14:20, 21. What a glorious prospect is here presented to us, of the future condition of the church and of the world! The beauty and luster of holiness shall then be spread over all we possess, and over all that surrounds us. The Spirit of the Lord shall be universally diffused, and every object will partake of a Divine consecration. The sciences will then be the handmaidens of religion, and their alpha and omega will be the glory of God in Christ. The arts will return to their primary destination, and be again devoted to the service of the living God. "The Lord will hasten it in its time."

The Reception He Meets

III. It must have been gratifying to Elijah to behold these sons of the prophets coming forth to meet him; and to hear, from their voices, an echo to his own ardent prayers, which, when his faith was weak, he had supposed to have no counterpart. It must have increased his own self-humiliation to witness such green spots still remaining in the moral desert, whereas he had thought the prophets all slain, and himself standing quite alone in Israel. He would now feel self-abased at the distrust he had expressed respecting the success of his labors. Truly his labors had not been in vain in the Lord. For here, notwithstanding the malignant influence of an Ahab and a Jezebel, and the apostasy of a whole nation, these blooming plantations of truth had thrived amid storm and tempest, in those parts of the country where Satan's seat had more especially been set up. It must have cheered the heart of the prophet to associate, with his hope of heavenly glory, the thought of leaving behind him such sturdy bands of champions on the side of the God of Israel.

On his coming with Elisha to Bethel, the sons of the prophets are already aware of the loss that awaits them. Probably the Lord himself had made it known to them, that they might know for certain how the course of this great man would end, and that their minds might the more willingly submit, having the comfortable assurance that the Lord of the church himself had taken him from them. With such feelings, as on this occasion, they had never before saluted their paternal master. How much did they need to establish their hearts in order to suppress all rising turbulence of feeling! For a delicate sense of propriety told them they ought not to let the master perceive that they knew of his approaching removal. They venture to disclose only to Elisha the secret of their mournfully affected souls, while beckoning him aside, and whispering with a trembling voice into his ear, "Knowest thou that the Lord will take away thy master from thy head today?" But Elisha, as if putting a still stronger seal upon their lips, signified to them that they should keep the matter to themselves. "Yea, I know it," said he softly to them; "hold ye your peace!" This happened at Bethel, and the same thing was repeated at Jericho. These are pleasing scenes, extremely delicate, and characteristic. Surely, even in the kingdom of God, there is something which the world calls discretion, and this must at least be reckoned among the odors and beauties which Sharon's roses and lilies shed around them.

22

The Passage Through Jordan

The king's daughter is all glorious within." In these sublime words, the inspired psalmist speaks of the true church of God on earth, Psa. 45:13. "A Christian is the highest style of man"; however little the world may acknowledge this. "The world" cannot receive the Holy Spirit, neither can it comprehend that which is Divinely great and glorious, it knows not how to appreciate the nature and actions of him who is born of God.

Great is the Christian in his repentance, for his repentance is an open rupture with sin and Satan. Great in his desires, for the supreme good alone is able to satisfy his heart. Great in his prayers, when he shakes off the dust of the earth from his feet, when with his "Abba, Father!" he mounts up to the heart of Jehovah! Great in his hopes, for he is looking for nothing less than a participation of the glory of the Divine Redeemer. Great in his tears, for they are tears of a fallen King, who mourns for the loss, and longs for the restoration of his crown. Great in his joy, for it is derived from another and a better world, and its objects are beyond the skies! Yea, much more might be said of the greatness of a true Christian; much more might be added in confirmation of this scripture, that "the king's daughter is all glorious within."

There is nothing more beautiful under heaven than the divine work of grace in a renewed soul. Consider it as it appears in a Moses, an Elijah, or a Paul, and you will agree with me, when I call the moral miracles, recorded in the Bible, far more wonderful than the physical ones; when I say that I look upon the inward excellency and

246

glory of these eminent servants of God with far greater amazement than upon the most splendid scenes and actions of their outward life. Indeed, the grand events of their external history almost cease to be surprising, when we consider the dignity and elevation of their inward characters. Let us bear this in mind, while we reflect upon the gigantic act with which we see the prophet Elijah concluding the wonderful chain of his miracles.

2 Kings 2:7, 8

> And fifty men of the sons of the prophets went, and stood to view afar off: and they two stood by Jordan. And Elijah took his mantle, and wrapped it together, and smote the waters, and they were divided hither and thither, so that they two went over on dry ground.

Having conducted this master in Israel through those valuable plantations of God, the schools of the prophets, we now again follow him to the solitary banks of Jordan, where new scenes of grandeur and beauty will open to our view. Let us contemplate for a few moments, I. The escort of the sons of the prophets; and, II. The passage of Elijah and his companion through the river Jordan.

The Sons of the Prophets

I. Here in the solitary wilderness of Jericho, where Israel's hosts first trod the soil of the promised land, Elijah and Elisha pass on together, and arrive at the bank of Jordan. Fifty men of the sons of the prophets followed them at a distance, and stood to view them afar off: and they two stood by Jordan. These sons of the prophets could not find in their hearts to remain that day in the town. It was their master's parting-day, during which they might still see him, but for the last time. They felt constrained to follow him, to behold him once more. They were sensible that no common loss awaited them.

We cannot doubt that these sons of the prophets, in expecting their master to be taken away, anticipated that he would be translated to happiness. So that, sorrowful as they must have been to part with him, their sorrow must have been strangely mingled with joy at the thought of his triumphant exit. Oh how true is this also of the surviving Christian friends of every departing saint! And how indescribably heart-rending is it, on the contrary, to see any beloved object going out of the world, without a well-grounded expectation of this good exchange! Truly the most valuable bequest which our dying relatives can leave us is a scriptural hope and confidence that they have fallen asleep in Jesus. We then no longer regard them as lost, but contemplate them as heirs with us of the future glorious resurrection. Yea, I know well the happiness of those of you who with this sweet confidence can cherish the remembrance of your departed relations and friends. I well believe you, that you would not lose, no not for all the treasures of the world, that comfort, which, like a blessed star of promise, shines over the graves of your departed ones, and unites you forever with those who for a time only are withdrawn from your eyes—Oh that all our tombs may be invested with such blessed hope to those we leave behind!

It does not appear that the sons of the prophets were witnesses of the ascension of Elijah to heaven. We cannot venture to say, with certainty, why this transporting sight was withheld from them. But it is easy to conclude, with respect to ourselves, why we are not made acquainted with all those circumstances of triumph which departing saints enjoy. For only imagine our longing and anxiety to depart, if we could see heaven visibly opened, wherever a righteous man died; if we could behold him enter straightway into the mansions of bliss; if glorified spirits were seen to surround his deathbed, as soon as his last hour was at hand, and if, among the glorious choirs of paradise, and guided by the angels of light, the redeemed soul ascended to eternal peace. We should then so languish for our own expected blessedness, as to be unfit for the duties of the life that now is. The present constitution of our nature cannot bear to become familiar with more than what faith is able to realize from the word of God. It is therefore an instance of the Divine wisdom and goodness that more than this is for the present withheld from us, and that darkness and the shadow of death are suffered to intercept the glories of the invisible world from our view, to call us to a patient continuance in this land of exile and sorrow.

That the sons of the prophets stood afar off, and did not advance nearer their departing master, is beautifully characteristic. They knew their spiritual father too well not to be aware that he was not desirous of any host of human witnesses at his approaching glorification, and they possessed sufficient delicacy of feeling not to intrude themselves upon him. Oh that among ourselves this more refined, spiritual decorum were less rare than it appears to be! There are many cases in which such delicacy is peculiarly appropriate; but persons in general are unhappily not acquainted with it. If, for example, we perceive the influence of Divine grace beginning to show itself in some person eminent for rank or talents, here is a case which calls for much discretion on our part. We ought to observe the thing as though we observed it not, and keep it among us as a pleasing secret; and if one or another should tell us of it, it ought to be said, as at Jericho and Bethel, "Yea, I know it; hold thou thy peace." Such persons, especially at their first setting out, must be dealt with discreetly, and the more so in proportion to the degree in which the fashion of this world has hitherto influenced them, and in which they have moved high in society; for should it come to the ears of such persons, that the report of their conversion is bandied abroad, it would naturally make them shrink back, and thus tend to retard them in the way of grace. But it is too common to disregard all this, and to forget that a shoot just springing up requires very different treatment from a full-grown tree. A variety of cases, wherein such delicacy on our part is required, might be mentioned here. But it is not difficult to understand that what is called in the world "refinement" and "good taste," may well have its counterpart in the kingdom of God; and that there is a nice attention to feeling and social decorum, which well befits the sons and daughters of Zion.

The Passage of Elijah and His Companion

II. Elijah having arrived with his companion at the brink of Jordan does not tarry there as if he doubted how he was to pass over the river. He had not forgotten Moses, who, with one stroke of his rod, parted asunder the water of the great deep, that the ransomed of the Lord might pass over; nor could he forget that Moses' God was also Elijah's God. A miracle similar to that of Moses now ensues. What a spectacle! The stream is divided. On one side it flows rapidly away; on the other it piles itself up like a wall of crystal, and the two prophets pass over, dryshod, to the opposite shore. As soon as they are over—lo! the watery heaps rush again down the channel, the invisible bounds are removed, and the unfettered stream flows on in its ordinary course. How great a God is our God, who rules so absolutely in the armies of heaven and among the inhabitants of the earth, and who does whatsoever pleases him! At his rebuke the seas dry up, and well-watered lands become a desert; the winds and the sea obey him. Happy the man whose refuge is in him! Yes, whosoever has this Rock of Israel for his strength, all things must tend to his salvation, even though it be against their natural tendency to do so. With this God we leap over every wall, and faith in his name removes mountains of difficulty out of the way.

The dividing of Jordan formed the last in the chain of wonders, which ran through the prophetic course of Elijah; and it serves to show that this man, with all his trials and fatigues, had not become decrepit in his faith, but held fast and maintained the beginning of his confidence steadfast unto the end. This last honor put upon Elijah's faith might serve a variety of valuable purposes. To Elisha, who was to inherit his master's mantle, it might serve to invigorate and encourage his faith. To the sons of the prophets it would be a final memento of the greatness of him at whose feet they had sat and whose instructions they had enjoyed. To the whole people it might serve as a new sign and demonstration that verily a prophet of the living God had been in the midst of them. To Elijah himself it would be a new token of God's loving-kindness, a new pledge of his faithfulness and truth. And to us it is a divine and glorious attestation of this truth, that the Lord is with his people even to the end. This act of the departing prophet resembled the ruby splendor of the evening sky, which tells us that the sun though it has vanished from our view, is not extinguished, but only departed to shine with renewed brightness in another hemisphere.

Elijah's passage over Jordan, while it reminds us of that of his forefathers over the same stream, seems far to excel it. At the passage of the Israelite host, what solemn arrangements and preparations were made for it! Here there was, so to speak, an acting on the impulse of the moment. There, the ark of the covenant was sent before, while the people followed at a measured distance; and it was only before the tabernacle of the Almighty that the waters yielded; here they yield before a folded mantle in a human hand. Had the Israelites, who passed over under Joshua, witnessed this wondrous act of Elijah, with what astonishment would they have beheld it! Would they not have confessed Jehovah as dwelling in very deed with man? And yet in this honor put upon Elijah there was but a faint representation of that which God has reserved for us!

When Elijah folded his mantle together to smite the waters of Jordan, he already seemed to anticipate a princely dominion over the earth and its elements. This act of his faith seems the effort of a soul aspiring to higher degrees of advancement, to full emancipation and liberty. He seems no longer to know anything of bondage to the elements of this world. He appears like one advanced to the dignity of a seat in the heavenly places with Christ; his faith would cast mountains into the sea, and pile up the sea to mountains, were it necessary. What is miraculous in the eyes of man appears to have become almost familiar to his faith. A new region must shortly be opened to his soul, for which this earth has become too narrow and contracted. You heavens, unfold! You boundaries of earth and time, retire; for his abode is no longer below!

Elisha's spirit too must have been strengthened and refreshed by all this that he witnessed and experienced at the side of his master. And here it may be observed that those who are especially honored of God, in any age of the world, are thus honored for the benefit of others around them, quite as much as for their own. From the Divine answer given to their prayers, our faith and confidence may learn to ascend with theirs on high. When they, in the night of their adversity, have new songs put into their mouths, is it not that the spirit of joy may take possession of us also, and that we may not sink under the weight of our worldly cares? When they pass in triumph through the valley of the shadow of death, how is such a sight adapted to encourage us, and to raise us higher on the vantage ground of faith! They seem almost to bear us away with them in their noble career. And, with reference to the peculiar times in which we live, let us remember that it is the Lord God of Elijah who rules all things, in the person of Jesus Christ, who is "the same yesterday, and today, and forever." He too has promised that a time shall arrive when the weakest shall be as David, and the house of David shall be as the angel of the Lord before his people, Zech. 12:8. "Yea," says the Lord, "I will strengthen the house of Judah, and I will save the house of Joseph; and they of Ephraim shall be like a mighty man, and their heart shall rejoice as through wine; yea, their children shall see it and be glad; their heart shall rejoice in the Lord," Zech. 10:6, 7. Such honor have all his saints. Blessed are they that wait for him! Amen.

23

The Great Request

W e come now to behold Elijah arrived just at the consummation of his life of faith, and anticipating the perfect enjoyment of that glorious liberty which is the future inheritance of all the children of God.

2 Kings 2:9, 10

And it came to pass, when they were gone over, that Elijah said unto Elisha, Ask what I shall do for thee, before I be taken away from thee. And Elisha said, I pray thee, let a double portion of thy spirit be upon me. And he said, Thou hast asked a hard thing: nevertheless, if thou see me when I am taken from thee, it shall be so unto thee; but if not, it shall not be so.

The hour in which the prophet is to be withdrawn from our view is at hand. The sacred narrative has brought us to the boundary of his earthly course. We have here his last words and his last work—a work indeed less evident to the senses than his former acts; but not inferior, perhaps more astonishing than those. The several matters which at present require our attention are, I. Their position after crossing the river; II. Elijah's proffer to Elisha; and, III. The request of the latter, with the answer he received to it.

Their Position

I. Elijah, whom we here behold beyond Jordan, may, spiritually considered, be regarded as now placed beyond the limits of sublunary evils and sorrows. These things, like the waters of Jordan, now lie behind him. His eternal Sabbath of rest is just at hand, and the remaining few moments of his earthly sojourn are now only a blessed waiting for the heavenly chariot. What an enviable situation! And yet it is in substance the same with that into which the gospel ought already to have brought us all. Whatever depths or difficulties there be still lying before us, if we had but faith, we might easily surmount them all, and spiritually leave them behind us. For faith substantiates what is hoped for, and evidences the things which are not seen. What is it that makes us tremble? Is it the waves of death? Let us embark only in the sweet promise of the Savior, "I will come again, and receive you to myself," and we have already surmounted them. Is it the storm of temptation? Let us commit the keeping of body, soul, and spirit to Him who has promised that he "will not suffer us to be tempted above that we are able, but will with the temptation also make a way to escape, that we may be able to bear it"; and the severest and most violent temptations will thus become powerless to us. Does the remainder of our innate corruptions dismay us, so that we are ready to ask, How shall we become perfectly holy? Let us reflect that Christ is "made of God unto us wisdom, and righteousness, and sanctification, and redemption." Are we disposed to entertain anxious presentiments of temporal and spiritual troubles? Let us remember that each day is ordered by almighty and everlasting Love, and brings with it that measure of the bitter and the sweet which, according to the judgment of infinite Wisdom, is most conducive to our true peace and welfare.

You see then, brethren, what glorious prospects are placed before us by Divine revelation, and how real they are to every sincere member of Christ. So that all such may securely look beyond the Jordan of death, beyond all the intermediate wilderness, toils, and temptations of their way, as if they were already there. Yes, those whose hearts are set upon gaining, by Divine strength, a complete victory over their innate corruptions may rest assured of their final triumph and say with the psalmist, "I will behold thy face in righteousness: I shall be satisfied, when I awake, with thy likeness," Psa. 17:15.

Elijah's Proffer to Elisha

II. When the two men of God were gone over Jordan, "Elijah said unto Elisha, Ask what I shall do for thee, before I be taken away from thee." This was something more than an affectionate parting word. He wished to communicate to him his last paternal blessing, and this no common one: "Ask what I shall do for thee, before I be taken away from thee." These are great words. But what kind of benefit did Elijah intend? Was it some valuable temporal good? Was it a large grant of worldly riches, honors, or gratifications? O no; he was thinking of good and perfect gifts that came down from above, from the Father of lights. Elisha is, therefore, invited to ask for blessings from the sanctuary; and here we discern a radiance of the glory of the New Testament in the Old. Bold as this expression is, "Ask what I shall do for thee," it was perfectly appropriate to the condition of the inspired prophet at the time, for he was evidently favored with an extraordinary outpouring of prophetic grace.

The words, however, of this address to Elisha serve to remind us of the words of our Lord to his disciples: "Verily, verily, I say unto you, Whatsoever ye shall ask the Father in my name, he will give it you: hitherto have ye asked nothing in my name; ask, and ye shall receive, that your joy may be full." You know what is commonly understood by praying in the name of Jesus. People say they pray in his name, when they so present their requests before God as not to hope for acceptance on the ground of their own worthiness, but on that of the merits of Christ and from free grace. They say that to pray in the name of Jesus is to pray in humble acknowledgment of our own entire unworthiness of any claim on Divine help, but to hope for it from the tender mercy of God through the merits and blood of Jesus Christ. Is this explanation the true and correct one? It is not exactly incorrect, but it is incomplete and imperfect. A person may really pray with the state of heart just described, and yet not pray fully in the name of Jesus. For if this expression signified nothing more than to pray, confiding in the merits of the Surety, why did Christ say to his disciples, "Hitherto ye have asked nothing in my name"? If the Savior would have had nothing more to be understood by praying in his name, than to pray as a contrite sinner, trusting in the merits of the Redeemer, then Abraham, Moses, Daniel, David, and others had certainly already prayed in the name of Jesus. But praying in the name of Jesus is here presented to us as something entirely new. The Savior himself speaks of it as a thing which was not known previous to his appearing upon earth, and which must therefore be regarded as one of the chief privileges of the New Testament dispensation.

If, in the painful consciousness of my desert of condemnation, I approach the eternal Father in prayer, and set Christ before me as my Mediator and Surety, regarding God only as a consuming fire, and considering that without Christ's mediation I should certainly be consumed before Him—have I not then learned the full import of praying in the name of Jesus? No, not if I consider the Father as still strange and distant with respect to me, and that I am protected only by Christ from his wrath; for then I am in the bondage of fear before the God of all grace. I ought to approach the Father with a firm belief that I am welcome to come to him in Jesus Christ, and that if I truly loathe myself for all my transgressions, and thus make confession to him, then my sins and iniquities are remembered no more. Here then may very suitably be applied to me the spirit and import of those words which he spake to his disciples:

"And I say not, that I will pray the Father for you; for the Father himself loveth you, because ye have loved me, and have believed that I came out from God." Let me then learn to cast all my care upon Him, fully assured, that in Christ I am not merely saved from wrath, through him, but am also numbered among "the children of God by faith in Christ Jesus." Surely to pray in the knowledge and belief of all this is something more than to pray to an offended God with a cold reliance, from necessity, on the merits of Jesus. We all know that to do anything in the name of another person is, in some sense, to represent that person; so that if you offer a request in my name, and you are refused, this would amount to a disparagement of me. For it is not in reality so much you that ask, as I. If the request be granted, it is from the respect belonging to and paid to me, that any such request is granted to you. This precisely is the case with respect to asking in Christ's name. Every answer to our prayers is primarily an answer to the intercession of Christ for us, and in him it is that we are accepted, answered, and blessed. Behold then what a blessed privilege the Savior imparts to us, when he encourages us to pray to the Father in his name.

Now he that is enabled, by faith of the operation of the Holy Spirit, to bring his requests before God with holy, filial boldness; not doubting that if he ask anything according to his will, he hears him—such a one prays in the name of Jesus. And in this wise the saints of the Old Testament and the disciples themselves had not yet prayed. Their insight into the mediatorship of Christ had never yet reached so far as to enable them to draw nigh to God in "full assur-

ance of faith." Indeed the condition of most of the Old Testament
saints, in relation to God, though the same in substance, appears to
have come far short of this in degree. They knew that, for the
Messiah's sake, they should not be condemned; they knew much
more than this, and in so far they rejoiced in their redemption. But
not many of them appear to have anticipated that fellowship with
the Father, and with his Son Jesus Christ, which was brought fully to
light by the gospel. They had not come to "mount Zion, the heavenly Jerusalem," but had come rather to "the mountain that might
be touched, and that burned with fire." Even of the most eminent of
them it is written that though they died in faith, "having obtained
a good report through faith," as yet "they received not the promise,"
Heb. 11:39. We have seen and heard what they only longed for from
afar—an infinitely blessed reality has taken the place of promises and
types, and the Lord says, that "the least in the kingdom of heaven is
greater than John the Baptist." We are therefore privileged to appear
before God, as children before their kind and loving Father; and we
need not wonder that our Lord mentions the praying in his name as
a new thing, which was unknown until he came into the world.

Nor ought we here to overlook the largeness of the promise which
our blessed Savior makes to his true disciples. "Ask, and ye shall
receive; that your joy may be full." And again, "Whatsoever ye shall
ask the Father in my name, he will give it you." "Ye shall ask what ye
will, and it shall be done unto you." What can we desire more?
Nothing in the world is so great, nothing so small, that we might not
every moment be receiving from the Father, if we only asked it in the
name of Jesus. What would you desire to have granted you? Is it to be
freed from any domestic trouble; as, for instance, that your sick child
should recover? Would you gladly see your whole household converted to God? Draw nigh unto the Father, and ask for it in Jesus'
name, and verily he will grant it you. But does not experience seem
to contradict this? We answer, it does not really do so. The deceit lies
within ourselves, through not really asking in Jesus' name. For let us
again call to mind what this asking in his name implies. You might
wish very ardently, it is true, for some peculiar interposition of God;
and you might express this wish in prayer, and, as you think, in Jesus'
name. But in this it is possible that you may be mistaken. A petition
is offered in his name, when it is offered in that faith which is of the
operation of God, and when that which we ask is according to his

will. Luther was enabled to pray in Jesus' name for the lives of his friends, Melancthon and Myconius, who were sick unto death, and already given over; and, lo! he received the petitions which he desired of God: and whatever we pray for, even if it be only gold or silver, it may be granted us when asked for according to his will. Thus the pious professor Franke prayed for means to erect his orphan house; and immediately the silver and the gold flowed in upon him, and he who on commencing was scarcely able to command a few pence, had soon enough to found that abode of orphan charity and education, whose praise has been in all the churches. The Lord had granted what his servant desired. It is to this effect that St. John addresses us, in his 1st Epistle, chap. 3 ver. 21-23, "Beloved, if our heart condemn us not, then have we confidence toward God. And whatsoever we ask, we receive of him, because we keep his commandments, and do those things that are pleasing in his sight. And this is his commandment, that we should believe on the name of his Son Jesus Christ, and love one another, as he gave us commandment."

What shall we say to these things? Alas! how little account do we make of such exceedingly great and precious promises! How lamentably is this shown by the low state of spiritual advancement in which most are contented to live! Were it otherwise, things would wear a very different appearance among us. The heavens would not so often be as brass over our heads, nor the earth beneath us as iron. The church would soon flourish like the lily; there would be more shaking among the dry bones, and a gracious rain would oftener refresh God's inheritance. Our poverty in spiritual things is our shame and our condemnation. It is still but too true of many among ourselves, "Hitherto have ye asked nothing in my name."

But much as these mighty words reprove us, they also serve to encourage us; for they unfold a glorious prospect of better days to the true church of Christ, whenever they shall generally unite in asking for a new and Pentecostal season, a general outpouring of the Spirit of grace and of supplications upon the professing church at large. This good work, we acknowledge, has begun to be engaged in by many a company of devout persons, in various places. But as yet, comparatively speaking, such union of prayer in the name of Jesus is but partial. As soon as it shall be full, and general, and fervent among all real Christians, then will the fullness of the desired blessing be poured out.

The same kind of observation applies to individual blessings desired by us. Is it the conversion of a child, or a beloved relative? We too often lament over the condition of such, without ever fervently praying in the name of Jesus on their behalf. It is well worthwhile, also, to be reminded of the duty of commending to God, in the name of Jesus, all our private cares. This is alike neglected by unbelief on the one hand, and spiritual pride on the other. "What is the use of it?" says the former; "God can hardly be supposed to concern himself about my private matters." And it is the notion of the latter, "That because God does concern himself about them, therefore I need not do it; neither need I make such things a subject of prayer to him." But be it remembered that he has ordained prayer in the name of Jesus as the means of obtaining and receiving our blessings. This is evident from Scripture, and from the experience of all ages of the church. If we are truly alive unto God through Jesus Christ our Lord, we shall feel that we can never enough value the inestimable privilege of being thus permitted to ask and to receive. If we do not value such a privilege as this, it must be because we are still unrenewed and dead in spirit; or because we have backslidden or sunk into a lamentable state of sloth and lukewarmness.

Lastly, it may be observed, that such boldness and access given us in prayer through the faith of Jesus Christ throws light and evidence on that great truth, "that when we were enemies, we were reconciled unto God by the death of his Son, and that, being reconciled, we are made the children of God by faith in Christ Jesus." For God, in thus answering our prayers, deals with us as with sons; hence the Savior calls him "his Father, and our Father"; and he says, "As the Father hath loved me, even so have I loved you: continue ye in my love."

Elisha's Request

III. The bold invitation to Elisha to ask what he would from the departing prophet indicates a state of heart toward God which was substantially the same with that we have now attempted to describe. Elijah rises high in making such an offer and Elisha seems to rise still higher in his expectation from it. "I pray thee," says he, "let a double portion of thy spirit be upon me"; that is, "I desire to be twice as much baptized with the Holy Spirit, and enriched with his gifts, as you have been." Let us not mistake the worthy Elisha in his request; however lofty it may sound, it proceeds from a humble and holy spirit. I do not believe that Elisha was here referring, as many expositors suppose, to the birthright of the first-born son, who inherited twice as much as his brothers and sisters, and that he only meant, "If others inherit a portion of your spiritual gifts, let this portion be doubled to me, to whom you have been more especially a father." Surely, he rather had his eye upon the loss which the church would sustain by his departure. This appeared to him immense! He thought that the earth contained no man at all comparable with Elijah. The idea that he, the inconsiderable husbandman of Abel Meholah, should fill up such a breach, or carry on the work of Elijah to its completion, was overwhelming to him. Therefore, if Elijah must depart, his successor would humbly implore sufficient help for his conscious inability. It seems then a feeling of the purest humility and self-diffidence which dictated this request. Perhaps, also, he foresaw by Divine revelation that his own future labors in Israel would be essentially different from those of his great predecessor and would bear a more evangelical character. After the mighty wind, the earthquake, and the fire, the still small voice of Jehovah's grace and loving-kindness was to succeed, and be conveyed through Elisha to Israel; and for such a vocation he needed very peculiar endowments. As he was to stand forth in the character of a messenger of the Divine benignity, it was necessary that this peculiarity of his vocation should reflect itself in his whole conduct, and beam as it were in his countenance. Perhaps he felt this also, and therefore said, "Let a double portion of your spirit be upon me!"

But, however this may have been, he desired this blessing only in order the more effectually to glorify Jehovah's name. The more any servant of God is humbled within himself, and lives by faith upon Divine grace alone, the higher will his wishes for the glory of God naturally rise.

Elijah's Answer

IV. To Elisha's request Elijah answered, "Thou hast asked a hard thing: nevertheless, if thou see me when I am taken from thee, it shall be so unto thee; but if not, it shall not be so." It is as if he had said, "It is no common favor that you ask; neither is it a favor that can be conferred on you by the will of man; it is a rare blessing, and such as few prophets ever have been, or ever will be distinguished with."

The condition upon which Elijah, by Divine inspiration, made the grant to depend, is also remarkable. "If thou see me when I am taken from thee, it shall be so unto thee; but if not, it shall not be so." "If thou see me at my departure, or in the act of departing"; as much as to say, "Do not expect the gift from me, but from Him, who is taking me away: moreover take notice of the sign which he appoints you for ascertaining his will in this matter; for by this sign you shall understand that the gift is purely of God's bestowal."

Let us conclude with noticing the superlative bounty of the New Testament dispensation. You know how frequently, in the first age of the church, the Holy Spirit fell on all them that heard the word, and they spake with tongues and prophesied; and how the common members of the New Testament church were often gifted with power to perform the most stupendous miracles. And thus, as St. Peter tells us, has commenced the fulfillment of "that which was spoken by the prophet Joel; And it shall come to pass in the last days, saith God, I will pour out of my Spirit upon all flesh; and on my servants and on my handmaidens I will pour out in those days of my Spirit; and they shall prophesy: and I will show wonders in heaven above, and signs in the earth beneath," Acts 2:16-19. How highly then should we value our privileges, as members of Christ, and partakers of the new dispensation, the heavenly calling! for behold how the glory of the gospel surpasses every thing that has preceded it! What are we that we should be thus favored! and "what manner of persons ought we to be in all holy conversation and godliness!" 2 Pet. 3:11?

24

The Ascension

There can be no doubt that the false and fashionable theology of the present day would not have occasioned half the mischief it has done, had it not assumed so specious an appearance of adhering to the doctrines of the church. The bulk of the people were unable to see through such delusion, and thus the adversary transformed into an angel of light, has, through his subtlety, corrupted their minds from the simplicity that is in Christ. It is true, there is scarcely any of the articles of Scripture doctrine which is entirely suppressed; but they are not taught in the power and beauty of the Bible, but mutilated and divided, so that the form only is retained, without the substance and power of the doctrine. Thus a Supreme Being is indeed set forth by them, but one with whom they would forbid us to hold communion. The revealed Son of God is refined into a personified idea, an unsubstantial image. Immortality and eternal life are spoken of also, but only so long as men are not in earnest in pressing after them. Alas, how is the apostolical warning forgotten, "Beware lest any man spoil you through philosophy and vain deceit," Col. 2:8.

But let us have the realities of the Bible, for the human heart needs realities, and the more palpable and substantial to our faith they are, the better. We want the knowledge of an intelligible God; and God is only intelligible to sinful man by the gospel, and by that manifestation of himself in our human nature which is revealed in the Scriptures. We want just such a knowledge of Divine providence as is taught by him who said, "The very hairs of your head are all numbered." We want a Divine Surety, who having obeyed, suffered, been judged and punished in our stead, has made a perfect and suf-

261

ficient sacrifice, oblation, and satisfaction for the sins of the whole world. We need a heavenly home into which we may be received, a kingdom which cannot be moved, a world more substantial than the present, which has become subject to vanity. We need a reunion of the soul with the body, changed indeed and glorified but still the body, for it is a component part of man; and, previous and preparatory to all this, we need a real change of heart, a renewal of the soul by the Spirit of God.

Such are some of those realities which our necessities require, and which alone can satisfy our hearts. I say we want these realities to remedy other realities which force themselves upon us in our actual experience. Far too real is the wretchedness which all men naturally and morally experience in the present life; disease and death await us; a body of sin oppresses and brings us low; conscious guilt confounds us; and nothing can avail to remedy all this but what is actually opposed to it. A paper shield gives no protection; the bread of dreams affords no support; we want the solid and substantial realities of Divine revelation. There and there alone are such realities to be discerned; and the more they are realized by our faith the happier for us. In the ascension of Elijah, which we are about to contemplate, we meet with one such solid demonstration of immortality and the life of the world to come.

2 Kings 2:11

> And it came to pass, as they still went on, and talked, that, behold, there appeared a chariot of fire, and horses of fire, and parted them both asunder; and Elijah went up by a whirlwind into heaven.

This passage of Scripture invites us as it were to a coronation, to witness an event most marvelous and most true.

The fact itself first requires our notice; and then its meaning and signification.

The Fact of the Ascension

I. We see Elijah and Elisha passing on together in the country beyond Jordan. It was comparatively a solitary region. God did not select the market-place of idlers for the scene of this wonder, but this secluded spot. While the two men of God thus walk on, engaged in holy conversation, "behold, there appeared a chariot of fire, and horses of fire, and parted them both asunder; and Elijah went up by a whirlwind into heaven. And Elisha saw it."

Well may we be astonished at beholding the glory and honor with which God thus crowns a poor sinner, for such is man "at his best estate" in this world. Let us however remember that it is not "flesh and blood," as such, that "entereth the kingdom of God; neither can corruption inherit incorruption." It is not Elijah as born after the flesh, it is not the son of Adam as such; but it is Elijah as born again of the Spirit, and as united to the Second Adam, the Lord from heaven, that is thus exalted. The free grace of God toward sinners is that which reigns and triumphs here. What does this wonderful scene indicate, but that the Most High regards and treats as righteous all who "believe in the name of his Son Jesus Christ, and love one another, as he gave us commandment?" Behold here then the effect of the meritorious sacrifice of Christ; behold the all-sufficient power of that blood, which speaks better things than that of Abel; behold the glorious consequences of the obedience and sufferings of the Lamb slain from the foundation of the world. And oh! learn also more impressively the exceeding sinfulness of sin.

Such honor, in substance, have all God's saints. "What is it for Him to send from on high to fetch me," (may every true Christian say,) "seeing he is willing to take me to his bosom as the Father of mercies, and the God of all comfort." He has in infinite wisdom and grace so ordered things, that it shall glorify his own holy name thus to deal with his obedient children. Having conformed them to the image of the only begotten Son who is in the bosom of the Father, it is a small thing with him thus to ratify their union with him forever.

We need not curiously inquire how Elijah, without dying, could be fit to be conveyed away, inasmuch as flesh and blood, in its present mortal and corrupt state, cannot enter into the kingdom of God. We are told of the mighty working of Jehovah Jesus, "whereby he is able to subdue all things unto himself," and whereby he will change this body of humiliation, that it may be like unto his own glorious body; we are told that at the last day "we shall not all sleep, but that we shall all be changed, in a moment, in the twinkling of an eye"; and we may be quite sure that such a change as this now passed upon the body of Elijah. This is enough for our faith at present. His mortality was swallowed up of life, and his corruptible nature had put on incorruption. It cannot further be described what his eye afterward began to see, his ear to hear, and his heart to conceive. God, however, has reserved the knowledge and experience of all this for them that love him.

Blessed servant of God, how unspeakable and incomprehensible is now your everlasting felicity; made glad as you are with the joy of God's countenance! Here you are gathered to your fathers with honor; and behold Abraham, and Isaac, and Jacob in the kingdom of God, and yourself numbered with them.

So then we have a patriarchal instance of complete triumph over death in the case of Enoch; an Israelite instance of the same in the case of Elijah; and, to crown the whole, the New Testament account of our Lord and Savior's resurrection and ascension; all serving to raise our faith to the certainty of a similar triumph. Let nothing therefore relative to death depress us. Let our faith in these truths become every day, by the grace of God, stronger and stronger; let us grow in gratitude and love, in obedience and patience, until our own faith also shall be swallowed up in vision, and our hope in enjoyment.

Its Meaning and Significance

II. The wonderful event here recorded is one of the most glorious, significant, and exhilarating facts which the world ever witnessed before the birth of Christ. It served to dispel much obscurity which might occasionally cloud the faith of dying saints under the Old Testament dispensation. It might serve to cheer the minds of many of the faithful but oppressed or afflicted servants of God, in those days, during the course of their earthly pilgrimage. For they would recollect that Elijah too had been thus oppressed and afflicted, and yet how gloriously did he triumph at last! Many a one, too, under deep conviction of sin, and whose faith could not always derive the comfort he needed from the typical sacrifices of the law, might have been preserved from despondency, by remembering this honor visibly put upon one of the penitent sons of Adam, as an encouragement to all who were like-minded with him.

This event also served to prepare the faith of true Israelites for the wonders of the New Testament dispensation. That prophetic invocation, "Thou hast ascended on high, thou hast led captivity captive," would thus be rendered more susceptible of its grandest import in the minds of those who should afterward wait from age to age for the consolation of Israel. The ascension of Elijah was surely intended to prefigure that of our blessed Savior. Yet, it became him, as Lord of all, to ascend, not in a fiery chariot waiting upon him, but by a visible manifestation of his own Divine power. Hence it is only said, that "he was received up into heaven," that "while he blessed them, he was parted from them, and carried up into heaven"; and that while the disciples "beheld, he was taken up; and a cloud received him out of their sight." Thus his ascension took place before the eyes of men in majestic simplicity and tranquillity, which may doubtless be ascribed to its superior glory, as compared with that of Elijah. For it was the ascension of the Lord from heaven, the Son of God.

In all generations of mankind, the present world has been too narrow for the capacious desires of the human soul. Hence men in every nation, however barbarous, have endeavored, by one way and another, to pierce the veil that conceals from us the invisible world and a future state. But what are the results of all these efforts of human speculation? They show that the spirit of man feels as it were its own immortal nature, though they show at the same time our universal need of Divine revelation. For let us see to what uncertain knowledge of a future state even those men only attained, who stood, as it were, on the very summit of philosophical learning. Cyrus, who had been educated in the schools of the most illustrious Persian sages, said at the approach of death to his children, "I cannot imagine that the soul lives only while it remains in this mortal body. I am rather inclined to think that when separated from this body, it will possess more understanding and greater purity!" Socrates, the prince of heathen philosophers, when his last hour was at hand, could only say to his judges, "We are about to part; I am going to die, and you to live. Which of us goes the best way is known to God alone." All that Cicero, the great and polished Roman, could say upon this subject was, "I do not wish that what I am about to write of a duration of existence beyond the present life, should be regarded as certain, like a Divine oracle. Upon this subject I entertain no more than conjectures." Neither have the wise of this world in our own day any better staff to lean upon, while they refuse to rest their hopes on the truths of Divine revelation. Their belief in a future state, if they believe in it at all, is in most cases so barren and comfortless that death is viewed by them in their reflecting moments as a formidable foe.

But while these wise men can show us nothing more, as the fruit of their deep and laborious speculations, than a poor and barren conjecture, that there is perhaps a future state and an eternal existence of the soul, it is the privilege of the Christian to exclaim, in his severest sufferings, "O death, where is thy sting? O grave, where is thy victory?" "We know," says the apostle, (and how many have been able since to adopt his words as their own!) "that if our earthly house of this tabernacle were dissolved, we have a building of God, an house not made with hands, eternal in the heavens." And if you ask the believer the source of this knowledge, he can refer you, not to an empty dream of his own imagination, but to the word of him in whose mouth men and devils endeavored in vain to find deceit; who confirmed his words by deeds of majesty and power; who, in proof that death cannot retain its prey forever, approached the tombs of the dead, and called them to life by a word; yea, who in his own person rose again and ascended visibly into heaven. Listen to him, when he says, "In my Father's house are many mansions: if it were not so, I would have told you: I go to prepare a place for you: and if I go and prepare a place for you, I will come again, and receive you unto myself, that where I am, there ye may be also." Here then is the veil that hides the other world from the eye of sense removed entirely to the eye of faith, and we have only to behold, rejoice, and be glad, at the glorious prospect thus opened before us by the Lord from heaven. And what he has thus revealed is plain and definite; which if we believe, we know in what we have believed. He shows us a house, a home, a heavenly paternal home; a real habitation, where we shall know one another, and be with one another upon terms of the most intimate fellowship and the dearest friendship. For the expression "My Father's house" indicates family community, familiar relationships, living with and in the presence of the Father. Oh how invaluable is the possession of such sure intelligence respecting our eternal habitation in the celestial world! and how quieting to the heart thus to know of a better country, that is, an heavenly, where peace forever reigns, where all is perfect harmony and love! How cheerfully do we continue our pilgrimage in this vale of tears, when we have had a glorious view of the world to come! However stormy the voyage, however high the waves, there is a haven beyond the skies, where we shall certainly arrive and anchor in peace.

Thus we see that a reflected image of the Christian's future glory is presented to us in the triumphant exaltation of Elijah, who was originally "a man of like passions as we are." They who are Christ's, who having crucified the flesh with its affections and lusts, are seeking those things which are above, where Christ sits at the right hand of God, who set their affection on things above, not on things on the earth, and whose life is hid with Christ in God—have in themselves an earnest and pledge of their future union with their Lord in glory.

But woe unto the impenitent and unbelieving, for it shall as certainly be ill with them! and this because the great salvation has been neglected, and the riches of Divine grace, and long-suffering, and goodness, and forbearance have been despised. Where this is the case, there remains no more sacrifice for sin, for it is to Christ's one sacrifice that Elijah and all the saints owe their triumph. God having "made him to be sin for us, who knew no sin, that we might be made the righteousness of God in him." "Worthy," then, "is the Lamb that was slain, to receive power, and riches, and wisdom, and strength, and honor, and glory and blessing!" Amen.

25

The Parting

Our Savior, Mark 16:14, upbraided even his own disciples with their unbelief: and what does he in general speak more strongly against? For unbelief is the occasion of all sin, and the very bond of iniquity. It does nothing but darken and destroy. It makes the world a moral desert, where no Divine footsteps are heard—where no angels ascend and descend—where no living hand adorns the fields, feeds the fowls of heaven, or regulates events. Thus it makes nature, the garden of God, a mere automaton; and the history of Providence a fortuitous succession of events; and man, a creature of accident; and prayer, a useless ceremony. It annihilates even the vestiges of heaven that still remain upon earth, and stops the way to every higher region.

But faith sees an invisible world dawning upon the visible, and beholds this earth as a theater of divine wonders. It everywhere traces the footsteps, operation, and government of the triune Jehovah. In the winds, it sees messengers commissioned by Him; in the lightnings, it beholds ministers sent forth in his service. It has eagles' wings for a worm in the dust, and opens the regions that lie beyond us.

Unassisted by faith, the mind of man, however bold may be its flight of thought, cannot soar beyond the limits of the visible world. For this purpose we must become as little children, sitting at the feet of Jesus, denying ourselves, and living by faith on his word. The poor and longing soul has then a place where it may find repose and shelter in the storms of this life, and becomes assured that whatever it loses of the blessings of Christian friendship by the stroke of death, shall be restored to it hereafter in tenfold excellence, to be lost no more.

2 Kings 2:12

And Elisha saw it, and he cried, My father, my father, the chariot of Israel, and the horsemen thereof. And he saw him no more: and he took hold of his own clothes, and rent them in two pieces.

Elisha Left Alone

I. Elijah, having now shaken the dust of the earth from his feet, Elisha, his faithful companion, is left alone in the wilderness, beyond Jordan. Who can describe the feelings of the forsaken man! Is he really awake? Is it only a vision he sees? No, he is certain of the contrary. He sees the mantle of the ascended prophet floating down from the sky, and his own hands take it up from the ground. It is all reality to the senses. His friend, his spiritual father, soars yonder in the chariot through the air, as really as Noah in his ark was borne upon the waters of the deluge, as really as Moses and the children of Israel passed dryshod through the Red sea. But oh, who had ever seen such a sight as this! In truth, he needed a Divinely supporting hand to keep him from sinking beneath the overwhelming feelings which he must have experienced at this solemn moment of his life.

Blessed was he to whom it was given to witness such a scene! But more blessed still are they, who are enabled to see by faith things which are hidden from the wise and prudent, and revealed unto babes. For verily there are those who, though endued with much strength of natural intellect, are, in spiritual things, as men without understanding; who, having eyes, see not, and having ears, hear not.

Elisha must have been filled with adoring wonder. New hopes and consolations must also have been suggested to him to allay his fears, and console him upon his loss of such a friend. His heart, however, was full, and he cried after the ascending prophet, "My father! my father! the chariot of Israel, and the men thereof." Probably the name of "father" had never before been pronounced on earth with stronger emotion or more affectionate tenderness. It is as if he would still draw back his departing friend from heaven. Elisha knew his worth. He had known him in private as well as in public life. He had found it good to be with him, and to enjoy the benefit of his intimate friendship. For he had shown himself, doubtless, in private life, what God had publicly owned him to be, a true servant of Jehovah; and thus had exhibited more than common disinterested love. Though

habituated to so much that was elevated and supernatural, he had
shown himself attentive even to the smallest matters which could
give real happiness to others around him: and if at one moment he
had stood terrible in the scene of conflict, with the drawn sword of
the Spirit in his hand, he had been ready the next moment to gather the little ones, the humble and teachable, under the wings of love,
and to cheer the timid with the utmost kindness. How much then
had Elisha lost in this one man! The happiest and most important
hours of his life had been spent in his society. Oh what recollections
would now hover about his soul! What surges of desire, affection,
gratitude, and regret are poured out in this exclamation, "My father,
my father!"

"The chariot of Israel, and the horsemen thereof!" or, "thou wast
Israel's artillery and cavalry"; its glittering legion, and its invincible
host. What a noble testimony! Yet what is there in this testimony
that is not true of the man whom God had made as an iron bulwark
about Zion, and as an armed host against Israel's foes? Think only of
the fire from heaven which this prophet, in his zeal for the house of
the Lord, called down upon the adversaries of God and of his people.
Think of the dreadful defeat, which, as with a waving of his hand, he
brought upon the destroyers of his people at mount Carmel. Think
of the awful thunder which he bore upon his lips for the blasphemers
of Jehovah, and of the mighty overcoming power which he was wont
to exercise against the proudest, the strongest, and most daring of
Jehovah's adversaries. He spoke, and the horse and his rider stood as
if thunderstruck. At his rebuke tyrants shrank back, pale and silent.
He commanded in the name of God, and fire and sword united their
force to destroy from the earth a whole royal race, both root and
branch, because it had taken the field against the kingdom of the
Lord. He was wroth in spirit, and his anger became a blazing flame,
which consumed a whole host of lying priests from the land of Israel.

And what a wall of protection was this man about the believers in
the land! How did he encourage the trembling and scattered
flock, by word and deed! How did he stand in the breach for them,
that their faith might not fail! What encouragement was afforded
them, both in precept and pattern, by this champion of the Lord!
And Elijah was not only their champion and standard-bearer; but he
was, at the same time, as a shield round about them in the name of
the Lord. More terrible was he to Ahab and to Jezebel, in his invis-

ible armor, than a whole host of Syrians and Philistines. Such was the man who had now departed! This phalanx of Israel and its bulwark was now removed! What would be the consequence? Who would now take the lead in the cause of God, and oppose the foe? O invaluable Elijah, alas that you have left us so soon! "My father! my father! the chariot of Israel, and the horsemen thereof!"

It is long since the church of God has seen such men as this language imports; while, on the other hand, the kingdom of darkness is in no want of champions. Yet still, accord to the promise, Zech. 10:3, 5, we wait for a time when "the Lord of hosts shall visit his flock, the house of Judah, and make them as his goodly horse in the battle; and they shall be as mighty, men, who tread down their enemies in the mire of the streets." But until that time, it must be said, "Herein is the patience of the saints."

In a certain sense, however, the honorable appellation of "the chariot of Israel, and the horsemen thereof," belongs also, even now, to all the faithful and the righteous, and especially to those who, in the spirit of the New Testament, are mighty in patience and prayer. Why was the destruction of Sodom and Gomorrah so long suspended? Was it not because of the prayer of one righteous man? for behold, what is testified of him. "I cannot do anything," says the Lord, "till thou be come thither." Who was it that interceded for Israel when they fought against Amalek? Was it not Moses, the servant of Jehovah? When he held up his hands in prayer, Israel prevailed; but, when he let down his hands, Amalek prevailed. It was not their own sword then that helped Israel; it was the prayer of Moses, the man of God. So, in like manner, did Samuel pray; and an inconsiderable band, under Judah's banner, discomfited their enemies. For, when "the children of Israel were afraid of the Philistines, they said to Samuel, Cease not to cry unto the Lord our God for us, that he will save us out of the hands of the Philistines. And Samuel took a sucking lamb, and offered it for a burnt-offering wholly unto the Lord: and Samuel cried unto the Lord for Israel; and the Lord heard him. And as Samuel was offering up the burnt offering, the Philistines drew near to battle against Israel: but the Lord thundered with a great thunder on that day upon the Philistines, and discomfited them; and they were smitten before Israel," 1 Sam. 7:7-10. Thus was Samuel Israel's artillery and armed force.

Behold, such help and deliverance can praying believers obtain for their fellow-men! For faith takes hold of the promise, and takes hold of the Divine strength in the promise, and thus can do great things. So, doubtless, at present, the faith of God's elect restrains many a vial of wrath; and happy is the place where such praying believers dwell. They are of greater service to such a place than walls of brass and ramparts of rock.

Happy the church whose pastors are the "chariots of Israel, and the horsemen thereof!" They are Israel's chariots, when, like Moses once, they ascend with you on the fiery wheels of intercession, through clouds and darkness, to the throne of grace. They are Israel's horsemen, when they send their arrows into your hearts, exclaiming, "Thou, thou art the man!" They are Israel's chariots, when, with a holy courage, they thresh every high place among you, that Christ alone may be exalted. They are Israel's horsemen, when, in the armor of God, they take the field in prayer for you, day and night, against the power of Satan and his seducing spirits. Pray for your own sakes, that God may anoint your teachers to be such men, and that you may be able to say of them when they are gone, "The chariot of Israel, and the horsemen thereof!"

Elisha's Grief

II. Elisha's eyes would still follow his master's triumphal car; but it is soon out of sight, and he is now left alone. Well might he now utter the lamentation of the psalmist, "Woe is me, that I" must still "sojourn in Mesech, and dwell in the tents of Kedar!" He rends his clothes, exclaiming, "My father! my father!"

We are not in a situation fully to understand and sympathize with Elisha's grief, because we have never had to mourn over the depar-ture of an Elijah. We must have stood at the grave of a Luther or a Calvin, in order to know something of it. We must imagine what it is to lose a beloved father or a tender mother, out of a family; and then apply this to the whole church of the saints.

But how different is the end of the ungodly from that on which we have now been meditating, and which, in substance at least, is the end of all Jehovah's saints! To the ungodly our God is a consuming fire, and their end will be destruction. "The wicked shall be turned into hell, and all the people that forget God." There will be weeping and gnashing of teeth; the worm will never die and the fire will never be quenched. Love will not dwell in those regions of darkness, neither will hope cast its cheering rays through the endless night. A scene will be realized there, far exceeding all our conceptions of woe. But blessed be God, the day of grace is yet continued to us. We still hear the voice of God, calling us to repentance, and saying, "Turn ye, turn ye; for why will ye die? As I live, saith the Lord God, I have no pleasure in the death of a sinner, but rather that he should repent and live." We still behold the open arms of a deliverer, which are kindly extended toward us. But, as everything has its time and its season, therefore, "work out now your own salvation with fear and trembling; for it is God that worketh in you, both to will and to do of his good pleasure." "Kiss the Son, lest he be angry, and ye perish from the way, when his wrath is kindled but a little." One of two events must follow our pilgrimage through this world; either an ascent to heaven, or a descent to hell. There is no middle state in eternity. Therefore, "O Lord God, Lamb of God, Son of the Father, that takest away the sin of the world, have mercy upon us. Thou that sittest at the right hand of God the Father, receive our prayer." Amen.

26

The Legacy

2 Kings 2:13-15

> He took up also the mantle of Elijah that fell from him, and went back, and stood by the bank of Jordan; and he took the mantle of Elijah that fell from him, and smote the waters, and said, Where is the Lord God of Elijah? and when he also had smitten the water, they parted hither and thither: and Elisha went over. And when the sons of the prophets which were to view at Jericho saw him, they said, The spirit of Elijah doth rest on Elisha. And they came to meet him, and bowed themselves to the ground before him.

We come now to an interesting act; the will of the departed prophet is unsealed, and Elisha is the heir of an inheritance, the like of which the world had seldom seen. Let us contemplate the happy man somewhat more closely in the enjoyment of his heritage, and consider Elisha, I. With Elijah's mantle; II. With Elijah's God; III. With Elijah's spirit; and, IV. In Elijah's office.

Elijah's Mantle

I. At the moment when Elijah was taken up in his fiery chariot, his prophet's mantle, unloosed by an invisible hand, fell from his shoulders, and floated down before Elisha. Although this was a trifling circumstance in itself, yet it is too significant to be overlooked. With his mantle Elijah had forever thrown off the burden of his commission. When formerly he cast his mantle upon Elisha at Abel Meholah, it was but as a preparatory vocation to the prophetic office. But Elisha, on inheriting this mantle, is henceforth called to take the place of his great master, and to carry on his work. This singular lega-

274

cy was therefore very significant to Elisha. The mantle came flying toward him heavily laden. But with the onerous commission he thus received, was connected the encouraging circumstance, that it came accompanied by such a precious memorial of his eternal master. It was now no longer the mantle of the feared reformer, but the robe of a blessed heir of heaven, borne thither on the wings of the cherubim. It would remind him, and others of the kindness and love of God to sinful men, expressed in a most unusual manner. The ascension of its owner to heaven had rendered it a truly festal garment; and thus it would contribute to refresh the spirit of Elisha in his arduous office; and, at the same time, to identify him as that gracious messenger of peace, who was to announce to the house of Israel, like the rainbow after a storm, Jehovah's good-will toward men.

It was also a significant circumstance to Elisha, that the official garment he was henceforth to wear was cast to him, as it were, out of the open heavens. What else could he perceive in it, but an immediate investiture and vocation on the part of the living God? And indeed, every priestly mantle ought to carry the same significance now. I mean that every clergyman, teacher, missionary, or whoever else labors in God's vineyard, ought to be able to say, with Elisha, "I have received my commission from Heaven—my call is of God." But, in the present day, people commonly make the mantle themselves, esteeming it as an idle tale that anything should fall from heaven but rain or snow, and looking upon the sacred office of a minister as upon any other profession, which may be taken up at pleasure, or for the sake of a maintenance. The parents decide for their child that he shall be a clergyman. The vain youthful student, especially if he be conscious of possessing some little talent, immediately thinks himself fit for the sacred office. How many young men proceed to universities to enter upon the study of divinity, without even the most distant thought of asking counsel of God, in order to learn by the directions of Scripture, by circumstances of Providence, and their own qualifications, whether it be his will to employ them in the work of the ministry! And when arrived at the university, how seldom do they meet with any pious counselor, such as Elijah was to Elisha, to take them aside, and inquire whether they had any other proof of their call to the ministry than their own notion and fancy, and the counsel of flesh and blood. Hence it is that we have now the mournful example of many a flock in Christendom, among whom grievous wolves fill the shepherd's office, to the subversion and ruin of souls. Is it then to be wondered at that the common mariner should occasionally seize the helm, when the pilot knows not how to govern the ship? The persecutors of such would do well to consider, that they are only opposing what they themselves have contributed to bring into existence.

Elijah's God

II. After Elisha had taken up the mantle in the name of the Lord, he commences his return to Jericho, doubtless much affected, and yet comforted; for not only Elijah's mantle, but Elijah's God remains to him. Of this he cannot doubt; but where is the faith which no longer requires a seal? "Show me a token for good," says the psalmist; and what comment of his is more often repeated than this? Elisha returns to the eastern bank of Jordan. He beholds the stream at his feet, and over it he must pass. Elijah is no longer at his side, and his mantle alone is not sufficient. Elijah's God must manifest Himself. We may easily suppose that he now heartily prayed, if not in David's words, "Show me a token for good"; yet in the language of deep submission and humble dependence on the Divine power and faithfulness. He takes the mantle of Elijah, folds it together as his master had done, and with it he smites the waters of Jordan, saying, "Where is the Lord God of Elijah?" What shall we say to this? It may sound strange in the ears of some: nevertheless it was a right way of proceeding; and "He that searcheth the hearts knoweth what is the mind of the Spirit, because he maketh intercession for the saints, according to the will of God," Rom. 8:27. The Lord was the portion of Elisha's inheritance, and not the prophet's mantle and commission only; and his faith could say, "Thou shalt maintain my lot." Thus Isaac inherited the portion of his father Abraham; and to Jacob God declared himself as the God of Abraham and of Isaac. To believers also of subsequent times he revealed himself as the God of Abraham, and of Isaac, and of Jacob; and thereby promised to them the blessings he had bestowed on those patriarchs; assuring them that he would bear them in his hands with the same faithfulness. Hence the Old Testament saints, when praying, directed their petitions to Jehovah as the God of their fathers.

And to whom do we direct our prayers? Thrice happy are we who have seen and known the "God manifest in the flesh," to whom we can pray with a degree of confidence, which the saints of Israel did not possess. We know that whatever the Lord of glory did for men in the days of his flesh, was to be a type and a pattern of what he will now do for all who diligently seek him. Oh how does it strengthen our faith, that we may say, when sin oppresses us, when affliction casts us down, or when poverty and want come upon us, "Where is the God of the penitent malefactor? where is the God of Martha, and Mary, and of Lazarus? where is the God of Paul, and of Peter, and of Mary Magdalene? where is the Lord, who after his resurrection, on the shore of the lake of Galilee, prepared a fire of coals, and bread and fish likewise, for his disciples, and who more than once fed thousands with a few loaves and fishes?" Yes, "this God is our God for ever and ever: he shall be our guide even unto death." "Jesus Christ the same yesterday, today, and forever!" Lo, he is "with us always, even to the end of the world." Amen.

Surely it is something very great and blessed, that we are permitted to call the God of all the favored individuals mentioned in the New Testament, *our God*. But the privileges of true Christians may be expressed in yet stronger language than this, because of their mystical union with the only begotten Son of God. They can say, "Where is the God and Father of our Lord Jesus Christ?" For what is it that Christ himself says of them in his prayer, to his Father? "That they all may be one; as thou, Father, art in me, and I in thee, that they also may be one in us: that the world may believe that thou hast sent me, and that *thou hast loved them, as thou hast loved* ME," John 17:21, 23. Oh, incomprehensibly glorious and adorable mystery of godliness! God indeed manifest in our flesh! We are therefore as true believers, who keep his commandments and do those things which are pleasing in his sight, warranted by his own express word, to expect, hope, and desire of God the supply of all our real necessities, as confidently and as assuredly as Christ himself, with respect to his human nature, was thus warranted during his sojourn upon earth. Think only, with humble and adoring gratitude, what unsearchable riches of blessing are implied in such a privilege as this. And shall it ever cease? No more than the love of the Father to Christ himself can cease. Such is his love to those who believe in his name. Live, my beloved brethren, daily in the faith of such a truth as this; and it will enable you to overcome every difficulty in the path of duty; to run and not be weary, to walk and not faint.

Elijah's Spirit

III. No sooner had Elisha smitten the waters of Jordan, than the manifestation of the Lord God of Elijah is vouchsafed. The stream of the river is again parted by an invisible hand, the course of the upper part of it is arrested by an unseen barrier, and the prophet descends with a firm and sure step upon its dry gravelly bed. It would be vain for me to attempt to describe to you the feelings which he must have experienced on this occasion. A deeply humble and contrite person, who experiences some sudden and evident answer to prayer; or a young and modest minister of God, who may have been tempted tremblingly to doubt whether he had received a Divine call to his office, but who sees in the first loaded fishing-net he draws to land, a Divine ratification, as it were, of his call to the ministry—such persons will be the first to sympathize with the unspeakable joy of Elisha, upon beholding the river divided at his word. In his wonderful passage across its bed, he must have experienced feelings something like those of Israel when passing through the Red sea; and of him also it may be said, that he was baptized in Jordan. Filled with the consciousness of God's nearness to him, he must have felt every doubt and scruple vanish away, like the mists before the morning sun. He now strikingly experienced that the Lord God of Elijah had caused a double portion of his spirit to rest upon him; God having given him the same power to exercise over the river, was an earnest of what he had granted him besides. How wonderfully also was his office as a prophet to Israel magnified by this miracle.

Upon his arrival on the other side Jordan, "when the sons of the prophets which were to view at Jericho saw him, they said, The spirit of Elijah doth rest on Elisha; and they came to meet him, and bowed themselves to the ground before him." This reverential homage had not so much reference to the man, as to the spirit that rested upon him, the Divine power which showed itself in him. These sons of the prophets not only perceived what was Divine, but they viewed it with affection and veneration. This was a beautiful feature in their character; whereas "the natural man receiveth not the things of the Spirit of God." Happy is it also for us, if we are affectionately and reverently affected toward Divine things, and toward those on whom the Spirit of the Lord rests. It is recorded of one of the most distinguished painters of former days, that when he was a mere boy, after viewing a painting by Raphael for some time, with silent transport, he suddenly broke out, with joy beaming in his countenance, as if he had found a great treasure, "I too am a painter!" He then left the picture gallery, mixed his colors, and afterward produced works, not unlike that which had kindled in him such enthusiasm for his art. In like manner, it may be regarded as a happy sign in ourselves when the spiritual image of an Abraham, an Elijah, or a Paul, transports us with affection, and kindles the ardent wish within us, that our hearts were formed like theirs. And if the consoling thought suggests itself, (I am speaking to those who love and keep the words of Christ,) that we also are the children of God by faith in Christ Jesus, that in us there is something of the same spirit which animated those eminent saints, we ought not to reject such a thought. For he who knows how to understand and appreciate those men, in their peculiar character, and embraces them with affection on account of their spiritual excellences, certainly indicates that something of their mind exists within him; for like is only understood and loved by its like. Hence the Lord says, "He that receiveth a prophet in the name of a prophet," that is, in the character of a prophet, or because he is a prophet, "shall receive a prophet's reward," for by this reception, he shows himself to be like-minded with him whom he receives.

Elijah's Office

IV. Elisha, with the spirit of his great predecessor, inherits also his office and his flock. Elijah had not commenced his prophetical course under such favorable circumstances. He had entered upon a waste moral wilderness; whereas his successor finds the fallow ground, as it were, broken up; he even sees here and there a blooming plantation, whose fresh and vigorous shoots already bear the promise of future blessings to Israel.

A minister of the gospel of Christ ought to esteem it no small advantage to find, on entering upon the care of a church, a little flock of really believing souls already waiting to receive him. However small their number, he discerns among them a little leaven, as it were, which is easily capable of further extension, and an echo to his instructions, his prayers, and his praises, from the hearts of affectionate brethren. In this consists the prosperity of a church, and not in earthly property and endowments. A church that is rich in the word of God, is rich indeed. It has then the keys of the invisible world; the weapons against death and hell; the universal remedy

for every evil; the wondrous staff that can divide every river; the tree
of life, whose leaves are for the healing of the nations; and the lamp
which lights the way through time into eternity. And even should
this precious treasure remain like an unemployed capital, still the
church by which it is possessed has much cause for thankfulness. It
lies at least within the territory of hope, and is like a field which has
received the seed into its furrows, although it has not yet sprung up.
The husbandman regards it with a hopeful eye, for it needs only that
the gentle showers fall, and it may by and by appear clothed in the
most beautiful foliage.

In many places the word has sprung up, and we have long had
among us many living men of God. If we look around us in our
church meetings, how many a brother and sister's face beams upon
us there! If we pass through our streets, where is there one in which
we might not somewhere or other greet a tabernacle of God with
men? Yes, there are quarters of the town in which house after house
is a pavilion of the Lord, and where we meet with groups of humble
and consistent Christians. And oh, how many a beautiful flower,
how many a lily of our valley, blooms in modest concealment,
known only to the heavenly Husbandman who refreshes it with his
dew, or perhaps to one or two among us by whom it has been acci-
dentally discovered! How many a holy soul walks in the midst of us
unobserved, and without talking or boasting; while few know the
rich treasures of grace it carries within, and the ardent love with
which it is attached to its Savior! Yes, were all who fear the Lord
among us to come together into one place, I believe we should be
astonished to see how numerous they are. It is true they are of various forms and complexions in outward respects; but they are of one
spirit, one faith, and one hope. Oh how we rejoice in being able to
call such husbandry ours! Blessed inheritance, which our never to
be forgotten predecessors have left us! To Divine grace alone belongs
the praise, honor, and glory.

But to return to Elisha, we left him on his way to Jericho, richly
laden with the fruits of the Spirit, to become a blessing to the land;
his own mind sparkling like the starry heavens with a thousand stupendous thoughts and hopes. Elijah's legacy to him may serve to
remind us of the better legacy which is bequeathed to every faithful
disciple of Christ. The mantle which our Savior has left to every one
of his followers is the robe of his own righteousness, a festal robe

indeed! It answers the purpose of armor here, and of priestly glory also, for our entrance into the holiest. It is so interwoven with personal holiness, that the two are always joined together; so that it constitutes the wedding garment of the soul, and sanctifies the members of the body for the service of God.

The God whom we serve is "a just God and a Savior," who "carries the lambs in his bosom," who deems not the angels too high for our ministering attendants, who combines his own glory and our happiness in one and the same everlasting love. The Spirit of holiness which he imparts to us, though he does not divide the waves of the sea, yet quells in us the troubled conscience; and though he does not act in us as a spirit of prophetic vision, yet "witnesses with our Spirit that we are the children of God." He does not excite us to call down fire from heaven, but he enables us to cry, "Abba, Father!" and though he does not make us workers of miracles, yet he makes us temples of the living God. Yes, and the office of ministers of the Spirit, as all true Christian ministers are, far transcends the office of any prophet of the Old Testament. For our ministry is that of reconciliation, which cries to men, "ye are complete in Him"; and that "there is no condemnation to them that are in Christ Jesus, who walk not after the flesh, but after the Spirit"; and that "he will not break the bruised reed, nor quench the smoking flax." We are not only Christ's messengers, but are commissioned to "beseech men in Christ's stead, to be reconciled to God." We are sent by him, even as he was sent by the Father. We act in the name of the Son of God, and carry not only the standard, but the keys of the kingdom of heaven, John 20:23. Behold, beloved brethren in the Lord, thus have we been remembered, in the will of Him who hung upon the cross. What a glorious legacy! What an unspeakably precious bequest! Let us rejoice always in these superior blessings of Divine grace; and, accounting that "the lines are fallen to us in pleasant places, yea, that we have a goodly heritage," let us pray and labor, and labor and pray, that we may live accordingly. Amen.

27

Growth in Grace

We know how much depends upon the hands into which a newborn infant comes, and how greatly its health and vigor in after life is influenced by the treatment it receives in its tenderest age. This is true also of newborn babes in a spiritual sense. It is no unimportant consideration to whose care they are entrusted. How many go haltingly all their days, through being placed under perverted guidance!

There is a religious party existing in the midst of us, which, because it does not receive the doctrine of sin and atonement in the apostolic sense, has no part in the blessed privilege of serving the Lord in gathering and bringing home the sheep of his fold. No icy heart melts under their teaching; no resurrection of the dry bones takes place under their ministry; yet is that party remarkable for its zeal to extend and increase itself, although it can only do so by building its wood, hay, and stubble on another man's foundation. The important work of awakening, and of conversion, it leaves to others. It does not begin its labors among the dry bones, but only where the stream of new life has already found its way; neither can it exonerate itself, with St. Paul, from the charge of entering upon other men's labors, 2 Cor. 10:15. Under its withering influence many a tender plant has pined away, and many a young and hopeful tree has been blasted.

In connection with this subject, we intend, in the course of our present meditation, to notice the character of genuine practical Christianity.

2 Kings 2:16-18

And they said unto him, Behold now, there be with thy servants fifty

282

strong men; let them go, we pray thee, and seek thy master: lest peradventure the Spirit of the Lord hath taken him up, and cast him upon
some mountain, or into some valley. And he said, Ye shall not send.
And when they urged him till he was ashamed, he said, Send. They
sent therefore fifty men; and they sought three days, but found him not
And when they came again to him, (for he tarried at Jericho,) he said
unto them, Did I not say unto you, Go not?

Let us, I. Consider *the historical fact itself,* which this portion of
Scripture presents to our notice; and, II. Apply it to the Christian's
growth in grace.

The Historical Fact

I. Elisha now finds himself among the sons of the prophets, doubtless with his heart deeply affected by what he had witnessed and
experienced beyond Jordan, as well as in crossing it the second time.
Endued with a double portion of Elijah's spirit, and destined to do
even greater works than his predecessor, his character appears, nevertheless, not to have been immediately comprehended by the
mourning sons of the prophets, however sincerely they venerated and
loved him, and submitted themselves to him as their new teacher.
They could not all at once consider their departed master as fully
replaced by Elisha; much less that in the husbandman from Abel
Meholah, an Elijah, even of a superior order, was presented to them
by the Lord! Nor was this to be wondered at, seeing it was perfectly
natural that the dazzling powers of Elijah should affect them more
than the less imposing appearance of an unassuming brotherly Elisha.
The abstracted gravity of the Tishbite seems to have corresponded far
more with the natural ideas of human greatness, than the condescending affability of his humble successor. Elijah appeared rather as
an instance of the glory of man through Divine endowment;
whereas the appearance of Elisha seemed to commend the greatness
of God's grace in human weakness. Hence we wonder not that the
sons of the prophets did not at once duly appreciate Elijah's
invaluable substitute.

From similar causes, the disciples of John the Baptist were slow to
perceive that Jesus was greater than his forerunner clothed with
camel's hair in the wilderness, who seemed to them to carry with him
more of the appearance of an ambassador from heaven, than the gen-

tle and affable friend of publicans and sinners. The ministry of the Baptist would also, at a superficial view, commend itself to those whose minds were not entirely freed from a legal disposition to establish their own righteousness; they would naturally regard it as the most impressive form of piety, and as most suited to their own necessities. The Baptist himself would appear to such persons as a sort of perfect man, entirely abstracted from the fashion of this world; and the works of reformation which he enjoined would be numbered up in a tangible sum total. But Jesus, on the contrary, appearing in the greatest simplicity, not withdrawing from the customary forms of life, describing his kingdom as not coming with observation, and insisting first of all on secret submission of the heart; promising moreover nothing of human glory to his disciples, and enjoining upon them the despised and neglected virtues of humility and love—was in the eyes of the careless world in general, and of the self-righteous in particular, "without form or comeliness," and there was to them "no beauty in him, that they should desire him."

That the hearts of the sons of the prophets were principally with their departed master, is evident enough from the urgent request they made to their new teacher, as soon as he had arrived at Jericho. "Behold," said they unto him, perhaps with tears, "there be with thy servants fifty strong men; let them go, we pray thee, and seek thy master: lest peradventure the Spirit of the Lord hath taken him up, and cast him upon some mountain, or into some valley." There is something ambiguous in these words. What did these worthy persons mean? Did they not know by Divine communication that he was that day to be taken from them? Certainly they knew it; but it is evident that the manner of his removal had not been revealed to them. They might, therefore, suppose either that God had removed Elijah to some solitary place, in order afterward to take him to himself; or that he was received into paradise only as it regarded his soul; but that his lifeless corpse might still be lying exposed in the wilderness. Perhaps they thought of the death of Moses, who, in the same region, on the top of Pisgah, was taken away in a mysterious, distinguished, and blissful manner, but whose body was secretly buried by the Lord. But whatever were their thoughts, their intention manifested that ardent love which could hardly believe he was really gone. It is also evident, from the urgency of their request, that they regarded the loss of their master as irreparable, and with all the high esteem they cherished for his successor, were far from believing that he could fill up the enormous breach.

It would have been easy for Elisha, by whom such thoughts and feelings of theirs could not well be unperceived, to have taught them something different. He could have said to them, "I come to you with messages and information, such as you have never heard from the lips of Elijah. I have facts to relate to you concerning the love of God to man, which have been hitherto unknown to the world at large, and will fill you with adoring wonder." But Elisha does not appear at this time to have taken a single step toward securing to himself such estimation. He was above those little sensibilities, which cause the slightest appearance of disrespect to affect us like the sting of a scorpion! Doubtless it was with sincere satisfaction that he witnessed the love and veneration with which the sons of the prophets adhered to their departed father; and was not vain enough to prefer his own honor in their esteem, to the wisdom which dictated his silence, for the present, as to what he had witnessed beyond Jordan, and which suggested a more convenient season for his strange and delightful communications.

Though we cannot fully explain why Elisha withheld from the sons of the prophets the account of Elijah's miraculous ascension, we cannot doubt that he had the wisest and best reasons for so doing. As a prudent steward of God's mysteries, he appears to have considered the capacities and wants of those whom he had to deal with, and to have reserved such matters for their proper occasion. Hence, though the sons of the prophets were increasingly urgent to obtain his consent to the sending out of fifty brethren in search of their departed master; all this did not induce him to disclose the secret. Their urgency was at length so great, that he was chained at their importunity, that is, he was embarrassed, and at a loss what to say to them. But he preferred yielding to their ill-advised purpose, and letting them go, rather than betray his precious secret before the time. It could at any rate do them no harm to convince themselves that neither their master nor his mortal remains were to be found any longer upon earth. By this means they would be the more disposed afterward to credit the intelligence of his corporeal ascension. So they went forth and searched for three days together through the wilderness country. But their journey proved a fruitless toil, and they returned to Jericho, downcast and weary. The only benefit they obtained by their laborious search was the gentle but salutary reproof of their master, "Did I not say unto you, Go not?" "Give instruction to a wise man, and he will be yet wiser," Prov. 9:9.

Sometimes we see it necessary to comply with the foolish wishes of wayward but beloved children, that they may learn, perhaps, by painful experience. And this is even exemplified, to our sorrow, in spiritual as well as in temporal matters. Thus, how difficult is it to persuade some that the righteousness which avails in the sight of God is quite near them—that Jesus Christ is nigh unto them, with all his righteousness to bestow on them, if they will only give themselves up entirely to him. They will still forget and undervalue him, and think well of themselves, and thus virtually seek justification before God in their own persons, instead of seeking it heartily in Christ. What their remains for us at last but to say, "Well, then, go to your own broken cisterns!" They may thus, for a while, torment themselves with the righteousness of the law, which only works wrath; and thus may learn by experience that they have chosen a path of peril, bankruptcy, and ruin—where there is no life, no progress, to reward their pains. They may then return to us with a trembling conscience, and welcome the confounding inquiry, "Did we not say unto you, Go not?" and thus Christ may become precious to them, and the gospel glad tidings indeed!

The Christian's Growth in Grace

II. It is evident from the portion of the sacred history we have just been considering that Elisha did not yet consider the sons of the prophets sufficiently prepared to receive the glorious message which he had to deliver. Though they were children of God, and had already partaken of the gifts of Divine grace, yet their master evidently looked upon them as standing in need of further spiritual education and improvement. We are reminded by this circumstance to say a few words on a subject, of which many Christians seem to entertain very limited views. I mean *"the growth of the children of God,"* of which the Scriptures speak so repeatedly, their increase IN THE GRACE AND KNOWLEDGE OF OUR LORD AND SAVIOR JESUS CHRIST. I know of no passage of Scripture in which the spiritual life of a true Christian is more fully and accurately described, than the words of the great apostle to the Gentiles (Phil. 3:12-14): "Not as though I had already attained, either were already perfect: but I follow after, if that I may apprehend that for which also I am apprehended of Christ Jesus. Brethren, I count not myself to have apprehended; but this one thing I do, forgetting those things which are behind, and reaching forth unto those things which are before, I press toward the mark for the prize of the high calling of God in Christ Jesus." This is the way in which the true Christian will think of himself: "Not as though I had already attained." Consequently, he will, with the apostle, follow after an increasing conformity to Christ; and he will never forget that this is the object for which he has been apprehended by Christ Jesus. Let us notice a little more closely these characteristic marks of genuine Christian faith.

Wherever there is life, real spiritual life, there is also progress in that life, from one state of knowledge and improvement to another. A plant, which makes no shoots or growth, is dead or sickly. Even the tree that has reached its full height does not remain as it is, but constantly renews and varies its outward appearance. Thus it is in the kingdom of nature; and so it is also in the kingdom of grace. "Be ye therefore renewed in the spirit of your minds," is the language of Scripture; and the fact in real Christians corresponds to it; for they can say, "Though our outward man perish, yet our inward man is renewed day by day."

"Not as though I had already attained, either were already perfect." Whose words are these? One would think they were the words of one who was but a beginner in the kingdom of grace, or who perhaps had not yet even entered the strait gate. But they are the words of one who had arrived at a height of spiritual stature, such as probably none among us has attained. Remember that this is the language of one who could also say, "I live; yet not I, but Christ liveth in me," Gal. 2:20; who could also say, "Who shall separate us from the love of Christ?" Rom. 8:35; who could say, "Brethren, be followers together of me, and mark them which walk so as ye have us for an ensample," Phil. 3:17. Here then is one who, at the very time that he was, with respect to the church militant, one of the brightest stars in Christ's right hand, freely and openly confesses that he had not already attained; and even repeats it with greater emphasis again, "Brethren, I count not myself to have apprehended." It is true, he is not speaking of what he is in point of justification before God, through faith in the righteousness of Christ; for he plainly teaches that the righteousness of Christ, laid hold of by faith, fully justifies us; and hence he could say, "Being justified by faith, we have peace with God, through our Lord Jesus Christ"; "It is God that justifieth: who is he that condemneth?" And in another place, "Christ by his one offering hath perfected for ever them that are sanctified." But the apostle, in the passages we have been noticing, is expressing his desire to see the life of his faith in Christ continually more and more manifested in the improved state of his heart and life. To appear, therefore, self-complacent and self-satisfied with our attainments, betrays ignorance of Christ, and lack of faith.

But, alas! how many are there among us who appear to suppose that they have "already attained"? Let us take as an instance, spiritual knowledge. There are many who are well acquainted with the fundamental doctrines of the gospel, and are perhaps able to defend them by argument, and have their memories stored with no small number of texts of Scripture, and pious psalms and hymns. We converse with such persons, and are glad to see them thus furnished. But a year afterward we converse with them again, and find them just the same. Two years elapse, and we come into contact with them again, but still no progress can be perceived—till at length the sight of them reminds us of a piece of wood-work carved in the form of a tree, rather than a living production of nature, for there are no fresh shoots nor any new foliage to be seen; on the contrary, the very same modes of speech, the same views and sentiments upon every point, and the same limited sphere of spiritual conception—no enlarged expansion of the inward horizon, not a single addition to the treasury of Christian knowledge. "But," say you, "what need we know more than we do know?" Ah, there it is! You have completed the circle of your knowledge; and in this respect, as you suppose, you are already perfect, and have already attained. But this is an indication of spiritual sickness. For if your souls were in health, and prospering, you would say with Paul, "Not that I have already attained"; you would be sensible of the imperfection of your knowledge; you would believe that thousands of precious things still lay hidden from you in the Scriptures; you would investigate the holy writings with increasing interest; you would continually find new glories while perusing the Testament of your Mediator; and when we see you from time to time, we should hear you exclaim, "Oh what precious things I have afresh discovered in my Bible! what a new and valuable light has been given to me upon this or that subject! what new and delightful views have I obtained of the glory and excellency of my blessed Redeemer!" And the more you thus grow in the grace and knowledge of our Lord and Savior Jesus Christ, the more valuable will the Scriptures become to you, the more sensibly will you be convinced that you might continue to search in this mine all your life, without exhausting it of the half of its treasures; and the more decidedly will you say with Paul, "Not that I have already attained"; and so much the more diligence will you give to search further and further into the inexhaustible riches of Christ.

But worse still than self-satisfaction in Christian knowledge is that stagnation of spiritual life which some betray by saying, "My sins were forgiven me; at such and such a time I received the assurance of it; and I know that the gifts and calling of God are without repentance!" The individual leads henceforth what is called a Christian life, performs his daily devotions, and supposes that everything is done, and that he has reached his aim. But was not Paul fully assured of his forgiveness and election? And yet he says, "Not as though I had already attained." We cannot too carefully remember that wherever spiritual health is enjoyed, the inward life is in continual progress. The child of heaven, the new creature, endeavors after the stature of a man, after "the measure of the stature of the fullness of Christ." There is, then, no end to its improvement. The life of faith in Christ is an increased abiding in him as its element. Hence there is less narrowness of mind, more love, more humility, more circumspection, more uniform zeal.

One word more upon our "not having yet attained." For St. Paul says, "I count all things but loss and dung, that I may win Christ, and be found in him; not having my own righteousness, which is of the law, but that which is by the faith of Christ, even the righteousness which is of God by faith." Here then we perceive that the righteousness of faith ought to be continually the aim and prize to which as believers we are to "reach forth"; I say, continually, and not merely at the commencement of our Christian course. And why are we to reach forth to it? Surely in order to enjoy it, to appropriate it, and to be invigorated by the belief of it to active love for Christ and for our brethren; and consequently to walk as He walked, and in perpetually doing good to men, both temporally and spiritually. And this requires perpetual self-denial and exertion on our part. It requires what the apostle calls "reaching forth unto the things which are before." For surely we cannot be ignorant that there are many hindrances to our attainment of this vigorous state of personal Christianity. To name only that single hindrance, our natural reluctance to rely simply on the merits and strength of our Divine Surety: is not this enough to awaken a holy jealousy against ourselves, and a vigilant spirit of prayer and diligence? We are prone so to forget the freeness of the grace of justification before God through the merits of the Redeemer, as to fall back in some degree upon the covenant of works. We are apt to imagine that some particular degree of holiness must first be attained before we can presume to rejoice in the free forgiveness of all our sins, and our reinstatement in the Divine favor; whereas, it is entirely through our Lord Jesus Christ that God justifies the ungodly. Forasmuch, then, as our whole peace, comfort, and strength depend primarily on our heartfelt belief of what we are and have in Christ Jesus, surely we have need to be constantly directing our endeavors after a full apprehension and heartfelt experience of the inestimable worth of Christ to our souls. For this is the only way to obtain complete victory over indwelling sin, and it is the main motive to adorn the doctrine of God our Savior in all things. Faith in the word of God concerning Christ our Savior is the healthful element in which a Christian spirit thrives. And how good is it always to remember that while we are endeavoring to apprehend the word of God, we are thus giving a proof that "we are apprehended of Christ Jesus," as St. Paul says. What a blessing is it always to feel that every desire after him is owing to his own previous love toward us, and to his gracious interposition on our behalf: and that each Christian should speak and think of him for himself, as the Savior who loved me, and gave himself for me!

Ever then let the wish and prayer of Moses, more and more, be ours: "I beseech thee, show me thy glory!" St. Paul being thus apprehended of Christ, follows after, "that he may apprehend that for which also he is apprehended" of him. And what is this which he so desires, but that with every increasing experience that in the Lord Jesus he has all righteousness and strength, he may become more and more like him, by keeping his words, and conforming to his precepts and example; by entering more feelingly every day into the spirit and meaning of all his gracious will and intentions. For his sake this holy apostle had thrown every thing overboard which he once had counted gain. All such things he had learned to account as loss for Christ, regarding them but as dross, "that he might win Christ, and be found in him." He therefore forgets himself with respect to all that he is by nature and by birth, and all that he has acquired by his own efforts. He has nailed to the cross the image of his whole former man, and cast away his specious advantages as a offscouring from his sight. He is willing to be nothing in his own eyes—nothing but a poor needy sinner; for he is not afraid to behold his own natural condition, because he knows that grace excels and repairs it a thousand times. He is much more afraid of the insinuating fancies of his own virtues and good works, because he is, once for all, resolved never more to admit any other consolation into his heart than that Divine one, that he is justified and complete in Christ. No, he goes still further in forgetting self. For even that which he had already enjoyed and acquired, in his dealings with the Lord, he regards among "the things that are behind."

Many have been tempted to spiritual pride, or else to spiritual depression, by the thoughts of their past experience in a life of grace. Some are very apt to indulge in melancholy recollections of a past and better state than that which they now enjoy. They laud the golden days of their espousals, the blessedness they knew when first they tasted that the Lord was gracious; and thus they stand like superannuated old men, who have left the fairest periods of their life behind them, and having no definite hopes for the future, only occasionally begin again to warm a little, when the past presents itself to their minds, and sends some sunny rays into their present winterly existence. Oh how different does St. Paul appear in this respect! Still brighter attainments of the confidence and joy of faith are the objects he keeps perpetually in view. He presses forward toward the mark for the prize of our high calling in Christ Jesus. He cannot be satisfied with beholding only a few glimmering rays of the Divine glory; nor with anything short of being "changed into the same image from glory to glory, even as by the Spirit of the Lord," 2 Cor. 3:18. He saw the fairest days of his spiritual life lying not behind him, but before him. Compared with what was yet to come, all the past was to him only as a foretaste; "an earnest of the inheritance," Eph. 1:14.

Behold, such was the mind of the great apostle! And is not this a pattern for us that may well awaken our desire to grow in grace? What remains, then, but that we be found living and walking in the

same spirit and in the same steps, that we may realize the same blessing, the same enjoyments? May He who says, "I am the Lord, thy
Physician," have mercy upon us, and having forgiven us our iniquities, may he also heal all our diseases. May He put away from
ourselves whatever hinders the free and joyful development of spiritual life within us. May He deliver us from the bonds of false and
hurtful notions, and grant that the love of Christ may be the main
stem, and faith in Christ the root of all we do. Yes, may the God of
peace and of all grace transplant every one of us from the sterile soil
of a false legality and self-righteousness, into the fruitful and well-
watered soil of his own gospel; and under the breathing of his
life-giving Spirit, cause us to flourish, that we may be perfect in love,
and "grow up into him in all things, which is the head, even Christ!"
Amen.

28

Elijah's Letter to Jehoram

An awful shipwreck of a royal vessel is recalled to our notice by the portion of Scripture selected for our present meditation. Let the wreck here presented to us be a warning against heart idolatry, that great evil of the present day. Let the affectionate words of the last surviving and aged apostle be now more heeded than ever: "Little children, keep yourselves from idols." Amen.

2 Chronicles 21:12-15

> And there came a writing to him (Jehoram) from Elijah the prophet, saying, Thus saith the Lord God of David thy father, Because thou hast not walked in the ways of Jehoshaphat thy father, nor in the ways of Asa king of Judah, but hast walked in the way of the Kings of Israel and hast made Judah and the inhabitants of Jerusalem to go a whoring like to the whoredoms of the house of Ahab, and also hast slain the brethren of thy father's house, which were better than thyself: behold with a great plague will the Lord smite thy people, and thy children and thy wives, and all thy goods: and thou shalt have great sickness by disease of the bowels, until thy bowels fall out by reason of the sickness day by day.

Elijah Rests from His Labors

I. Elijah rests from his labors. At the time of his departure to heaven, king Jehoram, the son of Ahab, sat on the throne of the kingdom of Israel. Jehoshaphat reigned in Judah, and continued to do so until the eighth year after the removal of our prophet. He also had now been gathered to his fathers, and first-born, Ahab's son-in-law, the degenerate Jehoram, of the same name with his brother-in-law, the king of Israel, had ascended the throne. To this Jehoram a writing comes, the contents of which were far from agreeable. The writing came from "Elijah the Tishbite," who had departed in the chariot of fire to heaven at least six years before.

It is said by St. Paul, that Abel, in a figurative sense, "being dead, yet speaketh." The quiet and godly character of this pious shepherd; his accepted sacrifice offered unto God in faith; his unnatural death, prefiguring to future ages what the children of God had to expect in this world; his blood, which cried to Heaven for recompense—all this is a kind of speaking, though without the use of words. And in this way many a pious departed person still speaks, though his tongue may have long been silent in the grave; and many a church and family is thus spoken to by the example of some departed member. What a cloud of such invisible witnesses encompasses us! How many never-to-be-forgotten pilgrims of God, whose names still live in our hearts or memories, still preach to us, encourage and comfort us, by their still remembered words and examples! Thus their influence on earth has not ceased with their earthly life. But here, it should seem, that the prophet Elijah did not speak merely by example to those he left behind: he spoke by a writing.

We are not, however, to expect that many will believe this in the present age, which has for some time been endeavoring to cleanse every corner of the earth from the belief of whatever is miraculous and supernatural. But we cannot conceal our belief that this is one scriptural instance which teaches us that between the kingdom of the blessed and the dark vale of our pilgrimage, there is not such a vast distance as most persons are apt to imagine. And are there not several other instances in Scripture which support this belief? Did not Samuel personally appear after his decease, and speak to Saul in common human language? Did not Elijah and Moses, more than a thousand years after their departure, meet their Savior and his disciples on the mount of transfiguration? Did not the apostles, when they beheld their Divine Master walking on the sea, and again when he appeared after his resurrection, imagine they saw an apparition from the invisible world; and did not our Lord, instead of reproving them for this, as mere superstition, only appeal to their senses to convince them that he was not such an apparition as they supposed him to be? Peter, too, after his deliverance from prison, was mistaken by the brethren for his spirit, as if they had thought he had died in prison; and is there a word said in Scripture to contradict any such supposed erroneous notion, namely, of the possibility of departed saints re-appearing in this visible world?

This awful writing comes to Jehoram, nearly eight years after Elijah's removal, and this is all we learn from the sacred text, for no explanation is given. How, then, is the fact to be explained? There are three different answers given to this question. The first is twofold: either that the name Elijah is here put for Elisha, because the latter came in the spirit and power of the former; or else that it is put for Elisha by a mistake of the transcribers. Now, neither part of this twofold answer is by any means satisfactory. The former supposition is unsatisfactory, because it is contrary to the whole analogy and simplicity of Scripture, in plain historical narration, that one man should be called by the name of another. The latter is unsatisfactory, because we have no evidence whatever that any mistake has here been made by the copyists, but all the evidence lies on the other side. For instance, the Septuagint version, which was very early made, and very widely spread, has it Elias; that is, according to its Greek, Elijah, and not Elisha, which latter word in Greek is Eliseus. Again, the Jewish historian, Josephus, in his Antiquities, a work also very widely spread in the world for ages, referring to this event, has expressly the word Elias, or Elijah.

The second answer that has been given to account for this writing coming to Jehoram at that time is that Elijah wrote it by prophetic prescience before he left the earth, and of course before Jehoram ascended the throne of his father, and either deposited it with the sons of the prophets, or committed it to the care of Elisha, and commissioned him to send it to Jehoram at a time prescribed. But as we have no evidence of such a fact, so we have no probable assumption for supposing it.

The third explanation remains to be considered; namely, that this writing literally came from Elijah the prophet, after his ascension from the earth. And why not, as well as by the agency of an angel, if it thus pleased God to make use of the prophet Elijah? In what manner it was done, we attempt not to explain, any more than we attempt to explain how this prophet appeared unto Peter, and James, and John, at our Lord's transfiguration on the holy mount. We ven-

ture not to explain how far the powers and sphere of action
vouchsafed to the "spirits of just men made perfect" are extended;
much less to assert that they bear no relation to the state of the
church militant here on earth. With this explanation we dismiss the
discussion, and proceed to the particulars of the narrative.[1]

Jehoram's Reaction

II. The awful writing which came to Jehoram contained unwont-
ed language for a monarch's attention. Doubtless it must have
occasioned momentary terror and alarm; but we read of no contrition, much less of true repentance on his part. Alas, to what
insensibility and obduracy can a man arrive by pride, infidelity, and
frivolity! Yet surely this warning was sent by a merciful God, in order
to alarm and awaken him to true repentance and conversion. Had it
produced such an effect, doubtless the awful threatening would have
been averted, as in the case of Nineveh; and, as in the case of his
own father-in-law, evil had been partially averted by Ahab's partial
humiliation. For God is slow to anger, good, and ready to forgive. He
has no pleasure at all in the death of a sinner, but rather that he
should turn from his wickedness and live, Ezek. 18:23. But, in case he
repented not, the sentence announced in this writing was a judicial
sentence; and this was awfully the case in the present instance.
Jehoram, when this writing came to him from Elijah the prophet, had
nearly filled up the measure of his iniquity; and yet two years elapsed,
after the arrival of the Divine message to him, before the threat was
fully accomplished in cutting him off from the earth. Such is the
patience and long-suffering of God.

Let us now review the contents of the writing which came to him
from Elijah. It commences with reminding him of his chief sins and
provocations. "Thus saith the Lord God of David thy father,
Because thou hast not walked in the ways of Jehoshaphat thy father,
nor in the ways of Asa king of Judah, but hast walked in the way of
the kings of Israel, and hast made Judah and the inhabitants of
Jerusalem to go a whoring, like to the whoredoms of the house of

---

1. *Note by the Editor*—The most current opinion amongst commentators is that
the Spirit of prophecy directed Elijah to prepare this writing, before his translation,
in the foresight of Jehoram's crimes; and that it was probably left with Elisha to
transmit it to him.

Ahab, and also hast slain thy brethren of thy father's house, which were better than thyself." How terrible this accusation! how abominable the sins here noticed! But be not deceived, as if the Holy Spirit of God can be vexed and grieved only with such sins as these of Jehoram. God can say to many among us, "I have given you the good word of life, and ye have heard it and read it; and yet have gone on in sin and vanity. I have sent you one messenger after another, but you have not hearkened to them; one affliction after another, but you heard not the rod, nor Him who appointed it: I reminded you of one commandment after another, but you have not laid them to heart!"

Elijah addresses Jehoram, "Thus saith the Lord God of David thy father!" This was to recall to his memory what God had done for his family in times past, and therefore to remind him the more forcibly of his own ingratitude. It was also thus intimated to him that he only sat on the throne because it had been promised to David that his house should continue to the coming of the Messiah; and, further, that he might have learned even from David's own history and language that with the Lord there is abundant forgiveness and plenteous redemption.

"Because," continues the writing, "thou hast not walked in the ways of Jehoshaphat thy father, nor in the ways of Asa king of Judah, but hast walked in the way of the kings of Israel." Here, therefore, is a remembrance of his own pious father and grandfather; and, consequently, an intimation of the so much greater heinousness of his guilt. Asa, his grandfather, had reigned forty-one years at Jerusalem, and had set an excellent example. "He had done that which was good and right in the eyes of the Lord his God, even as his father David had done: for he took away the altars of the strange gods, and the high places, and brake down the images, and cut down the groves." As a true shepherd of his people, he was not less anxious for their spiritual and eternal welfare, than for their temporal prosperity. By his own conduct and ordinances, he had called upon Judah to "seek the Lord, the God of their fathers, and to do the law and the commandment"; and the Lord had crowned these pious endeavors with the happiest results. Asa, as a thorough reformer, determined not to rest until the last idol in his land was burned, and every heathen altar thrown down. He had called his subjects back, from the groves and high places, to the altars of Jehovah; and the people had obeyed the call, "and entered into a covenant to seek the Lord God of their fathers, with all their heart and with all their soul." As a vig-ilant and indefatigable ruler, he labored to promote the social welfare of his people and the external security of his kingdom; and, as a valiant general, he obtained many a triumph over mighty foes, because he trusted in the God of Israel, and marched out with the watchword, "Lord, it is nothing with thee to help whether with many, or with them that have no power," 2 Chron. 14:11. Toward the end of his life, indeed, he on one occasion resorted to the vain hope of man, instead of looking supremely to the Lord, 2 Chron. 16:12; and he had to repent of it bitterly. But he slept in God, and the people consecrated his ashes with tears of gratitude and affection.

A still more illustrious king than Asa was Jehoram's father, the excellent Jehoshaphat. His example shines to this day as worthy the imitation of all rulers. The sacred historian records of him that the Lord was with him because he "walked in the first ways of his father David, and sought not unto Baalim, but sought to the Lord God of his father, and walked in his commandments," 2 Chron. 17:3, 4. He continued and completed the reformation which his father Asa had begun. The well-being of his people, in the highest and holiest sense of the term, was the great object which he kept continually before him. He, more than once, traveled through the land, from Beersheba to the mountains of Ephraim, to strengthen his people in the faith, and to bring back many to Jehovah, the God of their fathers; and the Lord gave great success to the labors of his royal mis-sionary. He sent also priests and Levites about the country, with the book of God's law in their hands, to instruct the ignorant, and to establish the better informed. And we read that "the fear of God was upon all the kingdom bordering upon Judah, when they had heard that the Lord fought against the enemies of Israel. So the realm of Jehoshaphat was quiet: for his God gave him rest round about," 2 Chron. 20:29, 30. "Also some of the Philistines brought Jehoshaphat presents and tribute silver, and the Arabians brought him flocks, and Jehoshaphat waxed great exceedingly," 2 Chron. 17:10-12. "And he set judges in the land throughout all the fenced cities of Judah, to watch over right and justice, and to determine individual disputes. And he said to the judges, "Take heed what ye do; for ye judge not for man, but for the Lord, who is with you in the judgment. Wherefore now let the fear of the Lord be upon you," 2 Chron.

19:5-7. If he went to war, his first preparation was by fasting and prayer, 2 Chron. 20:3. His army, distinguished both for discipline and courage, amounted to one million and eighty thousand strong, 2 Chron. 17:14, ff. Yet his wars were entirely defensive. He gladly remained at peace whenever the foe left him at leisure, to improve his country and to give fresh impulse to its prosperity by founding new cities, and by promoting education and commerce. Thus did this worthy descendant of David reign. Happy the country which is blest with such a governor! Let us not meddle with those who are given to change, but rather pray that the "powers that be" may ever be disposed to rule like Jehoshaphat. This is one of our plainest Christian duties. See 1 Tim. 2:1, 2.

Such were the honorable ancestors of Jehoram. He had been trained up in the very beams of such excellent examples. Nevertheless he had willfully yielded to his own natural vanity and pride, and by thus neglecting to hearken to instructors, and listening probably to flatterers, he gradually waxed worse and worse, deceiving and being deceived, till he became such a monster of iniquity that a worse monarch never sat on the throne of David. It seems as if he had made it his aim openly to set at naught the example of his excellent predecessors, by the disgusting contrast of his own; as if he had made it his chief employment to root up and tread under foot, in the shortest possible time, the seed sown by his pious father. No sooner had be buried his royal parent, and taken lawful possession of his throne at Jerusalem, than he threw off all disguise; and a horrible massacre opens the black catalogue of his crimes, followed by iniquity after iniquity. His brothers, who were all of them better than he, seemed to stand in his way, and he appears to have lusted for their wealth, but more especially to have feared the reproach which his heathen course of life would occasion him in their eyes; hence he hated them, and caused them to be massacred without mercy. Six of them thus died, and one or them only escaped. Many of the great men of the kingdom participated in their dreadful fate, as if the blood of his own brothers did not cry loud enough to Heaven.

Jehoram, under the influence of his wife Athaliah, the daughter of Ahab, was initiated in all the vices and abominations of heathenism. The long-suffering of Jehovah failed to send him serious warnings. The Edomites invade the country, and the City of Libna revolts from him. But Jehoram perseveres in sin and wickedness, and openly renouncing the God of his fathers, introduces the idolatry of Sidon, which had been expelled by Asa and Jehoshaphat, recalls the banished priests of Baal, erects altars, consecrates groves, invites his people to idolatrous festivals of licentiousness, and even compels Judah thereto with despotic intolerance. To this the words in this awful writing from Elijah refer: "Thou hast made Judah and the inhabitants of Jerusalem to go a whoring, like to the whoredoms of the house of Ahab." Do not be offended at this mode of expression. The Scriptures of Divine truth cannot employ such equivocal expressions as are used in modern days; its appellations strike always at the root of things; hence we are not surprised that its searching language and plain dealing should have always offended the hypocrite, the worldling, and the debauchee. When men depart from the living God and cleave to any idol of their heart, whatever name it may bear, whether that of superior light, philosophy, talent, or liberalism, the Scripture calls it whoredom, because it is nothing else; and, indeed, it is the worst and the vilest.

The "Maker" of the church is the husband of the church: its innumerable members are collectively his betrothed wife. This mystical union between Christ and his church is insisted on in Scripture throughout; and when any member of the visible church acts not according to it, but idolizes the honors, gains, or pleasures of this world, the Scripture calls his conduct adultery, and pronounces judgment upon it as a thing of Divine abhorrence. How awful then is the provocation of those who are not only guilty of this conduct themselves, but by influence or example, in word or in writing, pour the intoxicating wine of their spiritual fornication into the cup of others. How awful when parents or tutors do this with respect to those committed to their care! How awful, when ministers of Christ's religion teach, under the name of morality and philosophy, "another gospel which is not another," corrupting and denying the plain and express word of God! How awful when poets, journalists, and other popular writers endeavor, by every means, to seduce the people from the way of truth into deistical or atheistical sophistry! Awful indeed are the denunciations of Scripture against all such companions of Balaam! such murderers of souls! In the Divine displeasure against Jehoram, they may behold the same against themselves.

The sins and crimes of Jehoram having been thus reproved, the writing next announces to him the sentence of God. "Behold, with a great plague the Lord will smite thee. He will punish thy atrocities in thy people, thy children, thy wives, and all that thou hast, and finally, in thine own person. For thou shalt have great sickness by disease of thy bowels, until thy bowels fall out by reason of the sickness from day to day!" Oh fearful manifestation of the just judgment of Him who clothes himself with zeal as with a cloak, and repays his enemies to their face! Lo, smoke goes forth from his nostrils, and consuming fire from his mouth! How fearful a thing thus to fall into the hands of the living God!

Jehoram reads the tremendous announcement; but, instead of repenting, he makes his face harder than a rock, and his neck as an iron sinew. Verily, men become hardened and obdurate through the deceitfulness of sin, and nothing but the Omnipotence of grace is able to overcome this monster of man's corrupt nature. Without this grace the law is but as stubble in the fire, and the Divine judgments serve only to harden the sinner's heart. Jehoram affords a dreadful confirmation of this truth. Well might he shudder at reading such a writing. But it did not end in humiliation: and whatever will not bend must break.

The Divine curse, like a growing storm, soon discharges itself. First a hostile force of Philistines and Arabians suddenly attack the borders of his kingdom. Jehoram sends his armies against them, but they are defeated by the invaders. The blessing of God no longer attends the armies of Israel. With the faith of their fathers, their fathers' strength in war is departed. The enemy pours into the kingdom like a desolating flood. This was the first plague: the king was punished in his deluded and idolatrously revolted people. But this is only the beginning of his troubles; for his ears are too dull of hearing to discern the voice of the rod and him that had appointed it. The enemy advances to the capital, and Jehoram's host is vanquished wherever it shows itself. In a few days the conquering army of the heathen is under the walls of Jerusalem. The city is taken, and the remnant of the Jewish army scattered; the king's palace is stormed and taken, his treasure plundered, and all his wives, except Athaliah, who was reserved for a more tragic end, are carried away captive. Even his sons are obliged to leave their native land. Only one remains behind—Jehoahaz the youngest; for the Lord remembered his word, "David shall never want a man to sit on the throne of the house of Israel." All the rest go into miserable captivity.

Woeful example of the righteous judgment of God! Here is indeed "eye for eye, and tooth for tooth." The destroyer of the people becomes accursed of the people. The avaricious robber sees himself stripped of his family and treasures. The denier of Jehovah and his word is denied by him in return, and given up to his own way. The voluptuary and fratricide is visited with the loss of his own wives and children. But his plagues do not end here. Lest his impenitent heart should soon devise a false peace for itself, he is condemned to suffer also in his own person. The horrible disease in his bowels soon appears, and continues for two years together, baffling all the skill and wisdom of his physicians; so that "it came to pass, after the end of two years, that his bowels fell out by reason of his sickness; and he died. His people made no burning for him, like the burning of his fathers. Howbeit they buried him in the city of David, but not in the sepulchers of the kings."

Thus was every word of the Divine denunciation accomplished, and not a syllable of it remained unfulfilled. Let all who care not for God be admonished by it! A writing like that prophetic one lies at their very door. It begins, "Woe unto them that call evil good, and good evil; that put darkness for light, and light for darkness; that put bitter for sweet, and sweet for bitter! Woe to them that are wise in their own eyes, and pure in their own sight!" And again, "He that believeth not the Son, shall not see life; but the wrath of God abideth on him." It continues, "The lamp of the wicked shall be put out, and their feet hasten to destruction!" It concludes, "It is a fearful thing to fall into the hands of the living God!" So speaks the true and faithful Witness. Well may you tremble, you workers of iniquity, for not one of these words shall fall to the ground. Nevertheless they do not threaten unconditionally. There is appended to them the words, "Except they repent and be converted, that their sins may be blotted out." Rejoice at this. You may escape the curse which threatens you. Flee into the arms of Jesus. Hear the voice of the Good Shepherd; begin to follow him, and believe in him, and then you shall obtain through him, the forgiveness of all sins. But "there is no peace, saith my God, to the wicked."

29

The Mount of Transfiguration

There is perhaps none of the sons of fallen Adam to whom such a superabundance of honor has been granted as to that man upon whose eventful history we have for some time been dwelling with delight. After having been received up of God in a singular manner, without passing through the gate of death and the grave, and this at the close of a career of incomparably splendid deeds and wonders, and after having shone for several ages in the firmament of sacred history—new luster is all at once thrown upon his character, some hundreds of years after his departure from the earth, by his being introduced in one of the transporting scenes of that happy period, in the anticipation of which Abraham rejoiced, and which many prophets and kings had desired to see.

Malachi, the prophet of God, thus spoke to Israel, in the name of Jehovah, "Behold, I will send you Elijah the prophet before the coming of the great and dreadful day of the Lord: and he shall turn the heart of the fathers to the children, and the heart of the children to their fathers, lest I come and smite the earth with a curse," Mal. 4:5, 6. Hence the return of Elijah became, from the time of Malachi, one of the endeared objects of Israel's expectation. The saints, thenceforth, in faith beheld him, in the dawn of futurity, approaching as the harbinger of the day-spring from on high. At length, just before this day-spring began to visit the benighted earth, the people of Israel had their attention drawn to a voice crying in the wilderness, "Prepare ye the way of the Lord"; and announcing that "the kingdom of heaven was at hand." The Lord and Savior of the world shortly

afterward appeared, and in reference to the coming of John the
Baptist, he declared, "If ye will receive it, this is Elias who was for to
come!" Malachi's prophecy was therefore now fulfilled—yet only figuratively, and by way of prelude. That the whole meaning of the
prediction was not yet exhausted, is intimated in our Lord's saying,
"If ye will receive it"; and is still more expressly shown by the words
of John himself, "I am not Elias," John 1:21. John, therefore, was
called Elias because he appeared in the spirit and power of that great
reforming prophet. The words of Malachi have all along been understood by the Jews to predict a personal return of Elijah. Jesus, the son
of Sirach, appears to have understood them thus; for in the 46th
chapter of his apocryphal book, he says, "Thou, Elias, wast taken up
in a whirlwind of fire, and in a chariot of fiery horses; who wast
ordained for reproof in its season, to pacify the wrath of the Lord's
judgment before it broke forth into fury, and to turn the heart of the
fathers unto the sons, and to restore the tribes of Jacob. Blessed are
they that see thee, and shall be honored on account of thy friendship;
then shall we possess the true life."

And lo! all unexpectedly, this ancient prophet actually appears
again, on the mount of transfiguration, with Moses at his side—
both of them engaged in sacred converse with the Lord of glory.
What a wonderful event is here recorded by the evangelists! Did,
then, this event constitute the full and final accomplishment of
Malachi's prediction? I doubt it. For Malachi further said that Elijah
was to come in order to turn "the hearts of the fathers to the children, and the hearts of the children to their fathers"; but he has not
yet executed this commission; consequently, the ancient prediction
leaves us still to expect something more. It is already fulfilled in a
typical manner; but its entire fulfillment is yet to come. Are we
then still to expect the return of Elias? I am inclined to believe that
at the time of the restoration and conversion of Israel, he will again
appear upon earth in his glorified person, and that his future coming will signal a great and glorious epoch in the history of the
kingdom of God.

How wonderful to find a man once of like passions as we are, taking a part for thousands of years together in this world's history! "O
Elijah, how art thou honored!" we may say with the son of Sirach.
"Which of us is to be praised like unto thee? Blessed are they that see
thee, and will be honored on account of thy friendship!" Yet even

Elijah, what are you but a satellite shining with another's light, and setting forth the love and grace of Christ toward sinful men!

But let us now approach the mount of transfiguration, and may the scene prove a blessing to our own souls! It will disclose blissful objects to our view.

Matthew 17:1, 2

> After six days Jesus taketh Peter, James, and John his brother, and bringeth them up into an high mountain apart, and was transfigured before them: and his face did shine as the sun, and his raiment was white as the light.

The evangelists, Matthew, Mark, and Luke, all relate this wonderful event. It was not ideal, but real. The simplicity with which it is related is sufficient to show this. It affords us a glimpse of heavenly things, though very incomprehensible to us. Let joy, rather than impertinent curiosity, fill our souls in beholding this glorious event! Lo, we have here something more than the fiery sign on Carmel, more than the burning bush at Horeb, or the flames and voice on mount Sinai. "This is none other but the house of God, and this is the gate of heaven."

Let us devoutly consider this sublime occurrence, and may the Holy Spirit enable us to learn something of its excellent instruction! We will notice for the present, I. The probable intention of this event; II. The event itself.

The Probable Intention of the Event

I. The evangelists refer to the connection of this event with a conversation which occurred almost immediately before at Cesarea Philippi, when the Lord was on the point of commencing his last journey to Jerusalem. "Whom," said he to his disciples, "do men say that I the Son of man am?" They replied, "Some say thou art John the Baptist, some Elias, and others Jeremias, or one of the prophets." Jesus answered, "But whom say ye that I am?" Peter replied, "Thou art the Christ, the Son of the living God!" Jesus answered, "Blessed art thou, Simon Barjona; for flesh and blood hath not revealed it unto thee, but my Father, which is in heaven. And I say also unto thee, That thou art Peter, and upon this rock I will build my church; and the gates of hell shall not prevail against it." Never had the dis-

ciples stood on such an elevation of faith as now. It was therefore a
favorable season for introducing them deeper into the mystery of
redemption, and for disclosing to them the solemn truth that Christ
must suffer, a truth which they had hitherto been unable to bear.
"From that time forth began Jesus to show unto his disciples, how
that he must go unto Jerusalem, and suffer many things of the elders,
and chief priests, and scribes, and be killed, and be raised again the
third day." But the astonished disciples knew not what to think of all
this. They could not reconcile their minds to the notion of a suffering
and slain Messiah. Hence, Simon Peter fell back for a moment from
his exalted faith to the mere notions of a natural man; and, quite forgetting the humble relationship he had with the Lord, he takes him
aside, with unbecoming haste, and says to him in a tone of advice, or
rather of reproof, "Be it far from thee, Lord; this shall not be unto
thee." But the Lord, immediately perceiving from whence this "Spare
thyself" originated, replied with holy severity, "Get thee behind me,
Satan: thou art an offense unto me: for thou savorest not the things
that be of God, but those that be of men."

The manifestation, therefore, on the holy mount, appears to have
been vouchsafed, partly on account of the disciples, in order afterward
to cast a ray of light upon the gloom of Golgotha, by showing their
Master's resignation to his sufferings; and further, to show them who
he really was whom they were soon to behold crowned with thorns
and nailed to the cross. They might here learn that he would not fall
a sacrifice to unfortunate accidents, and that he could not fulfill the
mission upon which he came unless he voluntarily gave himself up to
death. They might here also learn that the voluntary death of Christ
was in harmony with the determinate counsel and foreknowledge of
God. The voice which they heard coming out of the cloud put it
beyond a doubt. Moreover, the transfiguration served to annihilate the
suspicion that there was anything in the establishment of Christ's
kingdom at variance with Moses and the prophets; for the appearance
of the heavenly envoys, and their converse with the Savior, testified
most unequivocally to the contrary. Behold then what a fullness of
Divine light and information was contained in this one fact. It served
to strengthen the faith of the disciples to such a degree, that they
might refresh themselves by the recollection of it during the rest of
their lives, as we find St. Peter does, 2 Pet. 1:16-18.

But let us not suppose that this manifestation was intended solely for the disciples. Not only earth, but heaven itself, participated in it. It was a spectacle also to angels, and to the spirits of just men made perfect. Edifying and joyous must it have been even to them to behold the glory of their abased King thus breaking forth as the light. From this glory there proceeded new occasion for heavenly praise.

Nor can we suppose that the transfiguration did not take place partly on account of the Son of man himself. Indeed its most important intention appears to have had reference to him, and him alone. For though, even in the days of his flesh, the fullness of the Godhead dwelt in him; yet he, with equal truth and reality, led a human life likewise. As a man, he had to believe, conflict, and learn obedience, even as his own disciples. His way, like ours, lay through manifold temptations, spiritual desertion, and darkness; seasons were not wanting to him, when like his people he really needed strengthening, comfort, and encouragement; neither did he despise even the sympathy of his disciples, Matt. 26:38. God had prepared him for his temptation in the wilderness, by the testimony he gave from heaven, "This is my beloved Son, in whom I am well pleased"; and as He was now approaching a still more portentous and awful conflict, the glory on the holy mount would serve to prepare him for it. Recollect the scene in John 12. Jesus has come to Jerusalem. The fire, which is to consume him as our sacrifice, is about to be kindled. The night is at hand; its approaching horrors are foreseen by him. His sacred humanity trembles, and the cry breaks out, "Now is my soul troubled, and what shall I say? Father, save me from this hour? But for this cause came I unto this hour." He submits to the will of the Father; and now he desires something else; "Father, glorify thy name." "Glorify thyself in me, and show that thou art my Father, and that I am thine Only Begotten." He speaks, and immediately a voice is heard by the people about him, who thought it thundered. "I have both glorified it, and will glorify it again!" Now the words, "I have glorified it," might partly have reference to the event in the holy mount. Thus, the transfiguration might have been intended as a means of invigorating the Son of man himself, in the prospect of his approaching hour of trial. For, sin only excepted, our good Shepherd was willing to pass through all the states and conditions of his sheep, and to labor like them, from day to day, in faith and dependence on his Father.

The Event Itself

II. The consideration of the transfiguration itself will afford us further instruction. "After six days," relates the evangelist, "Jesus took Peter, James, and John his brother, and bringeth them up to a high mountain apart." These three disciples he repeatedly distinguished above the rest: afterward he took them with him to Gethsemane, as into the holy of holies, to behold there the priestly altar and sacrificial fire; but here it was to view his regal splendor and glory. It seems almost as if the Savior in this respect also felt and acted as a man; that he showed that special affection, which the heart of one friend feels for another, and was nobly sensible of that lovely bond of tenderness which we call mutual *sympathy;* like that of Jacob, whose life was bound up in Benjamin's life. It is true that his children were all equally dear to him; he loved them all, even as the Father loved him. But there were two or three who seem to have stood nearer to his natural human feelings; and the nearest of these was evidently the apostle John, who is emphatically called in Scripture, "The disciple whom Jesus loved"; and the next to him were his brother James, and Simon Peter. And how amiable does Simon Peter appear, even in his errors and mistakes, on account of his ardent zeal for his Master, and his frank and ingenuous disposition! And who would not have been constrained to love James—the holy and warm-hearted man who was ready to be, and actually was, the first among the twelve to be martyred! And then John, that noble young branch in the heavenly Vine, that eagle spirit, who was named, with his brother just mentioned, a son of thunder, whose character nevertheless so beautifully resembled that of Jesus himself—a character full of tenderness and heavenly love, which seemed touched as with the live coal of the sanctuary; where has there ever existed, next to the "fairest of the children of men," a more lovely character than this disciple? The innermost chords of his soul harmonized with those of the human soul of Jesus.

Yet was our Lord's predilection for these three disciples only a subordinate reason for taking them with him to the holy mount. He had other reasons incomparably more important, which are to be sought for in the particular vocation of these three, and in their peculiar relation to the person of Jesus. For they undoubtedly appear as the Lord's more intimate circle, even as they were afterward selected to be the three principal pillars of the church. They were to be the first who should plant, in the midst of storm and conflict, the banner of the cross on the mountains of Israel; and, on this account, they peculiarly required such a signal preparation as they were now to receive.

The sacred narrative informs us that Jesus took these disciples with him to "a high mountain." From ancient times it had been the Lord's custom to select the retired summits of hills, those quiet islands amidst the ocean of worldly confusion, for the places of some of his most remarkable revelations. The mount on which the transfiguration took place is not definitely pointed out to us in Scripture. According to an ancient and not improbable tradition, it was Tabor, the most considerable and beautiful mountain in Galilee. This eminence, which a modern traveler found entirely covered with green oaks, and other trees, shrubs, and odoriferous plants, stands elevated in the wide plain of Jezreel, at no great distance from Nazareth and Cana; and it is said of it, that if there is anything beautiful in nature, it is this green and rounded mountain-pyramid of Palestine. Its summit is full three thousand paces in circumference, and presents one of the most extensive and charming prospects to be found in the world. To the right, the eye, after contemplating mount Carmel, that ancient scene of Jehovah's glory, looks over the vast extent of the Mediterranean sea. Northward appears the glittering snowy cupola of Hermon, with the black ridge of Lebanon beneath it. Toward the south the eye first rests upon the beautiful vista of luxuriant vineyards and orange groves, and further on, upon the mountains of Samaria; while to the left gleams the sea of Tiberias, intersecting the waving cornfields of the plain of Esdraelon. But why do we cast our looks into the distance, when something nearer at hand, of a far more interesting nature, calls for our attention?

The apostles subsequently called the mount of transfiguration "the holy mount." Yes, those are holy places, and must ever be so esteemed by us, where we once could say with Jacob, "I have seen God face to face, and my life is preserved." There are our Bethels and Peniels, where he whispered to our souls, "I have loved thee with an everlasting love!" or where he wiped away our tears, and crowned our supplications with his Amen. Such places are consecrated in our esteem. They are lovely spots in this vale of tears; and he who has many of them is truly rich!

Jesus commences the journey to the mount, followed by his three disciples. As the ascent required about a day, we may suppose the sun to have already set, and the evening twilight to have commenced, by the time they arrived at the summit. Solemn silence reigns all around. The disciples—weary with the journey, and at the same time mentally exercised by the conversation on the way, and by their solemn situation with the Savior alone, in the silence of night, on the solitary mount—recline themselves upon the ground and sink into slumber. The Savior prays to his eternal Father. What was the particular subject of his prayer history does not inform us; but it might be similar to that in John 12. "Father, glorify thy name!" or in John 17, "And now, O Father, glorify thou me with the glory which I had with thee, before the world was—that they all may be one; as thou, Father, art in me, and I in thee!" How sublime! how affecting! The Prince of life on his knees, before the face of the Almighty! the Son of the living God engaged in holy converse with the Eternal Father on the dark mountain-height! Surely, if ever the words, "stand at a distance!" were appropriate, it was here. And what ensues when Immanuel prays? His prayer must be successful. It is high as heaven in its ascent from the heart of the Son of man. And yet he is ever willing to mingle our supplications with his own intercession, and thus to give them full effect. You know how he said to his disciples, "Whatsoever ye shall ask the Father in my name, he will give it you."

Jesus prays; and what is the result? All at once it seems to the sleepers as if a bright light were playing about their eyelids, and as if the sound of a conversation penetrated down into the depths of their slumber. They stir—they awake; and well might they conjecture, in their sudden surprise, that the night was past, that the sun was in the highest blaze of noon. They look about them with amazement. But oh! what an incomparable spectacle! Behold him! behold him! Is that shining one yonder indeed their Master? Is the majestic figure which appears arrayed in Divine glory, he in whose company they ascended the mountain? The disciples are overcome with the sight. But it is not alarm or terror that they feel. This is not a Sinai, so as to cause them to say, "I exceedingly fear and quake." The glory here breathes only peace and joy. The heart is enlarged by it—the soul would gladly be entirely absorbed in it. Let our souls then be absorbed with the contemplation of this glory. Let our spirits rejoice in its wondrous light, and receive health and salvation. Oh how beautiful and glorious does He appear, the fairest of the children of men, who is not only the King of John, or of Peter, or of James, but my King also, and yours. Hallelujah!— Here is indeed more than Solomon in all his glory; here is more than Aaron and Melchisedek! When did ever a star shine on our benighted world like this! When brake ever a sun through the darkness of the earth like this! O incomparable brightness, which forces angels to fall on their knees and adore, and makes sinners rejoice and be glad! "This is my Beloved, and this is my friend, O ye daughters of Jerusalem." Oh contemplate the King in his beauty. Behold, there he stands! He himself is the Sun in the kingdom of spirits; he bears the source and fullness of light in Himself. There he stands on the solitary summit—and not He only, but the disciples also partake of the splendor of His transfiguration. Here we can in some measure anticipate, how the words of St. John, concerning the city of God, will come to pass: "And the city had no need of the sun, neither of the moon, to shine in it: for the glory of God did lighten it, and the Lamb is the light thereof," Rev. 21:23. Here also we have the key to that other saying: "It doth not yet appear what we shall be: but we know that, when he shall appear, we shall be like him; for we shall see him as he is."

"And Jesus was transfigured before them"; more literally, "He transfigured himself." The expression implies that the glory was not shed upon the Lord externally; but, as existing in him from the beginning, it only broke forth outwardly in the manifestation. Even then, while he still lay in the manger, as an infant, poor, and requiring assistance, and while laboring as the carpenter's son, the whole fullness of the Godhead dwelt in him bodily, though concealed and veiled behind the curtain of a servant's form. Single rays of this hidden glory had occasionally emanated from him, in deeds of omnipotent mercy, so that all who saw it were astonished, and said, "What manner of man is this? From whence is he?" But such an expansion of the rose of Sharon, as this on the mount, had none yet witnessed. Such a discovery of his hidden glory and majesty had hitherto not been made. But however indescribable, and beyond all earthly splendor this glory was, it was not the whole fullness of his beauty as the Son of God. In comparison with that glory, in which he will eventually meet us above, it was probably only as the early dawn compared with the perfect day. For he manifested his beauty only as far as mortals could apprehend and bear it. But since the whole scene on this sacred mount was only a manifestation of the glory which Jesus had in himself, therefore St. John, partly perhaps in allusion to this very event, speaks of the Word made flesh, taber-nacling among us, as the Shechinah, "full of grace and truth." The glory, in which he there appeared to them, was nothing borrowed, but his own most peculiar and real form; it was the visible reflection of the corporeal indwelling fullness of God, and consequently, a man-ifestation full of truth. But for what reason John calls this manifestation of the Son of God, a revelation "full of grace," he him-self must tell us, in order that he may completely comprehend it. The glory here manifested was a benign glory, a transporting reflection of pure kindness and love. Streams of peace flowed into the disciples' hearts; sweet and sabbatic repose breathed around them, and every ray that fell from his countenance upon them, affected their souls as a new expression of the love of God. No wonder that Peter exclaimed, "Lord, it is good for us to be here!" They would gladly have remained, forever remained, in this beatifying irradiation of Christ.

We leave the summit of the holy mount, in order soon to return thither with our meditation. Keep firm hold in spirit of the glory which has there beamed upon you. It will be to your faith and your love that which the vernal sun is to the first bud of nature. And what a blissful light does this scene reflect upon those great words of Jesus, "Father, I will that they whom thou hast given me be with me where I am, that they may behold my glory which thou hast given me!" What a meaning does it supply to that other promise, "The righteous shall shine forth as the sun, in the kingdom of their Father!" Oh let us now by faith build here a tabernacle for our souls! Let the summit of the holy mount be our oratory and our watch-tower!

30

The Holy Embassy

Matthew 17:3, 4.

And, behold, there appeared unto them Moses and Elias talking with him. Then answered Peter, and said unto Jesus, Lord, it is good for us to be here: if thou wilt, let us make here three tabernacles; one for thee, and one for Moses, and one for Elias.

Thus we stand again upon the holy mount—all around a solemn silence—before us, the King in his beauty. We would gladly yield up our minds to the contemplation of his glory; when, lo! a new appearance attracts our notice. There are three subjects which at present claim our attention: I. The heavenly embassy; II. Their converse with the Savior; and, III. Simon Peter's request.

Moses and Elijah Appear

I. The disciples stand in adoring astonishment, and in a kind of beatified contemplation of their glorified Master. But, all at once, new amazement overtakes them for they behold two other personages beside the Lord Jesus. We can imagine the surprise of the disciples. "Who are they," would they think, "and whence do they come? Did we not ascend the mountain with Him alone? And besides, these are not mortals, whom we behold;—the crown of life is already on their heads." And behold, the Savior begins to converse with these venerable strangers. The disciples listen, and find the one to be Moses, the other Elijah, possibly from hearing Jesus call them by their names. But how must this information have increased their

313

astonishment! They must have felt almost as if the earth had retreated from beneath their feet; and as if eternity had overtaken them unawares. For now they are certain that they behold, face to face, two happy citizens of the invisible world. One of them was now fifteen hundred years old, and yet fair and flourishing as a green palm tree, in eternal youth. It is Moses himself who here stands before us, he that was king in Jeshurun, the man who "esteemed the reproach of Christ greater riches than the treasures of Egypt, for he had respect to the recompense of the reward." And as for the other, it is Elijah who, nearly a thousand years before, ascended to heaven in the fiery chariot, on the other side Jordan. Behold, he suddenly appears again in bodily form, in the country of his ancient conflicts; but oh in what a different condition! How full of praise and raptured adoration within; how encircled with glory without! If he now called to mind the scenes of his former sufferings, how must they have appeared as the dreams of a night long fled!

Moses and Elias! how wonderful! For centuries they had been admitted into the more immediate presence of God; for centuries had the sabbatic peace of the upper world been their element. Through their hearts whole streams of bliss had already flowed, of which only scanty drops bedew this earth. What might not those messengers from heaven have told us! What new information might they have given us, respecting the invisible world! But they are silent; probably for the same reason that obliged Paul also to withhold from us the description of "the third heaven," into which he was caught up, 2 Cor. 12:2, ff. The strangely broken expressions which the apostle uses, when speaking upon this subject, show how much his heart was moved by the recollection of it. He seems struggling to express something which he counts among the highest and holiest things that had ever been disclosed to him. He knows it was no dream, no play of imagination, but a real translation into paradise. Where was he then, for he was away from the earth? Was it only in some blissful planet or star, from whence, like Moses upon mount Nebo, he could "behold the land that is very far off?" Isa. 33:17. No; he had been in the very heart of that land: he had been in "the third heaven." But as he gives us no description of that blissful place, so it may safely be said that his silence, implying his inability to describe what he had witnessed and experienced, is for us at present the best description of the glory of the third heaven. Every attempt at description would entirely fail:

both on account of the poverty of earthly language, and on account of the weakness of human capacity, and our want of powers of conception for such things. Indeed, to attempt to describe them, it would be necessary to dip the pencil in something that is terrestrial, however beautiful; and this would be to dip it only in gloomy shades. Another circumstance, which may serve also to give us some idea of the glory which he saw in the realms above, is the ardent desire with which we afterward behold him longing after those mansions of light. His conversation is henceforth in heaven. His hopes, his desires, his thoughts reside there, and the morning and evening song of his heart is, "I have a desire to depart, and to be with Christ." Death seems to him the most blessed messenger that could arrive; yes, death even in its most dreadful form; for he knows that when absent from the body he shall be present with the Lord. How joyfully does he now receive the cup of afflictions; "For I reckon," he exultingly exclaims, "that the sufferings of this present time are not worthy to be compared with the glory which shall be revealed in us." "To me, to live is Christ, and to die is gain." "I count not my life dear to myself, so that I may finish my course with joy."

Thus has the apostle, who heard "unspeakable words," animated us with expectations of paradise, which the more strongly excite our longings after home the less they are capable of being uttered in human language. It is in this indirect manner also that the two heavenly persons on Tabor afford us cheering information; being *themselves:* a living epistle of the things of the world to come. How sweetly does their very appearance address itself to that faith which still trembles, weak and uncertain, over the tomb! What a satisfying evidence is it of our personal and perceptible identity in another state of existence! And then the glory in which they now appear who were once so tempest-tossed; what a blessed testimony does this bear to us of complete "victory" over death, "through our Lord Jesus Christ!" 1 Cor. 15:57. It is indeed true that we have a greater witness of the other world than Moses and Elias. But as God has granted us these subordinate witnesses, let us thankfully receive them as the apostles of Christ.

Since the gate of Paradise was closed, heaven had scarcely ever visited earth in such a manner as here on the holy mount. What an assembly! The Son of eternal love clothed in majesty; before him, the two dignified ambassadors from the city of God; beside them, Peter,

James, and John, the pillars of the New Testament church; round about them, doubtless, the holy angelic hosts; and within hearing of the voice of the Eternal Father, whom no eye has seen nor can see. Where on earth was ever such a gathering as this? There had hitherto been wanting, even in the paradise of these triumphant saints, the delight of saluting the King of all kings, as a Brother and a Kinsman. Oh to behold Him now, whose day they had so long looked for! Him, by virtue of whose sufferings they had worn the crown so long beforehand! Him, the Lamb of God, whose sacrificial blood, so long before it was offered up, had blotted out their sins! Surely a new heaven would disclose itself, even to them, in such a contemplation of their Messiah!

The Conversation with Christ

II. Here also is a striking representation of the perfect harmony and unity between the economy of the Old Testament and that of the New. Moses appears as the representative of the law; Elias, as the representative of the prophets. As such they humbly and adoringly draw near to Jesus. The Law and the Prophets give witness to the Son of Mary. Such is the important meaning which we may behold in this scene. "Thou art he," exclaims the Law, "unto whom I as a schoolmaster would bring every man." "Thou art he," say the Prophets, "who wast the subject of our inspired song." And when both Moses and Elias disappear in the radiance of the "fairest of the children of men," that great truth stands embodied before us, that "Christ is the end of the law as well as of prophecy." Prophecy finds in him its fulfillment, for he is the substance of all the shadows. The Law ceases from all its judgments, threatenings, and condemnations, as soon as it finds the sinner in Christ.

Moses and Elias, we read, conversed with the Lord. Attend a little! What kind of discourse was it which they carried on with him? Did they announce to him that a chariot of fire, and horses of fire, stood ready to carry him away from the gloomy scene of earthly conflict, to his Father's house? No; the conversation is concerning a cross and a crown of thorns; an altar and its consuming flame. "They spake of his decease, which he should accomplish at Jerusalem," Luke 9:31. As envoys from the Eternal Majesty, they audibly affirmed that it was the will of the Father, that with his own precious blood he should make atonement for sin; "for without the shedding of blood there was no remission." They impressed, in God's name, a new seal upon the ancient and eternal truth, that the partition-wall which sinners had raised could be broken down by no other means than by the power of his sufferings; that He, as the good Shepherd, could only ransom his sheep with the price of his own life. Such was the substance of the conversation on the holy mount. We might almost imagine these blessed messengers trembling for the first time during a thousand years, at having to converse on such things with the Son of God. But they call his sufferings and death a decease, or exit, as if to comfort him with this expression; and they speak of the ACCOMPLISHMENT of this decease, or exit, as if they would present to his mind the prospect of his succeeding glory and joy.

Simon Peter's Request

III. The sublime interview between the Lord and the heavenly embassy is concluded. The glorified messengers are about to take their departure. But the three disciples, and especially Peter, naturally wished to have it otherwise; and, giving vent to his feelings, he exclaimed, for himself and his brethren, "Lord, it is good for us to be here: if thou wilt, let us make here three tabernacles; one for thee, and one for Moses, and one for Elias."

Peter has been severely censured, in various ways, by some writers, for this exclamation. Of such censures we shall take no notice, for we regard them as quite groundless. His request appears to have proceeded, confused as he was, from right and holy motives. Was it not really good to be there? Did not the most spiritual joy flow there; and was not the King in his beauty there? The unveiled face of Immanuel was there; in beholding which, even the inhabitants of heaven find their supreme delight. Their Lord's unspeakable condescension to sinners had never been displayed to them so clearly before. The glory of the Son of man had never been seen by them as now; neither had the love of the Father been so experienced as upon this occasion. They felt themselves abundantly satisfied in the contemplation of all this. They could have forgotten this earth altogether for the sake of it. They wished to lengthen this incomparable moment. "Whom have I in heaven but thee; and there is none upon earth that I desire beside thee!"

"Lord, it is good to be here." For where indeed is heaven? Is it beyond the stars? Is it where the seraph strikes his golden harp, or

318 Elijah the Tishbite

where the palm trees flourish in eternal youth? I think it is where the Beloved Son abides, where He reveals himself fully to the soul. So then, our knowledge of him here "in part," is indeed a part of heaven. What a lonely place in itself was this solitary mountain! But as soon as the disciples saw his glory, when he "was transfigured before them," they might well say, "It is good for us to be here."

There are some who are fond of inquiring what sort of an abode heaven is. But what need is there of such inquiries, if we only can be present with the Lord? How much more needful, then, is it for us to inquire, whether He is ours and we are his! He is verily our real heaven, and his nearness to us is our highest bliss. How comfortable are the words, "It is good to be here!" Whereas, under the old dispensation, it was said, "How dreadful is this place!" Gen. 28:17; and "We shall surely die, because we have seen God," Judg. 13:22. "It is good to be here!" said Peter. How seldom is this expression heard among thousands, who nevertheless profess to belong to the New Testament church! Alas! but few know the true element of peace and joy, and fewer still endeavor to breathe perpetually in it.

"Lord, if thou wilt," continues Peter, (which is the language, not of forwardness, but of submission,) "let us make here three tabernacles"; but for whom? "one for thee, and one for Moses, and one for Elias." He would have had then these two citizens of heaven to delay at least their return to paradise. This was a hard thing to ask. Yet he seems to have taken it for granted that Moses and Elias would willingly tarry forever where Jesus was. It seems expressive of humility that the disciples do not think of building four or six tabernacles, but only three; as much as to say, "We are willing to stand at a distance, and listen!" for the question, Who should sit at Christ's right hand, and who should sit at his left, in his kingdom? is not thought upon here. When we have a clear sight of the glory of Christ, our own pride lies in the dust. But perhaps their thought was to abide in the tabernacle intended for Jesus, for they would venture to enter there rather than into the others. And how truly do the hearts of God's children respond to this! A faithful man of God, well known to many, said, in his last moments, the thought of having to pass, in the other world, through all the radiant ranks of angels and glorified saints, almost made him afraid; but upon recollecting that he should immediately behold his Savior, his heart was again at ease, and he could depart with joy.

No tabernacles, however, were actually built upon the mount. The thick cloud soon hid Moses and Elias from their sight, and Jesus was left alone. The corn of wheat was first to fall into the ground and die, before it could bring forth fruit, John 12:24. They were to remember the vision for their own comfort, but to tell it to no man, till after the Son of man should be risen from the dead. Spiritually speaking, the tabernacle for whose delightful shelter Peter thus longed could only be erected above the cross. The sacred pavilion, however, is now really erected in this vale of tears—a wondrous, glorious, and incomparable temple. Its pillars embrace a world. Its upper story reaches to the stars. Its walls are invincible as omnipotence. Though heaven and earth be shaken, yet its foundations shall stand and remain unmoved. The natural eye cannot see this temple. This glorious building is visible only to the eye of faith. The light falls into this temple from above. There, no longer groping in the dark, we walk in the light of the seven-branched candlestick. It is no longer inquired, in this temple, "Wherewith shall I come before the Lord?" Here we know of an offering that justifies the ungodly. There is no longer any room for the saying of Cain, "iniquity is greater than that it may be forgiven."[1] Here it is said, " Where sin abounded, grace hath much more abounded." Here there is no longer any occasion for the exclamation, "Let not God speak with us, lest we die!" Here we learn exultingly to cry, "Abba, Father!" and to cast our cares, like children, on the Eternal God who cares for us. The robe, with which every one here is clothed, is a robe of righteousness. The bread that is here broken to us, is the bread of that peace which passes all understanding. The cup of blessing, of which we here partake, is a portion which no one takes from us. The air which is breathed here is the air of paradise. The incense of prayer and intercession kindled here, ascends as a sweet savor to the Lord. The songs which resound here, have for their burden, "I have obtained mercy!" The Preacher's instructions in this temple are, "Comfort ye, comfort ye my people."

If there be a happy abode under the sun, it is within this spiritual tabernacle. Happy are they who are in such a case, however poorly they may live as it respects the body! They need not envy kings upon their thrones, or the renowned of the earth in their pavilions of honor. Verily, they are the happy ones, who thus abide under the

---

1. Marginal reading of Gen. 4:13, with which the German agrees.

shadow of the Almighty, who are hidden in the pavilion, and in the secret of this dwelling-place, founded on the Rock of ages! Though they may have to pass through great troubles and to encounter great adversities in this life, they know whither their way conducts them. Verily, there is a reward for the righteous; there remains a rest for the people of God.

Who introduces us into this mansion of peace? One only who hears the key of David; He on whose worth the house is founded, as on an eternal rock. He still stands at the gate, ready to open it. O supplicate his mercy! Rise not up from his feet, until he has opened the door of his kingdom unto you, and until you also can rejoice in him, as "He that openeth, and no man shutteth; and that shutteth, and no man openeth." Amen.

31

The Shechinah

I am desolate!" complains the royal psalmist, Psa. 25:16. Here he spoke truth; but not the whole truth. He felt himself desolate; but feelings may deceive us. The Lord was still with him, behind the veil.

"I am desolate!" is a complaint frequently heard in the tabernacles of the righteous. But it ought not to be made so hastily. Have we forgotten who it is that said, "I will never leave thee, nor forsake thee?" And again, "Lo! I am with you alway, even unto the end of the world." Zion saith, the Lord "hath forsaken me, and my God hath forgotten me. Can a woman forget her sucking child, that she should not have compassion on the son of her womb? Yea, they may forget; yet will I not forget thee."

Many exclaim, in reference to the way in which they have to walk, "I am desolate!" Well, supposing it were so, and that the Lord led you by a way in which no others went, would that be a misfortune? If he does but lead us, then we may well be satisfied. Shall the clay say unto the potter, "What doest thou?" Still I believe, that even in this sense, no one can say, in reality, "I am desolate, or solitary." O, there are many that travel the same road; only we do not hear of it. Look into the Scriptures. There, at least, you will certainly meet with someone in whose way you may trace your own. The idea of being solitary or desolate tends to make us fearful and unbelieving. "I stand alone!" thinks many a one in respect of his faith in Christ; "I believe things which millions seem to reject as visionary and foolish." And then the doubt is ready to suggest itself, "Am I then right, and so many others wrong?" Yes; "Let God be true, though every man a liar."

"I am desolate!" No, indeed, you are not. Read the pages of history, and what do you there behold? Martyrs exclaiming at the stake, "None but Christ; none but Christ!" In the gloom of midnight dungeons, there have been heard songs of praise to Jesus Immanuel—God manifest in the flesh. Moreover, be well assured, that the number of those now upon earth who have, like yourself, enlisted under the banner of Christ, is not so small as it would often appear to the desponding heart. And even were it the case, is the race of beings that surround you the universe? Lift up your eyes on high! Behold the "ten thousand times ten thousand, and thousands of thousands," standing before the throne of God, and before the Lamb. Listen to the jubilant cry of the glorified hosts, which no man can number! These are the companions of your faith, like-minded with yourself, who stand on your side, and exultingly say with you, "Worthy is the Lamb that was slain, to receive power, and riches, and wisdom, and strength, and honor, and glory, and blessing!"

But, Christian, even if you knew nothing of this, still that word, that sure word of prophecy to which you give heed, as unto a light shining in a dark place, is a word confirmed and sealed so as none other is. Consider that all the best blessings of God under the sun have ever been found where this word is preached and received, and nowhere else. There is a golden thread running through the dark labyrinth of human history, and it has always followed the course of this word. There, and there only, love, joy, and peace, in their highest and truest sense, have been found. There only do men meet death, not only with calmness, but with heartfelt satisfaction, because they have had a desire to depart and to be with Christ. And should even your own knowledge and experience of all this be very limited, still your faith may well repose on the certainty of the word of God. Let us contemplate this as it is exhibited in the subject of our present consideration.

Matthew 17:5

While he yet spake, behold, a bright cloud overshadowed them: [and they feared as they entered into the cloud, Luke 9:34:] and behold a voice out of the cloud, which said, This is my beloved Son, in whom I am well pleased; hear ye him.

A new phenomenon now occurs on the holy mount. We have reached the most interesting part of the transfiguration scene. Let us collect our thoughts, in order calmly and adoringly to consider, I. The bright cloud; and II. The testimony which proceeded from it.

The Bright Cloud

I. "While Peter yet spake, behold, a bright cloud overshadowed them." This bright cloud had an important and sublime signification. It was the Shechinah, or Divine habitation, the sign of Jehovah's peculiar presence, like that vouchsafed in the early days of the Old Testament. In the time of Moses, a cloud, resembling a pillar rising toward heaven, formed the habitation in which Jehovah went before his people Israel in the wilderness. He also invested in a cloud the manifestation of himself on mount Sinai. At the dedication of Solomon's temple, "a cloud filled the house of the Lord, so that the priests could not stand to minister by reason of the cloud; for the glory of the Lord had filled the house. Then said Solomon, The Lord hath said that he would dwell in the thick darkness." But a cloud somewhat different from that on Sinai, and in the temple, was here. No stormy tempest accompanies it. It carries no rolling thunders, as on Sinai; no lightnings flash from it; nor is it attended with thick darkness: but glittering as if the sun shone behind it, and bordered with light as with the day-spring from on high. Thus this cloud appears as announcing the beginning of a new covenant period.

Moses and Elias enter with Jesus into the cloud, as into a presence-chamber, or as into a Father's house. How far from that ancient leader of Israel now is the expression, "I exceedingly fear and quake!" with which he once approached the darkness wherein God dwelt! Nor does Elias now cover his face as he did upon Horeb. Both of them have become strong to bear the nearness of the Eternal. They are so in Him who accompanies them, and who took them under the shadow of his wings.

The Testimony

II. "And behold, a voice out of the cloud which said, This is my beloved Son, in whom I am well pleased; hear ye him!" This voice came from no far distant height, but from the bright cloud which now overshadowed Jesus, Moses, and Elias. It is the voice of Him "who sitteth upon the throne between the cherubim, who clotheth himself with light as with a garment." It is the voice of the ever-lasting Father. He, from whom are all things, clothes his almighty voice in human language, and audibly testifies concerning the Son of man. Oh the blessed realities of the holy mount! Surely they are an anticipation of the fulfillment of the great prophetic voice out of heaven, "The tabernacle of God is with men, and he will dwell with them, and they shall be his people, and God himself shall be with them, and be their God," Rev. 21:3.

This testimony on the holy mount is unspeakably rich in meaning. First, it comprehends, in a very few words, the sum of the Old Testament, which, in Christ Jesus, is Yea and Amen. "This is my Son!" is from the book of Psalms.

"Thou art my Son, this day have I begotten thee." The addition, "In whom I am well pleased," is out of the prophets, namely, in Isaiah 42. The words, "Hear ye him," you will find in the writings of Moses. "A prophet like unto me, shall the Lord your God raise up unto you, of your brethren, like unto me. Unto him shall ye hearken." There is, moreover, in these words, a reference to the three offices of our Lord. "This is my Son," shows us Christ as a King. "In whom I am well pleased," points him out as the Mediator and High Priest, in whom God reconciles the world unto himself. "Hear ye him," represents him to us as that Prophet, to whose instructions we must listen. Finally, this testimony throws light upon the relative character which the Redeemer bears. The voice, "This is my Son," tells us who he is, with respect to his Divine nature and incarnation. The relation he bears to us is implied in the words, "In whom I am well pleased"; and in the injunction, "Hear ye him." So full of meaning are these Divine words; indeed, who is able to express all the fullness of meaning which is contained in them!

We already know the intention of this great testimony of God the Father. It doubtless addressed itself, first, to the five witnesses of Christ's transfiguration, before whom, as the representatives of the visible and invisible church, Christ is here solemnly proclaimed the priestly Head of the new kingdom; and his dominion over all things, and especially over the church, purchased with his own blood, was here formally ratified to him by the Father. We may, however, well believe that this testimony of the Father was also intended, like that at Jordan, for the Savior himself, and was to afford support to his faith, in the prospect of his approaching sufferings. And cannot we perceive that after each of these his Father's public acknowledgments, a new power appears in him, a new grace manifests itself in his discourses, a new ardor in his words and actions, and a more exalted state of mind for conflict and victory? Yes; in his human nature he grew like his people, and went from strength to strength.

"This is my beloved Son." The Father calls him his beloved Son, in a sense and meaning which can belong to no other being on earth or in heaven. This appellation bespeaks him to be no mere creature; it avouches heaven to be his throne, and earth his footstool. It evinces him to be the brightness of his Father's glory, and the express image of his person. It presents him to us as the Word that was with God, and was God, by whom all things were made and without whom nothing is made that was made; though now made flesh, and dwelling or tabernacling among us, as the true Shechinah, in whom dwells all the fullness of the Godhead bodily. Oh how happy are we to find our faith thus founded on God in Christ, and sustained by the immediate testimony and glory of God the Father. Everything depends upon the certainty of this article of our faith, "God manifest in the flesh." Upon this one prime truth the whole edifice of Christianity rests.

You know, Paul calls this mystery "incontrovertibly great," and certainly it is so, in whatever way we consider it. It is great in its amazing contents—God in man! Great by its mighty achievements—having cast down a thousand infernal strongholds and refuges of lies, by which the deceiver of the whole world holds men in the bondage of sin, fear, and temptation. Great by its unexampled operation—it plants a new creation in the old. Great by the continuation of its Divine power, it daily delivers fresh victims from the depths of Satan. Great on account of the glorious promises connected with it—for all the nations which God has made shall come and worship him through this mystery, and shall glorify his name. Indeed, what may we not perceive by the light of this single truth, "God manifest in the flesh"? We may see heaven open, and behold the eternal mansions of poor sinners prepared for them. We may see this earth, once the seat of the curse, hereby transformed into a residence of the glory of God, a scene of the greatest wonders of his love. We may see the fallen sons of Adam renewed unto holiness. We may hereby see the fountain of Divine mercy opened to us, of whose depths we formerly had no conception; and perceive a Divine and human Savior upon the throne of power, who is not ashamed to call us brethren; with the holy angels for ministering spirits to him and to us. Well, therefore, does the apostle call the mystery of "God manifest in the flesh," "the

pillar and ground of the truth." Certainly the whole temple of our
happiness rests upon this one truth.

The Father calls the Lord Jesus, "his beloved Son." But who can
fathom the depth of this expression, "My beloved"? In all human or
angelic love there is no parallel to this. Did you even know how
human glorified spirits love, yea, how angels love one another, still
this love of the Father would infinitely excel it all. Who, from a mere
drop of water, can learn the extent and depth of the ocean? Who,
from the dim light of a candle, can conceive of the blaze of noon,
and the extent of the solar rays? Yet these are but comparisons of
things finite with finite. And yet this beloved Son, O sinner, God
spared not for you: he SO loved the world, that he gave him for you,
that, believing in him, you should not perish, but have everlasting
life! Who shall comprehend the full import contained in that *so*?
Eternity alone can disclose it.

Again, who is it to whom the voice of the Father thus bears testimony? Is it not to him, who, as the Second Adam, is our
representative, our covenant Head and Surety? Surely this testimony
of the Father's complacential love is borne likewise in favor of all
who belong to Christ; that is, of all who abide in him, and keep his
commandments. Therefore, they may well refresh and strengthen
themselves with the same Divine love and kindness.

The declaration, "This is my beloved Son," is followed by the testimony, "in whom I am well pleased." The Father beholds his own
glorious perfections in him; and besides this, he beholds in him the
Mediator for us, and with this he is well pleased also. Jesus said, "For
their sakes I sanctify myself"; and the Father is perfectly complacent
in his so doing. Here, then, we see our own interest in the testimony given in the holy mount. Are we the devoted followers, the
obedient disciples of Jesus? Then the Father, who is well pleased in
him, is well pleased in us for his sake; is well pleased with us in him.

"Hear ye him!" is the conclusion of the voice from the cloud.
Christ is the Truth, as well as the Way and the Life. Had he not
come as the Teacher of this ignorant and benighted world, what
should we ever have known that is worth the knowing? We should
have been like poor forsaken orphans, and should have been ever at
a loss to know what we are, where we are, and what is to become of
us. We should have been forlorn wanderers indeed, in the valley of
the shadow of death. No prophet would then have carried a torch

before us. No apostle could have showed us the path of life. Moses, Isaiah, Daniel, and all the rest, shone not by their own light, but by the light of the Sun of righteousness. They were but as moons, some of them only in the first quarter, others more advanced, and some in full-orbed splendor. The same remark applies also to our teachers under the New Testament dispensation. The great office of them all is to bear witness to Christ, the Sun of righteousness.

"Hear ye him!" This needful admonition suggests a mournful reflection upon our present moral condition. Think only that to a race of beings who, spiritually considered, know not as it were their right hand from their left, a Savior is sent, who is as much at home beyond the stars as on this side of them and whose ministry, as proceeding forth from God, is sealed with proofs sufficient to astonish heaven and earth. This Savior comes, saying to the world, "I will remove all darkness and doubts from before you; I will explain to you the mystery of your existence; I will teach you the true nature of God and of man; I will unfold to you the remotest ages that are past, and the most distant of those that are to come; I will show you the way of peace, and direct you to the open gate of a New Paradise." Might we not reasonably expect that the whole world would immediately gather around him, and that all the race of Adam would sit, like Mary, at his feet; or be like Samuel, who said, "Speak, Lord, for thy servant heareth"? But how very different is the fact! There has been, alas, no lack of teachable disciples at the feet of erroneous teachers, false prophets and vain babblers; but in the church of the great dayspring from on high, there has always been room to spare, even to the present hour. Not as though there were any want of authentication of his doctrine. No: the sole reason of it is the entire corruption of the human heart; the deep depravation of human nature. Not as though the gospel did not exactly befit our human necessities; for nothing can be more suitable to them than the remedies it brings: but this is the cause—that the sinner neither knows nor cares to know his own most urgent necessities. Nor is it that the gospel is unintelligible; for it is, in all its most essential matters of faith, within the comprehension of a child. But it opposes the vain delights and desires of our fleshly mind, which loves darkness rather than light, that it may not meet with any check to its own willfulness. Neither does the Savior impose any heavy yoke upon man! Oh no! "His yoke is easy, and his burden light." But the degenerate creature, in its rebellion and pride, will not hear of any yoke at all, and will obey nothing but the dictates of its own fleshly will.

"Hear ye him!" How important a testimony is this to the whole of the New Testament revelation. Let us then learn to read and listen to every word of Christ, as if the testimony of the Father, "Hear ye him," were still sounding in our ears. When the Savior says, "Without me ye can do nothing"; and testifies, "I am the Way, and the Truth, and the Life; no man cometh unto the Father but by me"; when he promises eternal life to those who believe on his name, and threatens the unbelieving with the wrath of God, and with a fire prepared for the devil and his angels, forget not the voice of majesty which said, "Hear ye him." He then who refuses to hear the Son of God refuses to hear the Father. Not to hear him and receive his words, what is it but to make God a liar? But "he that hath received the testimony of Jesus, hath set to his seal that God is true," John 3:33.

But what kind of a hearing is it which the Father here enjoins? It is the hearing of our implicit and cordial faith. "He that believeth on the Son hath everlasting life; and he that believeth not the Son shall not see life, but the wrath of God abideth on him." This passage of Scripture is like the pillar of cloud and of fire between the Egyptians and the camp of Israel. It secures the salvation of believers, and the condemnation of unbelievers.

Let us only further notice how the apostles of Christ refer to this testimony of the Father, as one of the most powerful arguments for the truth of their doctrine. "We have not followed," says St. Peter, "cunningly devised fables, when we made known unto you the power and coming of our Lord Jesus Christ, but were eyewitnesses of his majesty. For he received from God the Father honor and glory, when there came such a voice to him from the excellent glory, This is my beloved Son, in whom I am well pleased." Let this testimony then remain ever present to our faith. If you are looking for a Pole-star amid the confusion of the present unbelieving age, it beams upon you from this testimony. The voice from the holy mount will serve to dispel all your doubts.

"There are," says an enlightened writer, "two sorts of persons that deserve the name of men of understanding. Those who serve God with their whole heart, because they know him; and those who, because they know him not, seek him with their whole heart." He adds, "There are in the world, spiritually considered, three sorts of persons. The first have found God, and serve him. The second have not yet found him, but seek him. The third live without either serving or seeking him. The first sort are wise and happy; the last sort are unhappy, wicked, and foolish. The second sort are wise, but not yet happy." "He that hath ears to hear, let him hear!" Amen.

32

None But Jesus

There are, through the mercy of God, many among us whose hearts bear them witness, that they have obtained the one thing needful, that they are believers. Happy are they! But I fear there are but few who know even a small part of the power, loveliness, and excellency of Him, "in whom" they have believed! This is much to be lamented. Not only in the world, but in the midst of his own family, the Savior is often but little known. Our acquaintance with him increases with the consciousness of our necessities; and the more we become acquainted with him, the more will the Divine nature be expanded within us.

Man is from his birth a degenerate being, blind and naked, alienated from the life of God, through the ignorance that is in him, and a willing servant of sin. He neither knows Christ nor feels his need of him. He cries "Peace! peace!" to himself and to others, when "there is no peace." Erroneous ideas of God and himself lull him into carnal security; but there are seasons when he has many misgivings, and when God appears to him in the light of a jealous God, a consuming fire. By the grace of God, many in this disquieted state begin to inquire in earnest after peace. They hear or they read of Christ. They find some consolation in the news of a Savior; but not of the true and right kind. They betake themselves to many means of amending their lives; but, alas! instead of trusting wholly in Christ, they lean upon their own performances. They make vows and good resolutions, and soon break them as easily as they were made. Thus they discover their own insufficiency and helplessness, and this teaches them to found all their hopes on Christ. By and by, however, they learn again that their faith, though real, is still very weak, by reason of their still looking partly to themselves. Some assault or trial of their faith serves to convince them of this. Temptation of some kind has proved too effectual; and now they begin to perceive that all their strength is in him, that they must maintain perpetual communion with him, that they must abide in him, or else they will bear no fruit, but wither. At last they learn to depend entirely on him, and thus their strength is confirmed, and their path becomes as the shining light. Thus do our necessities, from time to time, serve to promote our spiritual advancement; and thus the knowledge of Christ is found to keep pace with the sense of our own wants. It is great gain to suffer the loss of all things, that we may learn to depend on Jesus alone.

Matthew 16:6-8

And when the disciples heard it, they fell on their face, and were sore afraid. And Jesus came and touched them, and said, Arise, and be not afraid. And when they had lifted up their eyes, they saw no man, save Jesus only.

We are now arrived at the closing portion of this remarkable part of sacred history. The particular history of Elijah loses itself in that of our blessed Lord. Elijah leaves the earth a second time. When he will come again, the earth will shine in the nuptial ornaments of her heavenly glorification, and every hill and every mountain will be like Tabor. It remains for us to consider, I. The awful impression which the voice from the Shechinah made upon the three disciples; II. The relief which Jesus gave to their minds; III. Their subsequent experience.

The Transfiguration

I. The solemnity and grandeur of the transfiguration scene reached its height at the moment when the bright cloud overshadowed our Lord, with Moses and Elias, and when the voice of the Father's testimony proceeded from it. Up to that moment, the disciples had felt indescribably happy on the holy mount. But no sooner is their Lord and Master, under whose wing they had hitherto felt secure, enveloped in the cloud, and the voice from the excellent glory is heard, than their comfort is instantly at an end, and their rapture is changed into fear. They fall on their faces as if thunderstruck, and are sore afraid. So awful is the approach of Eternal Majesty to the sinner. "Let not God speak with us," cried Israel at the foot of Sinai, "lest we die. For who is there of all flesh, that hath heard the voice of the living God speaking out of the midst of the fire, as we have, and lived?" "When I saw his face," says Daniel, "and heard the voice of his words, there remained no strength in me, for my comeliness was turned in me into corruption, and I sank on my face to the ground." When Isaiah saw the glory of the Lord, he expressed his amazement by saying, "Woe is me, for I am undone! for I am a man of unclean lips." And even the disciple whom Jesus loved, at beholding the unveiled glory of the King of kings, fell at his feet as dead, and the arm of Omnipotence was needed to lift him up, otherwise he would have sunk under it. What is the reason of this terror in man, as soon as he perceives the nearness of God? Does it not betray alienation? By nature we are disposed practically to deny him. Our natural terror, therefore, at the thought of his presence, is, but too evidently, founded on our consciousness of our guiltiness in his sight. We think we are something; but when God's excellent greatness is suddenly opened to us, we sink before it. Besides, our present sphere of vision and conception is very limited. All our thoughts are earthly, and all our conceptions of spiritual things are derived from this world of sense; so that, when we behold such things in their real nature, it threatens, as it were, to break down the whole fabric of our ideas and notions. Hence it is no wonder that extraordinary manifestations of the invisible things of God should overpower us with amazement and terror.

But how could the disciples be so terrified, seeing they knew the Father, by having believed on him, and possessed in Christ their Head such a fullness of glory, that they could easily bear the loss of their own? We answer, that if self had been utterly annihilated in them in the presence of Eternal Majesty, they would have risen up only the more gloriously in Jesus; but as this was not the case, so, in more senses than one, Jesus was to them behind the cloud. Their insight into his mediation did not yet reach so far as to enable them comfortably to bear such a manifestation of God as this. They did not yet enter into the full import of the words, "Who is he that condemneth?" And how shall they, who have not yet learned the wondrous art of beholding and finding themselves in Christ alone, stand without terror in the immediate presence of the Divine Majesty? A word from his mouth, to the mightiest among us who is not thus prepared, is as the voice of the Lord, which breaks the cedars, and makes Lebanon and Carmel tremble. Were he only now to exclaim from the skies, in the hearing of the whole world, "I am Alpha and Omega, the First and the Last!" what a vast change would it instantaneously occasion in human theories and opinions! How different would be the view which men would immediately take of their present state of existence, and how different also the manner of life of many millions! A host of blasphemers would be, as it were, bound with the terrors of the Almighty. This will one day come to pass: "Behold, he cometh with clouds, and every eye shall see him, and all the kindreds of the earth shall wail because of him. Even so. Amen." But at present, it is in the way of faith that God chooses to be found of them that seek him. He will not thus forcibly manifest himself, till he shall come to the last judgment.

It was not only the voice from the clouds, and the unexpected approach of Divine Majesty, which so terrified the disciples upon the mount; but even in the testimony itself there was something awful, though it did not exactly tell them anything new. For though they had themselves confessed that Jesus was the Son of the living God, and had just seen his Divine glory on the mount, still this confirmation of his sonship, coming to them immediately from the excellent glory, might add to their belief in God incarnate, such vivid clearness of sensible demonstration as to overwhelm them with amazement and awe. All this is perfectly natural; and if the Lord were now suddenly to remove from our minds the shade with which our spiritual light is so greatly intermingled, and to elevate our faith to that clearness of demonstration which would amount almost to sight, the consequence would be that even the truths which we already believe and embrace would overpower us beyond measure; for instance, the truth that the babe once laid in the manger at Bethlehem is God incarnate, and the truth that the Son of God was ignominiously nailed to the cross *for our sakes*. For we at present behold all such truths in an attempered light; we see them only as in a glass darkly, or, as it were, through a veil, with which God moderates the overpowering effect they would otherwise have upon our present weak frame and faculties. Such things are far too wonderful, supernatural, and glorious for us to behold, except as through a veil; without which, in our present state, they would fail to produce the effect which God designs by them.

Jesus Speaks

II. The three disciples fell to the ground as dead, and could not venture to lift up their eyes, as long as they felt the immediate presence of the Eternal. But their Master again approached them, and at his approach "every valley shall be exalted." He is like a wise masterbuilder among fragments and ruins, or like a skillful artificer who forms vessels of honor from clay trodden under foot.

"And Jesus came and touched them, and said, Arise, and be not afraid." There was doubtless new vigor imparted by this touch, besides its natural adaptation to human feelings. The Sun of righteousness comes with healing in his wings. Remember the poor woman, mentioned in Matt. 9 and the believing language of her heart: "If I may but touch his garment I shall be whole." Her confidence was not put to shame. A touch of Christ is the only means of our own spiritual restoration. This must be obtained by faith in him, and fervent prayer in his name. This touch is, in other words, the work of his Holy Spirit upon our hearts and minds, producing inward peace and personal holiness, love, humility, meekness, self-denial, and activity to arise and labor for the glory of God and the good of man.

The Disciples' Experience

III. No sooner had Jesus touched the terrified disciples and spoken to them these encouraging words, "Arise, and be not afraid," than they are immediately delivered out of all their fears, and peace again takes possession of their hearts. "And when they had lifted up their eyes," relates the evangelist, "they saw no man, save Jesus only." Moses and Elias have returned, in the bright cloud, to their heavenly abode, to relate, to their companions in glory, the things they had seen and heard on the holy mount. The holy angels resume their ministrations before the throne, and their praises are increased. The Divine luster which, beaming forth from the Lord of glory, enlightened the darkness of the night, has withdrawn itself behind the veil of his servant's form; and it becomes again upon the mount, as it had been before, dark, solitary, and silent. The wind plays in the rustling foliage; the stars twinkle silently in the firmament; but, in the hearts of this little assembly, it is different. The Divine Redeemer, after his conversation with the heavenly messengers, anticipates more cheerfully the bloody baptism which awaits him. The glorified spirits above approach with an increased measure of holy boldness to the throne of Glory and Majesty; and the three disciples—how do they now rejoice more than ever in their Lord and Master! However brief are generally the moments which we may be permitted to spend on the mount, beholding the King in his beauty; they are moments which we justly reckon among the best and happiest of our lives. Though they may only momentarily enlighten our darkness, they are not lost upon us; a blessing remains from them which attends us in our path; a secret ministration of strength which is not soon exhausted; a light that lives in the storm, and helps to cheer the gloom of much temporal and spiritual conflict.

"And when the disciples had lifted up their eyes, they saw no man, save Jesus only." This circumstance serves to remind us of that state of mind, which, in the more immediate sense of the word, may be called gracious and evangelical. How desirable is it to have our distracting thoughts so banished and subdued, as to see "Jesus only!" Without this we cannot be vigorous, practical Christians. Learn, then, to look away from yourself entirely, and to "stand fast in the Lord." Divest yourself of all anxious care about the future, for that is safe in his hands. Yea, having committed "the keeping of thy soul to him in well-doing, as unto a faithful Creator," you have no occasion to tremble even at death itself. Think of those words, "I will come again and receive you unto myself, that where I am there ye may be also." Oh the blessedness of that peaceful position of mind, in which everything that is seen by us, is seen in Christ; not looking at the winds or waves, or ourselves, but Jesus only!

The disciples seeing no longer Moses or Elias, but Jesus only, may serve further to suggest to us instruction with respect to viewing Jesus as the true Lawgiver, and the true Restorer of all things. How happy is it, when the believer at length perceives that he has his sufficiency in Christ alone, and needs no other support. He then walks at liberty, keeping Christ's commandments with his whole heart. The peace of God which passes understanding, keeps his heart and mind by Christ Jesus. The terrors of the law no longer appall him, and yet he now learns to keep the law universally, and more steadfastly than ever.

"Jesus alone!" Yes, in that day when the "Lord shall be king over all the earth; and there shall be one Lord, and his name one," Zech. 14:9; then that which we have considered as spiritually significative on the holy mount, will be substantially realized. The whole world will then behold Jesus alone, as "fairer than the children of men," and will have his name written in their foreheads. All will bear his image; and everything will be dedicated to his praise. The very forms and creations of art shall glorify him; the halls of learning will be beautified with the wisdom which is from above; and the Lord alone will be the center and focus of all the sciences. The Lord alone will be exalted in that day; his love will form the sacred and inviolable bond of nations. How earnestly should we pray for the dawning of that happy day: "Hallowed be thy name; thy kingdom come; thy will be done on earth, as it is in heaven!" How should we rejoice at the thought that death will everywhere be swallowed up in the life of Christ, and all darkness be dispersed by the wonderful light of His beauty—when none other will be seen anywhere, but Jesus Immanuel alone! We thus close, for the present, our meditations on the history of Elijah; hoping to resume them one day more effectually in the city of our God. Let us be thankful for any consolation and benefit we have derived from these meditations; for to Divine grace alone is it to be ascribed. It was that the precious name of Jesus might be glorified in our souls that we began and continued these discourses. May the Lord graciously so dispose us all, that it may be said of us, in a blessed and spiritual sense, "When they had lifted up their eyes, they saw no man, save Jesus only!" Amen.